A Maverick's Defense of Freedom

T0124937

BENJAMIN A. ROGGE

A Maverick's Defense of Freedom

SELECTED WRITINGS AND SPEECHES OF
Benjamin A. Rogge

Edited and with an Introduction by Dwight R. Lee

Liberty Fund
INDIANAPOLIS

Introduction and index © 2010 by Liberty Fund, Inc.

Articles reprinted by permission.

Frontispiece used by permission of the Rogge estate.

C   10 9 8 7 6 5 4 3 2 1
P   10 9 8 7 6 5 4 3 2 1

Library of Congress Cataloging-in-Publication Data

Rogge, Benjamin A.
    A maverick's defense of freedom: selected writings and speeches of Benjamin A. Rogge / edited and with an introduction by Dwight R. Lee.
        p.   cm.
    Includes bibliographical references and index.
    ISBN 978-0-86597-784-6 (hbk.: alk. paper)—
    ISBN 978-0-86597-785-3 (pbk.: alk. paper)
    1. Free enterprise.   2. Capitalism.   3. Economics.   I. Lee, Dwight R.   II. Title.
    HB95.R6125   2010
    330.092—dc22

                                              2009049840

Liberty Fund, Inc.
8335 Allison Pointe Trail, Suite 300
Indianapolis, Indiana 46250-1684

CONTENTS

INTRODUCTION

Benjamin Rogge was indeed an intellectual maverick. Defending freedom with Rogge's power and persuasiveness automatically made him a maverick, given the intellectual climate of his day. During almost the entirety of Rogge's career as an economist, most intellectuals were skeptical of individual liberty and free markets and enamored with more government controls over people and the economy. Rogge would be much less a maverick today, especially among economists, in large measure because his influence and the influence of a few of his contemporary intellectual mavericks have made his views far more mainstream than they were during his lifetime. Rogge used his enthusiasm, persuasiveness, and keen economic understanding to relentlessly, and effectively, communicate the classical liberal principles of individual liberty, free markets, and limited government to an audience that never ceased to expand during his career.

As will be clear from some of the following chapters, Rogge was quite a good economic prognosticator, even though he was quick to point out that neither he nor any other economist had special powers to divine the future. But his most general forecast appears to be one he badly missed (though he wisely failed to specify the timing), although he would be happy to know he missed it. Rogge was pessimistic about the survival of capitalism for reasons he acknowledged came largely from the insights of one of his favorite economists, Joseph Schumpeter. For someone with the depth of understanding he had into how capitalism bestowed unmatched measures of prosperity, dignity, and liberty on those fortunate enough to live in capitalistic economies, it would have been easy to understand if Rogge had become confrontational and bitter, surrounded as he was in the academy by those who were some of the greatest beneficiaries of capitalism and its most vociferous critics. But he appears to have had no tendency toward confrontation and bitterness. Rogge coupled a wonderful sense of humor with confidence in his arguments and genuine regard for others that allowed him to separate his evaluation of an argument from his evaluation of the person making it.

Rogge's humor cannot be described; it can only be experienced. And one of the joys of organizing the writings in this volume has been experiencing that humor. Even critics of capitalism must have found it difficult to resist being charmed, and at least temporarily disarmed, by someone who started off a talk by predicting that the audience will soon be wanting to ask him, "Rogge, just what kind of nut are you?" and then defended himself by claiming that he was really a "Kiwanis Club–type conformist" whose "only attention-drawing eccentricity has been a tendency to give [him]self all putts under five feet." But Rogge's humor never distracted from the seriousness of his purpose or the intellectual depth of his arguments.

Rogge possessed a modesty that, while different from the intellectual arrogance that so often drives a wedge between academics and their audiences, was in harmony with the authority of his words. His arguments were clear and forceful without being dogmatic, and he could disagree with others without being disagreeable. As Richard O. Ristine, a former lieutenant-governor of Indiana, said at Rogge's memorial service on November 20, 1980, "He seldom criticized another person—though he might criticize that other person's ideas." Rogge's persuasiveness was based on his humor, civility, and ability to communicate his depth of understanding in straightforward language.

The contrast here between Rogge and many economists (and academics in general) is instructive. When supporting a proposition alien to most in their audience, economists tend to present it in the most controversial way possible—to state the conclusion in a way designed to shock, if not repel, the audience and convince them, at least initially, to reject it as completely wrongheaded. At this point most economists attempt to show how clever they are by employing complicated diagrams and mathematics to show that they are correct and the audience is wrong. Rogge's approach was more modest and gentle, and far more effective. Rogge treated his audience with respect by recognizing how reasonable people could hold views opposed to his and sprinkled his arguments with humorous observations and relevant examples to illustrate and soften the logic being used instead of using it as a club to bludgeon skeptics into submission.

Rogge could have made theoretical contributions to economics, but he didn't. But as all good economists know, great talent in one activity doesn't mean that one has a comparative advantage in that direction since one's talent in another activity may be even greater. Rogge obviously knew the theory of comparative advantage. That was easy. But he also knew and accepted what his own comparative advantage was, something many have difficulty figuring out and accepting. In a 1965 memorandum to the members of a committee on the Principles of Freedom (which, in addition to Rogge, included such economists as F. A. Hayek and Milton Friedman[1]), Rogge stated that if he had "any special talent, it is taking the materials of economics and making them more or less interesting and more or less meaningful to non-economists and to people who have no strong passion for economics." His comparative advantage in communicating economics was indeed a special talent, and a talent he used to full effect as a great writer, a popular speaker, and a beloved teacher. We should never overlook, however, the fact that Rogge was a teacher, and it was a calling he took very seriously. As his son, Ben Rogge, Jr., told me, "he was voted teacher of the year by the students several times. Students from all disciplines took his classes, and he usually had more student advisees than any other professor at Wabash."

In addition to Rogge's other activities, he was a valued advisor to important institutions and people. This is evidenced by his service on the boards of both nonprofit and for-profit organizations—organizations such as the Foundation for Economic Education, Lafayette Life Insurance Company, and Earhart-Relm Foundation. Also he was a longtime friend and advisor to Pierre Goodrich, the founder of Liberty Fund. Given his many impressive accomplishments, Goodrich clearly knew

---

1. Ben Rogge and Milton Friedman collaborated on the film *The Incredible Bread Machine,* which has been widely used in classrooms and other educational settings. Rogge narrated the film.

how to identify extraordinary people who could contribute to the practical and intellectual goals that meant so much to him. Rogge clearly satisfied this requirement. According to Dane Starbuck, "If anyone understood the mind and had the ear of Pierre F. Goodrich, it was Benjamin Arnold Rogge. Through their mutual attachments to Wabash College, Rogge and Goodrich established a close intellectual and personal friendship that lasted nearly thirty years."[2] Starbuck continues, "The thread that tied them together was the passion they shared for free-market ideas and their desire to see those ideas spread at Wabash and beyond."[3]

This "thread that tied them together" was durable because Rogge and Goodrich had complementary skills that amplified the effectiveness of each at spreading free-market ideas. Goodrich provided organizational skills and financial assets that created Liberty Fund and funded some of Rogge's travels for speaking and teaching, both of which served to expand Rogge's audience. Rogge's skills enhanced the effectiveness of Goodrich in less direct and obvious ways; yet Rogge clearly used his writing skill to amplify Goodrich's voice in their joint articles and through editing some of Goodrich's writing. And many of Rogge's ideas on intellectual issues, and likely even on organizational matters related to the formation of Liberty Fund, probably influenced Goodrich's decisions in important ways, although evidence on the particulars of this influence would be difficult to separate from the influence exerted by many of the impressive people with whom Goodrich consulted.

It would seem rather improbable that Rogge would become an economist with a passion for spreading free-market ideas given the prevailing views in economics when he received his formal education. He received his undergraduate degree in economics in 1940 from Hastings College in Nebraska while still a teenager—having skipped two grades in elementary school—and worked his way through college. So his undergraduate studies occurred during the Great Depression, when Keynesian skepticism toward market economies and their ability

---

2. Dane Starbuck, *The Goodriches: An American Family* (Indianapolis: Liberty Fund, 2001), 334.

3. Ibid., 335.

to sustain prosperity was beginning to infiltrate the economics profession. This skepticism had probably, at least to some degree, reached Hastings College during his time there. After serving during World War II as a captain and navigator in the United States Army Air Corps, Rogge earned a master's degree in economics from the University of Nebraska, began doctoral study in economics at the University of Minnesota, and taught as an instructor during 1946–47. Keynesianism, with its emphasis on encouraging consumption, was clearly dominant in most economics departments in the United States by this time, and in few places more so than at the University of Minnesota, where Walter Heller, a leading Keynesian who went on to serve as the chairman of the Council of Economic Advisors under presidents Kennedy and Johnson, was teaching in 1946. And no one can believe that the writings of Adam Smith received anything close to the attention as those of John Maynard Keynes in the economics department at Northwestern University, from which Rogge ultimately received his Ph.D. in economics in 1953.

As a student, Rogge may have been influenced by some of the relatively few classical liberal economists who remained in the academy, or maybe growing up in the poverty of rural Nebraska during the depression, he learned some harsh economic realities—such as that wealth has to be produced before it can be consumed—that immunized him from notions of spending as the key to prosperity. But Rogge's earliest writings show that he had the intellectual fortitude to stand up to the dominant views in economics with a deep understanding of the classical liberal principles that he believed provided the necessary foundation for economic prosperity and individual liberty.

From the early 1950s until his death in November 1980, Rogge wrote an impressive amount. Many of his numerous writings, however, have never been published, primarily because they were written as speeches, and many writings that *were* published are widely scattered over a variety of outlets and are no longer easily found. I believe that these writings are worth bringing together in a volume, making them conveniently available to the many people, including professional economists, who can benefit from Rogge's economic insights while enjoying the charm and humor with which those insights are communicated. It is this belief that motivated this volume.

The works in this volume were probably written between December 1951 and shortly before Rogge's death (some of the pieces have been impossible to date, however). They have been organized into six parts (with part 3 further divided into five sections), with the readings in each part (and section) connected by a common theme. Some of the readings are short editorials; others are longer articles or talks; and it is not clear whether some were written as talks, articles, or both. Some are concerned with particular issues of the day, and others will seem more general with respect to time. But even when Rogge is considering issues that seem more relevant to, say, the late 1970s than to current concerns (inflation, for example), his insights are more timeless than we might think. From at least Adam Smith to the present, the enduring insights of political economists have resulted from their interest in contemporary concerns, with those concerns continually reappearing in only slightly different guises.

In Part 1 ("Individual Liberty, Responsibility, and the Morality of the Market"), Rogge discusses individual liberty and responsibility, which form the foundation of his economic understanding. The first three chapters are speeches that Rogge gave to business and professional groups in the early 1960s. The first chapter is titled "The Case for Economic Freedom," the second "The New Conservatism," and the third, a previously untitled speech, I have called "The Only Economic System Consistent with Freedom and Responsibility." In these chapters Rogge considers the case for individual liberty and responsibility in maintaining the free-market economy; examines the fundamental difference between conservatism, what has become known as liberalism, and classical liberalism; and considers the risks associated with discarding the principles of classical liberalism, even to those who currently believe they are benefiting from doing so. The next chapter, "Intellectuals' Curse of Capitalism," is an editorial in which Rogge explains the tendency for intellectuals to criticize capitalism. In the fifth chapter, he discusses the importance of private colleges like Wabash, and private organizations in general, as bulwarks against the centralizing tendencies of government. The next two chapters are talks, the first one honoring Leonard Read, the founder of the Foundation for Economic Education (FEE), and the second pondering the future of FEE once the leadership of Read is over. These chapters provide another glimpse into Rogge's core beliefs and what he sees as crucial in the struggle for liberty. In the next chapter Rogge asks what actions government can legitimately perform and points out that he is not in total agreement with Adam Smith on this question. In the last chapter in Part 1, he examines the arguments that government is necessary to prevent private monopolies from controlling the economy while considering the question "Is economic freedom possible?"

Part 2 ("The Role of Economists") is fairly short, but some economists may think it is not short enough. No one can accuse Rogge of being unenthusiastic about economics, but neither can anyone accuse him of not having an independent mind. In these chapters, Rogge considers, among other things, just how useful economists are at either undermining or promoting free enterprise. Even if economists are important, maybe they are not as important as they think they are. In the first chapter in this part, which is undated and untitled (I have titled it "What Economists Can and Cannot Do"), Rogge gives his views on the limits to what economists do and provides an interesting response to those who think that conservative economists can help promote the ideals of capitalism. The next chapter, "When to See Your Economist," is an insightful and entertaining follow-up to the previous chapter. The chapter "Economists as Freedom Fighters" (my title) is a chapel talk that Rogge gave at Wabash College in March 1952 in which he puts forth an interesting perspective on defending freedom. The final chapter in this part is a 1976 editorial that discusses the views of an economist who could be considered an effective freedom fighter—Adam Smith.

The longest segment of the collection is Part 3, which contains chapters dealing with Rogge's views on a variety of educational issues and concerns, particularly as they relate to a free society. Instead of previewing each chapter in this part of the book, I shall provide a brief overview of each section. The first section ("Education in a Free Society") contains three chapters in which Rogge presents his views on the role of education in a free society and how much independence education should have from government (this in a chapter, also called "Education in a Free Society," coauthored with Pierre Goodrich); on what should be meant by academic freedom and ideological balance in education; and on what a college or university can realistically promise to students. This last chapter is a 1960 statement to the Wabash College faculty and administration produced by a committee of four administrators and professors from Wabash (deans Rogge and Moore, and professors Dean and McKinney), but the statement was clearly drafted by Rogge, who was the chairman of the committee. The second section ("Financing and Administering Higher Education") contains four short chapters: two on Rogge's views on how higher education should be financed; one on the issue of tenure for professors; and the last on who should have control over how a college or university is run. In the third section ("The Role of the Student") Rogge covers a number of topics relating to the responsibility of students in acquiring an education. These topics include hazing in fraternities and standing up for what you believe is right; to what degree undergraduates are prepared to understand classical liberalism; what college students can realistically expect to do with a college degree; and the importance of the average, as opposed to the honor, student in the educational process, and the positive-sum nature of academic competition.

In the fourth section ("The Role of Businesspeople and Intellectuals") Rogge shifts his attention away from students. The four chapters here consider the connection between businesspeople and academics; the effectiveness of businesspeople at defending capitalism; the idiosyncrasies of college professors; and the struggle among academics to influence young minds in the ongoing battle to preserve liberty. The final section ("Economic Education") contains two short chapters, the first of which discusses the difference between economists and the general public in their view on free markets, with an emphasis on understanding the moral as well as the productivity implications of markets. The even shorter second chapter consists of Rogge's comments on two papers on economic education at the 1956 American Economic Association meetings.

Part 4 ("Microeconomics, Labor Issues, and Political Foibles") moves more directly into consideration of public policy, beginning with "The Myth of Monopoly," which deals with the difference between competition and monopoly as discussed in textbooks and as they are found in the real world, with a discussion of the implications for antitrust policy. This is followed by a related and very short chapter, "Putty in the Hands of the Image-Makers," which considers the power of advertising to manipulate consumers. Next, in "Debating the Gold Standard," Rogge looks at an activity popular among economists for decades. Turning to labor issues in the fourth chapter in this part, "Job Creation . . . Whose Job Is It?" Rogge discusses the common concern that there are not enough jobs, and how this concern can lead to government policies on labor markets that are contrary to the expressed objectives of those policies. The concern with labor policy continues with a chapter on labor policy, "People, Problems, and Progress," that examines policy attempts to increase the compensation of labor. The next two chapters, "Union Wage Hike: An Economic Yes and No" and "Barriers on the Road to Employment," continue considering the effects of government policies that are widely believed to benefit workers. Changing the emphasis, but maintaining some attention to labor markets, in the next chapter, Rogge examines race in the marketplace in "Racial Discrimination and the Market Place." This is followed by a related chapter, "The Welfare State against the Negro," dealing with the effects of various public policies, justified in the name of compassion, on the well-being of racial minorities. Of interest here is that these last two articles were part of a larger body of work that Rogge shared with a young economist named Thomas Sowell. In an interview in the *Wall Street Journal,* Sowell gives Rogge's "fundamental idea that you could apply economics to racial issues" credit for inspiring much of his work on race and economics.[4] The role of the market in motivating workers is the issue examined in the next chapter, "Motivation and the Cost Squeeze," a talk Rogge gave to a group containing personnel experts and industrial psychologists—professionals who Rogge explains tend to have views on motivating workers different from those of economists. A short chapter follows on a connection that Rogge describes as "of turnips and energy scarcity." Another short chapter, "Yes, America, There Is an Energy Problem, But . . .", follows with more on energy problems.

Part 5 ("Macroeconomics: Policies and Forecasts") contains six chapters that deal with macroeconomic concerns that assumed critical importance in the last decade of Rogge's life and with some of the economic forecasts he made during that period with those concerns in mind. It would be a mistake to conclude that because the subjects

---

4. Jason L. Riley, "Classy Economist: The Weekend Interview with Thomas Sowell," *Wall Street Journal,* March 25, 2006.

highlighted in these chapters no longer dominate the economic news they have ceased to be threats to our future prosperity and freedoms. In the opening chapter, "Keynesian Policy," Rogge critiques some of the views on macroeconomic policy that dominated the economic profession in the 1950s. The second chapter, "Economics—Some Relationships of Theory and Practice," is a review of three books. In the last four chapters in Part 5, Rogge continues discussing macroeconomics principles and policies in a way that reflects the increasing sophistication of the profession's critique of Keynesian analysis through the 1970s. In these chapters Rogge ventures into economic forecasting and shows that he had quite a clear crystal ball, at least for the near term. In "The Outlook for the American Economy," based on a talk Rogge gave in December 1970, two contradictory views on macro stabilization policy are discussed, with a forecast following. The next chapter, "Misconceptions of the Cause and Cure of Inflation," is based on an untitled talk Rogge gave in June 1974 that begins with a forecast that would have been dismissed as impossible by many Keynesians of the day. In another untitled talk delivered in January 1977, which I have titled "Political Incentives and Continued Inflation," Rogge makes some remarkable forecasts of what inflation and interest rates will be at the end of the 1970s, forecasts even more remarkable given how outrageous they seemed when he made them. In the last chapter in this part, "The Political Economy of Inflation," Rogge sees continued inflation over a longer interval than he predicted before. What he didn't see was the appointment of Paul Volcker as chairman of the Federal Reserve System or the election of Ronald Reagan. The chapter contains a clever hypothetical discussion between President Carter and his advisors on inflation that rather accurately illustrates the political incentives that exist anytime a fight against inflation is considered.

Part 6 ("Foreign Policy and Economic Development") concludes the volume with five chapters, two on foreign policy and three on economic development. The Vietnam War is now more a memory (if even that, for many) than a pressing issue. But in the chapter "Should the United States Be in Vietnam?" written in 1969, Rogge makes an argument that unfortunately remains, and will remain, relevant to our conduct of foreign affairs, and that is deeply rooted in the same principles of freedom and responsibility that formed the foundation of his economic analysis. The next chapter, "East-West Trade," was written in 1967 and examines the issue of trade with the then Soviet Union, or with any collectivist country that is our enemy. This is very much a foreign policy issue, but one that Rogge considers from his perspective as a political economist. The first of the three chapters on economic development ("A Letter from São Paulo: They've Got an Awful Lot of Rogges in Brazil") is a short humorous piece Rogge wrote while on sabbatical in Brazil that touches on economic development and was intended for the Wabash College community. The second economic-development chapter (which I have titled "Haste Makes Waste in Economic Development") is excerpted from an untitled talk that Rogge gave to the Inland Steel Academy in May 1958. In this chapter Rogge draws on his experience in Brazil to consider why underdeveloped countries have so much difficulty developing their economies. The last chapter in this part, and in this book, was published in 1955 and is titled "The Role of Government in Latin American Economic Development." In this chapter Rogge takes issue with the overwhelming consensus in the 1950s that saw as necessary more government planning and control of the economies of underdeveloped countries if they were to experience economic growth.

The struggle for freedom with responsibility has been, and continues to be, a long and arduous one. It is Ben Rogge's dedication to the struggle for freedom that this book honors.

I would like to thank Amy Lynch of Liberty Fund for her diligence in finding and organizing copies of Ben Rogge's speeches, articles, and other writings. Without her hard work and competence, this volume would not have been possible. I would also like to acknowledge the Hoover Institute and Wabash College for extensive use of their archives in preparation of this volume. Also, I owe thanks to Marise Melson and Ben Rogge, Jr., for correcting errors and suggesting changes in earlier versions of this introduction, based on their knowledge of not just Ben Rogge the economist but Ben Rogge the father. Finally, I would like to thank my wife, Cindy Crain, for reading the first draft of the introduction and suggesting changes that I did not fully appreciate until I received almost identical suggestions from Marise and Ben.

Dwight R. Lee

Part 1   *Individual Liberty, Responsibility, and the Morality of the Market*

The Case for Economic Freedom

Writing just a few miles from here, Henry David Thoreau, the famous author of *Walden Pond* and other essays, once described government as follows: "Government is an expedient by which men would fain succeed in letting one another alone." Government in 1962 can best be described as an expedient by which one man would fain impose his will on another, preferably at the other man's expense.

Thoreau further said that "government never of itself furthered any enterprise, but by the alacrity with which it got out of its way. Trade and commerce, if they were not made of India rubber, would never manage to bounce over the obstacles which legislators are continually putting in their way; if one were to judge these men [the legislators] wholly by the effects of their actions, they would deserve to be classed and punished with those mischievous persons who put obstructions on the railroads."

Walden Pond is now a suburban development, and Thoreau himself just a memory, but the legislators of which he wrote are still with us. They are still with us and every day add to the vast network of intervention and control which now surrounds our economic activities. Why do they do this? Because they are evil, power-hungry men who are determined to subvert the American way of life? Emphatically no;

Speech presented to the Associate Industries of Massachusetts, October 25, 1962. Reprinted by permission of the Rogge estate.

they do this because we ask them to, because we insist that they do this if they wish to be re-elected.

We are moving away from the traditional system of free and private enterprise because, as a people, we no longer accept its fundamental premises. For example, we do not seem to believe that each man is the best judge of what is in his own interest. On the contrary, we believe that he must be guided, protected, encouraged, discouraged, manipulated, and maneuvered. The accepted approach is beautifully illustrated by the complaint against the television industry of Newton Minow, chairman of the Federal Communications Commission. His complaint is that the television industry is giving the viewers what they (the viewers) want.

Again, we do not believe that each man in pursuing his own self-interest is led as if by an invisible hand to serve the interests of others. For example, the businessman is urged to forget costs and revenues, to direct his actions not by the goal of maximizing profits but by the never-defined concept of "social responsibility." If you believe in the free market, as I do, you believe that the only social responsibility of the businessman as such is to make money for his stockholders. You believe that if a businessman wished not to make money but only to serve society, he could still have no better goal than maximum prof-its. If you don't believe this, you don't really believe in free private enterprise.

These and other premises of the system seem no longer to be accepted by the majority of Americans. Why is this the case? In part because the workings of the system are subtle and complex, and a majority of Americans never has and never will fully understand why and how the system works. But if Americans in the past did not fully understand the system, why did they still accept it and generally ask their legislators to let it alone? Because in the main the system seemed to be consistent with certain principles ("moral" principles) held by a good part of the American society.

Let me illustrate: the doctrine of man held in general in nineteenth-century America argued that each man was ultimately responsible for what happened to him, for his own salvation, both in the here and now and in the hereafter. Thus, whether a man prospered or failed in eco-nomic life was each man's individual responsibility; each man had a right to the rewards for success and, in the same sense, deserved the punishment that came with failure. It followed as well that it is explicitly immoral to use the power of government to take from one man to give to another, to legalize Robin Hood. This doctrine of man found its economic counterpart in the system of free enterprise, and the system of free enterprise was accepted and respected by many who had no understanding of its subtleties as a technique for organizing resources.

As this doctrine of man was replaced by one which made of man a helpless victim of his subconscious and his environment—responsible for neither his successes nor his failures—the free enterprise system came to be rejected by many who still had no real understanding of its actual operating characteristics.

I present this illustration in preparation for a statement of the central thesis of my comments this afternoon, that the most important part of the case for economic freedom is not its vaunted efficiency as a system for organizing resources, not its dramatic success in promoting economic growth, but rather its consistency with certain fundamental moral principles of life itself.

I say "the most important part of the case" for two reasons. First, the significance I attach to those moral principles would lead me to prefer the free enterprise system even if it were demonstrably less efficient than alternative systems, even if it were to produce a slower rate of economic growth than systems of central direction and control. Second, the great mass of the people of any country is never going to understand the purely economic workings of any economic system, be it free enterprise or socialism. Hence, most people are going to judge an economic system by its consistency with their moral principles rather than by its purely scientific operating characteristics. If economic freedom survives in the years ahead, it will be only because a majority of the people accept its basic morality. The success of the system in bringing ever higher levels of living will be no more persuasive in the future than it has been in the past.

Let me now present two sections of the case for economic freedom as I would construct it. The first section describes economic freedom as an ultimate end in itself; the second describes it as a means to the preservation of the noneconomic elements in total freedom.

The first section of the case is made in the stating of it, if one accepts the fundamental premise, I would put it as follows:

Major premise: Each man should be free to take whatever action he
wishes to take so long as he does not use force or fraud against
another.

Minor premise: All economic behavior is "action" as identified above.

Conclusion: Each man should be free to take whatever action he wishes
to take in his economic behavior so long as he does not use force or
fraud against another.

In other words, economic freedom is a part of total freedom; if freedom is an end in itself, as our society has traditionally asserted, then
economic freedom is an end in itself, to be valued for itself alone and
not just for its instrumental value in serving other goals.

If this thesis is accepted, there must always exist a tremendous presumption against each and every proposal for governmental limitation
of economic freedom. What is wrong with a state system of compulsory social security? It denies to the individual his freedom, his right to
choose what he will do with his own money resources. What is wrong
with a governmentally enforced minimum wage? It denies to the employer and the employee their individual freedoms, their individual
rights to enter into any voluntary relationship not involving force or
fraud. What is wrong with a tariff or an import quota? It denies to the
individual consumer his right to buy what he wishes, wherever he
wishes.

It is breathtaking to think what this simple approach would do to the
apparatus of state control at all levels of government. Strike from the
books all legislation that denies economic freedom to any individual,
and three-fourths of all the activities now undertaken by government
would be eliminated.

I am no dreamer of empty dreams, and I do not expect that the
day will come when this principle of economic freedom as a part of
total freedom will be fully accepted and applied. Yet I am convinced
that unless this principle is given some standing, unless at least those
who examine proposals for each new regulation of the individual by
government look on this loss of freedom as a "cost" of the proposed
legislation, the chances of free enterprise surviving are small indeed.
The would-be controller can always find reasons why it might seem
"expedient" to control the individual, and unless slowed down by

some general feeling that it is immoral to do so, he will usually have his way.

So much for the first section of the case. Now for the second. The major premise here is still the rightness of freedom. Here, though, the concern is with the noneconomic elements in total freedom—with freedom of speech, of religion, of the press, of personal behavior. My thesis is that these freedoms are not likely to be long preserved in a society that has denied economic freedom to its individual members.

The argument here could be drawn from the wisdom of the Bible and the statement that "where a man's treasure is, there will his heart be also." Give me control over a man's economic actions, hence over his means of survival, and except for a few occasional heroes, I'll promise to deliver to you men who think and write and behave as you want them to.

The case is not difficult to make for the fully controlled economy, the true socialist state. Milton Friedman, chairman of the Department of Economics at the University of Chicago, in his new book, *Capitalism and Freedom,* takes the case of a socialist society that has a sincere desire to preserve freedom of the press. The first problem would be that there would be no "private" capital, no private fortunes that could be used to subsidize an antisocialist, procapitalist press. Hence, the state would have to do it. However, the men and women undertaking the task would have to be released from the socialist labor pool and would have to be assured that they would never be discriminated against in employment opportunities in the socialist apparatus if they were to wish to change occupations later. These procapitalist members of the socialist society would have to go to other functionaries of the state to secure the buildings, the presses, the paper, the skilled and unskilled workmen, and all the other components of a working newspaper. Then they would face the problem of finding distribution outlets, either creating their own (a frightening task) or using the same ones used by the official socialist propaganda organs. Finally, where would they find readers? How many men and women would risk showing up at their state-controlled jobs carrying copies of the *Daily Capitalist*?

There are so many unlikely steps in this process that the assumption that true freedom of the press could be maintained in a socialist society is so unrealistic as to be ludicrous. Of course we are not as yet facing a fully socialized America but only one in which there is significant government intervention in a still predominantly private enterprise economy. Do these individual interventions pose any threat to the non-economic freedoms? I believe they do.

First of all, the number of coercive devices now available to any administration of either party at the national level is so great that true freedom to work actively against the current administration (whatever it might be) is seriously reduced. For example, farmers have become captives of the government in such a way that they are forced into political alignments that seriously reduce their ability to protest that of which they do not approve.

Secondly, the form of these interventions is such as to seriously threaten one of the real cornerstones of all freedoms—equality before the law. For example, farmers and trade union members are now encouraged and assisted in doing precisely that (i.e., acting collusively to manipulate prices) for which businessmen are sent to jail. The blindfolded Goddess of Justice has been encouraged to peek, and she now says, with the jurists of the ancient regimes, "First tell me who you are and then I'll tell you what your rights are." A society in which such gross inequalities before the law are encouraged in economic life is not likely to be one which preserves the principle of equality before the law generally.

We could go on to many specific illustrations. For example, the government uses its legislated monopoly to carry the mails as a means for imposing a censorship on what people send to each other in a completely voluntary relationship. A man and a woman who exchange obscene letters may not be making productive use of their time, but their correspondence is certainly no business of the government. Or to take an example from another country, Winston Churchill, as a critic of the Chamberlain government, was not permitted one minute of radio time on the government-owned and monopolized broadcasting system in the period from 1936 to the outbreak of the war he was predicting in 1939.

Every act of intervention in the economic life of its citizens gives to a government additional power to shape and control the attitudes, the writings, the behavior of those citizens. Every such act is another break in the dike protecting the integrity of the individual as a free man or woman.

The free market protects the integrity of the individual by providing him with a host of decentralized alternatives rather than with one centralized opportunity. Even the known communist can readily find employment in capitalist America. The free market is blind to politics, religion, sexual behavior, and, yes, race. Do you ask about the politics or the religion of the farmer who grew the potatoes you buy at the store? Do you ask about the color of the hands that helped produce the steel you use in your office building?

South Africa provides an interesting example of this. The South Africans provide a shocking picture of racial bigotry, shocking even to a country that has its Mississippi. South African law clearly separates whites from nonwhites. Orientals have traditionally been classed as nonwhite, but South African trade with Japan has become so important in the postwar period that the government of South Africa has declared the Japanese visitors to South Africa to be legally "white." The free market is a great force for creating tolerance and understanding among human beings. The controlled market gives man rein to express all those blind prejudices and intolerant beliefs to which he is forever subject.

I give you then the free market, the economic expression of man's freedom itself and the guarantor of all his other freedoms. I care not what claims may be made by those who would replace it or intervene in it. It is an essential part of man's hope for a better, freer, and more peaceful world.

The New Conservatism

First a note to explain my apparent vacillation in the choice of a topic for my comments today. As many of you know, a college dean is not paid to think—or, at least, not to think about matters extraneous to the operation of his college. For him even to continue an interest in his old, pre-dean discipline is thought by many to be evidence of a frivolous approach to administration. His job is to hire faculty members who will then do whatever thinking needs to be done around the place.

In line with this tradition, I have limited myself in recent years to one non-dean-type thought at a time, and I can never predict what that thought will be at a given moment. Two earlier predictions proved to be wrong; when I came to jotting down some notes for this talk, I found myself bemused by the new conservatism. Thus I had no choice but to make it my topic for today.

This choice of topic makes some sense in that I am considered to be a conservative by that embarrassingly small number of people who have thought me worth classifying. Also there is much talk and writing these days about the new conservatism or the "revival of conservatism" or, as some would put it, the "recrudescence of conservatism."

So to remove any element of suspense from this presentation let me say immediately that from the vantage point of my particular brand of conservatism much of the new conservatism is a hindrance rather than

Speech presented to the Nassau Club, December 6, 1961. Reprinted by permission of the Rogge estate.

an aid to the cause. Or, to put it differently, with some of these people as my friends, I don't need any enemies.

It should be obvious to you that we are now about to play a game of semantics. What is a conservative? What is a liberal? As speakers always say, that reminds me of a story. This is the story of three famous umpires discussing the calling of balls and strikes. The first one says, "I calls them as I sees 'em." The second one says, "I calls them as they are." The third one, and my hero, says, "They ain't nothing till I calls 'em."

I'm going to play the role of the third umpire and begin by saying that of course I am not properly identified when I am called a conservative. Rather I am a classical or, if you prefer, a primitive liberal. The distinguishing characteristics of a classical liberal are (1) a deep and abiding distrust of government and (2) a belief that an individual should be free to do and believe and say anything he wishes so long as he is not using force or fraud against some other individual. The political philosophy that follows from these beliefs is one that limits the government to the night watchman's role, the prevention of an individual from using force or fraud against another. The economic philosophy is basically that of laissez-faire. My intellectual mentors would be such men as Adam Smith, David Ricardo, the early John Stuart Mill, Frédéric Bastiat, Alexis de Tocqueville, Lord Acton, and, among the moderns, Frank Knight and F. A. Hayek, both of the University of Chicago.

If this be true liberalism, what then is true conservatism? The distinguishing characteristics of true conservatism are (1) a deep mistrust of human reason and (2) a belief that order and continuity are of paramount importance in nurturing and preserving the humane and civilized virtues of human beings in society. The true conservative sees society as always threatened by a return to barbarism, with the only effective restraints on brute man being those of religion, custom, recognition of an aristocracy of birth, and so forth. Thus an Edmund Burke sees in a French Revolution, not the coming of the new and enlightened Jerusalem, but a break in the pattern of society so violent that only barbarism or tyranny can result from it. I think it clear that Burke was right, and in fact, I find much with which I can sympathize in this, the true, conservatism. Modern representatives of this point of view are such men as Peter Viereck and Russell Kirk.

It is not, however, this kind of sophisticated and philosophical conservatism that is being revived. Nor can I forget that over the centuries, in actual operation this true conservative philosophy has brought man bondage, not freedom. The prototype of the unfree man has been the one living in a tyranny supported by religion, administered by an hereditary monarch, and made impotent by the deadweight of custom. The ancient kingdom of Sparta, a truly conservative state, lasted much longer than did Athens, but it is not a society I care to see reborn. I realize that the true conservative would say that Sparta was conservatism exaggerated and made rigid, but, alas, this seems so often to be the end of true conservatism in practice.

As I said before, though, the new conservatism is not the true conservatism. What then is it? It is in fact an odd mixture of many conflicting elements. It is, for example, a Robert Welch and a John Birch Society. A Robert Welch would give man his freedom in economic life, as I would. But he would not give man freedom to preach the end of freedom—for example, to preach communism—and I would. I do not know Mr. Welch, but I do know a number of the members of his society. They are serious, sincere people who see this nation facing a crafty and terrible enemy, an enemy so crafty, in fact, that he is able to enlist the witting or unwitting support of many of our own citizens. National survival then depends on exposing and defeating this enemy wherever he might be found. I say these people are serious and sincere, but so were the Athenians who sentenced Socrates to death for subverting the youth of the city. So were the men who devised the Spanish Inquisition; so was Martin Luther when he advised the ruler of a German province to shoot down like dogs the German peasants who threatened the stability of the society; so was John Knox, the father of the Presbyterian Church, when he urged that all Catholics in Scotland be put to death; so were the people who gave trouble to my German-born grandfather during World War I, in spite of the fact that he had a son fighting in the American Expeditionary Force; so were the Americans who ordered imprisonment for thousands of Japanese-Americans in World War II. So are they who, in fright, always hope to solve their problems by hunting out the "bad" guys and eliminating them.

Let us remember now the spirit of David Ricardo, the great classical economist of the early nineteenth century, who, born a Jew, turned

Quaker, yet spent part of his personal fortune to end the legal discrimination against Catholics in Great Britain. Freedom of belief and advocacy means exactly that—for communist and John Bircher alike.

A second much-talked-about element in the new conservatism is campus conservatism, or the phenomenal growth of conservative clubs on college and university campuses. There is much in this that I find interesting and attractive, but much that I find disturbing as well. Many of the young men and women, particularly those in the Intercollegiate Society of Individualists, seem to be concerned with the central issues of the individual versus the state. But many others, particularly in the Young Americans for Freedom group, seem to be only self-importantly and noisily anticommunist. They seem to see their tasks as those of identifying and exposing the left-wingers on the faculty and protecting the House Committee on Un-American Activities. The superpatriot is never a true friend of individual liberty, nor is he who would advance the cause of liberty by restricting the freedoms of all those who disagree with him.

I must confess that I can never be very optimistic about the contribution to the cause of freedom of college-age youth. Classical liberalism is essentially an end-of-innocence philosophy. It requires accepting the imperfect nature of man and, hence, the imperfect nature of all human constructs. It sadly, but firmly, insists that the New Jerusalem is never to be realized. It denies that man can consciously and deliberately plan himself into the good life and the good world. It places its restricted faith in the unpredictable and unplanned consequences of the individual decisions of free men and women.

This is a philosophy of the mature human being. It has little real appeal to the confident, hypercritical mind of the young person. It is the young who believe in the possibility of heaven on earth brought into being by the conscious exercise of their mighty power of reason—and who are prepared to sweep aside those whose feeble minds or weak wills make them an obstacle to the cause. It is later in life, if ever, that a man reconciles himself to living in an imperfect world in which imperfect people make imperfect decisions—and is willing to let them do so, so long as they do not infringe on his freedom and the freedom of others. In sum, while I am encouraged by the increasing interest of college students in the cause of individual freedom, I must confess that I think much of this interest is about as well grounded in philosophic commitment as their interest in panty raids and school spirit. If freedom survives in the decades ahead, it will be because age and not youth has had its way.

A third element in the new conservatism is reflected in a group of senators, particularly representatives in Congress, who belligerently identify themselves as conservatives. Some of these men I find very attractive, and, indeed, some of them seem to be consistent classical liberals. But most of them prove their conservatism by (1) urging the United States to use its military might to crush communism, (2) supporting all restrictive measures against domestic communists and fellow travelers, (3) vigorously upholding the right of the individual status to deny Negroes equality before the law, and (4) always supporting the "business" interest, whether it be by tariffs, right-to-work laws, fair trade acts, special tax treatment, or what have you. In none of this do I find any evidence of a true commitment to the principle of freedom and its corollary, the rule of law.

I am no more attracted by government intervention in economic life to give special treatment to business groups than I am to the antibusiness interventions supported by the modern liberal. This brings me at last to the other side, the belligerent nonconservatives, the authors of the New Frontier, the Fair Deal, the New Deal, and the New Republicanism. If I don't like my fellow conservatives, why don't I ally myself with those who are called liberals today?

The answer is that these people are no more liberal than my conservative friends. Admittedly they usually come down on the right (or freedom) side of the fence when the issue relates to freedom of speech or of press or of belief, although some of them are inconsistent even here. But they have absolutely no commitment to economic freedom, nor to any recognition of its relationship to all other freedoms. They are the would-be philosopher kings who are going to protect, guide, manipulate, subsidize, and control those who are less blessed with wisdom than they. They are the legal Robin Hoods, who in never-ending gallantry, are going to use the coercive power of the state to take from one man and give to another. They are the planners of great plans, whereby this country is going to achieve an annual growth rate of 6.12 percent, and all the underdeveloped countries of the world are to be brought quickly into the modern world. Their point of view is magnificently represented by Newton Minow of the Federal Communications Commission, whose complaint against the television industry is that it is giving the viewers what they (the viewers) want. Under this philosophy, workers and farmers are forced by law to do that for which businessmen are sent to jail. Under this philosophy, the blindfolded Goddess of Justice has been permitted—nay encouraged—to peek, and she now says with the jurists of the ancient regime, "First tell me who you are and I'll tell you what your rights are."

No, there is no commitment to freedom in this philosophy, nor is there any of that fear of the state, of government, upon which any philosophy of freedom must be grounded.

What then is left for a classical liberal? With which side is he to ally himself—the conservative or the modern liberal? In answer and in closing I would like to describe one of my favorite cartoons from the *New Yorker*. In the picture a mother is feeding a vegetable to a little girl in a high chair, and the little girl is obviously having none of it. In the caption the mother says, "It's broccoli, dear," to which the little girl replies, "I say it's spinach, and I say the hell with it."

Gentlemen, whether on the one hand it is called patriotism or true Americanism, or anticommunist, or probusiness, or antilabor; whether on the other hand it is called humanitarianism, liberalism, the wave of the future, economic democracy, the welfare state, the New Frontier, or the New Deal, I say it's spinach, and I say the hell with it.

The Only Economic System
Consistent with Freedom
and Responsibility

I am pleased, honored, and apprehensive at this opportunity to speak to members of the Indiana Bar. My apprehension about lawyers began with my proposal of marriage. My prospective father-in-law was a judge, and I was subjected to two and a half hours of interrogation from the bench—during which I took the Fifth at least a dozen times. I mean the Fifth Amendment, of course, because one of his concerns was whether I was addicted to the other kind of fifth. I could give him an honest no to that, because I was in graduate school at the time and unfortunately couldn't afford even a half pint.

I am comforted by the knowledge that the firm of Wernle and Ristine, which handles my own extensive legal affairs, is well represented here. In fact, this firm represents most of the faculty families at Wabash College, from which group they derive annual fees of approximately $32.15. When I first turned to Wernle and Ristine, they had just opened the office and this $32.15 constituted about one-half their annual receipts. Of course, that was before the sales tax—and it cost less to live then. Although I have been a friend of Dick's for some fifteen years, I am being urged by some to vote for Roger Branigin on the assurance that Roger's first act would be to exempt alcoholic beverages from the sales tax.

I am also apprehensive today because I am going to try to persuade you of the rightness of a philosophy which, if implemented, would

Editor's title. Speech presented to the Indiana Bar, June 27, 1964. Reprinted by permission of the Rogge estate.

cut the demand for the services of lawyers at least in half. My task is
like that of persuading a group of doctors of the rightness of Christian
Science.

Finally, I am apprehensive because I am going to speak as an economist, and as an economist, I am one of the losers. My brand of economics is now known as Brand X. What is my brand? I could say that it is
free private enterprise, but of course everyone is for free private enterprise. Perhaps I can make clear my own position by quoting from one
of my favorite scholars of the nineteenth century, Henry David Thoreau. The famous essayist and author of *Walden Pond* once wrote the
following: "government never of itself furthered any enterprise, but by
the alacrity with which it got out of its way."

Now that you know how hopeless my position is, let me go on to my
thesis. My thesis is that the legal and economic structures of a country
are both reflections of the basic philosophy about human beings generally accepted in that country; that the nineteenth century saw the full
development in England and in this country of a philosophy of individual freedom and personal responsibility, which was reflected in the
final flowering of the common law as the basic structure of law, and of
the free market system as the basic structure of the economy; that this
century has seen a continuing retreat from that philosophy of life and
from the common law and the free enterprise system; and that the consequences of this retreat could well be disastrous to both the freedom
and the economic well-being of the people involved.

I've just given my whole speech in one sentence, and I need to pause
for breath.

Let me begin the argument by sketching briefly the philosophy of
man which tends to be reflected in both the common law and free market economics. The central element in the philosophy is an essentially
religious view of man as a conscious, willing, and responsible entity.
As I personally accept this view of man, I do not deny that each of
us is influenced by the press of environment, by the dark and complex workings of the subconscious, by our parents—in fact, after a few
months in the dean's office, I was ready to recommend that henceforth
Wabash accept only orphans. But what this philosophy argues and
what I accept is that precisely what makes man man is his potential
to transcend these determinants to be something more than a pawn of

his id, his society, and his parents. It argues that given this potential each person is forever and terribly responsible for everything that he does, that the answer to the question "who's to blame?" is always "mea culpa"—I am.

Roscoe Pound, in his famous collection of essays, *The Spirit of the Common Law,* ties the later development of the common law in England and in this country to this Puritan ethic and sees its reflections in Coke in England and in Justice Field in this country. Pound puts it as follows:

> It [the Puritan-influenced common law] expresses the feeling of the self-reliant man that he is to make his own bargains and determine upon his own acts and control his own property, accepting the responsibility that goes with such power, subjecting himself to liability for the consequences of his free choice, but exempt from interference in making his choice. . . . It expresses the feeling of the same self-reliant man that neither the state nor its representative, the magistrate, is competent to judge him better than his own conscience; that he is not to be judged by the discretion of men, but by the inflexible rule of the strict law.

It was reflected in the languange of Blackstone when he wrote, "The public good is in nothing more essentially interested, than in the protection of every individual's private rights."

The relationship between this view of man, the common law, and laissez-faire economics requires no elaboration. It is self-evident—and it was this philosophy that largely guided the development of the legal and economic systems of this country in the first eighty years of the nineteenth century.

These concepts, however, came into direct conflict with the social reform movements of the late nineteenth century and the whole twentieth century. In fact, Roscoe Pound himself was one of the leaders in demanding that the law accommodate the rightful aspirations of the reformers, and his book *The Spirit of the Common Law* was published in 1921 for just that purpose. He argued that the reform movement could rest its case on a second element in the common law, feudal in origin, stressing the concept of "relation," affixing duties and liabilities independent of the will of those bound and on the basis of group or social responsibilities.

Pound has since come to regret his enthusiasm for society imposing its will on its individual member, but the movement of which he was an early leader has gone on apace. In effect, in both England and this country and throughout the world, an older ethic has been revived, the common law has been subjugated to administrative law, and the free economy has been replaced, in whole or in part, by the controlled economy.

The ethic that has been revived is that of man, not as the individual, but as the member of a collective, with primary responsibilities to that collective, with freedom to do only what the collective chooses to permit him to do, responsible neither for his own failures or difficulties nor for his successes, to be sheltered from the possibility of choosing wrongly, to be assisted if in trouble, and to be levied upon if successful.

The implementation of this philosophy has required the development of vast administrative structures and complex networks of administrative law—and most of you make some substantial part of your livelihood by trying to guide the stubbornly self-seeking individual human being through the maze that his economic and personal life has become. What I now wish to argue is that this has brought with it the virtual abandonment of both the rule of law and the time-honored concept of equality before the law.

Let me deal with the second of these first. For example, the reform movement has argued that both workers and farmers are handicapped in the economic struggle and must be given special privileges and immunities. Thus both have been permitted or encouraged or even forced to do precisely that—engage in collusion to manipulate the market price of what they have to sell—for which businessmen are sent to jail.

Here is the way in which Edward Chamberlin of Harvard University has put it:

> If A is bargaining with B over the sale of his house, and if A were given the privileges of a modern labor union, he would be able (1) to conspire with all other owners of houses not to make any alternative offer to B, using violence or the threat of violence if necessary to prevent them, (2) to deprive B himself of access to any alternative offers, (3) to surround the house of B and cut off all deliveries, including food (except by parcel post), (4) to stop all movement from B's house, so that if he were for instance a doctor he could not sell his services and make a living, and (5) to institute

a boycott of B's business. All of these privileges, if he were capable of carrying them out, would no doubt strengthen A's position. But they would not be regarded by anyone as part of "bargaining"—unless A were a labor union.

In effect, in America today, the blindfolded Goddess of Justice has been encouraged to peek, and she now says with the jurists of the ancient regimes, "First tell me who you are and then I'll tell you what your rights are."

I am not making a defense of collusion by businessmen, nor do I deny that such indeed does go on. As Adam Smith wrote in *The Wealth of Nations*, "People of the same trade seldom meet together, even for merriment and diversion, but the conversation ends in . . . some contrivance to raise prices." I am certain it can't be true, but I have even heard that lawyers sometimes send around suggested scales of fees for standard operations and use the state bar exams to exclude outsiders.

In all such cases, it seems to me, the common law had the right and only necessary answer: refuse to enforce collusive agreements at law. This is all that is necessary, because fortunately for the persons on the other side of the market, there are always members in every cartel who will cheat.

This is only one of many illustrations I could present to show the way in which the rise of government intervention in economic life has led to a breakdown of the principle of equality before the law.

A second consequence has been that of substituting the rule of men for the rule of law. I mean specifically that the fate of many of us is now largely determined by the whims and caprices of those who work in the agencies that are administering the programs of social reform. Moreover, assuming that they observe a minimum of formal procedure, their decisions are often exempt from judicial review.

The problems here can be best seen in England, where they are several decades ahead of us in creating the New Jerusalem. Here is what is said by George Keeton, dean of the College of Law, University College, London, in a book entitled *The Passing of Parliament*—a book that I strongly recommend to each of you:

> If Departments can today legislate beyond the reach of Parliament, and if,
> as they do constantly, they exclude the jurisdiction of the ordinary courts,

substituting for it the jurisdiction of their own departmental tribunals, is it not clear that they have effectively excluded the rule of law and the control of Parliament from increasingly wide areas of the subject's social existence? If this is so, is it not clear that "the rule of law" and "the sovereignty of Parliament" have both become polite, and increasingly meaningless fictions?

The factual reports of administrative high-handedness given by Keeton would be enough to make your hair stand on end, unless you had been prepared for them by appearances before trial examiners of the National Labor Relations Board or agents of the Federal Communications Commission or of six dozen other agencies you could identify for me.

Keeton himself felt that this country was less worse off than his own, but he did say, "nevertheless, most American administrative agencies are open to the same fundamental criticism as their English counterparts that they combine within themselves the functions of legislator, prosecutor and judge."

He closes his book with the following statement:

Behind the high sounding generalities of present-day politics, the issue is really a very simple one. It is whether we should accustom ourselves to the ant-like existence of the fully integrated and planned State, or whether we believe that individual initiative and increased opportunity are more likely to produce more tolerable conditions of life for the bulk of our citizens. In the long run, it is impossible to preserve freedom of the mind when the power to choose has been removed from the citizen in more and more areas of his daily life. In the end, there will have been produced something approximating to the planned stagnation of the Chinese Empire. That would be an odd fate for a people who built the common law and who were responsible for Magna Carta, habeas corpus, and dominion status. Yet the threat is real, and the hour late. Our present predicament presents a challenge which it is impossible to ignore.

What I am doing here is to echo his warning.

If time permitted I would argue that the positive welfare state has not produced welfare, but on the contrary has made it less likely that we are going to reduce poverty, maintain high employment, provide for economic security, or achieve a high rate of economic growth and the other laudable objectives of the welfare state.

Today I have concentrated on the side effects of the welfare state, particularly its impact on the traditional framework of the rule of law in this country. You lawyers have temporarily profited from the growth of the administrative state, but the time will come, if it is not already here, when your success will depend not on how well you assist the individual citizen to guarantee his rights in a free society, but on how effectively you can manipulate the men who make the decisions in the labyrinth of American bureaucracy. You may continue to make money, but if you are sensitive at all, you may find it a none-too-satisfying way of life.

In closing let me say again that I am not quarreling with most of the objectives of the modern welfare state. I am saying only that the free economy is still the only demonstrated path to the reduction of poverty, the provision of employment, the growth of the economy, and the true economic security of the individual human being. I am saying as well that it is the only economic system consistent with a true rule of law in a society of free men.

Intellectuals' Curse of Capitalism

Intellectuals are people who live by the power of the spoken and written word—and who have no direct responsibility for practical affairs. —Joseph Schumpeter, *Capitalism, Socialism and Democracy*

Do not snicker; that is what I am. So are Milton Friedman and John Kenneth Galbraith and Walter Cronkite; so too were Adam Smith and Karl Marx and John Maynard Keynes. We are the word people, the ones who talk and write rather than do. But by our words alone we can change the course of the world. As Keynes put it, "The ideas of economists and political philosophers, both when they are right and when they are wrong, are more powerful than is commonly understood. Indeed, the world is ruled by little else."

A self-serving exaggeration? Perhaps, but that ideas do indeed have consequences, few would contest.

Moreover, in the public policy area that is my area of interest the ideas of the economists and political philosophers seem to be largely in error. That is, most members of the intellectual community do not fully share my enthusiasm for that system of economic arrangements roughly identified as capitalism.

There are two possible explanations for this disagreement. The most embarrassing and most plausible is that the Galbraiths of this world are right and I am wrong. A second, more comfortable explanation is that

Reprinted from the *Indianapolis Star*, October 5, 1980, by permission of the Rogge estate.

I am right but that there is something about the mix of capitalism and the intellectuals that predestines most intellectuals to an anti-capitalist mentality.

What are these two elements—one in the intellectuals' view of the world, the other in the way capitalism functions—that might explain the anti-capitalist bias of the intellectuals?

I will describe the first by illustration. When he was head of the Federal Communications Commission, Newton Minow commented, "What is wrong with the television industry in this country is that it is giving the viewers what they (the viewers) want."

What should the television industry be giving the viewers? What we, the intellectuals, know to be best for the viewers and for society at large! After all, do we not read and write more books and score higher on I.Q. tests than the presidents of business firms?

Our sin is out at last, for all to see. The sin is that of arrogance, of a belief that we not only know best how to run our lives, but that we also know best how your lives should be run, including which television shows to watch. If we who know are not given the power to guide you less favored brethren, you will sit all day and most of the night in front of the soap-filled tube, moving only when the delivery service brings you your pink flamingos for the front yard or the junk food for your stomachs.

But the secret sin of capitalism, as seen by the intellectuals, is also out. It does indeed cater to the vulgar whims and caprices of the consumer; it does indeed give the consumer what he wants. In the free market economy, the intellectual can have his way only by persuasion and pleading.

But if the intellectuals can persuade the general public that for its own protection the public must give the intellectuals (now cast as bureaucrats) coercive power over what is to be produced or sold, the situation changes dramatically. The great wisdom of the intellectuals can be supported by the sheriff, and the New Jerusalem again becomes a possibility.

In other words, to many intellectuals, the great curse of capitalism is not that it doesn't work, but that it does; not that it doesn't give the consumers what they want, but that it does give them what they want.

The great attraction of controlled economies to many intellectuals is that such economies lend to the intellectuals in the society the coercive power of the state to put their great wisdom to use for the benefit of all. But what then of freedom? What then if the intellectuals prove to be wrong?

Voluntary Organizations in the Free Society

I wear several hats around this campus, and I would like to begin by wearing my Dean of the College hat. We are delighted to make the facilities of our college available to you for your annual meeting. In part, this is because we can make good use of the income from what would otherwise be empty dormitory rooms and an idle kitchen. But also in part because we take intense pride in this small college and are always pleased with an opportunity to show it off.

Those of you who know of Wabash College but know little about it might be interested in a thumbnail sketch of the place. Wabash is a college for men only, independent of both church and state. It does not accept federal aid and firmly intends to remain a private center of higher education.

The student body in September will number approximately 800. The freshman class is limited to 250 young men, and we closed the class on April 15 this year and will still end up with at least 10 more freshmen than we really wanted. The college offers only one degree, the bachelor of arts, and only one curriculum, the liberal arts and sciences. Seventy percent of our students normally go on to further education after graduation.

Some of our more distinguished graduates have been General Lew Wallace; Tom Marshall, vice president of the United States under Woodrow Wilson; Will Hays, of the Hays Office; Gene Beesley, president of

Speech. Source unknown; no date. Reprinted by permission of the Rogge estate.

Eli Lilly Co.; Ivan Wiles, formerly executive vice president of General Motors; Dave Gerard, creator of *Will-Yum;* Allen Saunders, creator of *Steve Roper, Ma Perkins,* and three other national comic strips; and Richard O. Ristine, lieutenant-governor of Indiana. Oh yes, another is Steve Crane, once husband to Lana Turner and father of the girl who killed Lana's friend Johnny Stompanato.

Last year the college was honored by being selected as one of eight small private colleges for major grants from the Ford Foundation. This was on a matching basis, and you may send your checks to anyone in our organization.

Along with organizations such as yours, this college is one of the many centers of private, voluntary action in American society. We at Wabash College are convinced of the importance of private centers of education. Our argument is the same as that used by John Stuart Mill in his famous treatise *On Liberty,* in which he wrote as follows:

> All that has been said of the importance of individuality of character, and diversity in opinions and modes of conduct, involves, as of the same unspeakable importance, diversity of education. A general State education is a mere contrivance for molding people to be exactly like one another; and as the mold in which it casts them is that which pleases the predominant power in the government, whether this be a monarch, a priesthood, an aristocracy, or the majority of the existing generation; in proportion as it is efficient and successful, it establishes a despotism over the mind, leading by natural tendency to one over the body. An education established and controlled by the State should only exist, if it exist at all, as one among many competing experiments, carried on for the purpose of example and stimulus, to keep the others up to a certain standard of excellence.

In the same way, I am convinced that the preservation of freedom depends upon the existence of numerous and strong centers of private action, formed on the principle of voluntary participation in the furthering of agreed-upon ends.

The central feature of the totalitarian state is that it absorbs all such organizations into the apparatus of the State, either directly or indirectly through control by the official state party. The Church, the schools, the trade unions, the luncheon clubs, the business groups (if any remain), the Boy Scouts—every single organization must give up its private identity and become a part of the system for complete control of the individual and the shaping of him to the ends of the State.

Your organization, then, has a significance far beyond the admittedly excellent work that you do in improving your communities, your states, and your country. You are a symbol of the right of the individual to freely join with like-minded men and women to promote causes of common interest.

The existence of such private centers of influence and opinion is, with our Constitution and our system of federalism, the bulwark against the centralization of influence, opinion, and power in a single, national government. No matter how benevolent may be the intentions of those who wield that centralized power, the very fact of its existence means the end of true freedom for the individual. The benevolent despot is still a despot, and history provides us with few examples of despots who have remained benevolent for any period of time. In the words of Lord Acton, "Power tends to corrupt, and absolute power corrupts absolutely."

Is our system of decentralized power and multiple centers of influence and opinion in danger at this time? If so, what is the nature of that threat and what forces or ideas have brought it into being?

My answer to the first question is quite simply, yes. What then is the nature of the threat and what forces or ideas have brought it into being?

The nature of the threat can be easily identified. It consists, in part, of the obvious and rapid centralization of governmental power in the hands of central government in Washington, D.C. In part it consists of the dramatic increase in the percentage of the national income that is seized by that government for the financing of its programs. Not only do these programs usually infringe on the freedom of the individual to make his own decisions (as in agriculture and in social security), but the progressive system of taxation leaves less money in the hands of precisely those groups in society that have customarily financed many of the private centers of influence and opinion—the private colleges and private charitable organizations being good examples.

The threat consists, in part, of the government taking over many of the functions that were once the reason for private organizations to exist.

Thus, community improvement is no longer thought to be the province of the private community organization—such as the Jaycees—or even of the local government; it has become the province of the federal government, with its huge programs of urban renewal and assistance to municipalities.

The influence here is both subtle and persuasive. A private, voluntary organization working for a better Indianapolis, say, is told that it can make use of federal funds to do so many of the things it has long hoped to do. Moreover, it knows that if the funds are not used to help Indianapolis, they will be used elsewhere—and, of course, the citizens of Indianapolis have paid some part of the taxes used to support the program.

Thus we see throughout the country, in case after case, examples of private organizations becoming propagandists for, or at least partners in, programs of federal aid to local activities. Each time a private organization becomes involved in such a way, it loses part of its independence and part of its significance as a private center of influence and opinion.

The same trend can be observed in the cases of hospitals, clinics, recreation centers, and so forth. In the great field of charity, the modern welfare state has largely replaced the individual charitable act, the private charitable organization, the voluntary service group. Charity is no longer in the domain of the individual conscience; it lies, rather, in the domain of compulsory redistribution of income.

I believe that this has great significance for the whole concept of the freely choosing, moral man. I believe that it can be destructive to both him from whom the money is taken and him to whom it is given.

But I am also convinced that each act of extending the reach of government in these areas reduces the room and the need for private, voluntary action. Each such step reduces the number and effectiveness of private organizations such as yours. Each such step brings closer the day when there remains but one center of influence, opinion, and power—the national government in Washington.

If this be true and if this be an undesirable outcome (as I passionately believe it to be), the relevant question then becomes one of what can be done about it. An apparently easy answer is the one given by organizations such as the John Birch Society: hunt out the rascals who have brought us to this position and prevent them from doing any more damage.

I can have no part in this answer. In the first place let us recognize that we all share in the blame. We have, each of us, at one time or another, given our approval to an action that seemed justified at the time without thinking of its long-run impact on individual freedom and the principle of voluntarism—and without thinking that we were leaving ourselves defenseless against the next steps. For example, Social Security was given the stamp of approval by many who are now leading the fight against Medicare. Yet once you accept the idea that the individual is not responsible for providing for himself in his old age, once you abandon reliance on the system of private charity to help those who are not able to help themselves, you have lost the argument over principle, and you have no real defense against a proposal to provide government medical care to the aged.

It is not evil men, not conniving socialists who have brought us to where we are; it is we ourselves who are willing to take the first easy, tempting steps and then find it difficult and uncomfortable to turn back.

I doubt if any great part of the problems of this world come from the actions of those who are consciously and deliberately seeking to do evil. Rather, most of the problems come from the actions of those who are generally well intentioned, but who are either careless or ignorant of what they are really doing.

But even if we were led to our present position by admitted socialists, the John Birch answer would still be wrong. After all, the socialists (most of whom are serious, well-meaning people) have an equal right to form their own private, voluntary centers of influence and opinion. To deny them that freedom is to deny the very principle for which we are arguing.

If the socialists are winning, it must be because they are being more consistent and more persuasive in presenting their case than we are. The answer is not to throw them in jail, but to look to our own case, to understand it more fully, and to present it more clearly and persuasively.

Specifically, how should we go about doing just that? To begin with, we can work constantly to improve the effectiveness of our voluntary organizations—our churches, our luncheon clubs, our charitable organizations, our private schools and colleges, our chambers of commerce and junior chambers of commerce. Every accomplishment of your organization is another finger in the dike holding back the flood of socialism. Every function well handled by private, voluntary action is an island of defense against further government encroachment in our lives. Every unselfish act of charity or public service is an attack on the argument for more and bigger government. This is something that you can do because you are even now doing it. Keep up the good work in this organization and in every such organization in which you are involved.

But this alone will not be enough. No matter how effective private, voluntary action may be in solving problems, there will always be those who cry for more, who insist that it is not enough. Against these cries there can be only one real defense and that is the defense of an America committed to the principles of decentralization of power, individual responsibility, and economic freedom—including the freedom of the individual to keep that which he has earned through honest means and his own effort.

The real battlefield is one of ideas, and that group will win which best understands its ideas and best presents them. How well fitted are you to join that battle? How carefully have you thought through your own position? What facts do you have to establish its validity? How much reading have you done lately on the principles of freedom? How many of you have ever read even part of the first great statement of the free market idea, Adam Smith's *Wealth of Nations;* of the classic statement on human freedom, John Stuart Mill's *On Liberty;* of the legal cornerstone of the free society, Blackstone's *Commentaries on Law in General;* of the best explanation of the greatest constitution ever written, *The Federalist Papers?* Don't expect the professional intellectuals to do your thinking and reading for you. They are equally human with you, and they may or may not lead you in the right direction.

Once you know what you believe and why, don't compromise on principle in your own behavior or your evaluation of others'. The road to socialism is paved with good intentions and compromises. Inform yourself so that you will not be fooled by labels or by pleas to be realistic, to relax and enjoy the inevitable. To illustrate this, and in closing, let me repeat one of my favorite cartoons from the *New Yorker* magazine: In this cartoon, a mother is trying to feed a green vegetable to a high-chair-age child. The child is obviously having none of it and the mother says, "It's broccoli, dear." To this, the sweet little girl responds, "I say it's spinach, and I say the hell with it."

In like manner, whether the expansion of governmental power is called liberal or progressive or humanitarian or industrial democracy or the wave of the future, I say it's spinach, and I say the hell with it.

Speech in Honor of Leonard Read's Seventieth Birthday

Let me begin by dispelling a myth that has been generally accepted here tonight. This is the myth that Leonard Read is seventy years old. How can any man pretend to be seventy whose mother-in-law is not only still alive, but whose selfsame mother-in-law has (within recent weeks) issued a personal challenge to fisticuffs (in the manner of Bill Buckley) to an official in a New York Giants football game? Anyone who has examined Read's current schedule of activities for a typical week or who is familiar with the tremendous output of his pen in just this last year or who has watched him curl at the St. Andrews rink or who has played golf against him within the last year (as I have) and lost money in the process (as I have) knows that, far from being seventy, he must be somewhere in his mid-forties.

If he wants to attract attention to himself by pretending to be seventy, all right. But by this little deception he's not going to persuade me to give him strokes when next we're out on the golf course. As a matter of fact, this guy Read is the kind of man who doesn't have to ask for strokes in any of the significant activities of his life, including, and especially, libertarianship.

I dislike manufactured words as a rule, but I rather like the manufactured word "libertarianship" because it expresses what seems to me to be the area of Leonard Read's greatest contribution to the cause he

Editor's title. Speech given at the Waldorf-Astoria, New York, N.Y., October 4, 1968. Reprinted by permission of the Rogge estate.

has served throughout his life. The word being of my own creation, I can give it the interpretation I wish. And my wish in using the word is to convey a sense of stance, of posture, of a method of standing witness to the truth of the libertarian philosophy—and it is precisely here that many of us record our largest single personal debts to the man we honor tonight.

He asked repeatedly that this evening not be devoted to a series of personal eulogies. Why? Because he is immune to the pleasures of formal flattery? Not at all. As a matter of fact I have known him, after sinking a long putt, to expect even the caddies to join in the applause. Rather his request is because of his libertarianship. His view of man and life warns him that he must be most on his guard against himself precisely when he has apparently been most successful, precisely when he is being most highly praised.

I want to return to that in a moment, but first let me attempt to put before you what I construe to be Leonard Read's fundamental proposition in libertarianship. It is that having once chosen a philosophy or a set of ends we are not then free to choose whatever means we wish to use in serving those ends. Rather, the choice of means is always implicit in the philosophy itself. Let me illustrate: at the end of one of the FEE weekend seminars, a participant in my discussion group stood up and said in absolute seriousness, "What we ought to have in every school and college in this country is a compulsory course in freedom." Let us not laugh too long at this well-meaning man until we have searched our own records to see how many times and in how many ways we have denied our own understanding of the philosophy of freedom by the means we have used to serve its cause.

I see in Leonard Read a man who is attempting to reflect in everything that he does his own particular philosophy of life—and herein lies his greatness. It is neither insulting nor trivial to add that from time to time he obviously must fail in the attempt. These words were not insulting, because they were spoken in love, nor were they trivial, because a central assumption in Leonard Read's philosophy is that every man, Leonard Read included, is now and forever imperfect. It is for this reason that he warns us to beware of listening to those who praise us. We may come eventually to believe what they are saying, to come to believe that we are perhaps an exception to the rule that all men are imperfect, or at least to believe that our own imperfections are so much less serious than those of others that we really differ from them in kind and not just in degree.

Most of us, particularly those of us who have wives and teenage children around the house, are not likely to be permitted to forget that we are imperfect. Read is at the dangerous stage when his children are grown and out of the house, and the wonderful Aggie, forgetting what a fool he must have been from time to time over the years, fills his days with obvious adoration. But I have confidence that nothing seriously corrupting is going to happen to the man who wrote these words:

> Any overassessment of self, for whatever reason, is corrupting and, thus, dangerous—at least to self, if not to others. The axiom, "power corrupts," doubtless can be explained by that overvaluation of self which the possession of power induces. Even that power to influence others which derives from a relative excellence—with its attendant adulation, flattery, applause—makes difficult a balanced judgment of self: the overesteem, unless consciously downgraded, is irresistible; it is so easily believable!

This is the kind of thing Leonard Read is always saying and that I'm always listening to and trying to apply to the concrete situations in which I find myself.

Here's another Read statement and the one that suggests the problem of method I want to struggle with in my few minutes here in the Waldorf-Astoria sun: "It is a simple, obvious, self-evident fact that ideas, understanding, wisdom cannot be coercively injected into the consciousness of another. Yet, such is the presumption of persons who employ the coercive techniques." That's the statement; here's the question: Does the public demonstration fall under the heading of forbidden techniques? Or are there circumstances under which it would be perfectly consistent for a libertarian to attempt to advance his cause by joining in a public demonstration?

This is not just an academic question; men and women calling themselves conservatives or libertarians have participated in picketing activities and public demonstrations of one kind or another. The man who curses the bearded flower children outside the Conrad Hilton Hotel may applaud the young men who are picketing the offices of business firms doing business with Communist countries. And how many of us are angry with the students in Eastern Europe and in Cuba and in Russia itself who have demonstrated against the Russian actions in Czechoslovakia? Is demonstrating fine and dandy if done by people on our side but an obvious breach of law and order if done by people who aren't on our side? This is what I'm struggling with, and this is the way the struggle goes.

First, is a public demonstration by its very nature a coercive technique? Certainly the leaders of most demonstrations in this country claim that they are following the way of nonviolence, and many a demonstration does take place with no unpeaceful acts having been committed. At the same time, the decline in the public interest in televised boxing and wrestling may come from the fact that now the citizen can always go down to watch a peaceful demonstration somewhere and see actual slugging bouts whose outcomes aren't determined in advance.

What is a public demonstration? It is a group of people collected in a given area to signify their united support of or opposition to something or somebody. Ostensibly, the idea is to communicate to somebody or other the nature of their position on the issues at stake. Why do they not simply content themselves with signing a petition, then? The answer might be given that this is a less dramatic (and hence less efficient) way of making certain that the message gets communicated. It might also be argued that in a democracy a demonstration is a kind of quickie Gallup Poll to show the makers of policy what will happen at the real polls if the demands of the demonstrators are not met. Whatever the argument (and this is at the heart of the thesis I am presenting here), I am persuaded that a group demonstration, by its very nature, partakes of the nature of assault. Even if not a blow is struck or a single piece of property is damaged, the emotional impact on those against whom it is organized is precisely that produced by a threat of assault in individual cases.

While in India during World War II, I saw at first hand a so-called nonviolent march through a city by the nonviolent followers of that man of nonviolence Mahatma Ghandi—and it was one of the most frightening experiences of my life. The flow of that stream of nonviolent individual particles was itself a warning and a symbol of violence unlike anything I had ever seen. From that night on, I have refused to accept as a disciple of nonviolence anyone who is prepared to use the instrument of massive public demonstration in support of his cause. Moreover, I would guess that most of those who organize and most of those who participate in massive public demonstrations know the truth of precisely what I have said. In fact, it is just this aspect of demonstrating that explains its appeal to the young of both the left and the right.

Young people are essentially potential energy, largely undirected and undisciplined. They delight in all kinds of excuses for that energy to be turned loose, from the pep rallies and half-time fights and campus hazing of the old college to the student sit-ins in the president's office of the new college. This is the kind of energy that can be used to destroy existing structures; it is not the kind of energy that can be used to bring about improved structures.

I repeat what I have said before in other settings: Those on our side who are looking to the young to lead this nation back to freedom will look in vain. For most of us, it is only with age, if ever, that we acquire the wisdom to be content to live under always imperfect rules that still permit us imperfect men to make our own imperfect decisions, with consequences for each man and for all men that no one can fully predict and that will always be something less than the New Jerusalem. It is the vision of a New Jerusalem, even if not clearly defined, or the vision of its opposite, of an existing total wickedness that must be destroyed, that brings people out into the streets. To my mind, the bringing of people out into the streets is not a part of the persuasive process. On the contrary, it marks the end of the persuasive process and the beginning of coercive action.

Of course, even if this be correct, it does not automatically solve the legal problems involved; that is, the questions relating to whether and in what form and under what circumstances public demonstrations should be permitted at law. Certainly, if they were to be viewed as I view them, as partaking by nature of the characteristics of assault, they would come under more vigorous control by law than is true at the present.

But whether legal or not, public demonstrations fall outside the border of acceptable techniques for Ben Rogge to use in serving the libertarian cause. Can you conceive of Leonard Read, joined perhaps by Professor Mises and the Reverend Ed Opitz attempting to make a point by picketing the home of, say, John Kenneth Galbraith? (Professors and ministers are big in the demonstration business these days; often they lead the charge, robes flying, to bring about the end of civilized society.) Or of Milton Friedman picketing the offices of the board of governors of the Federal Reserve System—perhaps carrying a banner on which he had painted in psychedelic colors some of his more telling regression equations?

If the libertarian goal can be defined as the victory of persuasion over force in human relationships, it can hardly be served by techniques that are coercive in nature, including public demonstrations. I will not march outside the offices of IBM or Firestone; I will not counter-demonstrate against the Mark Rudds and his faculty supporters; I will not join the demonstration outside the Soviet embassy. For so long as the channels for persuasion are not totally blocked (to borrow again from Leonard Read), I am committed by my philosophy to using persuasion alone in standing witness to my beliefs.

When we turn to Leonard Read for guidance on how best to stand witness, his answer is always the answer of Linus (the philosopher with a security blanket). Charlie Brown says to Linus, "Linus, suppose that nobody liked you or listened to what you were saying. What would you do? What would your answer be?" To this Linus replies, "I would examine myself very carefully to discover where my weaknesses lie and then I would attempt to correct them. That is my answer, Charlie Brown." To this Charlie Brown says, "I hate that answer."

And well he may, and well may we be irritated when Leonard Read tells us again and again and still again that we must always look to ourselves—to self-improvement, not to reforming others—if we wish to serve the cause of freedom. That he just may be right is testified to by our presence here tonight and because not an hour goes by but that somewhere in this world somebody is thinking or speaking or writing a word or taking an action under the direct or indirect influence of the life and the teachings of Leonard Read. May the rest of us be one part as effective and the world will again turn its face to freedom.

The Power of Tomorrow: Whither FEE?

The question before this house is, whither FEE? My answer to that question is that I do not know whither FEE. My answer is that you do not know whither FEE. My answer is that even Leonard Read (and this will shock you)—even Leonard Read does not know whither FEE. The reason for this universal ignorance is to be found in the fact that (as St. Augustine reminded us) God did not see fit to give any mere mortal the power of perfect foresight.

That Ben Rogge is a mere mortal will surprise no one. That Leonard Read is a mere mortal is somehow less credible. His denials to the contrary, we have come to expect *him* at least to transcend the boundaries of mere humanness. Leonard Read not know? How absurd; of course he will know. Yet by his own testimony, he has declared his imperfect knowledge of what in fact will happen in the years ahead to FEE, to the world, and even to his own physical self.

Let us be blunt and open about it. We are met at this time to discuss whither FEE? because we can no longer pretend that Leonard Read will always be here to tell us what to do and how to do it—and then to play the lead in carrying it out. Now don't panic and don't assume that I have knowledge that some of you do not have.

I fully expect Leonard Read to be in active leadership of FEE after others of us in this room have gone to the great FEE seminar up there in

Speech given at the Foundation for Economic Education (FEE) trustees meeting on November 18, 1979. Reprinted by permission of the Rogge estate.

the sky. But sooner or later, he is not going to be in active leadership of FEE, and the question is, what then?

My assignment here is not to answer that question, but to set in motion a discussion of that question. This I propose to do by offering up, as grist for your mills, a number of my own thoughts about what to do when Leonard isn't around to do it. I shall do so in the form of answers I will suggest to the following questions:

1. Should FEE be continued at all, or should it be given a decent, respectful burial?
2. If it is to be continued, should it follow the same general pattern of operation as in the past, or should we start planning even now to change its structure and its method of operating?
3. Should we look for some one person to give the post-Read FEE the same one-man leadership that existed under Read? If not, how should FEE be run and by whom?

The answers I now give you to these questions are not to be confused with the laws of Moses, brought down from the mountain. They are at best a beginning for a discussion or a debate, if you will, a debate that goes on in my own mind even as I speak.

Question 1

Should we plan to keep FEE going or should we close up shop? The temptation, even for me, is to rise up in anger at any suggestion that the doors of FEE be closed forever. However, let me read to you the words of one of my favorite speakers uttered on the occasion of FEE's twenty-fifth anniversary:

> The real danger to an organization of this kind is not that it will simply disappear, but that its form will long survive its soul. . . . Times change and people change and institutions change; it is as certain as death itself that sooner or later FEE will be, in spirit, something quite different from what it now is. Moreover, the chances are that that spirit will be significantly alien to the spirit that now moves this organization.
>
> When that day comes, if any of us are still around, let us have the courage and good sense to give FEE a decent burial, rather than yield to a pagan attachment to a body from which the spirit has already fled.

I meant those words when I first spoke them, and I am guided by them now. If it appears now or in the future that FEE can be kept alive only by compromising its essential nature, then, I say, close the doors and have done with it. That which carries the acronym FEE is a specific collection of people and things in a particular setting in time—and not a sacred vessel to be preserved at all cost.

Am I saying, then, that when Leonard can no longer be in daily command of FEE, we should bang the door shut, pension off the faithful, and bid FEE goodbye? I am not. I am saying only that to do so at some time in the near or distant future should be preferred to a saving of the acronym at the cost of its soul.

We return to the question, should FEE be continued? Perhaps we should first ask *this* question: is the fight for freedom so nearly won that a FEE is no longer needed—or so nearly lost that the activities of a FEE amount to little more than rearranging the deck chairs on board the Titanic? Does the passing of two propositions in California and the fact that college students have stopped burning down their college administration buildings mean that we can now relax and start work on a victory dinner? Hardly.

I am reminded of a story in one of Bernard Malamud's writings that seems relevant here. A small group of Jews lived in the Russian countryside under the tsars in a village that was situated in a rather deep valley. The elders of the group became concerned that when the Messiah came he would pass by their village and go right on. Their response was to build a high wooden tower out of the valley and into its morning mists. In that tower they placed the village beggar-handyman as a lookout. On detecting the presence of the Messiah, he was to shout loudly and draw the Messiah's attention to the presence of a flock of his chosen people in the valley below. Several weeks later, on one of his visits back to the valley, the lookout attendant was in conversation with a friend. The friend asked him about his new job, and he replied that it was all right. The friend then asked him about the pay, and he replied that although the pay wasn't so much he thought that he had found "steady work."

And so it is with us. It is quite unlikely that a Messiah, of either human or transcendent nature, will flood the world in a reign of perfect freedom in the near future. We do indeed have "steady work." The only question is how best to go about that work and what role, if any, should a FEE play in that work. Are there other organizations of similar, if not identical, purpose working in freedom's vineyard? Of course there are; in fact, almost every person in this room is involved in at least one, and many of us (including Ben Rogge) are involved in one way or another in a half-dozen or more organizations that are working the freedom side of the street. Let us face it: if FEE were to close its doors tomorrow, the fight for freedom would continue to be pressed by a great many organizations of solid structure, staffed by men and women of competence and courage.

If this be true, why then should we fret and stew about FEE? Why not just rechannel our energies (and our funds) through these other organizations that are even now in place and doing battle in freedom's cause? It seems to me that right here is the nub of our question. Unless there has been something unique in the way FEE has carried out its program in support of freedom, then there is little reason to put up any special fight to preserve it. Moreover, unless that which is unique can be carried forward into the years ahead, there is again little reason to make any special effort to see that it continues.

Our search, then, is for that which is unique and necessary for the cause in the operation of FEE. The first idea that suggests itself is largely the mortal person of its founder and only president, Leonard Read. We are not met here to celebrate Leonard Read; we are here to face facts and make plans. But for the purpose of our planning, is the uniqueness of Leonard Read the fact that overpowers all others?

I tell you in all honesty that it may well be. I do not seek to flatter Leonard Read; his ego has been reasonably well nourished for many years now. But the plain fact is that the running of an operation like FEE requires a man with a unique combination of gifts: the gift of understanding (without which nothing else matters), the gift of courage, the gift of eloquence, and at the same time, the capacity to handle the nitty-gritty tasks of raising money and managing people and things. If you think that combination isn't unique, make me a list of ten such people on our side of the street, and I'll give you a free copy of *Can Capitalism Surivive?* for each name on the list.

There are many people who can handle one or more of these tasks, but few who can handle them all. For example, in speaking of the administrative talents of one of the most brilliant of our freedom-loving scholars, Neil McLeod of Liberty Fund said "that man couldn't manage a two-car funeral." Yes, time may well prove that Leonard Read was and is our uniqueness and that, absent him, FEE has no great reason to exist. Nor would such an outcome reduce the significance of what all of us have been able to do under Leonard Read's leadership.

Just as Yankee Stadium, the House That Ruth Built, has survived the passing of the Babe himself, FEE, the House That Leonard Read Built, may be able to survive his passing from active leadership. Let us go back to our question: other than Leonard Read in person, are there unique ways FEE goes about its defense of freedom that would give real significance to its survival? I think there are, and I propose to identify them.

First, and most important, FEE has had one, and only one, philosophical position. As one of my colleagues who knows something about FEE said of it, "You know, Rogge, FEE may be wrong, but at least it's consistently wrong." Other organizations have been willing to embrace a wide range of views on the freedom side of the fence—and I make no criticism of that approach. For some purposes—for example, to influence public policy immediately and directly—this approach may be the appropriate one. But under Leonard Read's leadership, FEE has had the one position—"anything that's peaceful"; in a word, it has been predictable.

For example, before I ever heard Leonard Read pronounce on the subject, I knew exactly how he would respond to the voucher proposal in public education. Negative! Why? Because at best it can make more palatable an institutional arrangement (state-controlled education) that is, by its very nature, repugnant to the cause of human freedom. Quite frankly, I know of no other organization on our general side of the street whose position on any given issue is as predictable as FEE's No ifs, ands, or buts, no equivocation, just right down the line, ramrod straight for a society based on the principle of anything that's peaceful.

I believe this to be FEE's great, distinguishing characteristic. At the same time, I recognize that for each of us, there are particular questions of public policy—perhaps drug use or tariffs or zoning or the military draft or the Vienna State Opera—where FEE's unwillingness to bend or to recognize exceptions is a source of discomfort or unease. But it is my firm conviction that had FEE been willing to bend, it would not exist today. If Leonard Read had not been perfectly willing to say no to each of us when the occasion demanded, FEE's contribution to the cause of freedom would have been modest and transient.

I would identify the second of the unique features of FEE as its absolutely clear and unambiguous position on method: that is, it has placed itself in that part of the battlefield where the struggle is over ideas, over principles, if you wish. Or to put it another way, FEE has steadfastly refused to become an activist organization, to get involved in political campaigns or in popular movements.

The question is not whether activism is to be praised or condemned, to be used or not used. The question is whether an organization like FEE is going to work that part of the battlefield. As a board, following Leonard's lead, we have consistently said no—but not without some occasional signs of unease and halfheartedness.

FEE's nonactivist position can be (and has been) defended on the grounds that the battle of ideas is where it's at—that the activists can hope to win only when the idea base has been appropriately prepared; in other words, change the ideas and, sooner or later, the actions of the political leaders will change as well. But I would argue that it isn't necessary to accept that position to still agree with FEE's nonactivist position. It's very difficult—if not impossible—to participate in the day-to-day activist section of the battle and retain one's philosophical purity. (I offer in evidence the problems of Senator Goldwater's presidential campaign and the temptation to compromise that seems to confront Ronald Reagan's presidential aspirations at this very moment.) A candidate for public office almost inevitably comes to emulate Tell Binkley's nephew (as described by Hoosier humorist Kin Hubbard) who, when asked by the Plum Creek School Board in a job interview whether the Mississippi River flowed north or south, replied that he could teach it either way.

If one sees FEE's great strength in the battlefield of ideas (as I do) as lying in its philosophical consistency, then one tends to reject an activist role for FEE on purely practical grounds.

The third unique feature of FEE's posture, as identified by Ben Rogge, is its insistence that whatever others may do FEE does not intend to take its case to the masses. Here again one can argue (as Leonard Read does) that it is futile to attempt to win by so doing, that the real problem is a leadership problem, a problem of what Albert J. Nock called "the Remnant." It is not necessary, however, to accept that argument to still agree that FEE itself should make no attempt to take its case to the masses. It is difficult to communicate with the masses at that level of analysis and understanding appropriate to the battle for the minds of those who eventually, in turn, shape the opinions of the masses. If you don't believe this, just send copies of *Human Action* by Ludwig von Mises to the first ten names in your hometown telephone directory and see how many converts you make. In other words, not just on philosophical grounds, but again as a practical matter, by not attempting to reach the masses directly, FEE has been able to concentrate its resources on those levels of understanding and explanation appropriate to the Remnant that serves the leadership role in the defense of freedom.

In summary, I see FEE's uniqueness as consisting of these three characteristics: (1) steadfast adherence to one consistent, fully thought-out philosophical position, (2) an equally unambiguous choice of method, to wit, the search for basic principles and for the practical implications of those principles (as distinct from the method of activism), and (3) a clear-cut choice to not seek to reach the masses directly but rather to concentrate on those levels of philosophical inquiry where the inquiring few find the wellsprings of their own thought and action.

Quite frankly, I do not know of another organization working our side that offers us and the world this precise bundle of characteristics. If you believe (as I do) that just such an organization is an absolutely necessary part of freedom's forces, then you will join me in believing that it is imperative that we work together to see that FEE survives.

Question 2

If FEE is to be continued (as I have argued it should be), should it follow the same general pattern of operation as in the past, or should we start planning even now to change its structure and its method of operating?

It seems to me that, in a general way, this question has already been answered. I have argued that the general principles which govern FEE's operation are the source of its uniqueness and the reason for us to be concerned for its survival. This would seem to speak against any change in the basic principles which govern FEE's day-to-day activities. As a matter of fact, I would have no interest in participating in a project that would keep FEE alive but operating under significantly different general premises.

None of this should be taken to mean that the details of operation as they now exist are forever sacred and must never be changed. The actual details of operation are always changing and evolving in any organization in both planned and unplanned ways. Any significant event in an organization's history (of the kind we are discussing) is often a good time for a careful look at actual operational practice, to see what has become unnecessary or inefficient or what new techniques might be given a try. I have nothing to suggest at this time on my own, but I'm certain that there will be suggestions forthcoming for changes in practice in our session tomorrow morning.

In summary, my answer to question 2 is that we should not change those basic principles that have guided FEE's practice from the beginning but that we should encourage such changes in the details of practice as promise to improve FEE's overall effectiveness.

Question 3

Should we look for some one person to give the post-Read FEE the same one-man leadership that has existed under Read? If not, how should FEE be run, and by whom?

I do not know how to answer these questions. It seems to me that this is one of those situations where we might profitably draw upon the wisdom of Adam Ferguson and his description of outcomes "that are the result of human action but not of human design." I am not suggesting that we give no thought at this time to the leadership of FEE in the years ahead. What I am suggesting is that we not act in haste but rather that we give time for fortune to smile on us, as she seems to on those who are open to her surprises.

After all, at this moment we not only have Leonard Read but have in addition three good men and true who are perfectly capable of keeping FEE going ahead for X number of years in the future—and, most important, under the traditional principles of the founder. In Bob Anderson,

Ed Opitz, Paul Poirot, Bettina Greaves, Janette Brown, Mike Krenza, and others, Leonard Read has put together a magnificent group that even now does most of the work of FEE. Each of the three men first identified would be quick to point out that he is no Leonard Read—but who is, other than Read himself? I have no doubt that these three could keep FEE in full operation for a long time while the solution to the leadership problem emerges out of the course of events.

Again I am not saying that we, the members of the board of trustees of FEE, should do nothing but sit and wait. Certainly each of us individually should be giving thought to the situation that will some day confront us. Moreover it might be appropriate for there to be created a special committee of the board on long-range planning, with the leadership question as the principal item on its agenda. I am certain that other suggestions for action or thought to be taken will emerge from our discussions this afternoon and tomorrow morning.

In closing I return again to the theme that there has been created here in the Foundation for Economic Education a truly unique institution. It has been unique in its steadfast devotion to the cause of human freedom, human dignity, and the growth in human consciousness. It has been unique in the integrity with which it has served that cause. It has been unique in the influence over the minds of men that it has already exerted—and that it would continue to exert if its doors were closed tomorrow. If, after a full try has been made, it appears that those high standards cannot be maintained, then let us indeed close those doors. But let it never be said of us in this room and of the other many friends of FEE that we lacked the courage, the determination, or the dedication to the cause of freedom to make that full and vigorous attempt to continue the great work of the founder of the Foundation for Economic Education. Let us pledge ourselves in these two days to that most worthy and noble undertaking.

What Are the Duties of the State?

The topic that we are to discuss this morning seems to me to be uniquely appropriate to a session of the Philadelphia Society. The common belief that holds together this mixture of conservatives and libertarians is the conviction that in every country in the world today, not least our own, the agenda of the state has been grossly overextended. At the same time, I suspect that what often divides us is disagreement over what it is precisely that the state should do.

My own contribution will be precisely that—my own. It is Rogge's own personal philosophy that you are to be given. I describe myself as generally belonging to the libertarian wing, but I refuse to put a curse on other libertarians by identifying what you are to hear as *the* libertarian position or even as *a* libertarian position. Right or wrong, relevant or irrelevant, interesting or uninteresting, it is Rogge's very own, and you can make of it what you will. But don't misunderstand me: in saying this, I am not laying claim to any original analysis. This will be my own piecing together of fundamental theories and assumptions laid down by those who have done original work on this topic.

I begin with the assumption that man is imperfect, now and forever. Precisely what do I mean by this? I mean that he is imperfect as an intellectual agent—that is, in his knowledge of the universe around him and inside him; that he is imperfect as a moral agent—that is, in the

Speech to the Philadelphia Society, October 6, 1967. Reprinted by permission of the Rogge estate.

integrity with which he serves such values as he holds to be important; most important, that he is imperfect as a divine agent that is; he does not fully know what his purpose (if any) is on this earth; he does not fully know which values are the higher and which the lower.

Now, if this be true, does it not follow that one man's opinion in any of these roles is as good as any other's; or at least that, even with respect to the opinions of the best of men in any of these roles, there must exist an inevitable and terrible uncertainty? Indeed these conclusions could be drawn from the assumption as I have stated it. Where then do we go from here? I personally go from here to an explicit and apparently unavoidable leap of faith. Let me explain.

I simply cannot accept a view of the world in which one man's opinion as an intellectual agent is always as good as another's, in which one man's behavior as a moral agent is neither better nor worse than another's, in which one man's interpretation of man's purpose is as valid as another's. For life would then indeed be "a tale told by an idiot, full of sound and fury, signifying nothing." For my own sanity, almost for a reason to live, I must take the leap of faith and assume that there is indeed a better and a worse, a moral and an immoral, a more valid and a less valid. If you wish, there are absolutes, there are final standards, final benchmarks. There is a realm of the transcendental, if you wish. But now a libertarian word of caution: these absolutes, these ultimates, exist as rabbits to be chased but never to be caught. If every man is imperfect, then no man is ever to know them fully or to live by them completely. To the opinions and behavior and revelations of even the best of men must still cling the mortal, the human uncertainty.

It would seem to follow then that what counts is not the unattainable climax of catching the rabbit but the nature of the chase itself. If no one knows fully, if even those who come to be least imperfect in knowing and acting cannot be identified in advance (or even clearly identified after the fact), surely it follows that each imperfect man must be given (indeed, has) the right to follow his own imperfectly selected star in his own imperfect way, to march to the music he hears and not to the music that you and I hear. From this it follows that no man has a right to forcibly control another's march, another's search. Ah, but here's the rub: suppose one man's vision tells him that he must march forcibly over the body of another man and his code declares this to be a moral act? If all moralities are equally acceptable, whose morality is to prevail now?

This is really no problem. The man on the ground also has a right to march to his music; he also stands under the protection of the original premise, and the premise cannot be offered as a defense for denying the premise. As it has been put so many times before, my freedom to swing my fist is limited by the equal freedom of your nose.

But we live in a world in which some men are obsessive fist-swingers, and each of us is tempted on occasion to use the persuasion of the knuckles. This too is in the nature of man, and herein lies the duty of the state. The one and only duty of the state is to control the fist-swinging, to keep one man from using force against another.

I realize that there are those who believe that even this necessary social function of controlling the fist-swingers could and should be entrusted to men acting individually or through voluntary associations. They may be right, and many of these men are true lovers of freedom, but I think them wrong. With Professor Mises, I believe the state to be not only a necessary and desirable social institution but to be the most desirable of all social institutions, because without it, each man (or group) would be fist-swinging judge in his own cause, and life would indeed be mean, nasty, brutish, and short. But the state is fully useful only if it is limited in function to simply keeping the peace both within and on the borders of its jurisdiction. I repeat, this is its duty and its only duty. Or to put it another way, in the political society I deem to be the appropriate one, each individual is left free from physical coercion by others and by the state itself in the doing of absolutely anything that's peaceful, either alone or in voluntary association with others.

Let me enumerate some of the activities of the state in this country that would be eliminated under this rule.

1. All actions, all legislation relating to economic life except those involving force or fraud (which is just a special case of the use of force). Comment: In case there should be any doubt, this would mean a privately provided money supply and a totally private educational system, as well as no TVA and no minimum wage laws.

2. All regulation of peaceful, personal behavior. Comment: This means no laws regulating noncoercive sexual behavior, use of alcohol, use of narcotics, and so forth.
3. All forms of state censorship of the press, the stage, the radio, TV, and so on.
4. All restrictions on freedom of speech.
5. All restrictions on entry to the country, not only of goods but of people as well. Comment: It is only the welfare state that must limit immigration. A non–welfare state can benefit from immigration, as our own experience in the last century indicates.
6. All official state positions on religion, for or against. After all, why should the chief of police be appointed as divine agent?

Even though this list of proscribed state activities is just a sampling, it should make clear that the influence of the state in Rogge's world would be somewhat less ubiquitous than it is at present. But at the same time, I would like to argue that the state is now doing far too little in its one legitimate area, that of keeping the peace. Let me cite three kinds of cases. One is just simply that of keeping the criminals, the hooligans, and the toughs under control. Surely I don't need to tell this group about fear in the streets. A second type of case is the violence, the destruction of property, and the denial of property rights that are now permitted if committed by those who are thought to be serving a good cause. This is the single most dangerous doctrine of our times. I trace its real origins to the special privileges granted trade unions in the 1930s, symbolized by the inactivity of the state in the face of the sit-in strikes. When the state did not immediately use its full force to evict these people, the whole concept of private property was brought into question, and the age of lawlessness began. In today's riots, we see the natural consequences of this strange philosophy that a criminal attack on persons and property is not criminal if committed by well-meaning people.

A third type is the long-continued failure of the state to curb what is now termed "pollution." For one man to impose the smoke from his factory or even the exhaust from his car on another is a direct violation of that person's rights. Reduced costs of output that are obtained by shifting some of the costs to innocent third parties are a snare and a delusion, and we are now paying a tragic price for our neglect in this area. Yet all that was ever required was a proper protection of persons and property.

In other words, the state has done far too little to carry out its one legitimate function, while assuming one inappropriate function after another.

One further comment on this: we pay the men and women who carry out this necessary function of keeping the peace less than the market would require. Thus our police departments are manned by some of the least competent individuals in our society, and we have to coerce men into our armed forces, like slaves and not like free men.

Two further comments and then I'm through. In arguing that the state should not legislate, say, against homosexual activity between consenting adults, I am not expressing approval of this activity, nor am I asking you to approve, nor am I asking you not to criticize it or to use all your persuasive powers, including social ostracism, to reduce it. Just remember though, that the laws we now enforce would have sent almost every one of the great philosophers of ancient Greece to jail.

What I am asking for is precisely what men like Albert J. Nock have asked for in the past—that the society be distinguished from the state and that the society not be absorbed by the state. Society, with its full network of restraints on individual conduct—based on custom, tradition, religion, personal morality, and a sense of style—and with all of its, indeed, powerful sanctions is what makes the civilized life possible and meaningful. I am not proposing an anarchic society; on the contrary I am essentially a conservative on most questions of social organization and social process. I do believe in continuity, in the important role of tradition and custom, in standards for personal conduct, and in the great importance of the elites (imperfect though they may be).

But unlike the political conservative, I do not wish to see these influences on individual behavior institutionalized in the hands of the state. As I read history, I see that everywhere the generally accepted social processes have been made into law, civilization has ceased to advance. For one, the penalty to be paid by the innovator, which is severe even without the law, and perhaps properly so, is made so severe (even including death) as to stop that healthy and necessary and slow process of change through which civilizations move to higher levels of achievement.

For another, the elites, if given the power to implement their views with the use of force, are almost certain to be corrupted by that power and to cease playing their essential and beneficial role in society. The pages of history are strewn with the wreckages of superior men who have been undone by the corrupting influence of possession of the power to coerce.

I repeat: my goal is not to bring the anarchic society; rather it is to so separate society and the legal right to coerce as to permit that appropriate tension between the essential societal restraints on individual conduct and the equally essential, disruptive behavior of the innovator.

One final comment. To say that the state should be limited to maintaining law and order might seem to imply that this is a simple, unambiguous task. I know full well that it is not. For example, my lawyer friend Pierre Goodrich has made me aware of the great difficulty at law of defining what constitutes assault. There must always be boundary problems, and for these I would rely on the method of one of the greatest works of civilized man—the common law. In its case-by-case approach, with precedent as the guide, it seems to me to have been the best of all legal approximations of the society of free and responsible men and the associated human right of private property. Our march into collectivism can be measured in part by our march away from the common law and into administrative law.

A second example. What guidance does this philosophy give the state in carrying out its duty to protect its citizenry from aggression from outside its borders? For example, what does it have to say about American involvement in Viet Nam? This too is one of those difficult boundary decisions. I am opposed to the American presence in Viet Nam because (for one of many reasons) it seems to me to reflect an intent to use force to keep others from falling into sin—an intent quite out of keeping with any form of libertarian philosophy. At the same time, I recognize that it can be argued that it is simply a necessary step to protect our own borders from eventual attack—and many of my libertarian friends do support the American position in Viet Nam on this precise basis. In other words, there would still exist difficult boundary problems in even the Rogge-type world.

But, at least, in such a world, the individual imperfect man would be left far freer than he is today to make his own imperfect decisions, enjoying the fruits of his successes and suffering the agony of his mistakes; he could at least fully attain to the dignity and tragedy and comedy that come with being a man; and the great and unpredictable and mysterious processes of civilized society could work their way through historical time, perhaps to levels of achievement that no one of us now can even comprehend.

Is Economic Freedom Possible?

The real debate on domestic policy in the United States at mid-century concerns the proper role of government—and those who wish for less government in economic affairs are obviously losing. The judges, in this case the voters of the United States, have been giving verdict after verdict to those who argue for more government intervention.

Those of us who are losing the debate often ascribe our losses to the work of men in academic life and elsewhere who are preaching socialism and trying to subvert the traditional American system of free enterprise. This easy and tempting explanation implies that our un-American opponents should be silent, and thus permit true American principles to prevail.

This explanation is both untrue and dangerous. It is dangerous because it could lead us to impose restraints on freedom of speech and of press that would indeed be un-American. It is dangerous because it leads us to relax our efforts to prepare and present our own case as powerfully and persuasively as possible. It is untrue because not one in five hundred of those who favor more government intervention is a committed socialist or even basically opposed to free private enterprise. On the contrary, most of them are committed to the free market arrangement and believe that their proposals are designed to strengthen rather than to weaken it. Specifically, they argue that the market arrangement

Reprinted from the *Freeman* (April 1963): 14–23, by permission of the publisher, Foundation for Economic Education, Irvington-on-Hudson, N.Y. All rights reserved.

can survive only if certain of its weaknesses and failures are offset by appropriate government action.

For example, it is alleged that the free market economy tends to be unstable, alternating between boom and bust, and that this instability will destroy the economy unless corrected by appropriate government action. Though this is a serious charge, I believe that both the analysis and the call for government action are mistaken.

What I prefer to discuss here is an equally serious charge made against the free market by its friends.

Their charge is that economic freedom, though desirable, is not strictly possible—that in an unhampered market the individual would not be truly free but would be imposed upon by monopolies of various kinds and degrees. This charge appears in the preamble to one piece of interventionist legislation after another. Thus, the worker is said to need special protection because of the monopoly power of the employer. The farmer must be protected against monopolies on both sides of his market. Certain kinds of business firms must be protected against certain other kinds. Certain price decisions must be influenced by government because of the monopoly power of the firms involved. And on and on it goes. Clearly, if private monopoly is indeed this ubiquitous, a presumption is established in favor of a substantial role for government.

In my opinion, however, and this is to be the central thesis of my argument, the unhampered market tends to be a competitive market. In fact, strong action by government is all that can prevent its being a competitive market.

Phrased another way, my thesis is that positions of monopoly power tend to be short-lived and relatively ineffective, except as they receive the positive assistance and protection of government. Or phrased still another way, government in the United States has done far more to promote monopoly than to promote and permit competition.

Good for Others, Not for Me!

In developing the argument, I admit that there are certain very human attitudes which tend to work against competition. Although each of us may approve of competition as a general principle, we are less than anxious to face competition in our own personal activities. Competition is good in principle, we say, but not in our particular industry or occupation, or not when it comes from overseas, or not when it comes from people improperly trained in this occupation.

A natural outcome of this attitude is the attempt to reduce competition by cooperative action among would-be competitors. This tendency was clearly recognized by Adam Smith, the father of free market economics. In *The Wealth of Nations*, published in 1776, he wrote as follows: "People of the same trade seldom meet together, even for merriment and diversion, but the conversation ends . . . in some contrivance to raise prices."

A second reason for questioning the possibility of a truly free economy is the influence of advancing technology on the size of the firm. The continuing technological revolution has produced a situation in one industry after another where, to be efficient, a firm must represent a large accumulation of capital, translated into buildings, machinery, and distribution organizations of great size and complexity. This growth in the size of the efficient firm is another challenge to the maintenance of the competitive economy.

A third reason often advanced for skepticism about competition is the difficulty of keeping oneself informed on the alternatives facing him in the multiple markets in which he operates, and the associated difficulty of retaining the mobility to shift his course of action in response to changes in those market alternatives.

A Temptation to Connive

The modern economic world is indeed a complex and confusing world, and these charges deserve serious attention. Let us take the charge that collusion rather than competition tends to be the distinguishing characteristic of the unregulated market economy. It is true that men are always tempted to practice collusion. However, it is equally true that the same forces which lead to the formation of cartel agreements tend to destroy those agreements.

The principal force involved here is simply the desire to make money. For example, suppose that a number of farmers agree to hold livestock off the market in a local area. The effect of this, of course, is to cause livestock prices to rise in that area. But with each increase in price, the individual farmer is under greater temptation to break the rules of the cartel and sell his hogs or beef cattle. At the same time, each increase in price attracts more livestock to that local market from farms outside the agreement area. The members of the cartel must then battle both their own members and outsiders to maintain the effectiveness of their operation.

In the same way, if a number of business firms agree to divide the total market into exclusive territories, the resulting price increase tempts each firm to try to increase its sales so as to increase its profits. However, each firm's own territory provides only limited opportunities for increased sales, and the temptation is enormous to expand sales by poaching on the neighboring forbidden markets.

Cartels in America

The history of cartels in America is a history of brief initial successes followed by increased cheating on the agreement, then serious internal conflict, and eventual breakdown and dissolution of the cartel. This was the history of cartels long before the government made such agreements illegal per se, when the only restraining influence was the time-honored common law practice of court refusal to enforce cartel contracts. I could provide one case history after another to support my thesis. At the same time, I know of no cartel agreement in the history of this country that has been both effective and long-lived except those that have had the explicit support of government.

The farm program in this country in the last 35 years has been nothing more nor less than a government sponsored and operated cartel arrangement among otherwise competing producers. The nonfarm citizens have had to pay both the higher food and fiber prices and the cost of operating the cartel producing those higher prices.

In the same way, the trade union, a cartel arrangement among otherwise competing sellers of the services of labor, has been given the explicit support of government. In addition, trade unions have been permitted methods of enforcing their cartel rules that have made a mockery of the legal prohibition against assault.

In the same way, certain business and professional groups have been given legal protection in their cartel arrangements through licensing and franchise protection and through so-called fair trade laws.

Justice Encouraged to Peek

The seriousness of these actions by government lies not only in the economic consequences but also in the violation of an important cornerstone of the free society—equality before the law. The union member, the farmer, and certain businessmen have been encouraged and assisted in doing precisely that for which other businessmen are sent to jail. The blindfolded goddess of justice has been encouraged to peek, and she now says with the jurists of the ancient regime, "First, tell me who you are, and then I will tell you what your rights are."

To summarize the point: although there is a natural tendency toward collusion among those who otherwise would be competing, there is an equally natural and ultimately stronger tendency for such collusive agreements to break down. The greatest contribution the government can make in this regard is to stop assisting and encouraging cartel groups.

Adam Smith followed the words I quoted above on "people of the same trade," and so forth, by saying, "It is impossible indeed to prevent such meetings, by any law which either could be executed, or would be consistent with liberty and justice. But though the law cannot hinder people of the same trade from sometimes assembling together, it ought to do nothing to facilitate such assemblies; much less to render them necessary."

We have in the traditions of our common law refusal to enforce cartel agreements all that is really needed to prevent such agreements from destroying the basic competitiveness of the American economy.

Growth in Size of Firm

I turn now to the second argument: the threat to competition that is said to be posed by the growth in the size of the firm. Here again, there is no disputing the fact that advancing technology has led to larger and larger firms in many industries. However, in some industries, advancing technology has made it possible for small, even household, units to compete successfully with the giant firms. The development of efficient and relatively inexpensive tools, for example, has made it possible for many a husband to run a basement factory for producing furniture, at least for use in his own home.

But rather than rest the case on this possibility, I would further point out that the growth in the size of the firm often has been matched, or more than matched, by the growth in the size of the market. It is the size of the firm relative to the market that is important, and not the absolute size of the firm. Advancing technology also has been at work in transportation and communication, and this has had the effect of widening all markets.

For example, as a result of the automobile, no giant supermarket today has as much control over its market as did one small store in the small Midwestern town where I was raised. The United States Steel Corporation has less control of its market than did many a small backyard iron foundry in the last century. Transportation costs shielded the backyard operation from competition located no more than a few miles away. U.S. Steel, on the other hand, faces competition from firms in every steel-producing country in the world.

In the same way, the worker living in a small town with only one major employer usually has the real alternative today of driving no more than twenty-five miles to dozens of other employment opportunities. Thus, in many cases, improved transport and communication facilities have widened markets more rapidly than firms have grown in size, and competition has increased rather than diminished.

A second way in which markets have been widened by advancing technology is through the development of substitute products and materials. Thus, the major steel companies, in almost every use for steel, face tremendous competition from substitute materials—aluminum, wood, concrete, plastics, even glass. In fact, it is quite unrealistic to speak of this arrangement as the steel industry. There really exists an entire complex of firms and industries, and no one firm—no one industry even—approaches monopoly power when so used. The typical textbook, man-on-the-street way of defining industry—and hence, of evaluating monopoly power—is both unrealistic and dangerous. It leads to a gross exaggeration of the market power actually possessed by the firms involved.

But again, let us not rest the case on these possibilities of widening markets. In spite of these powerful influences, there still can exist situations in which a given firm, or small group of firms, dominate a given market—no matter how wide that market has become. Do these not constitute hard-core cases of monopoly, calling for government action to break them up or offset their consequences by creating counter monopolies of labor or agriculture or other business firms? My answer is no!

Success through Service

To begin with, it is extremely unlikely that a firm can acquire market power except by laudable efficiency in serving the wishes of consumers. Is this firm to be rewarded for its efficiency by government antitrust action? And, if so, what of the consumer and the service he has been receiving?

Furthermore, if this firm uses its market power to raise prices above the competitive level, other firms will be tempted to enter the industry. These other firms can include large, diversified companies with adequate capital to invade any market. In this country in recent years we have seen many cases of large firms in a given industry suddenly finding themselves facing the competition of other large firms, already established in other fields, but coming into this market to reap the rewards of diversification and higher profit margins. The result is that even the powerful firm in a dominant position in its own market must behave as if it faced immediate important competition, because a failure to do so would soon attract that competition.

Beyond this, the very process of technological progress which may have created this dominant firm tends, over time, to weaken its position. Other firms with newer, better ideas will come into the field, and the original firm will find its share of the market shrinking. Thus, in spite of the fact that the Supreme Court decided long ago against breaking up the United States Steel Corporation, that company's percentage share of steel sold by American producers has declined steadily from more than 75 per cent to around 35 per cent.

It is the little foxes, indeed, who nibble away at the market, who improvise and experiment, whose administrative simplicity permits daring moves, who reduce the stature of the giant to one quite consistent with almost any meaningful definition of competition. This process of short-run market power being replaced by someone else's short-run reign, in turn supplanted by a third, and so on, was eloquently described by the late great Austrian and Harvard University economist Joseph Schumpeter. He argued not only that the dominance attained through technological advance is short-lived but also that it is this possibility of at least short-run market power and security that induces firms to undertake the technological explorations which are revolutionizing the modern world.

In summary, then, although the process is not perfect nor instantaneous, there are powerful forces always at work in the modern world to create a dynamic and effective competitive process, protecting each element in the economy from each other.

"Individuals in Modern Economy Lack Knowledge and Mobility"

Turn now to the third charge, to the claim that individuals in the modern complex economy do not possess the necessary knowledge and mobility to force competitive practices on those with whom they deal.

I would first say that the modern economy, with its advanced techniques of communication and transportation, provides the individual with more information and better and cheaper means of transport than ever before in the history of the world. But beyond that, it is not necessary that all individuals in a given market be completely informed and completely mobile for adequate competitive pressures to exist.

For example, I know almost nothing about the workings of a television set. What protects me, then, when I buy a television set or have one repaired? It is the fact that there are a substantial number of men who do have the required technical knowledge. The television dealer who expects to prosper and survive must meet the demands of all with whom he deals or quickly lose out to other more reputable and reliable dealers. On the other hand, in certain areas I am the better-informed buyer, and in these areas I protect the less well informed.

In the same way, I have a personal commitment to the college where I work and the community where I live, which seriously reduces my mobility. Here, I am protected in part by the good will of those who employ me, but I am protected as well by the fact that the college must offer a general program of working conditions and salaries that will retain the uncommitted and that will attract the appropriate staff replacements and additions.

Not All Must Move at Once

This same process works to effect the many adjustments that must continually be made in a dynamic economy. Usually, in a dying industry or area, not all workers must leave at once. The process customarily takes years. The adjustments are made by the sizable mobile element in every workforce, thus protecting the less mobile from exploitation or loss of employment. The adjustment process can be left to each individual and does not require that everyone have complete knowledge and complete mobility.

Another variant of this argument is the charge that the consumer is deliberately misled and confused by advertising and, hence, falls easy prey to noncompetitive sellers. I have heard this argument presented by many people from all income levels and all walks of life. But I have yet to find one of them who would admit that he himself was the helpless victim of Madison Avenue. It is always "they"—a vague and never identified "they"—who are thus bamboozled. The fact is that advertising itself is competitive, an expression of the basic competitiveness of the American economy, a process through which all of us receive the necessary information for the making of decisions.

In summarizing my answers to the charges that have been made against the possibility of a truly competitive free market, let me repeat, I do not insist that the processes at work produce instant pure competition, in every market in the country, at every moment of time. I say only that the forces are sufficiently strong, and work in good enough time, to give us a workably competitive economy, an economy that does not need government action to offset the noncompetitive elements.

More Harm than Good

When I have admitted that the system is not perfect, does this not leave a case at least for government antitrust legislation to handle the imperfections that remain? In theory, a case might be made for this, but in practice, I see no evidence that antitrust legislation and action ever can be devised to correct the few imperfections without the greater possibility of destroying dynamic competitive firms.

How is one to distinguish between the firm that has acquired temporary market power through greater efficiency and the one that has acquired power without being efficient? To break up the firm that is efficient is to work against true competition rather than to promote it. Nor can we seek to maintain competition by maintaining competitors. This has been a common thrust of our antitrust action. Yet, in fact, it thwarts competition rather than promotes it. Under true competition, the resources come under the control of those firms which have proved themselves the most efficient in serving the interests of consumers. The weeding-out process is severe and effective. To stop that process, to try to maintain a given number of competitors, is to promote inefficiency, not competition.

Another direction taken by our antitrust laws has been that of prohibiting unfair competition. Unfair competition has been defined as selling below cost in order to drive out rivals and thus gain a dominant position in the market. In practice, though, it is virtually impossible to distinguish between low prices that are a natural part of competitive maneuvering and those that are designed to establish market dominance. In practice, then, this legislation has done much more to reduce the competitiveness of the economy than to enhance it. In addition, it has contributed to a general climate for business decision-making characterized by uncertainty and confusion. Thus, one major electrical manufacturing firm recently was under indictment for charging prices that were thought to be too high and at the same time for charging prices that were thought to be too low.

Antitrust legislation generally has been subjected to such varied interpretations that the most experienced legal staff in the country cannot, with any certainty, advise a company on what practices will be illegal under the legislation. Surely, this reflects the basic philosophical and practical weakness of the antitrust approach itself.

In conclusion, then, I would offer as the only meaningful definition of monopoly the following one used by Adam Smith: "Monopoly is a government grant of exclusive trading privileges." If this definition be accepted, it follows that what the government must do, and all that it must do, to promote competition is to stop fostering and protecting monopoly, whether it be in business, or in the professions, or in agriculture, or in labor. In the words of the great Belgian historian Henri Pirenne in his study of the emergence of competitive capitalism from the blight of the government-protected guild economy: "Capitalism is not in itself opposed to the tendencies of human nature, but its restriction is. Economic liberty is spontaneous."

Part 2　*The Role of Economists*

What Economists
Can and Cannot Do

We begin with the obvious fact that capitalism is indeed on trial. In common with all other social systems, it is on trial before the court of public opinion each hour, each day, each year, now and forever. Moreover, it is a trial in which no final verdict, binding on all parties, is ever rendered. It is a test case that can never be won, once and for all—nor can it be forever lost.

The general question for those who are inclined to think well of capitalism is how best to conduct the continuing defense of capitalism. The specific question that I wish to explore here is this: just what can the economist, as an economist, do to be of help? I come before you as a practicing, certified, licensed, Ph.D.'d economist, and the question is what, if anything, can I do for you? My purpose in exploring this question is not simply to find an answer but, in the process, to throw further light on what must be done by whom in the ongoing defense of the marketplace.

I intend to argue that, in general, in this undertaking, more is expected of the economist than he can hope to deliver, that his role is not only just one of many but that his may not even be the leading role in the defense of capitalism. All of this not withstanding, and in a desire not to spoil the market for my services, I intend as well to identify the specific ways in which we economists may be helpful in the cause.

Editor's title, source unknown, no date. Reprinted by permission of the Rogge estate.

If we are to identify what the economist can do in defense of capitalism, we must first understand just what an economist as an economist can and can't do. An example might be helpful. Can an economist tell you whether it was good or bad policy for the United States government to bail out Chrysler? No, he cannot. Why not? Is he a coward, afraid to take a stand? A coward he may or may not be, but the fact is that there are severe limits to what he can profess to know as a scientist. As a scientist, all that he can do is to tell you what he believes to be the most likely short- and long-run consequences of that bailout. You may then put that information together with your own set of values to decide whether you think it was good or bad policy. In other words, in common with all other scientists, the economist's jurisdiction is over means and not over ultimate ends. He can tell you which means seem most likely to serve your ends, but he cannot speak to the quality of those ends.

You must now be saying, "Surely, Professor, you jest. I hear economists, including you, praising and condemning policies all the time." I freely confess that we do offer verdicts of "good" or "bad" on questions of economic policy, and for this I offer two explanations. One, we are often describing policies as "good" or "bad" in terms of whether they promise to serve or not to serve what we take to be the generally accepted goals of our society. In other words, we are using your values, not necessarily our own. Second, we are indeed human, and as human beings we are much given to that all-too-human temptation so well described by Charlie Brown. In a critical moment in one of his baseball games, Charlie, as the pitcher, is the recipient of advice on what to do by each of his teammates; as he finally faces the batter on his own, he speaks to himself as follows: "This world is filled with people who are anxious to function in an advisory capacity." And so it is, and so do we economists yield to that temptation to advise when our proper role is simply to analyze and describe.

"But surely," you ask, "those of you who teach conservative economics can at least tell an ignorant world that capitalism is the best of all economic systems—and why?" Sorry, but no. There is no such thing as conservative economics or radical economics or Christian economics or Buddhist economics—anymore than there is Christian mathematics or Muslim chemistry. There is only economics—period. Its tentative conclusions are not moral or immoral; they are only correct or incorrect or some of each. Did the real incomes of the greater part of the workers of England go up during the early Industrial Revolution (as I believe to be true) or did they go down (as Marx and Engels thought they did)? This is a question of analysis and fact, not of value judgment.

What am I saying? I am saying that the economist as a scientist is neither for or against capitalism, anymore than the mathematician is for or against the high probability that two plus two are equal to four. Where then does this leave the economist as an assistant in the struggle to defend capitalism? When, if at all, should he be called to the witness stand?

Let me outline my answer to that question by running through a number of the familiar defenses of and attacks on capitalism, asking in each case whether the economist should be called or left in the wings.

I begin with one of the defenses of capitalism, in fact with the one that is alone sufficient to lead me as a specific human being to prefer the capitalist economic arrangement to all others. It is that man is endowed with the right to be free of coercive restraint in the doing of anything that is peaceful, whether singly or in pairs or in groups as large as IBM or the Mormon Church, and that capitalism, as the system of voluntary exchange, is the economic embodiment of this freedom. If this basic premise of the primacy of freedom to choose be accepted, there is nothing more that need be said. No economist need be called to explain the consequences of a legislated minimum wage. It stands condemned by the very fact that it is a coercive intrusion into what would otherwise be a voluntary exchange between employer and employee. In the words of Adam Smith, "It is a manifest encroachment upon the just liberty both of the workman, and of those who might be disposed to employ him" (Adam Smith, *The Wealth of Nations*, Modern Library Edition, p. 122).

What am I saying? I am saying that I believe that the primary argument to be advanced in the defense of capitalism is that it is the system under which the individual is "free to choose" (in the words of the title of Milton Friedman's new film)—and this is an argument that does not rest in any significant way upon the work of the economist. It stands on its own.

True, the economist may point out, as Milton Friedman does, that limiting the individual's freedom to choose tends to reduce economic efficiency and to produce results directly contrary to the intent of the framers of the action. But this is embroidery on the argument. In a society in which the weight of public opinion supported the idea of freedom of choice (in this sense of freedom from coercion) for its own sake, the economist would never need be called to the witness stand—the philosopher or the political theorist perhaps, but not the economist.

Moreover, I am persuaded that capitalism can survive in meaningful form only in a society in which most of its members accept on principle a presumption in favor of freedom of choice, personal responsibility, and private property. If each time a proposal is made that contradicts one or more of these principles (say, a requirement that peanuts may be grown on a given piece of land only if that piece of land has been "licensed" for peanut growing), each citizen has to consult his economics textbook to discover the likely long-run effects of such a law on real growth, unemployment among black teenagers, and the survival of the family farm, the cause is as well as lost.

To begin with, the great masses of the people are never going to understand the intricacies of economic analysis, anymore than Ben Rogge is ever going to fully understand the conflicting theories of the origins of the universe. What the man on the street *can* understand is the statement of the farmer, "This land is mine, by God, and I should be able to grow peanuts on it if I want to!" Or the statement of the landlord, "This is *my* property, *my* apartment house, put up with *my* money, and the government has no right to tell *me* what rent I should ask for an apartment." If these gut feelings (or "societal presumptions" as they might be called in polite society) in favor of freedom of choice and property rights guide the making of policy in society, capitalism will flourish without a word needing to be said by Ben Rogge or Milton Friedman. If they don't, nothing that Rogge or Friedman might say is going to make much difference.

But how are such societal presumptions created or destroyed? Do they arise in ways beyond the control not only of the economist, as I have implied, but of rational designers of whatever kind? Is the thrust to freedom of choice, to private property, to acceptance of personal responsibility built into each of us—or does each of these run counter to other equally potent and contradictory impulses in the dark recesses of the human soul? Don't ask me; I'm just an economist.

Go ask Robert Ardrey. In his book *The Territorial Imperative* he argues that he finds a deep sense of private property (or "turf") imbedded in all forms of animal life, and presumably, then, in Homo sapiens. But other anthropologists tell us that our early ancestors were communalists, with no itch for individual or even family property rights. Or go to Dostoyevsky's Grand Inquisitor, who tells us that man dreads nothing more than freedom and the responsibility that goes with it. Or to Thornton Wilder, who, in *The Ides of March,* puts these words into the mouth of Julius Caesar:

> Since childhood I have been attentive to the attitude which men bear to those who have been placed over them and who are in a position to restrict their movements. What deference and loyalty proceeds from man's gratitude that his superior relieves him from responsibility and from the terrors of weighty decisions; the contempt and hatred from his resentment against the man who limits his freedom. During a part of every day and night even the mildest man is, however obscurely, the murderer of those who can command his obedience. . . . the central movement of the mind is the desire for unrestricted liberty and this movement is invariably accompanied by its opposite, a dread of the consequences of liberty.

Let me summarize by stealing several paragraphs from an earlier paper of mine.

> Most people are going to judge an economic system by its consistency with their moral principles rather than by its purely scientific operating characteristics. If economic freedom survives in the years ahead, it will be only because a majority of the people accept its basic morality. The success of the system in bringing ever higher levels of living will be no more persuasive in the future than it has been in the past.
>
> Let me illustrate: the doctrine of man held in general in nineteenth-century America argued that each man was ultimately responsible for what happened to him, for his own salvation, both in the here and now and in the hereafter. Thus, whether a man prospered or failed in economic life was each man's individual responsibility; each man had a right to the rewards for success and, in the same sense, deserved the punishment that came with failure. It followed as well that it is explicitly immoral to use the power of government to take from one man to give to another, to legalize Robin Hood. This doctrine of man found its economic counterpart in the system of free enterprise, and, hence, the system of free enterprise was accepted and

respected by many who had no understanding of its subtleties as a technique for organizing resources.

As this doctrine of man was replaced by one which made of man a helpless victim of his subconscious and his environment—responsible for neither his successes nor his failures—the free enterprise system came to be rejected by many who still had no real understanding of its actual operating characteristics.

Again, what am I saying? I am saying that the survival of capitalism may rest largely upon frames of mind, views of man, sets of values, and similar elements largely beyond the purview of the economist. It may require a fierce desire for individual freedom—yet there is no certainty that man is moved at all times and for all purposes by such a desire. It may require a visceral attachment to individual property rights—an attachment that may or may not be innate to the race of man. It may require a willingness and a strong desire to accept individual responsibility, to say with William Ernest Henley, "I am the master of my fate; I am the captain of my soul." But the terrors of personal responsibility may far outweigh its allure on those obscure scales in the gelatinous substance that is the human brain. In other words, the survival of capitalism may require a set of attitudes and instinctively accepted beliefs that may not come naturally to the human race and that we may have no clear idea of how to produce by precept or example—or even by witchcraft.

Well, now we are in a pretty pickle! Rogge has told us that whatever it is that he and Friedman and others of their ilk do, it is never going to be fully understood by all and wouldn't be all that important if it were. Where then is help to be found? Who is to be called to the witness stand?

In brief, I would urge us to call to the witness stand those voices out of the great traditions of our civilization that have preached freedom and responsibility—and the moral nature of property rights. Let us call a Sam Adams who, in 1768, penned the following words, "It is an essential, unalterable right in nature, ungrafted into the British Constitution, as a fundamental law, and ever held sacred and irrevocable by the Subjects within the Realm, that what a man has honestly acquired is absolutely his own, which he may freely give, but cannot be taken from him without his consent." Let us call a John Adams for these words,

"Property is surely a right of mankind as really as liberty. . . . The moment the idea is admitted into society that property is not as sacred as the laws of God, and that there is not a force of law and public justice to protect it, anarchy and tyranny commence."

These are but brief snippets from the great precepts that have served to create the free societies of the world. If we would defend capitalism, let us channel our energies and our funds at least as much into those activites that would keep these precepts bright and clear before our people as we do into the activities of the economists.

But let us teach by example as well. Would a measure before us that seems expedient restrain the peaceful conduct of others? or erode the right of others to use and dispose of their property for peaceful purposes? or take from others some significant part of the responsibility for their own lives? If we do not stand firm against such proposals, how then can we come into court to defend capitalism with clean hands? I would wager that each of us in this room has in the past given support to (or is even now supporting) practices and proposals that encroach upon the freedom of others, or their right to control their own properties, or their responsibility for their own lives. Can it be that the fault lies more with those of us who do not practice what we preach than with those who preach that which would destroy us and our civilization? If such be the case, the remedy seems obvious.

So far so good, perhaps, but to paraphrase a Sondheim lyric, "and where are the economists? there ought to be economists." Indeed there ought to be, and it is now time to bring them in from the wings, where they have been impatiently waiting, pelting each other with statistical data and computer printouts. But what are they to do? That is the question.

I would describe the role of the economist in the defense of capitalism as largely that of reassurance. After all, for a society to permit its members great latitude for individual action, full control over their own properties, and full responsibility for their own lives requires a great "leap of faith." Even to the most knowledgeable there must often come an occasional crisis of confidence. If we tell people that they can do anything they please with themselves and their property so long as its peaceful, and that they are responsible for taking care of themselves, how can we be sure that anything will get done, that food will be produced and houses built, and that children will not starve in the streets of the city? Who will save us from the Great Depression, from the monopolist, from the terrors and privation of old age?

The economist has now been called. Each of these questions is but one of many that could be drawn from the pool of the one big question! Does the marketplace work?

One answer to this question is that if the marketplace—that is, economic freedom—is right in principle, and if the world is not absurd, then of course it will work. The world may be "a tale told by an idiot," but if it isn't, then that which is right in principle must indeed work—and that which is wrong in principle cannot work.

But most of us demand more than this metaphysical kind of reassurance; we want numbers and cases—hence, the economist. The economist's role on the journey of capitalist enterprise over the rough seas is like that of the crew member on the ships of Columbus, whose duty it may have been to quiet the fears of the sailors (who expected any day to sail right off the end of the universe) by demonstrating to them just why a ship could get to the East by going west. The economist deals with an equally mystifying paradox: how to achieve an efficient order in economic life without any king or parliament or commission whatsoever issuing a single order—other than "keep it peaceful." In other words, the economist deals with the consequences of free markets—and unfree markets. It is in this role that he is quite properly called to the witness stand.

To illustrate: there is presented to the court a charge that in the uninhibited marketplace the economy would be subjected to violent swings from boom to bust, with disastrous consequences on the lives of those most affected by these disturbances.

What do you do about that? Call Friedman, or if you can't afford him, call Rogge. In the witness stand, I would testify that the violent swings from boom to bust that have indeed taken place are not inherent in the marketplace but have been produced by government's mismanagement of the money supply, particularly by its almost irresistible temptation to pay for some part of its spending with newly created money. I would bring forth evidence indicating that in those times and places where governments have had little or no discretionary control over the money supply, the economies, though not perfectly stable, have not been subject to violent swings from boom to bust.

Or another: comes now a spokesman before the court who charges that in the uninhibited market it is often not freedom of choice that prevails but, rather, monopolistic restrictions on freedom of choice. What would Rogge say to that? I happen to have in front of me a copy of what he has already said to that: "Competition does not have to be created or protected; it inheres in the very nature of man. It can be reduced or eliminated only by coercive acts of governments. All that a government need do to encourage competition is not to get in its way."

I would then bring forth evidence to indicate that the dynamic nature of an uninhibited market serves to confront all participants in the marketplace, no matter how large—even as large as the Chrysler Corporation—with the warning to continue to try to improve their products and services to their customers or face decline and extinction.

But what of this: here is a spokesman before the court who alleges that market freedom is really the freedom of the rich man and the poor man alike to sleep under the bridge, or, in other words, that under capitalism some at least are condemned to live lives of desperate need and misery. How would Rogge respond to this? Secretly, I would be rejoicing that the question had been raised. Why? Because quite honestly I do not know of a single charge against capitalism that can be as easily refuted as this one.

I would begin by presenting before the court a chart that would match "bread" on the vertical axis and "freedom" on the horizontal axis. I would be using "bread" as a proxy for "rate of increase in the per capita income of the masses of the people," and "freedom" as a proxy for the extent to which the society was operating under the rules of private property, individual freedom, and limited government. I would then place dots on the chart to represent the positions of various countries at various periods of time. The result: a configuration of dots that would indicate, in impressive connectedness, that the more "freedom," the more "bread." Compare West Germany to East Germany since World War II, or England in the nineteenth century to England since World War II, or Hong Kong or Taiwan to mainland China, or the Ivory Coast to Guinea, and on and on. Of course, precise numbers are hard to come by for the making of such a chart, but the evidence of the chart is given additional credibility by that most telling of all pieces of concrete evidence—the direction in which people move when they vote with their feet.

I do not know of a single mass migration of people from less to more socialized lands. Which way do they swim around Hong Kong at night? Which way do the guns point on the Berlin wall? Why do the blacks of southern and central Africa try desperately to get into Rhodesia and South Africa proper?

As a scientist, I do not know of a more clear-cut relationship than that between capitalism and improvement in the standard of life of the masses. Now, after six decades of socialist trials, there is not a single example of a socialist economy that through its socialized sectors has been able to bring to the masses of its people a significant increase in the things of this world. When some improvement has taken place, it can usually be traced to the vestigial capitalist elements in the system, such as the famous "private plots" of Soviet Russia, which, with less than 2 percent of the arable land, produce almost 40 percent of everything eaten in Russia.

Ah, but the previous witness counters with the argument that even though the masses may have made progress under capitalism, nevertheless (as one of the opposing panel members said in one of the Friedman film discussions) "there is still a lower 20 percent." True, true. Even at Wabash College, with its carefully selected student body and its outstanding faculty, each year approximately 50 percent of our seniors are graduated in the lower half of the class. I assume that at the great state universities they do better than that.

But I do not take lightly this charge that there are always some at the bottom who are in at least a relatively deprived situation and often in an absolutely deprived situation as well.

The questions before the court would now be, Why, at capitalism's mighty feast, do some find that, for them, no plates are laid? Why must they beg at the back door for the scraps from the table?

Comes now Rogge with the following answer: In a truly uninhibited market, those who, for whatever reason (for example, those newly arrived from Eastern Europe in America in 1910), are on the bottom rungs of the income ladder will know that they must themselves be the instrument of their own survival and advancement. This incentive, when permitted to operate in an open market where the labor of all the members of the family, young and old alike, may be exchanged for income, tends to produce an upward movement on the income ladder.

In recent decades we have made it far more difficult for this process to work. To begin with, we have created a welfare system that takes from the family much of the incentive to work and achieve. (The evidence to this effect is becoming more abundant and convincing each day.) Next, by minimum wage laws, absurdly restrictive child labor laws, high fringe costs imposed on employers, and in a dozen other ways, we have made it difficult or impossible for the low-income family to use all of its man- and woman-power as in times past. In addition, through the special privileges we have granted to trade unions, and the restrictions and costs we have imposed on the founding and operating of small-scale enterprise, we have narrowed the channels through which the upwardly mobile can make their way to the higher rungs on the income ladder. (I might add that in the process of doing all of this, we have also done much to strip the individual of self-responsibility and, hence, of self-regard—but this is Rogge the citizen, not Rogge the economist speaking.)

Enough is enough. I have said to you that there is indeed a role for the economist in the defense of capitalism, and that that role is to provide reassurance that, yes, the marketplace does work. This reassurance may be helpful to those whose instincts lead them to be generally open to the capitalist persuasions. It may even induce some who are poised on a knife edge of indecision to move in the capitalist direction. But I doubt if economic argument alone is ever going to be persuasive with those who do not accept the principles of individual freedom, private property, and self-responsibility (or free will, if you wish). To a nineteenth-century Proudhon, to whom property was theft, or to a modern B. F. Skinner, author of *Walden II* and *Beyond Freedom and Dignity*, who sees each of us as the helpless pawns of the conditioning forces around us, the arguments of the economist are not likely to be persuasive.

Nor are they likely to be persuasive with the great masses of the people in society, whose knowledge of economic processes is never likely to be much superior to a monkey's understanding of the workings of the watch he has been given as a plaything.

I close as I began. Capitalism will survive and prosper only in a society that is committed to those fundamental moral principles and assumptions—individual freedom, private property, and personal responsibility—that define capitalism as the only morally acceptable way of organizing economic life. In the creating of a society so committed, the economist can play but a supporting role, as the agent of reassurance as to the workability of the market process. The great task of moral rearmament, if so it may be called, will have to be the work of others, including each of us who professes to accept those fundamental principles of human life. How best to go about that task, I do not know, but I do know these two things: (1) We are not likely to be persuasive in bringing others to our view if our practice is significantly at odds with our preachment. Let us at least begin our decision on any issue by asking whether or not what is proposed would restrict the free and peaceful behavior and property use of others or would deny to the individuals involved the dignity of responsibility for self.

(2) What we are fighting for is not just gasoline for a Sunday drive, or a television set for the children's room, or even just food for the hungry and shelter for the cold. What is at stake is the opportunity for us and for the generations to follow to live lives of some fullness and dignity and significance. It would seem to be eminently worthy of our attention and concern.

When to See Your Economist

Gentlemen: I'd like to begin by telling you how pleased I am to be finally a part of your activities. For some time now, I've felt like a new boy on the block, standing around watching the other boys play and hoping that he'll be asked to join in. Like this same boy, I feel compelled to do something that will attract your attention, something that will prove I really belong to your gang.

I'm a little old now to ride by you on my bike without holding on to the handlebars. In fact, it's one of the frustrations of my life that I've never been able to do that; so I'm forced back on somewhat less positive evidence of my ability to participate in your games. I'm confronted then with the disturbing question, Just what am I able to do that would justify your asking me in?

Well, currently I'm playing two kinds of games—dean's office games and economist's games. Now a dean is never invited to play in other people's games; in fact his presence alone is repulsive to most players. A dean is at best a necessary evil, and in your activities he's not even necessary. It seems clear, then, that if I'm to be asked to join in it will have to be as an economist. This may be little better than the deanship gambit, but it's all I've got left, and I intend to fight it through on this basis.

My purpose this morning is, first, to describe what an economist can and can't do, and, second, to convince you that what he can do is

Speech given at the Professional Development Program in Indianapolis, Ind., March 16, 1956. Reprinted by permission of the Rogge estate.

important to you in this particular undertaking of yours. Now of course this undertaking is a liberal arts-type game, so I'll need to prove that economics really fits the pattern. This will involve me in a few remarks on the nature of a liberal arts game, and here my colleagues will recognize that my position is the same as our president's, as presented in his faculty lecture Tuesday night. I might explain that since I've assumed my new duties, I have made it a point to disagree with the president only when he's wrong. As a consequence I haven't been in a good argument in a month and a half, but perhaps I can start something here.

I am calling my remarks this morning "When to See Your Economist." This title may start a trend, and you may soon be hearing Harry Cotton or Tom Altizer on when to see your metaphysician, George Lovell on what to do 'till the psychoanalyst comes, Vic Powell on ten years a country elocutionist, and Ralph Caplan on bookbirth without fear.

We might begin by asking whether it's respectable to ever visit an economist—in other words, whether economics is a respectable calling. The fact that I'm engaged in it proves nothing, for as Talleyrand once said, "A married man with a family will do anything for money." Or as my father once said, "Son, if you're going to be a shiftless ne'er-do-well, as I suspect you will be, at least have the decency to pose as a college teacher or insurance salesman so as not to bring shame on your mother and me."

This line of inquiry might prove embarrassing, so let us try another. What problems should not be taken to the economist? I hate to disappoint you, but my first answer to this question would be, any problem of personal finances (or lack of them). The economist cannot tell you how to get rich or even how to avoid being poor. The economist can no more tell you how to get rich than the physicist can tell you how to build a bridge or the ballistics expert can tell you how to play golf. Getting rich is an art, and the economist is the scientist, not the artist, of economic life. If you want to know how to secure a loan from the small-loan department of your local bank, I can tell you from personal experience, but that's as far as I can go. When I first approached this department in a local bank I was told, "Physician, heal thyself." This may explain my sensitivity on the point under discussion.

Now if economics is not directly designed to prepare you for making a living, it would seem to have passed one of the tests for admission to the charmed circle of the liberal arts. In his faculty lecture of Tuesday night, our president identified the liberal arts in terms of the ends sought (and I would agree with him that this is the only way of distinguishing the liberal from the non-liberal arts). The goal of making a living did not appear in his listing of the ends sought in liberal education. With this too I am in complete agreement.

But now let me add the paradox: I am convinced that the liberal education, though not designed to prepare a man for making a living, is yet the only practical education for making a living in our world of today. True, a certain amount of vocational training, of specialized study, may be a useful supplement to the liberal education, but it is the liberal education itself which fits a man to make the best progress in a given specialty and, more important, to adapt himself to the rapidly shifting tides of his personal economic environment. Economic security in a dynamic situation comes from adaptability, and this the liberal education tends to foster, and specialized education tends to reduce.

Some of my colleagues (yes, even at Wabash) are somewhat embarrassed by any allusion to the vocational benefits that may flow from a Wabash-type education. It seems to them to be profaning something that should be kept pure and undefiled. This attitude makes no more sense to me than would the attitude of a man or woman who loved to watch the ocean, but who regretted that the sea was also quite useful as a transport medium. If our type of education, which we believe can be justified on nonvocational grounds, also produces as a by-product certain vocational advantages, we should rejoice rather than lament. I would agree with my sensitive colleagues that concern over the by-product should not be permitted to distort the program for achieving the primary and direct goals of a liberal education, but the experience in this program last summer would seem to indicate that such distortion is neither necessary nor desirable in achieving vocationally oriented results.

Here I am back in the dean's office when I'm trying to sell myself as an economist. Let's try to say something germane to the issue again. I have established to my own satisfaction, which is what counts of course, that economics is not designed to prepare you to make a living. But this alone would not qualify economics for admission to the liberal arts any more than not being black is proof that something is white. What is economics designed to accomplish? What can the economist do?

The fact is that the economist as a person plays many roles, not one; these roles may be grouped under three headings: (1) as a scientist; (2) as a social philosopher; and (3) as a social reformer.

Now only the first of these roles is a necessary characteristic of the economist, and it's on this role that I wish to concentrate.

The central concern of the economist as a scientist is with what may be called the economic problem. The economic problem is nothing more than the gap between what people want and what they're able to get, nothing more than the obvious fact that there isn't enough of everything to go around. Does anyone wish to challenge this, to deny the existence of the economic problem? Who here has everything he wants? (Watch these hands carefully, Mr. President; we may be able to effect a saving in the payroll next year.)

That question was not quite as nonsensical as it may have sounded. A number of people, while not denying the present existence of the economic problem, would deny that it need exist. One group of dissenters would argue that the problem can be eliminated by the simple expedient of eliminating or limiting wants.

A man named Ruskin once said that "the true progress of a nation consists in extinguishing a want." This thesis is often advanced by poets, philosophers, and employers (at salary reconsideration time), and with these men I have no quarrel, at least in my role as a scientist. They may be right as to what should be, but the central concern of the scientist is not with what should be but with what is, and I feel safe in assuming that man still has unsatisfied wants. It may well be that man's true happiness is not increased one iota when he gets what he thinks he wants, but that is Harry Cotton's concern and not mine. As a scientist, I observe that men are moved to action by the desire for more, and if I am to understand the world about me, I must understand how men go about trying to get more. To the scientist, it is important to know how a dog chases rabbits, even the rabbits it doesn't catch.

In my role as a social philosopher I am concerned with ends as well as means, with morality as well as motion. In this role, I at least say that it is "good" when one or more men can get more of what they want without anyone else having to get less of what they want. If you study this thesis carefully, you will note that it contains a value judgment and hence is social philosophy and not economic science.

But let us go on. Others deny that the economic problem need exist, even today on the grounds that our production potential is so great that we have the ability to satisfy all the wants of everybody. This thesis is often stated thusly: We have now solved the problem of production; all that's left is to solve the problem of distribution. Gentlemen, this is not only arrant nonsense, but productive of great mischief as well. I submit that the gap between what people want and what they're able to get is little narrower today than it was three thousand years before the birth of Christ, and I predict that five thousand years from now it will be but little narrower than it is today.

My argument rests on man's virtuosity and elasticity as a wanter. How many of you have wanted a television set twenty years ago, in 1936? How many of you now look on it as more or less essential to the good life? As Gandhi said, "Today man wants to visit England; tomorrow he will want to visit the moon." This analysis led Gandhi to reject the goal of getting more, and to recommend the goal of wanting less. It leads me only to accept the existence and permanence of the economic problem. I may have fears about the future of the economist, but of one thing I'm certain: he's not going to be made obsolete by an early disappearance of the economic problem.

You might well ask at this point, If you don't think we've made much progress as yet in narrowing this gap, and don't expect us to make much progress in the future, how can you get excited about economics at all? This is a fair question, and I'll try to answer it. In the first place, as I indicated earlier, in my role as a scientist I am interested in man in motion, and it makes little difference whether he's on a treadmill or actually getting somewhere. In the second place, as a social philosopher, I am interested in what man wants, and economic progress, even narrowly defined, permits man to want more of such things as leisure and liberal education, and this I believe to be good. In other words, while the total of unsatisfied wants may be undiminished by economic progress, the new level of wants brought into being by such progress may be a higher level than the old. In the third place, and most important, I am convinced that the way in which men go about satisfying their wants has an important bearing on the extent to which they will be free men, that there is an important and inevitable connection between economics and freedom. It is freedom and not more bathtubs that attracts me to a study of economics. I suppose that what I'm saying is that if I weren't a social philosopher and social reformer, I wouldn't be interested in economic science. Now of course these value judgments that move me to action may reduct my effectiveness as a scientist, but this I believe to be a price that must be paid. If we had science without emotion, we would have no science.

If this be true, we must be cautious not to reject something important just because it comes from a source we suspect of bias; we must not be too quick to react like the man who said, "I cannot hear what you are saying for what you are is roaring in my ears."

But I must drag myself back to the central topic. Economic science starts with the economic problem. Where does it go from there? Well, the existence of a gap between what people want and what they're able to get, between the resources available for producing things that satisfy wants and the resources needed to satisfy all wants, means that decisions have to be made. The decisions that have to be made are the following: (1) Which wants are going to be satisfied? In other words, what goods and services are going to be produced and in what amounts? (2) Which resources are going to be used at each of the tasks involved in producing these goods? In other words, to which task is each unit of labor, land, and capital to be assigned? And (3) once the goods and services are produced, how are they to be divided among the members of the society? How do you split the pie once it's baked?

The system used to make these decisions in any society is called the economic organization of that society. Various systems can be used to make these decisions. Economics is a study—analytical, comparative, and historical—of such systems.

"Aha," you say, "at last I see what you can do; you can tell me which is the best type of economic organization." I hate to disappoint you again, but that's not quite right. All I can do as a scientist is tell you how each system is supposed to work, what it involves, what conditions must be present if it is to work efficiently, what it can and can't accomplish, what problems arise under each system, what history tells us about each system, and so forth. Then you take your pick. No one economic system is best in an absolute sense. It all depends on what you think is important. For example, as a citizen, I favor the enterprise system, not primarily on economic grounds but because a study of the way in which it works (or might be made to work) convinces me that it is the only system which operates in a way that is consistent with personal and political freedom. In the same way there are others who believe an equal distribution of income to be an ethical imperative. These men reject the enterprise system because it necessarily involves an unequal distribution of income. It's all a matter of taste. You come into my shop, tell me what you want, what you think is important, and I'll show you the economic system you should select. But don't simply ask, "You're an economist; should I select socialism or free enterprise?" I can answer that as a citizen, but not as an economist.

The economist in America devotes most of his time to a study of the enterprise system. He does so because it is the system we're at least trying to use. He studies how it is supposed to work, what conditions must be present if it is to work efficiently, how it has worked in the past and how it is actually working now, what problems arise under this system, and what solutions will cure the disease without killing the patient.

Now of course each of you is involved in this system in one capacity or another; in fact you must feel that you are more in touch with the pulse of our economic system than an academician could ever be. I have often been asked, "What makes you think you know the answers to these questions any better than I? Did you ever meet a payroll? Run a factory? Or a bank? Or a punch press? Or a trade union? Just what contact have you had with the real business of economic life?"

My answer is, "very little." My only advantage is one of vantage point. I spend my days looking at the forest; you spend your days looking at a selected few trees. You know each of those trees better than I, but, if I'm worth my salt, I know the forest better than you.

Some of you might now want to ask, But if you are to know how the system actually operates, something more than pure theory, don't you need to know something about the trees? The answer is yes; I do need to know something about the specific economic institutions through which the enterprise system works in America, the corporations, the trade unions, the banks, the insurance companies, the stock markets, the business customs, and so on. But I do not need to know each particular company, each bank, each trade union in detail. I need to know only the general characteristics of such institutions. I need to know only enough to determine whether the institution is helping to make the system work or preventing it from working in the proper way. I do not need to know how to run a bank, a corporation, an insurance company, a punch press. Each of these activities is an art, and I am not the artist of business life. I am the scientist of business life. I am interested in the broad complex of causal relations and not in the specific techniques of business. To advise a business corporation I would need to know techniques; in fact I would need to know the specific problems and techniques of the specific corporation. This I do not gain through a study of economics. True, my general understanding of economic institutions might be of some help, but it would be neither necessary nor sufficient for the problem at hand.

This then is my case for being admitted to your very select company. I am an economist, and economics is a study of an important aspect of the total universe in which men live. If the purpose of a liberal education is to increase one's understanding of that universe, then economics belongs in the curriculum of that education, and I belong here.

If you're still not convinced, I might add that I'm a good, sociable drinker, I play a decent hand of bridge, and I'm just as willing to discuss a subject without knowing anything about it as any man in the crowd. If that isn't enough, you're just being difficult.

Economists as Freedom Fighters

Today I shall discuss the sad plight of the economist; in moving language, I shall describe to you how he has been denied a role in the greatest drama of the age. I shall show you the grievous bruises and lacerations that he has received as punishment for daring to criticize the way in which the actors are playing that drama. If there is a dry eye in the house when I finish, I shall have failed of my purpose.

The great drama of the age is, of course, the struggle between freedom and tyranny. The stage is the world; the actors, some professionals, some amateurs, are the people from all walks of life in all the countries of the world. The audience is limited to a few scattered tribes of aborigines who do not seem to care whether it comes out one way or the other.

The leaders of the forces of freedom I shall describe by telling you what they are not—they are not economists. Political scientists, historians, psychologists, philosophers, politicians, military men—these they may be, but not economists. But pray, you ask, why has the economist been excluded from this distinguished company? Why indeed. Because the economist, when he insists that he, too, is a fighter in the cause of freedom, is told, Begone. This is a struggle for freedom—not for free markets. While your cause may or may not be a worthy one, it is irrelevant to this, the greatest of all undertakings. Moreover, with your crass materialism and your ranting and raving about free enterprise, you embarass us, and you might shock and alienate some of our sensitive

Editor's title. Speech originally titled "Chapel Talk," given at Wabash College on March 12, 1952. Reprinted by permission of the Rogge estate.

friends. As if that were not enough, you insist on interrupting our strategy meetings to tell us that this or that will not work as planned. Go peddle your free enterprise elsewhere.

Now of course, these noble men may easily ignore economists, but they can not ignore economics. Thus, their strategy always calls for some strange and wonderful creations in the realm of economic strategy that, like Duz, promise to do everything—maintain full employment, provide security at a high level of living to every man, woman, and child, induce great strides in technology, reduce income inequality, stabilize exchange rates, correct fundamental disequilibria in the balances of international payments, promote the free movement of goods and services in international trade, and develop the underdeveloped areas.

Then they come to the economist and say, Now this plan is a wonder to behold, and we would like you to write a few words in praise of it for the next issue of *Popular Economics*. Then, when the economist refuses to do so, when he refuses to use his cunning to prove that two and two are equal to five, when he insists that many of these goals, while desirable in and of themselves, are mutually exclusive, he is branded as unrealistic, reactionary, and isolationist.

The kinder critics of the economist say that while his message may have meaning in the long run, it is not relevant to the present time of crisis. This may easily be the case. However, it must be pointed out that the present time of crisis is really concerned with a secondary drama—to wit, the struggle for survival of the American people. This struggle is only incidentally a struggle for freedom, as witness the fact that various lesser tyrants are joined with us in this fight against the strongest tyrant, Soviet Russia.

The unfortunate fact is that the leaders in the struggle for freedom have not distinguished their fight from the struggle for survival. This has led us to such absurd actions as rejecting Chiang Kai-shek because he is reputedly undemocratic, while clasping first Tito then Franco to our bosom. If the immediate problem is survival, then we are in no position to ask to see the credentials of those lined up on our side. The man who is set upon by cutthroats in a dark street does not care if his rescuer is Jesse James, Willie the Actor, or Harry Emerson Fosdick—the important thing is to survive.

In the same way, a nation that needs strong allies to survive, that finds itself with weak allies who must be strengthened by aid, is in no position to ask if the recipients of that aid are socialist, communist, fascist, or free enterprisers—the only important questions are (1) Is this nation anti-Russian, and (2) Is it potentially a strong ally?

A nation faced with great and immediate danger from abroad must select its domestic economic policy on the basis of what is politically feasible at that time, not according to what is economically the most desirable over the long run and may be politically feasible at some time in the future.

While all this may be true, it is also true that if and when the survival crisis is reduced in urgency, attention must then be directed to the even greater struggle for freedom. In that struggle, the choice of allies is determined by the answer to the question, Are these people dedicated to the preservation of freedom? Moreover, if the thesis that I shall present in a moment is correct, this struggle also demands that serious attention be given to questions of economic organization.

My argument proceeds as follows: The economic life of any society consists of using resources to produce goods and services to satisfy human wants. Because the resources are always scarce and the wants unlimited, the economic problem of any society is that of using each resource in such a way as to satisfy the greatest possible number of wants. This in turn presents two problems: how is the resource owner to know which are the most productive uses for his resources? and how can he be induced to put his resources to those most productive uses?

There are only two ways in which the first question can be answered:

One is the free market solution in which prices serve as the guide to resource owners. The other is a planning solution in which some central authority determines the use to which each resource is to be put.

If we assume that men are and will continue to be largely self-seeking, then the second question can be answered in only two ways: One is the free market solution in which resource owners are induced to place their resources in the best uses by the lure (largely) of pecuniary rewards— higher wages or higher profits, for example. The other solution is to compel resource owners to place their resources in the best uses.

Two comments on the significance of these statements are now in order:

First, under the planning solution, the economic well-being of each individual is under the control of a central authority. Now if it be true, as history so clearly demonstrates, that control of a man's economic life permits control of all other aspects of his life as well, and if it be true that power corrupts, as history again demonstrates, then it follows that economic authoritarianism is but the first step to total authoritarianism.

Second, if the only alternative to the "carrot" method of inducing resource owners to place resources in the best uses is the "stick" method, it follows that a planned economy can be efficient only if the leaders are willing to be ruthless in forcing individuals to do their bidding.

Now of course, if a people are content to permit gross inefficiency in the conduct of economic affairs, then a departure from free markets to some form of so-called democratic socialism may not lead inevitably to tyranny. I point as evidence to Britain under the Labor Party. This group led Britain to abandon even those vestiges of free market economic organization that remained after long years of state intervention in markets, but, steeped in the spirit of British democracy, this group could not bring itself to that ruthless disregard for individual wishes and individual liberties which alone can make a planned economy efficient.

This conclusion now follows: While other forms of economic organization may be able to provide either freedom or economic efficiency, the free market type is the only one that can provide both freedom and economic efficiency. Further, if it be true that an economically inefficient nation is vulnerable to attack from authoritarian groups both without and within the country, it follows that the free market form is the only one that is consistent with maintenance of freedom over the long run.

Further, planning within a given country can be efficient only if that country is economically isolated from the rest of the world—otherwise the constant intrusion of changes from outside forces makes planning impossible. Thus, economic planning is not consistent with that increased economic cooperation among the freedom-loving nations which could do so much to strengthen these nations in the fight against tyranny. Evidence of this isolationist position of planning nations is to be found in each issue of the daily paper.

In conclusion, I submit that the struggle for freedom and the struggle for free markets are indivisible, but two sides of the same coin. I submit as well that most of the great struggles for freedom in the past have involved, as an associated element, attempts by groups and individuals to escape from the dead hand of economic authoritarianism. I submit further that the great virtue of the free market type of economic organization is not its tested ability to bring a high level of living to those who work under it; rather, it is the fact that it is the only type of economic organization which is consistent with the maintenance of those individual liberties which are to be prized more dearly than the material benefits of an efficient economy. Have I made myself clear?

The Bicentennial of Economic Liberty

In this year of 1976, we celebrate two bicentennials: the birth of the American nation and the publication of Adam Smith's book *The Wealth of Nations*.

Adam Smith is hardly a household name in America, and the school children of this land hear more of Thomas Jefferson than of the Father of Economics. However, I am prepared to argue that Smith deserves equal rank with the Founding Fathers in the honor roll of those who have helped to make this a nation of freedom with order—and with general prosperity.

I could write of his support of the American colonies in their dispute with the mother country. After all, he was the principal spokesman against the mercantilist policies of England, of which her treatment of the American colonies was a part.

He urged the British government either to invite the colonies to send representatives to Parliament or, better yet, grant them their total independence.

Proper Attitude

I choose rather to concentrate on Smith's advice to us on the proper attitude to take toward the businessman. A popular misconception is

Reprinted from the *Indianapolis News*, February 27, 1976, by permission of the Rogge estate.

that (as one writer put it) "Smith was an unconscious mercenary in the service of a rising capitalist class. He rationalized the economic interests of the class that was coming to power."

It is, in fact, absurd to speak of Smith as if he were a puppet of the business interest. His book *The Wealth of Nations* was written first and foremost as an attack on the ruling system of mercantilism—a system which was characterized by an alliance between the government and particular business interests.

Smith warned us that "the proposal of any new law or regulation which comes from this order (the businessmen) ought always to be listened to with great precaution, and ought never to be adopted till after having been long and carefully examined, not only with the most scrupulous, but with the most suspicious attention."

This did not lead Smith to call, as do many modern demagogues, for government action against the businessman or his firm. Rather, he called for the government to neither restrain nor give privilege to the business (or any other) interest: "All systems either of preference or of restraint being thus completely taken away, the obvious and simple system of natural liberty establishes itself of its own accord."

He is telling us to reject both the absurd arguments of, for example, the dealers in alcoholic beverages who would have us lend the support of the police to their price-fixing schemes and the equally absurd arguments of those senators who would have us send out the police to "break up" the large oil companies.

Smith is telling us to grant the businessman (as to all men) freedom within the law—no more and no less. Under this arrangement, the self-interest of the businessman would lead him to the service of society.

To those who ask the businessman to act less on self-interest and more out of a sense of social responsibility, he had already given the answer: "I have never known much good done by those who affected to trade for the public good."

My Way

I would add that I trust the businessman only when he's out to make money—because then he's going to want to do things my way. When he's out to do me good, he is going to do it his way.

Nor is there any need for the government to direct the decision making of the businessman or his customers—quite the contrary. "The statesman who should attempt to direct private people in what manner they ought to employ their capitals, would not only load himself with a most unnecessary attention, but assume an authority which could safely be trusted, not only to no single person but to no council or senate whatever, and which would nowhere be so dangerous as in the hands of a man who had folly and presumption enough to fancy himself fit to exercise it."

Here, I submit, was wisdom of a high order. To the extent that we have chosen to be guided by it, we have had freedom, order, and prosperity. To the extent that we have turned away from it, we have had tyranny and disorder and economic distress.

Fortunately, as Adam Smith himself counseled us, each man's effort to better his own condition "frequently restores health and vigor to the constitution, in spite, not only of the disease, but of the absurd prescriptions of the doctor."

Part 3 *Education*

SECTION 1

Education in a
Free Society

Education in a Free Society

The question is this: what would be the ideal educational arrangements in human society and, in particular, in a society of free and responsible beings?

Some Explanations and Assumptions

First of all, the presence in the question of the word "human" immediately takes from the word "ideal" any sense of the utopian. The question that we are asking is not how to produce philosopher kings or Übermenschen, but, rather, how to do the best that is possible with the imperfect material that man now (and forever) represents. Our search is for a description of the optimal, not the perfect. Even the optimal in human affairs must, of necessity, reflect the underlying imperfection in the human raw material. But even this optimal set of arrangements is only a guideline, a Polaris to be used as a reference point by the navigator and not a position likely to be reached in fact.

Why then bother with an attempt to define that which would be less than perfect even if attained, but which is thought probably unattainable as well? Because without a reference point, the navigator is condemned to aimless wandering in an almost limitless sea of choice. *The identifying of an ideal is a matter of absolute practical necessity in all rational decision making.* Far from being the impractical, time-wasting pursuit of

Cowritten with Pierre F. Goodrich and reprinted from *Education in a Free Society,* ed. Anne Husted Burleigh (Indianapolis: Liberty Fund, 1973): 53–93.

the dreamer, an attempt to define the ideal is the first step of the rational man concerned with the conduct of each day's practical affairs.

Second, what precisely is meant by the word "imperfect," as used above to describe the human condition? First, it is assumed that man is imperfect as an intellectual agent, that is, in his knowledge of himself and of the human and physical world around him. Next, it is assumed that man is imperfect as a moral agent; that is, he is of less-than-perfect integrity in serving whatever guidelines of ethical conduct he may recognize, in serving whatever ultimate purposes he may select. Next, it is assumed that man is imperfect as a divine agent; that is, he does not fully know or understand *what* he is, *why* he is, or what his role is in the cosmic scheme of things. In a word, he is not God. As John Locke said, a man cannot be a judge in his own cause. Finally, we accept the Acton thesis that it is man's nature for these inherent imperfections to become even more pronounced as he exercises power over others, particularly the power to coerce.

To summarize, in defining man as imperfect, we are describing him as an ignorant, weak creature, somewhat lower than the angels, with a strong predisposition to be corrupted by power. None of this is written as a hymn of despair or as a criticism of man or as the preface to a sermon to man to mend his evil ways; it is written as a description of that which is and will be. Man is not now God; he cannot acquire godship; his greatest corruption is his desire to play God. In all this he seems not to have changed since the time when we first have knowledge of his characteristics. It would seem safe to assume that it is this imperfect raw material out of which must come whatever results can be obtained in human affairs. Again, to say this is not to despair; those who have truly lost hope for man are those who abandon him as he is and will be and create dreamworlds peopled with creatures that never have been and never will be on the face of this earth.

Third, we shall describe as "educational" any process that results in growth in understanding for a particular human being. We direct your attention immediately to our conviction that education is something that happens within an individual. No matter how formally educational the setting or the process, if nothing happens to the supposed learner, nothing educational has taken place. (*It should be apparent from this definition that perhaps the greater part of the activity now undertaken by supposed teachers and supposed students is not, in fact, educational at all.*) At the same time, something educational can take place far removed from a classroom, a teacher, a degree-granting institution, or any of the other paraphernalia of organized schooling. It would be difficult to overestimate the importance we attach to the ideas that we have introduced in this paragraph (and which we will develop at greater length in a later section of the paper).

Fourth, given the almost infinite variability of the members of the human race, it seems safe to assume that we differ, one from the other, in our capacities to become educated, to acquire understanding in the various areas of knowledge. One will be more generally educable than another, one will be highly responsive in one area but not in another, one will respond to an educational technique to which another is unresponsive, and so forth. It would seem to follow that no *one* approach to education would be optimal for all. Rather, the ideal set of educational arrangements we are seeking to describe must somehow take into account the fact of human differentiation.

Finally, the "educated man," as we have implicitly defined him here, is not necessarily also the "virtuous man," the "good man," the "great man," or the saint. We are not certain precisely how man does become virtuous or good or great or saintlike (perhaps through "revealed" knowledge?), but we are certain that it is not the necessary end product of education, not even of the ideal education that we hope to describe here. We are reluctant to believe that a man can be truly good, yet essentially ignorant (witness the many economic and political catastrophes wished on us by the apparently well intentioned but uninformed), but we do suspect that the saint and the scholar are not necessarily one and the same.

It might be possible to argue that the extensive knowledge of consequences of human actions which would come from being truly educated would lead a man to choose virtuous behavior, if on no other grounds than that of efficiency, the knowledge that right action succeeds while wrong action fails. But the Faust myth still rises to challenge us, and we cannot be comfortable with the assumption that the knowledgeable man will also be the noble or virtuous man. In fact, in the Faust myth, it is precisely the most learned who is most susceptible to the temptations of the Devil, to the lure of temporal power over others. (It is tempting to explain the behavior of many modern intellectuals in somewhat this way.)

We are aware, then, of the limitations of even the ideal that we hope to describe; even the best of all possible educational arrangements cannot make man into God or into a saint—or even into a good, decent human being. To be educated in the sense we have in mind here is something, perhaps a very important something, but it is not the alpha and the omega of human existence.

From these words of introduction, we turn now to our task. We shall ask, first, what are the purposes to be served by the educational arrangements we have in mind; then, what economic and political arrangements for education would seem best to serve those purposes; finally, what kinds of specific educational techniques we would expect to be emphasized in the ideal arrangements we seek to describe.

The Purposes of Education

A Preliminary Statement

Our concern is with, and only with, the purposes of education in a society of free and responsible men. Quite obviously, the purposes of education in an *un*free society are going to be directed to the needs of the ruler or the ruling group, whether it be a personal dictator, the dictatorship of the proletariat, the rule of the priest-kings, or what have you.

Some interesting technical questions are posed by the role and nature of education in unfree societies—questions that shed some light on the role of education in a free society. For example: Would it be in the interests of the rulers really to encourage (or even permit) growth in understanding among the ruled? Or would all so-called education be, in fact, nothing more than training for the particular roles to be filled in the command-determined structure of society? Can all growth in understanding really be prevented, even by an apparently omnipotent state? Some of the great masterpieces of the human spirit that have been composed within prison walls would seem to testify to the durability of the desire for understanding and wisdom, at least on the part of the few. Further, there are questions of whether a dictatorship that really succeeded in stifling all true learning would not inevitably come to be staffed by men of such brittleness and inflexibility as to fall easy victim to some more imaginative foe.

Interesting though these questions may be, they are not our concern here. Here we seek to know only what would be appropriate in a free society. *By a free society, we mean precisely one in which each individual is free to do that which is peaceful,* or, put another way, one in which the state is limited to the role of the night watchman.

Put still another way, the properly educated citizens of a free society are those who are committed to living as responsible members of society, free from intimidation both by individuals within the society and by other nation-states as well. (The question of how such a society should deal with those in its midst who are unwilling or unable so to live deserves serious attention, but will not be dealt with here. Briefly, it might be said that the hoped-for solution would lie in the growth in self-responsibility that often seems to follow upon the *necessity* of being responsible for self. The junior author of this paper is somewhat more optimistic about this coming about than is his partner.)

In such a society, the purpose to be served by any peaceful activity, whether it be educational, economic, religious, or what have you, is not a proper concern of the state; definitions of purpose lie wholly within the jurisdiction of the individuals involved. For example, whether the individual pursues an education for the sheer delight in learning or to acquire knowledge for personal decision making and action or to better serve his God—or even to do no more than flaunt his learning before others—the choice of purpose (as well as means) is *his* and not society's.

In this sense, it is not only unnecessary to define the purposes of education in a free society, it is logically inconsistent to attempt to do so. The very meaning of the free society is a society in which questions of goals, ends, and purposes are left to the individual, and questions of means are of concern to the state only if the means used depart from the peaceful.

It would seem to follow from this that all that need be said about the educational arrangements in a free society is that they should be left to the free decisions of the individuals in the society, that the state should not interfere with any man's attempt to find the educational arrangements best suited to his purposes or with any man's attempt to offer educational arrangements that he thinks others might find attractive.

The Apparent Paradox

Comes now the seeming paradox. If, in a society already free, the state takes no action with regard to education, how can there be any assurance that the citizenry will know and understand the desirability of freedom, the various legal and other necessary structures of the free society, the undesirability of the unfree society? How will a citizenry not deliberately educated in the ways of freedom be able to withstand the constant temptations and pressures to abandon freedom in the hope of some transient advantage? In other words, does the survival of the free society require that its citizens be unfree in at least one area, the area of education? Must they be compelled to acquire at least some minimum understanding of the nature of the free society and its alternatives? Must all discussion of the alternatives to freedom be critical in nature, or can freedom be expected to win out in any open argument? Can even the free society afford to let educational arrangements be determined at the whim of its imperfect citizens?

Most self-styled free societies have chosen to abandon freedom to some degree in the field of education. Most have enacted compulsory school attendance laws; most have used the coercive power of the state to obtain the funds to support some part or all of the formal educational programs in the society; most have dictated in one way or another, in one degree or another, what is and what is not to be taught in their schools and colleges.

A central argument of this paper is that *all* such interventions by the state in the educational process are both unnecessary and undesirable. We intend to argue that the best way for the people of a free society to assure that the educational arrangements of the society serve the cause of freedom is for the society *as a political unit* to have nothing whatsoever to do with those arrangements—except, of course, as the state protects the citizen from force and fraud in this area, as in all others.

We oppose state operation of educational programs at any level; we oppose state financing of such programs at any level, in any form (including tax relief); we oppose state coercion of participation in such programs, whether public or private. We believe that education must, by its nature, be a part of the *private* sector of society. We can hardly put our position more plainly or more forcefully.

But if the state (the night watchman) is not to educate for freedom, what persons or what agencies will? We remind the reader of two facts: (1) In even the largely free societies, the most effective spokesmen for limited government and individual freedom have usually *not* been the paid agents of the state. We offer the great historical examples of John Locke and, later, the authors of the *Federalist Papers*. (2) To grant to the government of even a free society authority over education, even for the intended purpose of educating for freedom, is to extend the power of fallible, corruptible men. And history reveals all too clearly how these men may yield readily to the temptation to turn education to the purposes of expanding state power (and, hence, their own power), rather than of restricting and limiting that power. Witness the many "civics" or "government" courses in modern America that are training grounds not for the defense of freedom but for attacks on freedom and limited government, in the interests of whatever social causes may be of current interest to the instructors.

We repeat: the task of educating individuals for freedom, if done at all, will be best done by *private* agencies and institutions, manned by individuals deeply committed to that cause. Admittedly, in a free society there will also exist private educational programs dedicated to restricting or eliminating freedom, alike manned by deeply committed individuals. Without being so naive as to believe that the truth must always win in an open contest, we still insist that the risk in this arrangement is far less than the risk run in a system where the agency of coercion (the state) is expected to educate the citizenry in the desirability of limiting the power of the state—a most unlikely act of self-denial!

In the words of one student of these questions, "every politically controlled educational system will inculcate the doctrine of state supremacy sooner or later, whether as the divine right of kings, or the 'will of the people' in 'democracy.'"[1]

1. Isabel Paterson, *The God of the Machine* (1943), 271–72.

Whose Purposes, the Child's or the Parents'?

We have now made clear our insistence that the purposes of education are not to be defined by the state; they are rather to be defined by the individuals who participate in educational activities. This seems clear-cut enough in cases where the individuals involved are adults, assumed to be capable of making their own decisions. Certain questions arise when the participants are children.

Quite obviously, the infant is incapable of choosing a good part of what and how it is to learn, to grow in understanding of itself and of the world around it. But as the infant becomes the child and the child the young person and the young person the young adult, he (or she) tends to develop not only the capacity to make his own decisions but an ever-stronger will to do so as well.

Who should be entrusted with the decision making on educational questions for the infant and the child?—the parents or the legal guardians? voluntary agencies concerned with child welfare? the state? Who should decide when and to what extent the developing young person is to be permitted his or her own decision making on educational matters?

There is a strong presumption among those who would use the state to bring about the good society to distrust the decision making of the family in many areas, particularly in the rearing and educating of the young. In almost all of the better-known utopian schemes (e.g., those of Plato, Fourier, Robert Owen, and Skinner), the children are to be taken from their parents at an early age so that their upbringing can be under the control of the all-wise agents of the state, rather than of the foolish and primitive family circle.

Needless to say, while recognizing the serious, and at times tragic, imperfections of the family system of child raising, we reject all arrangements that would substitute for the imperfect family the even less perfect state. It is appropriate for the state to intervene in the family relationship when improper force is used against the child, and it may be necessary at times for the court to resolve questions of legal guardianships for orphan children. But except for those obvious cases, the state has no jurisdiction over the relationship of parent and child, including all questions of the education of the child.

The question of how much freedom of decision making is to be granted the child by the parent is also a question for the parent to answer—not the state. Some parents will grant their children early and substantial freedom of decision making on educational matters; others will insist on making all such decisions, even for offspring beyond the legal age dividing the child from the adult. Either attitude on the part of parents can be carried to absurd extremes, but it ill behooves us to ask the state to intervene in such cases, in view of the strong presumption we hold against state intervention in the peaceful activities of its citizens.

We repeat: imperfect as it may be, the family still seems to be the *least* imperfect agency for the making of educational decisions for the young.

The ideal is that any given decision is to be made by the person or persons responsible for the consequences of the decision. In the case of education, this would seem to require that the parents (or guardians), for so long as they are financially responsible for the children, be permitted the associated right of making educational decisions for them. The child who becomes financially responsible for himself is no longer a child in this sense and should then be free to make his or her own educational plans.

Summary of the Purposes of Education

We have insisted that the very essence of a free society is that questions of purpose are to be resolved by the individuals involved. The purposes of education, then, must be personal and individual, to be chosen by the person directly involved or by those legally responsible for that person.

Even those of us who are deeply committed to the ideal of a society of free and responsible men and who would wish to see this ideal become a part of the understanding of all are restrained, by both principle and knowledge of consequences, from asking the state to make this ideal a part of the education of all. Our hope must rest in the uncertain outcome of competitive educational programs, free of state control. In a later section, we shall speculate on the nature of the noncoercive educational program that would seem to be most likely to develop in its participants an understanding of the free society and a commitment to it.

The Economics of Education

Some part of the education of each human being comes as the unintended by-product of the daily experiences of life. (See, for example, *The Education of Henry Adams*.) Education so gained may be painfully acquired, but in an economic sense, it is costless; that is, no resources were taken from other possible uses to make this result possible. The opportunity cost of education so acquired is zero.

But the greater part of the education of a human being requires the use of resources (if only the time of the person seeking the education) that could have been put to other uses. The questions that arise out of this fact are the ones now under study.

Types of Educational Activities and Institutions in a Truly Free Society

We begin by assuming a society in which the state plays no part in the educational process. Gone would be all state colleges and universities, all public elementary and secondary schools, all public libraries and public opera houses, and so forth. What would we expect to find in their places (if anything)?

Let us be honest. We do not know nor can we ever know, except by trying the experiment. As F. A. Hayek has demonstrated, it is impossible to predict the precise nature, the details, of what men will create under freedom.[2] Nor can we predict solely by studying the private sector of education under current arrangements. Under those arrangements, structure and performance of the private sector of education are distorted by a host of state interventions, including the awesome competition of a public rival who can give away that for which the private sector must ask a price.

We are not totally at a loss, though. We have been able to observe the private sector at work under relatively free circumstances in other lines of activity, and we can make some very rough guesses about the general nature of the educational arrangements under freedom.

---

2. F. A. Hayek, "The Use of Knowledge in Society," *American Economics Review* 35 (1945): 519–30.

First, we would expect enormous variety in the kinds, the forms, and the qualities of educational opportunities offered. For example, we would expect to see far more use than at present made of the relatively less expensive techniques of education—books, journals, tapes, films, televised lectures and discussions, and so forth. It has been in the interest of the educational establishment in this country to promote the demand for its own services (particularly the classroom teacher and the formal textbook) by emphasizing formal schooling over the almost infinite variety of less formal approaches to education. They may teach the children the story of the self-education of such greats as Abraham Lincoln or Thomas Edison, but only to emphasize the great disadvantage those men had to overcome in being denied the opportunities of the modern classroom, complete with its teacher with at least two degrees and thirty or more hours of course work in how-to-teach (but, perhaps, no true education). ("Just think what Lincoln could have accomplished had he been able to go to college!" was the statement of one such enthusiast to the senior author of this paper.) Capitalist enterprise has so reduced the cost of reading material that only the most desperately insolvent need now be denied at least this form of educational experience.

Next, we would expect many of the educational enterprises to be run for profit, hence to be more efficiently run than the not-for-profit enterprises that now control the greater part of education. (It is interesting to note the experiments now being conducted by some school boards, which, in their search for an answer to the gross inefficiencies of public education, are turning to private, profit-making educational organizations to run their schools on performance-guaranteed contracts!) More on this later.

We would expect the formal schools in a free society to reflect at least as much variety as we now see in the private sector. Some would be operated by religious groups, some would be aggressively secular; some would be specialists in serving the gifted student, some in serving the slower students; some would have a variegated student body, some a homogeneous student body; some would offer only the liberal arts, others only the vocationally oriented materials, still others some mixture of the two. Actually, we would expect even more variety than that which now characterizes education; the current arrangements (as will be discussed later) do not lead schools to be consumer oriented; the private school of the free society we have in mind would tend to reflect that same consumer orientation that has characterized the private sector in other areas.

The Financing of Education

A convenient way to examine the issues under study here is to ask how education should be priced and whose funds should be used in paying that price.

The traditional view, even in largely free societies, is that education is somehow different from other goods and services and that this difference calls for special pricing and funding arrangements.

The differences are usually said to derive from two particular attributes of education: (1) the spillover of benefits from the individual to all of society, coming from the advantage of a better-educated citizenry; and (2) the unique importance of education to career opportunity and, hence, to providing some kind of equal opportunity for all.

These two claims have been discussed elsewhere by one of the authors of this paper.[3] To summarize the objections we have to these claims to special treatment of education: First, both the fact and degree of spillover benefits from education are open to serious question. In effect, what happens here is that A decides that C has benefited from the education of B and that, therefore, C should pay some part or all of the costs of B's education. This is a denial of C's basic right to make his own decisions (in this as in other cases) about benefits supposedly flowing to him and to act accordingly. As a matter of fact, as two of the C's in modern America, we deny that we have gained from the schooling provided the B's; in fact, inasmuch as most of that schooling, as it relates to citizenship, has been antifreedom, we believe that we have been *damaged* by the schooling of the B's. For the state to tax us to support the teaching of collectivist ideas is a real violation of our freedom.

If the C's of this world believe that they would benefit by the B's understanding a specific educational activity, they are free to transfer

---

3. B. A. Rogge, "The Financing of Higher Education in the United States," *Wall Street Journal*, editorial page, May 1 and 4, 1959.

resources directly or indirectly to the B's for that purpose. As a matter of fact, many of the schools and colleges of this country were founded by the C's on exactly this basis.

To the argument that the C's must pay for the education of the B's because, otherwise, the B's would not have an equal chance in the race of life, we reply: given the infinite variability of the species, there is no way in which all individuals can start as equals, let alone end up as equals. To seek to provide so-called equality of opportunity would literally require the application of constant coercion to the human condition. *The only equality that is consistent with freedom is equality before the law;* in fact, this form of equality is a necessary condition for freedom to exist. All other forms and types of equalities can be brought into being (if at all) only through the use of force.

To put this another way: it is often said that each B has a *right* to an education. If a right exists, it must run against someone else—that is, against the C's of this world. This implies that each B that is brought into this world brings with him a blank check drawn on some collection of C's, to be cashed for whatever purposes society may decide appropriate. This is a monstrous perversion of the concept of natural rights—at least of the traditional interpretation of the natural rights idea.

Under the natural right concept as it flowered in the seventeenth, eighteenth, and nineteenth centuries, A, B, and C do indeed have certain rights with which they were endowed by their Creator, but those rights do *not* include rights to the goods and properties of each other. In fact, to John Locke, the right to one's own property is one of the natural rights; for another to claim that property as a right—to further his schooling, say—would be a denial of the *true* natural rights of man.

What B does have a right to, in the field of education, is to seek his education (or not seek it) by any peaceful means, free of the restraint and coercion of his fellow men. Not too surprisingly, this particular right is denied him daily by precisely those same A's who would award him an automatic claim on the goods and services of C for the purposes of education. (For example, in many states, the parents of a child are not permitted to provide schooling for that child in their own home, with themselves as the teachers.)

The concept that all must be assured of some form of education, regardless of desire or financial ability, is thus rejected in principle. We would also question the practical argument that schooling is necessary to opportunity. We would argue that much of the apparent relationship between schooling and income either does not establish causation or reflects state action that has required degrees and diplomas as cards of admission to various careers.

Below-Cost Pricing and Efficiency

An additional pragmatic argument against providing "free" education to all is that this method of pricing produces gross inefficiencies in the educational process. (This argument is developed at length in the Rogge article previously cited.) First, under the system of tax-derived financing of schools, there is no natural process by which the efficiently run schools may grow and prosper and the poorly run schools be weeded out by the competition. One of the great achievements of the market process is that it does not suffer fools gladly, that it rather quickly takes the control of resources from the hands of the incompetent. One need not be a serious student of public education to be aware of the fact that a substantial part of the educational resources of this country are in the hands of the incompetent—yet this is inevitable under the current arrangements.

Next, this method of pricing does nothing to weed out those students who have no desire to learn. The storekeepers (teachers, counselors, deans, and so on) must keep constant watch to see that the would-be customers do not slip out of the store without the merchandise that someone else has purchased for them—an absurd predicament. Admittedly, the young, under any system, are sometimes less than anxious to submit themselves to the discipline of education, but the problem is made much more severe (particularly at the secondary school level) by the fact that those who are anxious to learn are surrounded by the many who are not. Willingness to pay the price is one measure of strength of motive; when the price is zero, the motivation is often its equal.

In addition, with the income of the teacher coming *not* from the student but from a general subsidy, the teacher is under no real necessity of serving the interests of his students. One obvious manifestation of this is that in most public schools in this country, excellence (or lack of it) in teaching has absolutely nothing to do with the salary of the teacher. As Adam Smith put it:

> In other universities the teacher is prohibited from receiving any honorary or fee from his pupils, and his salary constitutes the whole of the revenue which he derives from his office. His interest is, in this case, set as directly in opposition to his duty as it is possible to set it. It is the interest of every man to live as much at his ease as he can; and if his emoluments are to be precisely the same, whether he does, or does not perform some very laborious duty, it is certainly his interest, at least, as interest is vulgarly understood, either to neglect it altogether, or if he is subject to some authority which will not suffer him to do this, to perform it in as careless and slovenly a manner as that authority will permit. . . . In the University of Oxford, the greater part of the public professors have, for these many years, given up altogether even the pretense of teaching.[4]

In summary, then, *tax-supported education tends to make of our schools and colleges a collection of nonstudents under the tutelage of nonteachers and the administration of the incompetent.*

Summary of the Economics of Education

We reject, then, the view that education must be treated as a special case and insist, rather, that it be given precisely the same status as any other good or service in the marketplace. Let each man choose among the alternatives open to him; let each would-be supplier offer his wares in the marketplace, subject only to the general rules against fraud.

Note: In all probability, thanks both to the workings of the market and to the explicit application of the law against fraud, those conducting such educational programs would be brought to a higher level of integrity and honesty than now characterizes such men and institutions. The arrangements currently existing in both public and private schools and colleges tend to induce administrators to deceive the students, the parents, the governing boards, the taxpayers, or the donors to their institutions as to the true nature of the school's operations. In particular, most college administrations have found it desirable, shall we say, *not to emphasize* the fact that on their campuses the students will be confronted

4. Adam Smith, *The Wealth of Nations* (Modern Library, n.d.), 717–18.

by faculties far more liberal or left-wing than the *prevailing point of view* among parents, trustees, taxpayers, and donors. In how many college catalogs do you find prospective students and their parents given *any* information on the social philosophies to which the student is exposed on that campus? Do they say, Send your son to College X and he will be taught by five Marxist, burn-down-the-buildings activists, fifteen non-Marxist, just-seize-the-buildings activists, one hundred left-of-center modern liberals, ten Ripon Society Republicans, and two eccentric conservatives just reaching retirement age? As Professor George Stigler of the University of Chicago has said, "the typical university catalogue would never stop Diogenes in his search for an honest man."[5]

Quite obviously, there are dishonest men and men of questionable integrity in all occupations, but both competition and the law tend to weed them out over a period of time in the market sectors of the economy. However, no such process works as vigorously in the not-for-profit sectors. A thoroughly dishonest man can probably last longer under the umbrella of occupational blessedness in teaching or in the ministry than in the world of business.

To continue with the summary of the economics of education in a truly free society: again, we cannot predict with accuracy the pattern that truly free men would develop to serve their educational desires. In general, though, we would expect a mixture of for-profit and not-for-profit institutions to prevail, with the for-profit institutions largely setting the pace, at least in terms of the economics of the operation. For example, we would expect that education would come to be priced in a market fashion—that is, with the equilibrium price being one that covers all costs, including a normal rate of return to ownership. Even the not-for-profit institutions would probably find it efficient and equitable to set prices at market levels, with subsidies going to individual recipients rather than to institutions. Few who wish to give bread to the poor think it wise to do this by starting a bakery and selling the bread to all (or even just to the poor) at below cost. Most find it more efficient to subsidize the individual (but not by the state) and then let him buy his bread where he will—and so we would expect it to be in the system we are describing here.

---

5. George Stigler, "The Intellectual and the Market Place," *Selected Paper,* no. 3, Graduate School of Business, University of Chicago, February 1967, p. 7.

We would also expect school and college administrators to demand that teachers *really* serve the interests of students. We do not mean by this that the students would run the place but only that, as the ultimate consumers of the product, their decisions to stay or leave would determine whether the institution itself would survive. The faculty members who today can consistently shirk their teaching responsibilities just wouldn't be tolerated under the arrangements we have in mind, unless, of course, they could find some private source of funds to support them in whatever it is they are doing (such as research) other than teaching. (*Note:* Research and teaching are not necessarily mutually exclusive activities; in fact, the teacher who is not actively engaged in a continuing search for more understanding is not likely to be an effective teacher. We would expect some part of the financial reward for research to come in the form of the higher fees that students would pay to study with such teachers.)

The income of teachers, then, would be determined by the effectiveness with which they served the purposes of the employing institutions, not by seniority or degrees earned. Needless to say, the tenure arrangement would disappear. Both of the authors have discussed this topic in other writings.[6] Suffice it to say here that tenure is not needed by the competent and, hence, shields only the incompetent. We are not dissuaded from this position by any arguments with reference to so-called academic freedom. *We simply do not believe in academic freedom.* We do believe in the idea that each man should be free to say what he will, but we don't believe that anyone has the right to say what he will and be paid for the saying of it by someone else who doesn't wish to so pay him! In this sense, academic freedom is, in fact, a denial of freedom—the freedom of each man to expend his resources on only those uses that he sees fit, including the choice of sources of learning.

We have no way of knowing how the advantages and disadvantages of horizontal and vertical integration would serve to shape the nature and form of educational institutions. Perhaps chain-store and full-line education would emerge as the most efficient; perhaps the independent or specialty shop would prove the more flexible and innovative. We simply don't know—but we do know that whatever would emerge

---

6. B. A. Rogge, "The Financing of Higher Education"; Pierre F. Goodrich, *Education Memorandum, 1951–1969.*

could not help but be many times more efficient than the present arrangements.

We must summarize by saying that *a truly private educational system, rather than being more costly than a public one, would surely provide more and better educational opportunities at a far lower cost per unit of delivered product (i.e., per unit growth in knowledge) than the current system.*

We repeat: let each family, using its own resources or resources voluntarily made available to it by others, pay for such educational programs for its children as it sees fit—whether that which is purchased be a book, a television set, or four years at Harvard College. Let each adult, again using funds acquired by peaceful exchange or gift, make his or her own educational decisions, acting on them in the educational marketplace. If freedom of choice is desirable for individuals in most aspects of their lives, why is it not imperative that freedom of choice be granted them in one of the most important aspects of their lives: their growth in understanding of themselves and of the world around them? To the collectivists we say, if you insist on controlling something, make it the peanut butter or hula hoop industries, but for God's sake, leave education alone!

The Ideal College

In this section, we intend to describe in some detail what we believe would be an ideal college. Let us say a number of things immediately:

1. These are no more than our own thoughts on what we would consider the ideal college. In a free educational marketplace, consumers might or might not select *our* ideal as *their* ideal—and their choices would be the ones that would prevail.
2. For "ideal" we are using this criterion: Does this arrangement maximize the likelihood that those who are exposed to it will come to be committed to the free society and, equally important, come to know and understand precisely what they are for and against and why? In other words, we are not interested in the purely emotional, unreasoning convert to our point of view.

Some might wish to argue that what we are proposing is a propaganda mechanism, not an educational program. To this we would make two replies: First, in the sense that there are no truly "objective" teachers or collections of teachers, all educational institutions have some kind of planned or unplanned slant or point of view. For example, most of the so-called places of true learning in this country today are, in fact, dominated by the philosophies of the left and, hence, giant factories of left-wing thought and opinion. Our position would be openly declared, for all to know, rather than concealed under the guise of objectivity. Second, it is our conviction that any person of reasonable intelligence who studies the human experience in the manner appropriate to true learning will probably come to the conclusion that the optimal organization of society is that of free and responsible men under limited government and the rule of law. Admittedly, some may not agree; certainty is rarely encountered in human affairs. Others may agree in principle but find the attractions of power for themselves too great to resist. (Compare, for example, the Woodrow Wilson who said, "The history of human liberty is the history of limitation of governmental power," with the Woodrow Wilson in the presidency, who added enormously to the power of government in the domestic economy and who used his position to bring America's entry into a tragic foreign war. The poet Kipling reflected some rare insight in his poem "The Gods of the Copybook Headings," published in 1919.) In other words, we believe that true growth in understanding is likely to turn the learner's head and heart in the direction of freedom; the educational dice do not have to be loaded in our favor, although it may be necessary that they not be loaded against us, as they now are.

3. We have chosen the college-level kind of institution, not because it is necessarily the most important, but because we feel that we have had more experience with and know more about this kind of education than we do about, say, elementary schooling.

We would add only that we believe the same general principles would apply at all levels of educational activity. In a truly free, competitive educational system, we would expect a great variety of elementary and secondary educational programs to evolve, some involving the formal classroom, others not. What we *would* expect to happen is that the young and the very young would come to some level of competence in the basic skills of language and number use at an earlier age and at far less expense per pupil than under current arrangements.

4. We are restricting our model to what might be termed (in a very rough sort of way) the liberal arts college.

We are not contemptuous of vocational training nor do we deny that much vocational training can also lead to true growth in general understanding in the liberal arts sense. However, the training of doctors or electrical engineers or lawyers need not have any close relationship to the question of freedom. Our concern is with those forms of educational activity that do seem to have a close tie to questions of human freedom. (Actually, we are convinced that the training of doctors, accountants, lawyers, engineers, or what have you, would be improved if greater general understanding were required of them. When the accountant, for example, encounters problems of inflation or of political control of his work, he stands in need, *even to be a better accountant,* of kinds of understanding not usually taught in courses in accounting.)

The Structure of the College

The college would be private, of course, with ownership and, hence, control residing in a specified person or group of persons. *Note:* Many of the problems of today's colleges and universities flow from the ambiguous nature of ownership and, hence, control. With students, faculty members, alumni, administrators, board members, taxpayers, donors, and the general public all laying claim to some authority, it is no wonder that it is sometimes difficult to determine who really is in charge.

The firm could be for-profit or not-for-profit, with our preference being for the former.

All decisions of policy would be made by the board and implemented by the administration. As in any successful firm, customer (student) and employee (faculty) opinion and responses would be made a part of the general information on which policy-making decisions would be based, but in no case would any ambiguity about the location of final authority be permitted.

Personnel Policies and Practices

Faculty members would be selected for their promise as teachers, in the sense of encouraging and contributing to growth in understanding in others.

The greater part of them (perhaps all) would be men and women who are also deeply committed to the philosophy of the free society: If we believe (as we do) that the outcome of true learning is likely to be such a commitment, then it would be inconsistent of us to seek to find true scholars and teachers among those not so committed. However, in recognition of our own fallibility and of the responses of students to what seem to be loaded dice, it might not be inappropriate for the faculty to include some who are critics of the free society.

Faculty members would serve at the pleasure of the administration, with only such recognition of time in service as is usually appropriate in any organization.

The income of faculty members would be directly related to their effectiveness in serving the purposes of the college. In effect, if they failed to attract students to their lectures or their seminars, or if nothing educational seemed to happen to those who did so attend, the man would be fired, or his salary not increased, or what have you. (An alternative arrangement would be for the greater part of faculty income to be in the form of student fees paid directly to them, after students have paid the college proper a basic fee to cover overhead expenses.[7])

The Curriculum

The educational program of the college would consist of three basic elements: (1) individual study by students, (2) seminars on assigned readings, and (3) lectures delivered by members of the faculty (or visitors).

Students could choose among the alternatives available to them, with only these provisos: (1) any student whose behavior in class or on campus created problems for others would be asked to leave; (2) any student who wished to participate in a given seminar would be expected to have read the assigned material. On evidence that he had not read the material, the seminar leaders would ask him to leave (or perhaps, become an observer only).

For any given term, the college would publish a list of the seminars to be held and of the lectures to be given. These lists would be the bases on

7. John Fischer, "Preface to the Catalogue of Curmudgeon College," Harper's, June 1970, pp. 75–78.

which students could plan their programs. On such questions, students could consult counselors explicitly provided by the administration, or any member of the faculty who would consent to serve. Students would also be given a list of suggested books and other materials, including not only those to be explicitly discussed in seminars but readings that would contribute to the students' general understanding. Some of the books that might be listed (in either category) are given in the *Liberty Fund Basic Memorandum,* part 6.

Students could continue for as many terms as they wished, given proper behavior in the classroom and on campus. *No degrees would be given or diplomas awarded.* The college would exist to serve students truly seeking knowledge, not those seeking only a degree or other meaningless relics from the current system.

Neither courses nor teachers would be organized by departments or divisions. Quite naturally, some range of interests in the faculty would be deliberately sought, but the artificiality of departmental lines would be avoided. *Note:* The *fact* of departmentalization for administrative purposes is not the great evil; it is the *spirit* of intellectual departmentalization that we would seek to avoid.

The Educational Process

Students would involve themselves in reading, discussing, and listening to lectures—and we would put them in that order, both in terms of importance and of the chronological order in which they should take place. In effect, students would be sent off to do some guided reading, then brought together for small group discussions under trained Socratic leadership, then more reading and more discussion. Finally, the students would be ready to listen intelligently to lectures presented on the topics under study—then more discussion, more reading, and so forth.

Students who wished to receive an evaluation of their progress could make appropriate arrangements, including payment of fees recognizing the extra work involved in such an evaluation. They could write papers or examinations to be read by members of the faculty and used as the basis of evaluation. No grades in the usual sense of that term would be given, except at the request of the student or his parents (or some person or agency providing the student with financial assistance).

We suggest this arrangement not because we are opposed to competition for excellence among students, but because the real purpose of education is for each individual to make the maximum progress possible *for that person*—for this, relative judgments are not significant.

The Student Body

The student body would be made up of those who would be attracted by this kind of educational program and who would be willing to pay the full cost of participating in it. Without the artificial lure of degrees, college dances, and campus sit-ins, an appropriate student body would be self-selecting.

In Loco Parentis?

The remarks made above should not be taken to mean that we object to young people going to dances or doing other things that they find enjoyable. We are not opposed to fun; we just don't believe that it is the business of the college to organize, sponsor, or finance it.

The college would not take responsibility for the general lives of its students; it would not serve *in loco parentis*. Some colleges might choose to do so (for a price), but not this one. Parents who might wish to see their sons or daughters under what they would think appropriate supervision could undoubtedly arrange with local families or landladies for this supervision to be given.

We give you then Free Society College, a sample of the kind of school that might emerge in a free educational marketplace. If this particular college is not to your liking, you need have no fear that it would be the only kind available. We would expect every conceivable type of formal and informal educational program to be available at a wide range of prices. One of the great advantages of the economic marketplace over the political marketplace is that the majority does *not* rule. Every minority opinion that can be served with any hope of profit can and will be served.

Summary

We have argued in this paper that the educational arrangements currently in use in this country are grossly inefficient, inequitable, contrary to human rights, contrary to human nature, and destructive of the society of free and responsible men. We have sought to construct a general picture of those arrangements in education that would be ideal, in terms of being consistent with the principles and practices of a free society and of tending to produce individuals knowledgeable about and committed to that free society. We have rejected any possibility that the ideal could involve state participation and have argued that the ideal arrangements must be found within the jurisdiction of the private educational marketplace. As an example of the kind of school that might emerge under freedom, we have sketched the general features of a college program that we believe would serve the cause of its students and of the free society.

It seems unlikely that the American society will move rapidly (if at all) in the directions we have indicated. But this we do know: if there are none in the society who stand ready to hold out the ideal of a more hopeful arrangement, real progress is not only unlikely—it is forever impossible.

Complexity in Hades

It was a simple story of good against evil. After a strenuous tussle, the good guys won. The leading lady in the drama was a high school social studies teacher; at issue was her right to make the classroom a free marketplace of ideas.

The casting was excellent. One look at the pictures of the bad guys and you knew which side *they* were on. The cast of good guys included a tough old crusading newspaper editor and a courageous widow. As virtue triumphed in the end, all right-thinking people in the audience leaped to their feet to applaud.

As a partisan, I too cheer the verdict of the voters of Paradise. But as a critic of social-message drama, I am forced to insist that the structuring of the issue was too simple and too pat. Let me rewrite the story in several other forms to illustrate my meaning here.

Setting for Virtue

In the story as it was written, the teacher was exposing her students to almost all of the modern social philosophies from far left to far right, and apparently without throwing the weight of her opinion behind any one position. Let us now have her present all sides *but* in such a way that anything to the right of Arthur Schlesinger, Jr., is made to appear

Reprinted from *Teachers College Record* 65 (May, 1964): 654–57, by permission of the publisher.

as unrealistic nonsense or nascent fascism. Do the bad guys now move from black to shades of gray?

Or let her present all sides but with the reverse twist, with anything to the left of Fulton Lewis, Jr., being labeled as socialistic and un-American. What a scrambling of roles *this* might call for! The bad guys now become the defenders of academic freedom. Would all right-thinking people in the audience now leap to applaud a verdict for freedom in the classroom? Some of the left-thinking people in the right-thinking group might well be able to restrain their enthusiasm.

The story line could be made even more complex by arranging for the teacher to present only one side to her students, with little or no exposure to contrary points of view.

It is tempting at this point to conclude that "proper" teaching in the social studies requires the approach of Mrs. Franklin in her Paradise High School classrooms, that the issue as drawn in the dispute that developed around her is the only relevant one, and rest the discussion with some confidence that virtue so defined will usually win out in a democracy.

Comfortable as this conclusion might be, it is open to serious question on grounds of both practice and philosophy. In practice, it requires a degree of neutrality on fundamental issues to be expected of only a minority of teachers. The teacher who is truly neutral, who has no opinions of her or his own, is likely to be a cold, uninformed, uninterested and uninteresting fish. The only kind of teacher who is likely to evoke much real response from students is the one who cares, who has thought through the issues and who has taken a position somewhere on the social philosophy spectrum. To demand that this person conceal this commitment from the students is to demand sainthood of mere human beings. Some few can do it—apparently Mrs. Franklin is one of the few—but most of us are unlikely candidates for canonization.

Crusader vs. Huckster

The plain fact is that the most effective teacher is likely to be the one who has firm convictions, perhaps even some of the fervor of the crusader. If this be true, how then can the classroom be the "free marketplace of ideas" we seem to desire? Perhaps more important, who is to decide what brands of crusaders the students are to be confronted with in the classroom?

An immediate answer to the first question might be to shift the focus from the individual *classroom* to the *school*. This would permit us to demand only that the school be a free marketplace of ideas. The school could offer its students a mixture of brands, with all important points of view represented on the teaching staff.

As a college dean who accepts the validity of this approach, I can say right now that this is easier to do in theory than in practice. The staffing of a faculty is influenced by so many factors—what you start with, staff contacts, coincidence, what's available at the time you can make a change, current staff preferences, etc.—that the maintaining of any kind of "balance" is a precarious business at best.

Then let us recognize another fact of school and college life: for whatever reasons, the majority of teachers who have taken a position on social policy have lined up on the modern liberal range of the spectrum. The number of effective teachers of conservative persuasion is limited, and chance alone tends to bring a school or a college a staff with a majority of modern liberals. A nice 50–50 balance can usually be obtained only by roughhouse techniques and only by turning to some teachers who are conservative but incompetent. (Personally, as an academic dean *and* as a conservative, I refuse to let social philosophy substitute for basic competence.)

The facts of academic life in this country today would seem to indicate that the typical school or college is *not* going to be an equal-time, free marketplace of ideas—either in the individual classroom or in the school as a whole.

This fact alone accounts for a substantial part of the current tension in school-society relations. Those members of society who are most concerned with the schools and colleges and most conscious of the social philosophies taught there are generally more conservative than the teachers and school and college administrators. Nor is this group of critics of the schools and colleges made up exclusively or even predominantly of the John Birch Society and American Legion members involved in the Paradise controversy.

Most of them are serious-minded, thoughtful citizens who are concerned by what they deem to be the one-sidedness of American education, by the failure of teachers to give equal time and respect to the traditional economic and political arrangements of the pre–New Deal USA.

Conservative and Liberal

Let us see where this puts us in terms of the questions raised here. Does society (or at least the active, articulate element in society) really wish the schools and colleges to be a free marketplace of ideas? Probably, no; at least in the sense that it thinks the teachers should not be neutral but, rather, should come down squarely on the side of traditional, i.e., conservative—American social philosophy and practice.

Now the teachers might argue that modern liberalism is indeed within the American tradition, and they could make a good case for this point of view. However, if a significant, perhaps decisive, element in society does not accept this argument, what then for the teachers? Who is to decide what brands of social philosophy, what crusades, are to be presented in the classroom?

Here at last is what I believe to be the central issue. In the last analysis, whose servant is Mrs. Franklin? Her own? Society's? Her students' parents?

Let us take first the answer that the teacher is no one's servant, that the teacher serves only the truth as he or she sees it, and that to make the teacher subservient to *anyone* else is to deny the principle of academic freedom. This is a point of view often expressed by teachers, but its logical implications may be distressing even to teachers.

To begin with, it implies that the teacher, unlike all others in our society, is to be judge in his or her own cause. The product of the teacher is to be judged only by its producer and not at all by its consumer— the students, the parents, society. It implies a self-perpetuating, self-evaluating group of philosopher kings to be supported *by* society but not to be responsible *to* society.

In fact, of course, a case can be made for this position. It can be argued that the teachers constitute an elite of the knowledgeable and that this elite is better fitted to judge what is best for society than is society at large. Moreover, this position would make good sense if society were not also forced to consume the teachers' services through compulsory, tax-supported schooling. The teacher (or group of teachers) who were to say "I shall decide what to teach and you can patronize me if you wish" would be clearly entitled to the academic freedom that that posture would embrace.

That the teacher as a human being has a right to take and argue for a given social philosophy can never be questioned, and in fact freedom so defined is literally worth dying for. But it does not follow that the teacher or any other individual has a right to speak what he wishes *and* be paid by others for doing so. Certainly, Paul Robeson should have a right to sing the Communist "Internationale," but I am not denying him any inherent right or freedom when I refuse to pay for the privilege of listening to him.

In Society's Service

The very existence of a public school system in this country is based on the (debatable) presumption that it serves social as well as personal goals. If it were serving only personal goals, then free public education could be defended only for the indigent. But if the school system is designed to serve social goals and is financed by universal taxation, those who teach in it cannot claim immunity from social decision-making, nor can they insist, on the grounds of academic freedom, that they alone must be permitted to define and interpret those goals. If the voters of Paradise, California, had voted *against* Virginia Franklin, they would have been exercising a right that is naturally and properly theirs. A school system cannot be public for tax-levying purposes and private for the teachers for the making of all other decisions. To be consistent, a teacher or school system that wishes all other decisions to be private must argue as well for a private and voluntarily financed school system.

Let me now hasten to add that I believe that, although they had the *right* to do so, the voters of Paradise would have been acting very unwisely had they voted against Virginia Franklin. The case for academic freedom is not a case based on natural rights but on educational efficiency. The best education is one in which the student is exposed to a variety of points of view, in which the school is a free marketplace of ideas. A neat 50–50 balance on all issues is neither possible nor necessary, but representation from all significant and relevant positions is both possible and important.

I would add that because I believe a public school system must by right be subservient to the public, and because I believe the public to be often wrong and intolerant, I attach great significance to the *private* sector of education at all levels. If the bad guys of whatever persuasion gain the ascendancy, as so often happens to societies under stress, let there be islands of at least temporary resistance to the trends of the day.

The Promise of the College

In this age of Madison Avenue–license in the making of promises, it ill behooves a college to promise its customers (students, student families, and society at large) what it can never hope to deliver. In this age of exceptional stress on the financial resources of a college, it ill behooves a college to promise and deliver services only remotely related to its central purpose.

No intensive research is required to establish the fact that the typical American college is not living by either of these precepts. Wabash College (in company with all other institutions of higher education in this country) is now promising more than it can possibly hope to deliver. It is assuming responsibilities both too various in number and too demanding in nature to be consistent with the realities of the college experience and the college budget.

Perhaps it should not be too harshly condemned for this. In large part, it has but responded to the flattering assurances of the parents of its students that it can indeed make silk purses out of sows' ears— and to the flattering assurances of society that all of the ills of an obviously ill world can be cured through applications of the magic salve of education.

Extenuating though the circumstances may be, they do not excuse this or any college for its failure to develop an honest and explicit statement of what it can do and of what it proposes to do. Existing

Letter to the faculty at Wabash College, July 11, 1960. Reprinted by permission of the Rogge estate.

statements of this nature in various Wabash College publications are obviously unsatisfactory and include patent exaggerations of the quality and quantity of consequences that can be expected to follow from exposing even a reasonably bright young man to four years of college. In addition, various practices of the college reflect an ambiguity in the college's conception of its responsibility to and for the student and take the college far afield from its central task.

The following statements of purposes, assumptions, and procedures are presented with a view toward stimulating discussion on the issues involved here. They are not assumed to be ultimately and exclusively definitive, but they do represent carefully considered and sincerely held opinion.

The Central Purpose of the College

The central purpose of Wabash College is to provide opportunities for young men to develop a solidly based and continuing interest in the life of the mind. The best of colleges can do no more than assist the student in preparing himself for the lifelong task of becoming an educated man. Thus the emphasis of this college is not on turning out the educated man (an arrogant and patently fraudulent promise) but rather on seeking to turn out the man with a strong desire to continue his education and with some idea of how to go about it. This in turn implies that no matter how apparently efficient it may be, an educational program that does not lead eventually to the student's assuming responsibility for his own education is grossly inefficient.

The Promise of the College

Wabash College promises to its constituencies that it will make an unrelenting effort to maintain and improve on the quality of the opportunities with which it challenges its students. It does not promise that all its students will respond fully (or at all) to the opportunities it provides. It does not promise to make scholars (or even acceptable students) of all who come. It does not promise to inculcate in each student the "right" set of values. It does not promise that each of its graduates will be better prepared to serve as a citizen in his society. It does not promise that the opportunities it offers will of necessity produce men of great leadership potential. But as an act of faith, it does express its confidence in the ultimate consequences of exposing free men to the challenge of opportunity.

The College and Values

Wabash College is not the agent of any given general value system. It does not propose to manipulate and mold its students to serve the interests of some one pattern of thinking about ultimate ends. It takes this stand as a matter of principle, but it would be prepared to argue that it could not hope to deliver on a promise to produce young men of a certain value orientation, even if it were to make such a promise.

This does not mean that its staff members will be value neutral, or that its students will not be encouraged to explore value-loaded questions. On the contrary, an important element in the life of the mind is an awareness of the significance of the choices made by men among alternative value sets. Moreover, the life of the mind imposes a morality of its own; it requires of those who would participate in it the minimal character traits of personal integrity and self-reliance. Thus the college will seek to conduct its affairs and to set its standards in such ways as may be most likely to promote in its students these personal characteristics.

Implications for Curriculum Building

The academic program of the college must reflect the central purpose of the college. If the purpose of the college is to encourage the development of the self-propelled scholar, then its academic program must move the student as quickly and fully as possible from a dependent to an independent status vis-à-vis the classroom, the teacher, and the grade book.

Thus the college grants to each student maximum freedom to choose among alternatives in his intellectual life, consistent with its definition of the intellectually concerned man. It assigns to the student a progressively larger share of the responsibility for planning and carrying through his intellectual and aesthetic ventures.

The college defines "the intellectually concerned man" as one who has

a. demonstrated his capacity to respond to challenges over a broad range of the spectrum of intellectual and aesthetic inquiry;
b. demonstrated his capacity to respond in depth to the challenges in one or more of the narrow bands in that spectrum; and
c. given evidence of his awareness of the significance of the choices made by men among alternative sets of intermediate and ultimate ends.

It will grant the bachelor of arts degree to a man who meets these criteria and who has not given evidence of character traits that would vitiate the significance of his work as a scholar.

Implications for the Personal and Extracurricular Life of Its Students

The college's formal responsibility for the personal and extracurricular life of its students must be narrowly defined and must be directly related to its central purpose—that is, to the development of the life of the mind and its associated virtues.

The college assumes that the vital and continuous friction of undergraduate minds contributes in a most important way to intellectual growth. With this in mind, it is proper for the college to see to it that there are available to its undergraduates living arrangements, whether fraternity or dormitory, that will facilitate this process of learning from each other.

So too should Wabash provide within reason the facilities for those extracurricular activities which augment the academic program. However, the college must leave in the hands of the undergraduates the central responsibility for carrying out the activities and must grant them maximum freedom in doing so, consistent only with the good name and integrity of the college.

Although the mental and physical health of an undergraduate bears on his potential for intellectual growth (as does his high school preparation, his family environment, and so forth) such problems fall outside the central responsibility of the college as defined above. For example, funds that might be expended for professional counseling, for medical and psychiatric care, or for remedial work—all available in the community or nearby communities—can be more wisely employed to improve the intellectual opportunities available to students; for example, to augment faculty salaries or add books to the library. If certain personal services are not available in the community, it is not inappropriate for the college to provide these services at cost to its undergraduates.

The college is in no way responsible for promoting the social life of its undergraduates. However, it is not inappropriate for the college to make certain facilities available to student groups for essentially social purposes. In the same way, the college should not interfere in the social activities of its students, other than asking of the students that in this, as in all else, they meet the minimum standards consistent with the good name and integrity of the college.

This standard—behavior consistent with the good name and integrity of the college—applies at all times and in all places during the undergraduate's career at Wabash. But even this standard must be ever judiciously invoked and should never be invoked in contradiction of the central purpose of the college—that is, in such a way as would inhibit the free development of the student's intellectual and aesthetic interests.

The other standard relating to personal characteristics was identified earlier and was described as a demand that the student not display such lack of personal integrity as would vitiate his work as a scholar. These two standards are the only ones, other than academic competence, that will be applied in the granting or not granting of a degree. The college would not deny to society its right to invoke other standards and values in evaluating individuals, but it does not propose to serve as the agent of society in invoking those additional standards in evaluating its students.

Concluding Statement

Nothing in what has been said above should be taken to mean that the staff members of the college will be isolated and unavailable to the undergraduates. On the contrary, once the student has assumed almost complete responsibility for his intellectual life, he can then meet the faculty member in a relationship dignified by his independent status. The relationship can then be one among equals, as it were, each of whom is a member of the community of those who seek knowledge and understanding.

Nor should this statement of the purposes and procedures of the college be taken to exclude the natural human concern which one individual must feel for another with whom he is engaged in a cooperative endeavor. Here too the greater dignity which attaches to the student who has been granted both greater freedom and greater responsibility can lift this human concern to a level above what it has not attained—which is so frequently a level of paternalistic, almost maudlin concern for the student, reflected in an expensive and formal structure for the administration of synthetic kindness.

In narrowly and explicitly defining its goals and in carefully delimiting its promise to its students, this college is *not* reducing its potential contribution to the individual student and to his society. On the contrary, by ceasing to pretend to do that which it cannot do and by directing its time, effort, and funds into their central and most significant uses, it should be able to move to ever higher levels of service to its various constituencies.

Financing and Administering Higher Education

What Price Education?

To subject higher education to economic analysis may seem to be laying profane hands on a sacred symbol.

Yet "the vulgar calculus of the marketplace" still remains as the most humane method man has yet devised to solve those problems of allocation and division which are ubiquitous and permanent in human society. How does below-cost pricing affect the college and university system of this country?

To most observers the only problem presented by below-cost pricing is the financial problem—the deficits that must be underwritten by the taxpayer or the private donor. Admittedly the financial problem is a serious one. This fact is clearly evidenced in the increasing tendency for college and university presidents (even of tax-supported institutions) to be fund-raisers first and educational leaders and scholars second.

But the financial problem is not the only problem presented by below-cost pricing, nor is it even necessarily the most serious. At least as serious is the rationing problem which comes from selling educational services at well below the price which would clear the market.

The price of a good or service in a free market is not only a source of funds to cover the costs of the good or service. It is also the instrument which answers the question of to whom the available supply is to go. That is, price rations the total number of units available among those who wish to buy the product. It does this on the principle that the

Reprinted from the *Wall Street Journal*, May 1, 1959, by permission of the Rogge estate.

product is to go to those who are willing to give up the most (i.e., pay the highest price) to obtain it.

Practical Questions

The acceptability of this principle need not be debated here. It is important only to note that it is a device for rationing. Moreover, it is a device that clears the market and that operates without any need for the seller to choose among buyers on some personal basis.

To set a price below the market price is to create an excess of quantity demanded over quantity supplied, whether the product be sirloin steak, rental housing, or education. This in turn requires of the seller that he find some way to determine whose requests for the product are to be granted and whose denied.

The problem of rationing the available educational services is fast becoming one of the major problems of higher education. This has brought into sharp relief the issue of the rationing principle to be used. The generally accepted principle is that educational opportunities are to go to those possessed of the greatest potential for intellectual growth. This principle has an immediate rationale in that education certainly involves intellectual activity. But closer examination reveals that it can be questioned on both practical and theoretical grounds.

If the principle is accepted, the first task is to measure potential for success in college. No one who has served on the admissions committee of a college or university would argue that this is a simple task. On the contrary, it is one of the most difficult tasks of college administration. Techniques for measuring potential are being improved each year, but mistakes are still made and continue to be made under the best of measurement programs.

The rationing technique under discussion here—whether applied in the selection of students for admission or in the selection of those to continue—operates in such a way that it often appears to the rejected student as a personally discriminatory technique. The rationing system of the free market at least has the advantage of operating as does the system of justice represented by the blindfolded goddess holding the scales. It does not ask "Who are you?" or "What kind of person are you?" or "Did your mother or father attend this college?" but only

"Are you willing to pay the price?" Cruel as this may sometimes seem in practice, it would appear on balance to be less cruel and less humiliating than the personalized techniques of non-marketing rationing.

But even if potential for intellectual growth and general success in college could be measured with complete accuracy and in such a way as to leave no room for personally discriminatory decisions, there would still exist serious questions of the appropriateness of this principle. It seems to rest on the assumption that large jars should be filled with the purest wine, while smaller jars should receive nothing but such rainwater as they can catch from the skies. If education is opportunity for personal growth, are we to deny it in some arbitrary way to those unfortunate enough to start from a lower level or to possess less absolute capacity for growth? Is 30% growth for the bright student more to be preferred than 30% growth for the less able student?

Is it not possible that the brighter student is more capable of educating himself than the weaker student; that in fact it might not be nonsense to say to the quick-minded, "Go educate yourself," and to the less-gifted student, "Come, we will try to help you"? As a matter of fact, current practice on United States campuses is moving toward independent study programs for the gifted students—a back-handed recognition of the fact that to such students the traditional apparatus of the college may not be important. This is not to argue that admission should be limited to the poor student, but only to indicate that the principle that admission should be limited to the good student can be questioned.

Suppose this same principle of making educational opportunities available only to those with high potential to benefit from those opportunities were applied to other goods and services. The sale of opera tickets would then be restricted to those who could establish ability to enjoy opera. Wine would be sold only to the recognized connoisseur.

Under the price system, a unit of any given product goes to the one who is willing to give up the most to get it. This is a rationing principle which tends in part to be a measure of strength of motivation. It tends to weed out those who have no great interest in the product. The effect of far-below-cost pricing in higher education is to admit many who have no strong desire to be educated—thus, the curious situation exists in which professors and deans must be constantly belaboring students to take that which they profess to desire.

Impact on Teachers

But the effect on the motivation of teachers is equally significant. To the extent that their incomes come from sources other than student fees, they are freed from some part of the necessity to really attend to the interests and wishes of the students. It is curious how irritated teachers become at any suggestion that their product be evaluated by their customers. They seem to really desire that each teacher be judge in his own cause, or at worst that he be judged by his colleagues (who of course should not be so vulgar as to consult student opinion of his work as a teacher).

In sum, then, while the student may find it pleasant to have his education subsidized, the price he pays for this is loss of control over his education. He who pays the piper will call the tune, and if the student is not the one who pays the piper, he cannot call the tune. Moreover, the divorce of teacher income from student fees has a tendency to encourage inefficient and ineffective teaching and to encourage teachers to treat their teaching duties as a necessary evil to be disposed of quickly as possible so as to permit them more time for more important activities.

In sum, the effect of below-cost pricing is to make of our colleges a collection of students, many of whom have no real desire to make use of the opportunity, and a collection of teachers who are under no real necessity to provide a high quality of teaching services.

"Below-Cost" and "Freedom"

The problems to be examined next are usually discussed under the heading of Academic Freedom. However, academic freedom is really a misnomer. It should not be confused in the sense of those rights which are guaranteed to Americans in the Bill of Rights. It is altogether fitting and proper that a person should be free to worship as he pleases (or not to worship at all), to think as he pleases, to speak and write as he pleases without fear of reprisal by government. In fact, these rights are the very cornerstone of the free society, and they are literally worth dying for.

But to say that Paul Robeson should be free to sing the Communist "Internationale" is a far different thing from saying that we must pay him for singing the Communist "Internationale." We may believe that William Z. Foster should be free to publish books on the Communist line, but we are not violating his freedom when we refuse to buy them. Now perhaps we are missing a chance to become better educated by refusing to buy them, and that brings us to the point here. So-called academic freedom is really a question of educational efficiency, of the improved understanding which comes from being exposed to a variety of points of view.

No teacher has an inherent right to present a point of view and to be paid for presenting it. If his customers wish not to pay to hear his point of view, this may be unwise on their part, but it it is not a violation of any inherent freedom. In fact, to force them (say) through the taxing power of the government to pay a teacher to present a point of view which they do not wish presented is a violation of an important freedom—the freedom of each man to spend his money as he pleases.

But insisting that what is called academic freedom does not really involve freedom is not to minimize its importance. On the contrary, even though it is really a question of educational efficiency, it is a very important question. It is important that students be given an opportunity to hear and read a variety of points of view, particularly on questions of social policy. In the words of John Stuart Mill, "There is always hope when people are forced to listen to both sides; it is when they attend only to one side that errors harden into prejudices."

This brings us back finally to the matter of below-cost pricing. The necessity for finding funds to fill the gap between student fees and total costs is always potentially dangerous to the integrity of an institution, to its continued ability to offer a program which embraces a wide range of social philosophies and which is otherwise educationally efficient.

The reasoning runs as follows: While the piper must inevitably be subject to pressure from those who pay him, his opportunity to play a varied and personally satisfying concert is the greater the more numerous the sources of his support and the less dependent he is upon the support of one payer or one group of payers. In other words, his best protection lies in a wide diffusion of the economic power which he confronts.

In sum, below-cost pricing combined with public or private subsidy creates a situation in which the integrity of the educational institution is not protected by that diffusion of economic power ranged against it which is the real protection of all units—households and firms alike—in a competitive market economy.

Financing Higher Education

Two primary arguments are advanced in support of below-cost pricing.

The traditional thesis is that the student "captures" only a part of the gain that flows from his college education. Some part of the gain flows to society at large.

The student tends to push his purchases of education only to the point where the private gain from another unit would be equal to the cost of another unit. However, it is in society's interest that he push his purchases beyond this to the point where the social gain from another unit would be equal to the cost of that unit. This requires that the student receive a subsidy sufficient to induce him to purchase the additional units of education.

The subsidy could be provided directly to the student to permit him to pay the market price to whatever institution he chooses to attend. We have implemented our desire to provide bread to those who do not have the means to buy it, not by asking bakeries to sell all bread at below-market prices and then subsidizing the bakeries, but rather by providing a direct subsidy to the families involved. In particular, we have not insisted on the government actually operating bakeries to take care of this problem.

The second argument advanced in support of below-cost pricing is that equality of opportunity must be assured and that this demands equal educational opportunity for all.

Reprinted from the *Wall Street Journal*, May 4, 1959, by permission of the Rogge estate.

Support and Effects

In the first place, it should be pointed out that this, too, would justify only subsidy in some form and provides no specific support for below-cost pricing of the services of higher education. On the contrary, below-cost pricing is a technique that subsidizes the sons and daughters of the wealthy as well as the sons and daughters of the poor. If the goal is to make education available to those who cannot afford it, below-cost pricing is a very blunt and wasteful instrument.

But the thesis that equal access to higher education, regardless of financial ability to pay for it, is a sine qua non of equality of opportunity is not of unquestionable validity. Support for this thesis usually involves pointing to the demonstrably higher lifetime earnings of college graduates vis-à-vis non–college graduates.

One of the most important principles of statistics is that correlation is not the equivalent of causation. In this case, the high correlation between years of education and lifetime earnings may derive in part from the fact that those who attend college possess a generally higher potential to achieve than those who do not attend college. Thus these same people would attain to higher-income positions even if they were not to go to college.

Moreover, those who wish to be educated do not face just the one alternative of formal classroom education. Each person in our modern society is surrounded by opportunities for acquiring the knowledge, skills and understandings that are the end product of higher education.

In other words, there is no clear evidence that income-earning possibilities are a direct function of education. But even if this could be established, it would still be difficult to prove that formal college education is the only kind of educational opportunity which promotes this end.

Admittedly, there are certain professions (e.g., law, medicine and engineering) which are open only to those with a certain minimum of formal education. But in most of these cases, the lifetime earnings of those who received the training would easily permit them to pay for their education on a deferred-payment basis. All that is needed here is a capital market that will permit the treating of professional education as an investment in personal capital.

Confirmation of this thesis is found in one unexpected place: in a book whose central thesis is that higher education must be even more subsidized than at present, including a substantial increase in federal aid to higher education. The book is *A New Basis of Support for Higher Education,* and the author is Thad L. Hungate, Controller and Professor of Education, Teachers College, Columbia University.

In one paragraph he says, "While students and parents may continue to finance student living costs, neither fees nor living expenses should bar a student who has met defined state standards and has been admitted to and accredited for attendance. State aid should supplement family means as needed for this purpose." Yet in the very next paragraph he adds, "It is considered likely that each beneficiary of a college education so lifts his lifetime earnings that the increased taxes he pays will more than repay to society the initial capital it has invested in him."

But if his increased earnings will permit him to repay the taxpayer, they will also permit him to repay a lending agency on the private capital market. Far from establishing a case for public subsidy, this statement weakens the case for public subsidy and strengthens the case for letting each student finance his own education from some combination of current and anticipated resources.

It might be argued that the primary inequality associated with less than universal higher education is a social inequality, that the non-college person is denied entry to the social circles of the college graduates.

This may or may not be true. Certainly there is some evidence that many Americans look upon the college degree as little more than a card of admission to "polite" society. This case is usually stated less boldly by the philosophers of American higher education. Their stress is upon the "democratizing" influence of our educational system.

Pandering to Envy

It may well be that the college degree available to all has a levelling effect on the social system. The colleges and universities may be primarily institutions dedicated to the task of giving young people membership cards in an eventually universal club of college graduates.

If so, it is serving a futile purpose. Nothing is surer than that man will develop forms of social differentiation, and if one form is eliminated, another will take its place. To pander to envy is hardly a useful and noble role for higher education.

Nor is it likely that the quality and nature of its services will remain unaffected by this goal. Already there is good evidence of the impact of the demand of education for all on the qualitative characteristics of higher education. It would be interesting to speculate on what would happen to the quality of a "prestige" car like the Cadillac if we were to endeavor to make one available to each family so that no family would have to feel inferior to another.

If the arguments developed here were to be accepted as valid, what policy changes would seem to be required? Would these changes not call for an unrealistic assumption of the willingness on the part of the American people to modify the traditional arrangements in higher education?

Certainly, it is true that traditional arrangements cannot be changed quickly or with ease—and this is not an unmixed evil. A certain caution in making changes is usually wise.

It is particularly difficult to secure any reduction of subsidies to special groups, and in particular to secure reduction of subsidies coming from public funds. Those who lose the subsidy lose a considerable sum per capita; those who are relieved of paying for the subsidy gain only a small sum per capita. Thus, the subsidized tend to be much more vocal and aggressive than the subsidizers.

Clearly, any changes would have to begin with the charges of state-supported schools. The private colleges and universities cannot hope to move much closer to full-cost tuition charges until the tuition charges at state-supported schools are increased substantially. The differential in tuition costs already operates to place the private schools at a serious competitive disadvantage.

The Beginning Steps

The first step would seem to be for state-supported institutions to set up a pattern of tuition increases designed to increase the percentage of costs covered by tuition payments. This pattern could call for a final position in which the revenues from tuition fees would be approximately equal to total costs. This could probably be done only if the state were to also provide an increasing supply of straight grants or loans to students. It would seem to be desirable to move as quickly as possible to the use of loans only to students pursuing strictly vocational courses, and to increase the ratio of loan money to grant money for all students. These loans and grants could also go to students attending privately operated colleges and universities.

This would certainly be consistent with the general principle, but the private colleges would probably be able to bring students in touch with private sources of loan or scholarship money and would probably prefer to do so. In fact, there would be good reason for the state governments to vacate the lending position as rapidly as the private money market could service the needs of students.

This study is basically neutral on the question of whether government aid should come from local and state units or from the federal government. However, the principle of diffusion of power would seem to establish a preference for local and state units. Also, the general reduction in the financial responsibilities of government for higher education under this plan would largely dissipate the case now being made for federal aid to higher education.

It is probably unrealistic to expect that higher education in this country could be recast in the ultimate pattern implied in this study. But it is not unrealistic to suppose that progress could be made in bringing all tuition charges closer to the level of full cost, in greater use of loan techniques in the financing of all education and in the financing of vocational education in particular, and in making greater use of the private capital market in the financing of investments in education. These changes would also tend to place an increasing emphasis on private as compared to public sponsorship of institutions of higher education.

If the arguments advanced here are valid, all of these changes would work to the benefit of higher education and of the American society.

Tenure

Those of us on the faculty who prefer drinking coffee in the Scarlet Inn to working are much exercised these days over the topic of tenure. Each of my boorish colleagues is so insistent on having his own say on this topic that I have had great difficulty getting my own superior views before the group. I welcome this opportunity to present the definitive statement on the topic.

1. I do not believe in tenure. It is a device to protect the inefficient. The primary cost of this practice is borne not by the college, but by the students who have to put up with the incompetent teacher. (I am not saying that all who are in fact refused tenure are incompetent. If nothing else, administrators still make mistakes—as Rogge did when he was in the Dean's Office.)
2. It may be cruel to dismiss an incompetent teacher after a number of years of service, but it is equally cruel to impose him on many generations of college students.
3. To the argument that the reason for tenure lies in the cause of academic freedom, I reply that I do not believe in academic freedom. I believe that it is each man's right to say his piece, but that this does not include a right to be paid for doing so with the money of those who would not choose to listen. Must Morehouse College hire or continue to employ an avowed racist? Brandeis

Reprinted from the *Bachelor* 68 (February 18, 1972): 1 and 12, by permission of Wabash College.

University, a neo-Nazi? Earlham College, a raving militarist? Freedom exists only when each individual and each institution in society is free to hire (or not hire) any person on any basis whatsoever, including length of shoestring. A good part of the so-called civil rights legislation of recent years dealing with employment represents a gross denial of freedom.

4. It may be wise educational practice for a college to confront its students with a variety of points of view, but this is a matter of pragmatic judgment and not of principle. What *is* a matter of principle is the right of those who put up the money to control its use, including the question of to whom it is to be paid.

In brief, the ideal arrangement would be that of Curmudgeon College: as a condition of employment, each faculty member, on being hired, would be required to sign an undated letter of resignation. Thus, if the college administration thought a given professor was off campus too much to be useful, or possessed of such peculiar ideas of laissez-faire economics as to be no longer relevant, it could get rid of him with no fuss and no muss.

More coffee, anyone?

Student Power and All That

The question is this: To whom does Wabash or any college or university belong? To the current students? to the alumni? to the faculty? to the administration? to the Board of Trustees? to "society"? to some mixture of these agencies?

The answer to this question is of some importance. Perhaps, though, it should be made even more specific: Where does sovereignty lie in a given college or university? Who's in charge around here?

Rogge-type answers:

A college exists, in theory, in whole or in part, to serve its students. In the same way, Steck's Men's Store exists, in part, to serve the students of Wabash College. But Steck's Men's Store does not belong to its customers, and Wabash College does not belong to its students (past or present). "Student power," in the sense of a claim by students of a right to make decisions that relate to their college or university, is thus of no substance or standing.

This is not to say that a college or university administration is always acting wisely if it ignores the wishes and the recommendations of its students. It means only that, when the chips are down, the students can rightly be told to get the hell out of the administration building and to stop interfering with the conduct of college business.

The faculty members of a college are employees of the college, and, by definition, a college does not belong to its employees. Again, this is

Reprinted from the *Freeman* (September 1969): 519–21. Originally published in the *Bachelor* 63 (February 16, 1968): 2, used by permission of Wabash College.

not to say that a college administration is necessarily unwise if it delegates authority over (say) the curriculum to its faculty. But again, when the chips are down, the college can rightly say to any faculty member for any reason whatsoever, "Go away!" A human being has a right to believe in and espouse communism or laissez-faire capitalism or any other piece of nonsense, but he has no right to be paid by someone else for doing so, against the will of that someone. So-called academic freedom is in reality a denial of freedom—the freedom of those to whom a school belongs to put the resources under their control to the uses they believe appropriate. Again, a school is surely unwise if it refuses to permit a wide range of views to be presented to its students, but it is not denying anyone his natural-born right if it takes this unwise position.

Administration-Delegated Control

The members of a college administration are also employees of the college—hence, they cannot be the ones to whom the college belongs. In practice, they are the ones to whom control is usually delegated by the "owners," and they are the visible source of authority on the campus. Unfortunately, many college administrations in this country seem to have abdicated (not delegated) their authority to some combination of students and faculty members (or athletic departments). The result is a kind of tragicomic anarchy—although for short periods of time on some campuses it can be very exciting (even intellectually exciting) for everyone involved. A college should be actually run by the administration—not the faculty. As Sidney Hook has put it, "Give the intellectual everything he wants—but power."

Does it follow that it is to the Board of Trustees that a college or university really belongs? In the case of a private college the answer would seem to be yes. It is this Board that has legal control of the assets that the college has acquired. It is this Board that, in theory, is responsible for seeing that the assets are used for the purposes for which they were and are made available to the college.

In the case of the public college, the answer is somewhat more complex. Here the Board must ultimately answer to those who largely pay the piper—the taxpayers of the jurisdiction involved. When the taxpayer in California screams, "We've got to get those Lefties and Hippies out of Berkeley," he may not be evidencing much knowledge of educational processes—but he is exercising a right that is essentially his. After all, it's largely his money.

Claims of Society Invalid

But what of the claims of society? Do not the institutions of higher learning in any society really exist to serve the interests of that society? In a word, No. In the first place, the word "society" is filled with ambiguities and difficulties. As a matter of fact, in these cases, those who use the phrase "the interests of society" usually mean the interests of society as seen by their own minority group, whether it be the National Association of Manufacturers, the National Education Association, or Americans for Democratic Action. But more than that, the best example of a university system serving the interests of its society would be the German universities under Hitler or the Russian universities of the last fify years.

Neither society nor the students nor the alumni nor the faculty is or should be in charge at Wabash College. The administration is and should be in charge, acting under the authority delegated to it by the Board of Trustees and serving the purposes of the college as defined in its charter and interpreted by that Board over the years. And if you think things probably aren't this simple and clear-cut in practice, you're right.

The Role of the Student

Thursday Chapel: Rogge
Raps Pledge Training

It seems to be my fate this year to play the role of the stand-in who appears on stage only when the star cannot appear. Earlier I substituted for our President, and today it is Rogge for a flu-stricken Calkins. The switch was made yesterday, and so my comments of this morning were written in haste. But I assure you that the ideas involved were not developed in haste, but rather represent a position that has been developed slowly over a period of six and one-half years as a straight teacher at Wabash and of almost two years in the Dean's Office.

My subject this morning is fraternity life at Wabash College, with particular reference to the handling of freshmen. Let me confess immediately that I cannot profess to speak of this problem as a recognized authority. My own undergraduate campus had no fraternities. Not only have I had no personal experience as a fraternity man, but moreover, even as a Dean, believe it or not, there are things that happen in our fraternity houses that I know nothing about.

Let me also make it perfectly clear that even though my remarks will be largely critical, they do not reflect opposition to fraternities per se. On the contrary, I am convinced that the net is clearly in favor of the fraternity system—at least as it operates on this campus.

Finally, though I expect this to be greeted with at least a mild skepticism, my critical comments do not portend dramatic and far-reaching action by the Dean's Office. Monter's editorial was quite right. We do believe in voluntarism. My comments are offered in the frank hope that

Reprinted from the *Bachelor* 50 (November 8, 1957): 2, by permission of Wabash College.

they will lead to student-initiated and student-directed changes in the operation of fraternities on the Wabash campus.

So much for the preliminaries; now for my thesis. My charge is that Wabash fraternities, though largely manned by first-rate men, are run as second-rate institutions, and that this is both reflected in and partly caused by the handling of freshmen in the houses.

I would like to postpone discussion of my charge that the Wabash fraternities are second-rate institutions until I have made specific my criticisms of the freshman programs.

In the first place I am convinced that the total demands made on the time and energy of a fraternity pledge on this campus are excessive by any standard that might be applied. I am not charging that these demands make it impossible for a freshman to do satisfactory course work. This may well be the case, but the evidence is confusing and contradictory. Also, I am perfectly aware of the fact that many a freshman has used the pledge program to excuse his own failure to make good use of his time and talents. Many a freshman has cried "wolf" at the pledge program when the real wolf is inside himself.

When I say that the time and energy demands are excessive, I have in mind two problems of the freshman. One is the problem of getting enough sleep. Don't quote statistics at me and don't answer that even the upperclassman has this problem. The upperclassman who studies late or participates in a late-hour lineup or supervises a 1:00 A.M. window-wash can usually be found on his sack the next afternoon (or the next morning) while the pledge is busy at housework or compelled to keep his bloodshot eyes steadily fixed on his CC text. The evidence to support this charge that the pledge does not get enough sleep has come to me in a dozen different ways and from a dozen different sources—including the statements of you upperclassmen when you were freshmen.

The second problem related to excessive time demands on the pledge is that he almost never has time that he can really call his own. So-called free time in the day seems to really be open season on the freshmen in the house. To maintain his own integrity, his own individuality, each human being needs to have some time each day that is truly his own—when he is not subject to the formal and informal pressures of others, but rather is free to listen to his own inner promptings, be they good or bad, wise or foolish.

This leads me to my most serious charge against the typical pledge program. It is degrading, both to the freshmen and to those who administer it. It is degrading because it does not recognize the individuality and integrity of the man, because it consists essentially of the tyranny of one man over another. This is not too serious in those aspects of a pledge program that represent essentially rule of law, e.g., in the requirement that freshmen enter the house by a side door. It is terribly serious in those parts of a pledge program that consist of one or more upperclassmen harrassing one or more freshmen. From the testimony of freshmen, this is the really demanding aspect of the typical pledge program.

To some men in each house each year, the pledge program is a magnificent opportunity for them to compensate for their own inadequacies by tyrannizing the freshmen. Rarely have I heard of an upperclass Little Caesar who was himself a success at anything—as a student, as an athlete, as an activities man on campus. He is the professional fraternity man who finds in abusing freshmen that sense of power which he could never reach through his own talents and resources. His viciousness can be disguised as "helping those pledges shape up" or "making good Wabash men out of those dumb Rhynies." These are the men who shout loudest at the lineups, who demand the most personal service of pledges, who find good humor in the spectacle of an awkward and frightened young man trying to do fifty push-ups right after a heavy meal.

What distresses me equally is that most of their brothers are embarrassed by these tactics, yet do nothing to stop what's going on. I know for a fact that the Storm Troopers are a minority in every house on campus, but they seem to be free to carry on their assaults against the dignity of man without even a chiding word from the majority. The majority, having condoned these actions, then feel compelled to justify and defend them.

In sum, whatever noble words may be applied in describing the purposes of the pledge programs, in fact they operate not to improve but to degrade, not to inspire creativity and individuality but to enthrone conformity and mediocrity, not to promote the real brotherhood of equals, but to glorify a mushy, insincere, maudlin love of dear old Sigma Kappa Pi and of Brother John, who may in fact be a slob of the first order.

I have often been told that the freshman pledge program, while it may be difficult for the freshman while he's going through it, is really a great builder of men, that he's a better man for having gone through it. Gentlemen, that is bunk. I have never seen the slightest evidence that those who did not go through such a program were poorer men than those who did. Nor have I seen any evidence that the men who did go through the program were better men as a result.

I have been told that it promotes brotherhood and that brotherhood is the unique contribution of the fraternity system. Gentlemen, real brotherhood can come from life in a dormitory or in a college rooming house off campus, or from a tour of duty in the armed forces, or, for that matter, from a stretch in the State Pen. The real virtue of fraternity life is clear and obvious—it can be a very pleasant and exciting way to spend your four years as an undergraduate. I think this is an important virtue; I do not believe that college is just preparation for life. I believe it can also be a wonderful four-year section of life itself, and that being in a fraternity can help to make it wonderful. That's why I hope that Wabash men will always have the option, and that's why I am so disturbed that Wabash fraternities now seem to be run as second-rate institutions.

The freshman pledge programs reflect the general sloppiness in the conduct of fraternity affairs. This is reflected as well in dozens of other aspects of fraternity operations, including the refusal to discipline an upperclassman who makes a fool of himself and problems for the fraternity. If this were a long chapel, I would run through the evidence.

I think it sufficient to show that Wabash fraternities are less well run, from pledge programs to table manners, than most other fraternities in the country. Now I also think that Wabash fraternities are clearly better than most other fraternities in other respects (for example, in avoiding becoming social clubs for sons of the wealthy), but it is still true that at least two representatives from national fraternity offices have told us in the last year that Wabash fraternities are ten to fifteen years behind the times in pledge programs.

But now some might argue that Wabash men have always been unique and that Wabash fraternities are simply carrying on the glorious traditions of those fraternities in the past. I would urge those who believe this to get the facts from those who were in fraternities on this campus in years past. Ask Willis Johnson, Myron Phillips, Ed Gullion or Warren Shearer. Actually, some of the strongest criticisms of Wabash fraternities have come from men who were themselves members of Wabash fraternities in years past.

Take, for example, the myth that the Wabash tradition prescribes a tee shirt and jeans as the proper dress for dinner. The fact is that in the hell-roaring Wabash of the 1920's every night was dress dinner in every fraternity on campus, and any man who came down to eat without coat and tie was told to eat in the kitchen.

Moreover, in that same period, a man who perennially came into the house drunk or who insisted on heavy drinking in the house was kicked out of the house. Today no crime short of murder (or danger to the house point average) seems sufficient to get an upperclassman kicked out of the house.

True, there was inexcusably brutal physical punishment of freshmen in those days, but at least it was quick, and for a good part of each week the freshman was his own boss.

Gentlemen, there is nothing in the Wabash tradition that sanctifies sloppy personal behavior or sloppy administration of fraternity affairs. Particularly, there is nothing in the Wabash tradition that gives to each petty tyrant the right to vent his own frustrations on freshmen.

What is in the Wabash tradition is the guts to stand on your own principles, to take stands that may be unpopular. This is a tradition that I would urge on freshmen who may not like what is happening. If you don't like what is being done to you in your fraternity, get out. No one has a gun at your back forcing you to stay in, and, if a few of you do this, it may produce some changes.

This is a tradition that I would urge on you, the majority in each fraternity house, who are worried and embarrassed by what is going on in your own house. Have the guts to stand up and be counted. In the long run you'll help yourself in that you'll be able to look yourself in the eye when you shave; you'll help your fraternity in that you'll assist it to become what it should be—a wonderful place to live for all, from freshmen on up; finally you'll help your college in that you will make its principal living units collections of first-rate men in first-rate institutions. What about it?

Youth's Cause

I must confess that I can never be very optimistic about the contribution to the cause of freedom of college-age youth. Classical liberalism is essentially an end-of-innocence philosophy. It requires accepting the imperfect nature of man and hence the imperfect nature of all human constructs.

It sadly, but firmly, insists that the New Jerusalem is never to be realized. It denies that man can consciously and deliberately plan himself into the good life and the good world. It places its restricted faith in the unpredictable and unplanned consequences of the individual decisions of free men and women.

This is a philosophy of the mature human being. It has little real appeal to the confident, hypercritical mind of the young person. It is the young who believe in the possibility of heaven on earth brought into being by the conscious exercise of their mighty power of reason—and who are prepared to sweep aside those whose feeble minds or weak wills make them an obstacle to the cause.

It is later in life, if ever, that a man reconciles himself to living in an imperfect world in which imperfect people make imperfect decisions—and is willing to let them do so, as long as they do not infringe on his freedom and the freedom of others.

In sum, while I am encouraged by the increasing interest of college students in the cause of individual freedom, I must confess that I think

Reprinted from *Michigan Daily,* March 18, 1956, by permission of the publisher.

much of this interest is about as well grounded in philosophic commitment as their interest in panty raids and school spirit. If freedom survives in the decades ahead, it will be because age and not youth has had its way.

Well, So You're a College Graduate: What Tricks Can You Do?

Mr. President, members of the Class of 1980 (1981), teachers, friends, and admirers of the Class of 1980 (1981), and a special greeting to the members of that greatest class in the history of the College, the Class of 1940. Surely a commencement speaker is permitted one modest exaggeration. In return, let me save you from another exaggeration. Do not attach any great significance to the pompous title I carry around. That is the kind of thing that small colleges like Wabash and Hastings hand out to senior faculty members—in lieu of cash.

To have been selected as your commencement speaker for today was an unexpected and undeserved honor—but that did not stop me from a quick affirmative response, as you can see by the fact that I'm here. Later at the second-thought stage of my reaction to the invitation, I was humbled to my total inability to recall the name, sex, age, or message of the commencement speaker in June of 1940. All that I could dredge up from my defective memory bank was the great sense of relief we all felt when the speaker, whoever it was, finally stopped talking and the important business of the day could commence.

Why then do colleges continue to go through the ancient ritual of "the Commencement speaker," and why do invited speakers continue to agree to speak? I suspect that for the colleges involved, this routine has much of the character of the saying of last rites over an unhearing and unheeding patient. It may be of no help to the patient, but at least

Reprinted from *The Wabash* [yearbook] (1981): 90–94, by permission of Wabash College.

the survivors feel that they have done the best they could. But why do people like Rogge stand ready to play a part in this charade? I find a possible answer in a statement from one of the better young philosophers of the day, to wit, Charlie Brown.

Charlie Brown is the pitcher in a baseball game, and he is saying to himself, "It is the last of the ninth, the bases are loaded, there are two outs and the count is three and two on the batter. If I get him out, we win." The next box shows all of his teammates around him, one saying, "throw him a curve, Charlie Brown," etc. In the next box, Charlie Brown is again alone on the mound, saying to himself, "This world is filled with people who are anxious to function in an advisory capacity."

And so true that is, and no group is more likely to be victimized by that instinct than young men and women of promise of the kind you represent today. With this in mind, I shall address my remarks directly to you, the graduating seniors. There's no point in trying to influence your parents or the members of the faculty. They are beyond hope.

My remarks directed to you, the seniors, will relate to the general question of what the degree that is to be conferred on you today signifies. What can you do with it that you couldn't do without it? All of this is often summed up in the mildly cynical question, "Well, so you're a college graduate?"—in effect asking, "What tricks can you do?"

What does it all signify? Just what will the degree behind your name signify? That is our question. I begin with one obvious answer. It signifies at the very least that you were in a position to cover the costs, from whatever sources, of four years in college, including the very important opportunity cost of forsaking the income that you could have earned had you chosen to go to work instead.

Instead of going to work, you have been given the privilege of spending some four years of your life in what most young people consider to be a pleasant and exciting fashion. The classroom, the dormitory, the playing field, the college lovers' lane—all these are usually more attractive to the late teenager than an apprenticeship at a local factory or a job at a fast-food emporium. To put it another way, to the students involved, "going to college" is very significantly a "consumer good," a value unto itself, quite apart from whatever long-run advantages may be forthcoming. An important part of the benefit for you from going to college comes to end as of today.

College administrators and faculty members are usually reticent to speak of this aspect of college life. It is perhaps embarrassing to admit that we are engaged in serving such apparently frivolous purposes as friendship, excitement, sentiment, and love. For myself, I see nothing wrong in so serving—and this in spite of the fact that for many of you this aspect of "going to college," this source of rich memories through-out your lifetime, may well prove to be the major part of your benefit from having spent four years on this campus.

Ah, you say, "But surely a college is something more than a four-year camp for aging teenagers!" Of course it is, but don't be disappointed if some of the other benefits of going to college prove modest indeed.

For example, the person who offers the sardonic question, "So you're a college graduate?" may well have in mind that you see yourself as entitled to certain rewards, such as employment that recognizes your great potential to produce (or even better, to lead the others who will do the producing). It is certainly true that college graduates tend to make more money than non–college graduates, but don't make too much of that point. One of the things that you may have learned in these last four years is that correlation does not prove causation. Those who go to college do make more than those who don't, but was it the going to college that caused the higher income?

The kind of person who has the brains and, yes, the financial back-ing to go on to college would undoubtedly have made more money than others even if he or she hadn't gone to college. Some professions and some activities are open only to college graduates, but fortunately many avenues to the high-income suburbs, to fame and fortune, are open to all comers. As a matter of fact, as you may be discovering, there may well be a surplus of college-trained men and women; i.e., there may even now be more persons seeking the kind of employment and income associated with degree-holding than there are positions of that kind available. Even when you, the degree holders, drop your aspira-tion levels to employments not requiring a degree, you may encoun-ter the response that you are overqualified for such positions. In other words, some of you may well find that your lifetime earnings, deduct-ing both the direct and opportunity costs of these last four years, will have been little if at all improved over what you would have earned absent the degree. But of course, a true education has nothing to do with the making of money, except as a very direct and far-from-the-certain by-product.

Does this reduce these last four years to simply an unprofitable, though pleasant, consumption expenditure? For your parents, does this reduce the gains from their sacrifices to what Adam Smith in *The Wealth of Nations* described as the gain to the parents from sending a son on the Grand Tour of Europe, to wit: "By sending his son abroad, a father delivers himself, at least for some time, from so disagreeable an object as that of a son unemployed, neglected, and going to ruin before his eyes." During your stays on campus, your parents have at least been given relief from the ear-drum-threatening sounds escaping from your stereo sets.

Surely there is more than that. Cannot the degree holder and his parents at least take some satisfaction in the fact that they have participated in a process that has prepared you for citizenship in the challenging, complex world of tomorrow? Who knows, perhaps the best way a college could deliver on this promise would be to teach you how to live off the land following an atomic diaster. Ah! you say, but perhaps the college can equip me to help save the world from an atomic disaster. Don't be too certain of that. The two countries most likely to launch an atomic disaster (one being our own) pride themselves on the literacy of their citizens and on the excellence of their programs of higher education. The system of higher education in Germany was the wonder of the world, copied in one country after another (including this country), and its scientists designed, among other things, the ingenious gas chambers at Dachau and Auschwitz.

I am not saying that education and good citizenship are inversely related. I am saying only that a strong, positive, and direct relationship has yet to be established. It may well be that the citizen whose education has come more from experience and from deep commitment to values than from the brittle world of on-campus intellectuality may be just as good a citizen as any of us with our college degrees. At the very least, this promise can be no more than the expression of a pious wish until more evidence can be collected.

But comes now the writer of the typical college catalogue (who, by the way, would not usually lead Diogenes to believe that at long last he had found a truly honest man), with his reply that, for its leadership roles, a society almost invariably turns to the college trained. True, true, but again the question of causation is not resolved, and many of our great leaders have had very little formal education—Abraham Lincoln being the most obvious example.

As a matter of fact, the directions in policy-making urged on us by many of our college-trained leaders of recent decades and today give promise, as I see it, of doing at least as much harm as good. The intellectuals in that group (by which I mean those who live by the spoken and written word and who have little responsibility for the conduct of practical affairs) tend to have, as an occupational disease, the belief that, in their wisdom, they know not only what is best for themselves but what is best for all the less-wise others as well. I am convinced that a considerble part of the smothering bureaucracy, of the restrictions now placed on our "freedom to choose" (the title of the recent book by my friend and colleague Milton Friedman) has come out of this unwillingness on the part of those who think themselves wise to permit the average man to make his own imperfect decisions in his own imperfect way, paying the price for his mistakes and enjoying the rewards of his successes. But enough of my now-revealed biases.

Now where are we? "So you're a college graduate?"—but you won't necessarily make more money than those who aren't, nor are you necessarily prepared to be uniquely competent in your citizenship role, whether as follower or as leader. How now can the investment of these last four years be justified? Does nothing go with you beyond today, other than a non-real sheepskin?

There is indeed something that you should be taking with you from this fine old college, and here is what I believe it to be. You have benefited from a good faculty and a good group of fellow students. If you have worked (and the fact that you are to be given a degree would indicate that you have), you are now leaving this place knowing more than when you entered it. That's it; that's all there is. Or I can put it this way, you have all the personal advantages of knowing over not knowing. Moreover, you now know how to go about knowing even more for the rest of your life; you may even know what it is that is worth knowing and what it is that isn't worth knowing.

Hopefully, you will as well come to know how little you know, in fact how little is known, about man and his world by even the most knowledgeable around you. This is to say that you may come to carry with you through life a deep sense of wonder and of awe, not of what you do understand, but of the deep and mysterious processes which neither you nor anyone else fully understands.

A brief interjection here: One of the ways in which colleges (and college faculties in particular) have become corrupt in recent years has been the way in which they have sought to woo their students to their personal causes by assuring the students that they, the young, are possessed of a mystical wisdom, a godlike, compassionate understanding of life denied all over age twenty-two, except of course those few adults who share the vision. This I believe to be nonsense.

Young people, and I mean you, are capable of being intelligent, courageous, selfless, and dedicated but are not usually marked by the qualities of wisdom, tolerance, kindness, and true compassion. I cannot urge you too strongly to beware of all adults who flatter you and tell you of your wisdom: we seek but to enlist you in our causes, whether of the left or the right or the middle, and we do not honestly believe you to be wise—nor are you, as a matter of fact.

To know more, yet to know how little you know—is that all there is to it?

Yes, that's about it. To know more may not be much, and it may not be directly useful in the way the world measures usefulness, but at least it's something. To know more is at least to live an examined rather than an unexamined life; to live in an examined world rather than an unexamined world. In a world in which most human beings are said to live lives of quiet desperation, surely there is something to be said for this increased awareness, this increased perception of shades of meaning, of shades of beauty and ugliness and dissonance, of shades of dignity and integrity and vulgarity and hypocrisy.

Nor is respect for style an unimportant by-product of knowing more. This sense for style, for how things are said or done, is often thought to be peripheral to the gutty business of life—or even of education. In fact, it seems to me to be one of those terribly important, self-imposed restraints which man has designed to keep himself from slipping back over the precipice into barbarism. Civilization is the most contrived, artificial, and delicate of man's creations, and its survival rests upon such slender reeds as man's cultivated sense of style—one of the by-products of a true education.

With this education, this knowing more, should come as well a life-long habit of observing all that happens, even what happens to you with a certain detachment, a certain objectivity, a certain curiosity. In a sense, this may be a handicap to you, holding you back from passionate commitment to any single-track cause or single-minded interpretation of human experience—or if you do get so involved, you will occasionally be aware that what you are doing or saying may possibly be a trifle absurd.

What else? Let me conclude this somewhat rambling survey of the advantages of knowing more over knowing less with one more comment. Hopefully, the college will also have helped you, in the process, to become very careful about words. Words are the raw material of knowledge and, in fact, of much of life, and they deserve to be treated with respect. The educated person will always attempt to use them carefully and precisely and to demand of those who would communicate with him that they do the same. He will have learned that words can be used to inform or to deceive or to inspire or to confuse or to manipulate or to set into action—and will examine each important word used by another with the care and the suspicion with which an oriental peasant examines the fruit in a street market. When he finds a false one, he will reject it as convincingly as one of my favorite heroines of modern literature—and with this I reach the end.

This favorite heroine of mine is a little girl in an old cartoon in the *New Yorker* magazine. She is being fed by her mother but is obviously rejecting whatever it is that is being offered her. Finally, in desperation, her mother says to her, "It's broccoli, dear." At this, the little girl in her chair looks her mother in the eye and replies, "I say it's spinach, and I say the hell with it."

May the next years be exciting and productive for you, and as you go on through life, may you gradually come to the knowledge of the difference between broccoli and spinach, and may you acquire the courage to challenge those who confuse the two.

All Who Play Can Win

In the years that I have known him, I have developed a great respect for your headmaster, but as of today, I am beginning to doubt his wisdom. Any man who would schedule an honors convocation on the afternoon of the seventh game of the World Series is obviously lacking in judgment. I would be exceedingly unhappy with him if it weren't for the fact that he didn't set the date at all—I did. This will give you some idea of the level of wisdom you can expect from me this afternoon.

But there is another reason to question Headmaster McCluskey's judgment: What this school obviously needs today is not another speech maker—the place is crawling with them as it is; what this school really needs today is another carpenter or bricklayer or landscape gardener—or millionaire. As a member of the board, if I had to choose, I'd settle for the millionaire.

But incomplete though this new campus may be, it is even now an exciting and handsome physical environment for an independent school. And the campus itself is only a visible symbol of an absolutely serious determination on the part of your headmaster and of those of us on the board (and of others responsible for and interested in Park School) to make of this one of the very finest places of learning, not just in Indiana or the Midwest, but in the country itself.

Editor's title. Honors convocation talk at Park School, October 12, 1967. Reprinted by permission of the Rogge estate.

If you who study and teach here have not yet caught the spirit of this vision, have not yet been caught up in this dream that is to be a reality, then we have failed in our communications with you. This vision, this dream, should lend an excitement and a meaning to what each of you does here each day that would literally change your lives. There is an old saying that the road is better than the inn, and I know from my association with Wabash College that there can be far more excitement in a school that is making its move to excellence than in one that has already achieved it. Park School is now a good school, but it has the potential to be a great school, and it is on all of us that the responsibility falls for seeing that it becomes so.

You see, for this dream to come true, it will not be sufficient for the board to will it. It will be necessary for every single human being connected with Park School to will it and to order his or her life here accordingly. I am quite serious when I say that you seventh-graders are as much a part of this as the seniors or your teachers or your headmaster or the members of the board. The pride that you take in your class work this year and in the years ahead, your behavior as young people—everything that you do—will reflect in part the quality of this school, and what you do and how you do it will in turn be in part a reflection of the pride and love you feel for this school. Fine students make a fine school, and a fine school in turn induces high performance from its students. It is a full circle of cause and effect. You can take the initiative right now by doing better tomorrow than you did today, so that those who evaluate Park School on the basis of your performance as students and as young people will be led to a strong, affirmative judgment of the quality of this school.

For better or for worse, you are Park School's product, and the school will be judged by what you do and by how well you do it. The diligence of purpose with which you study your lesson this very night will help in its own way to shape the future of this school. If you believe in this school and if you wish to see it become known as (and become in fact) one of the great independent schools in America, each of you can do something each and every day of this school year to bring this dream closer to reality.

Ah, but you say that you are not one of the top students of the school and never will be, no matter how hard you try. You will never be honored at a convocation of the kind that is being held here today. Let me tell you something: the quality of a school is not really determined by how good its top 10 percent is; the top students from the best schools and colleges in America are not always distinguishable from the top students from the weakest schools and colleges in America. What really distinguishes a Phillips Exeter Academy or a Princeton University is that even its lowest 10 percent in each class is made up of young men of excellent quality, good self-discipline, and good characteristics as human beings. It is on the quality of you so-called average students of Park School that this school will be judged in the years ahead. If you have become accustomed to pressing yourself to the limits of your potential, if you have acquired habits of diligence and self-discipline, if you have permitted your natural human desire to know more to move you in your studies, if you have set high standards for your personal conduct both on and off this campus, Park School will come to be identified as a great school, and its greatness will in turn inspire all who follow you here in these buildings in the decades and centuries ahead.

You may be curious as to why, at an honors convocation, I am addressing myself to what I term the average student. It is in part because I believe the honors student to be somewhat less in need of being sermonized at than the non–honors student. It is in part because I am afraid that we often overlionize the top students—as if schooling were a footrace or a golf tournament with prizes going only to the winners. Schooling is not a foot race, and its prizes or rewards go not just to the winners but to all who participate with a will.

We often seem to be saying to the nonwinners, the non–honors students, that their accomplishments do not count and should not be recognized. This can discourage the nonwinners and lead the winners to an unjustified conclusion that they are God's chosen people. To me, one of the distressing characteristics of many of the students who come to Wabash as freshmen, most of whom have been top students in their schools, is their arrogance, their attitude that Wabash College has indeed been blessed by their willingness to enter the school. But in part we adults have brought this on by the extreme emphasis we have put on the winners and on their achievements.

Of course we have done this in large part out of good intent, out of our desire to stimulate every boy and every girl to work to his or her limit to enter into the ranks of the winners. Unfortunately, though, no matter how hard all the students at a school may work, only 10 percent of the class can be in the top 10 percent. Don't misunderstand me. I am not a bleeding heart who is distressed by competition and by the fact that for there to be winners there must also be losers. But I repeat: education is a game in which all who play can win.

Now a word to the most-visible winners, the ones for whom this session is convened. In spite of my earlier words, I'm not really against you. On the contrary, I wish to congratulate you and to tell you that you have every reason to take pride in your accomplishments of last year. Nor would I be unhappy if you were to come to Wabash, arrogant or no. You're the ones who make the teachers look good, whether or not we deserve any of the credit.

I do wish to say to you that you have a particularly important role to play in creating the greater Park School. By the challenge that you present to others, by the example that you set for others, you can help to lift the quality of student performance on this campus.

But two words of warning: (1) Even if you are first in your class, but with still only a 70 percent effort—as is possible for the very gifted— you are not taking full advantage of your opportunities nor are you helping to bring the better Park School. Your pride in yourself, your pride in this school, and your hopes for this school should lead you to a maximum performance in everything that you do—and your exceptional talent demands no less of you.

(2) No matter how good you are, what you don't know is still infinitely greater than what you do know—or will ever know. Each new hill that you conquer intellectually will simply reveal more clearly the vast areas of unconquered territory that surround you. This need not induce discouragement—just humility.

Or to put it another way: no matter how proficient in any field you become this year or in your lifetime, the odds are that there will always be at least one man or woman who is still more proficient than you. Again this should be a source of humility and inspiration—not of discouragement.

You students may now be impatient with me for concentrating my whole attention on you. Why don't I recognize that perhaps some of your weaknesses derive, not from you, but from your teachers? The reason I don't recognize this is that, as a general rule, I don't believe it. I'm not going to argue that teachers are of no importance, but I am going to argue that education is primarily a process of learning and not of teaching.

Each student controls the doors to his own mind, and if he keeps those doors closed, there is little the teacher can do to penetrate into the interior. On the other hand, if those doors are open they will be open, not just to the classroom teacher, but to the whole world of learning possibilities around each of us.

One way we will know when Park School has begun to reach its full greatness will be when we see each student progressively assuming more and more responsibility for his own education, exhibiting more real independence in his search for knowledge, with less reliance on the formal classroom and the institutionalized prodding of the teacher. In fact, no educational program is worth its salt if it leaves the student, at the end of the program, still totally dependent on a classroom and a teacher. Once the critical point is passed, the process of education, as in atomic reactors, should be self-sustaining.

What then is the role of the teacher? To begin with, of course, the formal classroom and the explanations and the undisguised prodding of the teacher are usually necessary for all students in the earlier phases of their schooling. In addition, even the student who has largely become self-directed in his learning needs—indeed must have—a chance for dialogue, preferably with someone who knows more than he. It is astonishing what errors we can fall into when we have no chance to expose our ideas to the critical vision of others.

But in all these roles, the most important characteristic of the good teacher is that he himself be a lover of learning, that he himself be so excited about the materials of his field that students will be induced by his example to open the doors of their minds and to share in his excitement. To somewhat overstate the case, the good teacher is not a teacher at all: he is an excited learner, and his students catch his excitement and join in the chase. This idea is hardly new. In the *Canterbury Tales,* Chaucer says of the poor clerk of Oxenford, "and gladly would he lerne, and gladly teche."

You may call this a romantic notion, but I insist that it is not only practical: it is the only practical approach to education. With any other approach, the doors of the mind stay firmly closed, and the teacher is really doing little more, even in giving exams, than taking class attendance.

What I am saying is that if there are weaknesses in Park School's education at this time the real place for each of us to look for the reason is inside himself. As some of you know, I am a great admirer of Charlie Brown. In one of the strips, Charlie asks Linus what he would do if he thought that no one liked him. Linus replied that if he thought no one liked him he would examine himself objectively to identify his weaknesses and faults, and then he would attempt to correct them. "That's my answer," he says to Charlie Brown. To this, Charlie Brown replies, "I hate that answer!"

In fact we all hate that answer but it is still the correct one in almost all human affairs, including the current performance of all of us connected with Park School. Let us seek to correct our individual weaknesses and faults and, in so doing, participate in moving this school closer to our vision of what it should be.

If all of us, members of the board, friends of the school, faculty members, administrators, and students of Park School can bring a true sense of excitement for learning to our particular responsibilities connected with the school, there is literally nothing that can stand between Park School and real greatness. From the seventh-grader to the senior, from the lowest-ranking student in the class to the honor student, from new instructor to the headmaster, from the newest board member to the chairman of the board, this is the challenge to each of us, and today is as good a time as any to get started in meeting it.

The Role of Businesspeople and Intellectuals

Speech in Honor of Charles D. LaFollette on His Retirement from Wabash's Board of Trustees

The first question before the house this evening is one on which I refuse to speculate. That question is, "Why me?" I know only that when my personnel file reaches the Great Evaluation Committee up there in the sky, pride of place will be accorded to the entry reading as follows: "Whatever his flaws and weaknesses, let it be noted that for a few brief moments one evening, he was admitted into the fellowship of the humane and liberal arts." Much as we of the social sciences deny it in curriculum discussions, and as loudly as we announce the social usefulness of the social sciences, deep down in our grubby, model-building, hypothesis-testing hearts we know, we know—and what we know is that the humanities lie at the very center of a liberal education.

I approach this gathering, then, with some of the same mixture of anticipation and apprehension that reportedly was felt by my mentor Adam Smith when, in 1775, he was invited to join the London Literary Club (more accurately, simply The Club), presided over by Lafe LaFollette's friend Samuel Johnson and including such distinguished members as Goldsmith, Boswell, Reynolds, Garrick, Burke, and Gibbon. True, he had once lectured on rhetoric and belles lettres at Edinburgh and Glasgow, and, true, he was the author of *The Theory of Moral Sentiments*. But the editor of a literary magazine of the day stated that on the subject of poetry, Smith seemed "not to have been endowed with a gleam of taste." And Wordsworth said of Smith the literary critic that

Editor's title. Speech, October 28, 1977. Reprinted by permission of the Rogge estate.

he [Smith] "was the worst critic, David Hume not excepted, that Scotland, a soil to which this sort of weed seems natural, has produced."

Smith's poetic sensitivity is clearly revealed in a comment of his on blank verse: "They do well to call it blank, for blank it is." He continued, "I myself, even I, who never could find a single rhime in my life, could make blank verse as fast as I could speak." Not too surprisingly, none of Smith's blank verse has survived the test of time. At the same time, this view of Smith's on blank verse was seen by Johnson as Smith's redeeming grace. Johnson is reputed to have said of Smith, "Sir, I was once in company with Smith, and we did not take to each other; but had I known that he loved rhyme as much as you tell me he does, I should have hugged him." Smith in turn had once been quoted as saying that he "was no admirer of the Rambler or the Idler, and hinted that he had never been able to read them."

The gulf that separates the social scientist from the man of letters and that impresses itself on my sensibilities tonight was well described by Smith's friend the Earl of Buchan, who wrote that Smith was "too much of a geometrician" to have "any perception of the sublime or beautiful in composition." As consolation, though, he did add that Smith "had the greatest perception of moral beauty and excellence."

But we have come here tonight, not to celebrate or even to criticize either Adam Smith or Samuel Johnson. We have come here to celebrate our great good fortune in having had Lafe LaFollette in our midst for lo these many decades. We are also met to share in the exciting news that there has been established the Charles D. and Elizabeth S. LaFollette Distinguished Professor of Humanities Chair at this, our college.

In serving these purposes, we are also met to intone yet one more time, and in unison, the Wabash College version of the prayer of the Pharisee: "We thank thee, Lord, that we are not as other colleges!" There are very few campuses in this country where a gathering of this kind would be likely to take place. Cheek by jowl, the poet and the banker, the historian and the industrialist, the artist and the telephone executive have chewed their meat and drunk their wine and talked "of shoes—and ships—and sealing-wax—/Of cabbages—and kings—"

Does this mean that we, the professor and the businessman, are now as one, that the lamb and the lion do now indeed lie down together in peace in our time? It does not. There must always be a tension between the intellectual and the man of affairs, and it is to why this must be true that I intend to speak tonight. I speak to this topic, not to exacerbate our inevitable conflicts; on the contrary, I do so in the hope that by recognizing why there must always be tension between us we may better discover and pursue those terribly important ways in which we can and must be mutually useful to each other and to the greater society.

I begin with the obvious. On this campus and on every campus, however we may romanticize the relationship, you, the trustees, are the employers, and we, the teachers, are the employees. The significance of this to our personal relationships is similar to that of the teacher-student relationship, as described by that wisest of modern educators, Jacques Barzun, in his work, *Teacher in America*—a work, that in my opinion, contains more and better advice to would-be teachers than 120 hours of graduate work in Columbia Teachers College.

> Let me say bluntly, as I do not hesitate to do when my students broach the subject, that friendship between an instructor and a student is impossible. This does not mean that the two should remain strangers; there can exist cordial, easy relations, tinged perhaps with a certain kind of affection; but friendship, not. For friendship has strict prerequisites, among them, freedom of choice and equality of status. Neither of these can exist in the teacher-student relation. The absence of equality may horrify the sentimental but it is a fact nevertheless. Consider only a few of the things a teacher must do—he must judge work done, decide passing or failing, order tasks, reprove mistakes, discipline conduct, and *deal impartially* with all similar cases. These, I submit, are not the acts of a friend, even if—as equality would demand—the student were allowed reciprocal privileges.

In the same way, you stand in immediate judgment over us, or at least you appoint those who do or, at least, who should. Judgment is, after all, a principal responsibility of organizational administration. The occasional friendships that break through this barrier between the judges and the judged, including some involving Lafe LaFollette and Wabash faculty members, prove only that all generalizations are certain to be in error in some specific parts.

At the same time, when seen in the longer perspective, we (the professors) stand in judgment on you (the men of affairs), not just in your roles as college trustees, but as participants in the social process. Most of you are aware of this role reversal, and some of you are even now involved in activities designed to try to persuade us (the intellectuals) that what you do is indeed in the social interest.

Moreover, in this relationship where we are the judges and you the judged, we are inevitably acting as critics of what is, a "what is" of which you are an important part. I quote now from a modern mentor of mine, the late great Austrian-born Harvard professor of economics Joseph Schumpeter, as he writes of intellectuals and the critical attitude:

> Intellectuals are people who wield the power of the spoken and written word, and one of the touches that distinguish them from other people who do the same is the absence of direct responsibility for practical affairs. The critical attitude [of the intellectual] arises no less from the intellectual's situation as an onlooker than from the fact that his main chance of asserting himself lies in his actual or potential nuisance value. The intellectual group cannot help nibbling, because it lives on criticism and its whole position depends on criticism that stings.

Schumpeter seems to be implying that the critical attitude of the intellectuals to the societies of which they are a part is wholly self-serving, and there is much that is self-serving in our attacks on what is. But both Schumpeter and I would argue that a society without critics would do well to hire its devil's advocates, like the church of old. The uncriticized life is not worth living. As the late Professor Walter Fertig used to say, "We professors are often accused of being subversive and indeed we are. That, in large part, is our function."

True enough, and it is a role we take to with a relish and a will—in a way that you must often find at least moderately disturbing. Put us down in Eden, and in two days time, we would have a demand for reform—nay, we would have a dozen conflicting demands for reform. Put us down in Soviet Russia, and we are critics—and pay the terrible price by dying in the rime ice of Siberia or in Solzhenitsyn's First Circle or, if we are lucky, in exile. Put us down in the United States in 1977, and we are critics—and you, as the men of affairs, are inevitably a part of that which we criticize. Are our criticisms often in error, do our judgments sometimes miss the mark, do we tend to grievously misunderstand what you are about? Of course—in the same way that you often grievously misunderstand what we are about.

So here we meet in mutual suspicion and in mutual and inevitable judgment, each of the other, just as parent and child and husband and wife confront forever the frightening knowledge of mutual and continuous judgment. The wonder is not that we are occasionally in conflict; the wonder is that our relationship, like marriage itself, survives at all.

But survive it usually does and for a very good reason: we are in great need, each of the other, and it is to that mutual dependency I now turn.

In what ways are we, the professors, in need of you, the men of affairs? To somewhat exaggerate, without you we'd starve to death or be eaten by the trolls. Without the businessmen to make certain that we are fed and clothed, without the foundation managers to assist our research activities, without the officers of government to protect us from the trolls, both domestic and foreign, most of us would not last out the week. It is not just that these are not our specializations; it is also that, by nature, we are not adept at getting things done. We are not even very good at such management tasks as our own work requires. In the words of John Fischer of *Harper's* magazine, in one of his "Easy Chair" columns, "Preface to the Catalogue of Curmudgeon College":

> The college is governed by President Curmudgeon, period.
>
> He may from time to time consult members of the faculty on administrative matters, but feels no obligation to take their views seriously. Early in his career President Curmudgeon learned that the typical professor can't administer his way out of a paper bag. As he observed in his now-famous paper on collegiate governance:
>
>> The true scholar is inherently incapable of running anything. By temperament, he loathes the very concept of authority; hence he is always opposed to the administration, but is even more opposed to the idea of exercising authority himself. When confronted with the necessity of making a decision, he habitually falls into a spasm of self-doubt, takes refuge in a faculty committee which argues for three months, and then resolves to defer action until further information becomes available. He can never learn Rule No. 1 of management: "A good executive is one who always acts promptly and is sometimes right."
>
> Consequently our faculty is limited to its proper functions: teaching and research, in that order. Managerial decisions are handled by the responsible executive, *i.e.*, me. Students participate in governance the

same way that customers participate in the governance of Macy's. If they don't like the goods offered, they can go to Gimbel's.

Byron Trippet, former president of this college and one of the greatest of all college administrators, felt strongly that the man of affairs (the businessman) was also capable of contributing to the discussions of what should be taught—that is, discussions of questions of academic substance. In his view, many of these men of affairs (such as Lafe La-Follette) were good journeyman scholars and could bring to such discussions a useful and different view from the "too-close-to-the-forest" vision of the professional scholars.

My great friend, and long-time Wabash trustee, Pierre Goodrich, an easily infuriated man, was particularly infuriated by the easy assumption of most faculty members and some college administrators that college trustees should be consulted on questions of roofing material for buildings or portfolio investment policies but should be left out of all discussions of serious academic matters, such as curriculum or faculty. I think, on balance, he was more right than wrong.

Yes, need you we do, most clearly and most emphatically. But how, if at all, do you need us? How can we, the teachers of the Greek tragedies and of the philosophy of Immanuel Kant, assist you in making sausages or tranquilizers or commercial loans?

The first part of my answer to this question comes from a paper prepared by a certain Charles D. LaFollette for delivery in October 1960 to a conference of the boards of trustees of the community colleges and institutes of the State University of New York.

> Some time ago, I came upon the following list of traits desired in a business leader—I think they hold for leadership in any field.
>
> (I am reminded of the judgment that to borrow from one author is plagiarism. To borrow from many is research.)
>
> 1. Good judgment—decisions based upon facts and not emotions
> 2. Ability to plan—outline an orderly course
> 3. Fairness in dealing with all men—justness
> 4. Open-mindedness—encouraging and listening to suggestions
> 5. Initiative—the ability to be a self-starter
> 6. Decisiveness—after getting the facts, take a position
> 7. Enthusiasm—inspire to act

8. Courage—to explore and lead

9. Ingenuity—the ability to find new methods of solving problems

10. Resourcefulness—the capacity to meet emergencies promptly

To these definitions, I should like to add:

A leader must understand people—their motives, problems, spiritual and secular; their strengths and weaknesses. He must be able to communicate clearly or his understanding will not be translated into action. He should possess an intelligent curiosity leavened with patience. And, above all, he must be strong enough never to compromise with truth. He will not make a decision solely for the reason that it seems to be within the limits of the law.

Having listed the desired characteristics of a leader, may we turn to the question—Can a liberal arts education help develop these qualities?

His answer to his own question: an absolute affirmative. This same affirmative is given by the fact that we have here at Wabash, in the Wabash Institute for Personal Development, a program based on the assumption that, soon or late, there is indeed a relationship between the materials of a liberal education and the bottom line on a business firm's income statement. What happens and why? Quite frankly, those of us who have been involved in this program from the beginning don't really know. All we know is that most of the men and women who participate in this program, and most of the companies that send participants to the program, are convinced that the men and women who go through this three-year exposure to the liberal arts come out as more effective human beings and hence more effective businessmen and women. In other words, the liberal arts education, the only true education, the education that is not designed to train anyone for anything, proves finally to be eminently practical and useful in the conduct of practical affairs.

To many of us who teach in the liberal arts, this conclusion is shocking and outrageous. Have we not for centuries insisted that what we are about is nothing so vulgar as training, but is nothing less than the pursuit and transmittal of truth? Of course, and we were right. Our intent is not to train, but if training of great usefulness comes as an unintended by-product of what we do, why should we not rejoice rather than lament?

Should those of us who take such intense pride in the utter uselessness of our subject matters be encouraged by the fact that business recruiters seem no longer to be interested in the liberal arts graduates? In my opinion, not at all. The obsession of recruiters today with those who already know how to do something is but a reflection of a general environment of inflation, taxation, regulation, and uncertainty that has led business decision-makers to shorten their planning horizons, to apply a higher rate of discount to future returns—and it is in the long run that the liberally educated human being makes his or her unique contribution to the success of the business enterprise.

But your dependence on us, the word people, the practitioners of the liberal arts, runs well beyond considerations of the profitable or the practical. It is we indeed who largely shape the idea systems within which you live and work and by which you chart your own lives. I offer in support the words of one whose own influence on the contemporary world bears testimony to the truth of the words I now quote:

> The ideas of economists and political philosophers, both when they are right and when they are wrong, are more powerful than is commonly understood. Indeed the world is ruled by little else. Practical men, who believe themselves to be quite exempt from any intellectual influences, are usually the slaves of some defunct economist. Madmen in authority, who hear voices in the air, are distilling their frenzy from some academic scribbler of a few years back.

These are the words of the late celebrated English economist John Maynard Keynes, whose influence is as current as yesterday's meeting of the Council of Economic Advisers to the president of the United States. But our influence is not just with other word people or other leaders of opinion. Even that most representative man of affairs, the businessman, comes under our sway. As Schumpeter described it, not only does the businessman tolerate his critics, not only does he provide the funds for the education of his critics, not only does he send his own children to be brought up in the creeds of his critics, he himself comes finally to be educated by them and begins to repeat their slogans—creeds and slogans that Schumpeter was convinced were almost certainly destructive of the business system itself.

But whether destructive or not, the ideas are what count, and when you deal in ideas you are on *our* turf—and on our turf, we are tough to beat. If it is an intellectual who is most likely to produce the ideas that threaten to destroy that which you hold important, it is also some other intellectual who is most likely to produce the counterforce. If you are to be given protection from the furies and emotions of the masses, it most probably must come from us and not primarily from you. Just as you did not unleash the fury of the masses, you quite probably cannot cause it to subside. As Schumpeter has put it, "A genius in the business office may be—and often is—utterly unable outside of it to say boo to a goose, whether in the drawing room or on the platform. Knowing this, he wants to be let alone and to leave politics alone. Without protection by some non-bourgeois group, the bourgeosie is politically helpless and unable not only to lead its nation but even to take care of its particular class interest."

Let us admit then that we, the intellectuals and the men of affairs, are in a symbiotic relationship. If one perishes, so must the other. At the same time, let us not romanticize the relationship. It is certain to be marked by tension, by mutual suspicion, and at times by open conflict.

But let us also be inspired by the example of Charles LaFollette to recognize that understanding, patience, and civility can go a long way to make this difficult marriage of disparate types the fruitful and finally satisfying relationship that it is capable of becoming. To our friend Lafe LaFollette, then, I propose this toast: May those who teach and those who learn at this college and those who guide its destinies in the years ahead be forever mindful of your example, forever aware that the finest product of a liberal education is that rarest of creatures, a truly civilized human being.

It's Nice, but It May Never Sell

Q. *Dr. Rogge, why do you profess such pessimism?*

A. I think the chances are no better than three out of ten that capitalism as we know it will survive the twentieth century. I'd be even more depressed if I did not detect a pronounced shift taking place in the way professional economists view the system. I see a shift to the right. And it's obvious today's students have a greater appreciation of the system than they used to.

Q. *Doesn't that cheer you up?*

A. Certainly. Intellectual support for capitalism is growing. There is a definite swing among economists and political scientists in the direction of the marketplace. If you don't think so, talk to the economists and intellectuals of Eastern Europe, where they have tried to do without markets. I mean, it is so obvious that the non-market schemes all over the world—including those in this country—simply have not worked that even the intellectuals are noticing it.

Q. *But anti-capitalist theory seems to be getting a lot of attention?*

A. Sure. Any time you have an upheaval, people come out of the woodwork to tell you how you got in such a mess. Once in a while, they'll even tell you how to get out of it. But rarely. There is always a fringe group. Indeed, Paul Samuelson says we ought to know Marx. But I think Paul is farther from Marx today than he was

Reprinted from *The Changing Challenge: General Motors Quarterly*, Spring 1975, by permission of the Rogge estate.

fifteen years ago. As a matter of fact, the great body of economists is very clearly moving to the right. Unfortunately, it will take a while for that school of thought to exert strong influence on economic policy. You see, the people who have been calling the economic shots in this country were raised on Depression economics. They have been applying 1930's remedies, which are not remedies at all.

Q. *Are you talking about price and wage controls?*

A. That's one remedy, yes. And it's a good example of why the public is so confused. I mean, the effect of price and wage controls is the destruction of the free market system. Everybody knows that. Some people are happier about it than others. Yet, it wasn't so long ago that the National Association of Manufacturers and the Chamber of Commerce and even General Motors favored controls. They won't make that mistake again. But the harm has been done to public understanding. I think we'll see periodic wage and price controls over the next ten or fifteen years, along with an increasingly hampered economy and accelerating inflation and rising interest rates. So that, eventually, the American economy will come to look very much like the English economy of today.

Q. *What can be done about it?*

A. I suggest the system needs defending. It needs defenders. Unfortunately, the average worker does not defend it, because he doesn't understand how it affects his welfare. Intellectuals do not defend it, because capitalism is anathematic to aristocrats, which is what all intellectuals fancy themselves. Joseph Schumpeter said the capitalist achievement does not typically consist in providing more silk stockings for queens but in bringing them within the reach of factory girls. And businessmen are poor defenders of capitalism for a number of reasons. First, they are doers. They are more concerned with getting something done than in why they do it. They would just like to be left alone to do their thing. Secondly, they are no good at articulating something like the role of profits, for example. And they have even been taught by intellectuals to feel guilty about their successes.

Q. *If businessmen are such poor defenders of the system, won't exposing them to students via career-related programs do capitalism more harm than good?*

A. No. There's no doubt that contact with businessmen in their own setting will produce a better understanding of our economy and how it works than anything a student might learn in a liberal arts classroom. The classroom study of economics is better than nothing. But a lot of students don't even get that. They pick up what they know about the system from their English and foreign language and history professors. The best thing about all these real-world programs is that students get a chance to meet the businessman on his own turf. And that's where he is the most effective, or should I say the least ineffective.

Q. *He's better at showing than telling?*

A. Something like that. The typical businessman tends to be weak in understanding how the total system works and weak in communicating that which he does understand. But he's magnificent in communicating what he does, what happens inside his particular enterprise. Unfortunately, that's not enough to make him an effective spokesman for capitalism. This new thrust in partnership arrangements with academia represents a real challenge to him. But I'm pessimistic that many businessmen will accept the challenge, that they'll take the time to do the things necessary to make themselves more articulate.

Q. *Where does that leave the students?*

A. As I said before, I think students are somewhat less critical of the market economy today than they used to be. Certainly they are more aware of how the economy affects them personally. The easy assumption that a person with a bachelor's degree could automatically find a job is gone. So students have come to realize they cannot afford to be ignorant of the working of the system. Despite what you read about the interest in various radical approaches to economics, I think young people are more sensible today than they were, say, five years ago, when a lot of them seemed willing to believe that the troops were in Viet Nam because America was a capitalistic system.

Q. *Do you mean students today are less likely to be swayed by the views of their professors than they were yesterday?*

A. I certainly would not characterize today's college student as gullible. He is still largely uninformed about economics, though. And much of what he does know comes from liberal arts professors who have distorted views themselves. I mean, when a teacher uses a Cesar Chavez speech in a Spanish literature class, he's teaching economics. I'm not saying that's bad. I think teachers have a perfect right to do that. And the totally objective teacher has never existed and never will. I'm only disturbed when a teacher presents himself as objective when he is not.

Q. *How do you handle that matter in your classes?*

A. I warn the students of my biases. I don't try to conceal my opinions. That's a lot of the fun of it for them as well as for me. We have some great arguments in my classes, some really good ones. It's not that students necessarily like my point of view. But I think they like the fact that they are dealing with somebody who has one.

I Remember . . .

There are a number of signs of advancing age in the human male. One is a tendency to shortness of breath after exercise, as, for example, after leaning over to tie one's shoes in the morning. Another (and the one that prompts my comments) is the growing temptation to start writing one's memoirs. I find myself increasingly living in the past these days—perhaps because, like Archy the Cockroach, I am more optimistic about the past than I am about the future.

In any case, my remarks will appear as a chapter in my memoirs under the heading "Wabash College, September 1949." The book itself will have some such title as "The Memoirs of a Loser" or "The Story of an Economist Who Tried to Sell a Brand X Product in a Brand Y World."

I turn to my reminiscences about Old Wabash with some misgivings, knowing that my own seniority here does not match that of some of my colleagues—Willis Johnson, for example, who was born in a log cabin on the site of what is now Waugh Hall, or Jack Charles, who came here just after the Peloponnesian Wars. Dean Shearer's tenure is so well known as to require no comment, except to note that he and Caleb Mills were the best double-play combination in the history of faculty athletics.

With apologies to these, my betters, then I begin. When I arrived here in September 1949, the president of the College was Frank Sparks,

Reprinted from *Old Wabash: Bulletin of the National Association of Wabash Men* 65 (February 1968): 16–17, by permission of Wabash College.

businessman-turned-educator. That he had not completely forgotten his earlier training was evidenced in his first words to me, which were: "Rogge, I'm glad you're here, but I do have one regret; I think I could have gotten you for $200 less." As a matter of fact, he was absolutely right.

The College then had two deans, but only one was really active in day-to-day administration. George Kendall, after serving as *the* dean for some fifteen or more years, had set a pattern to be followed by at least one of his successors by returning to teaching, carrying with him the largely honorific title Dean of the Faculty. Kendall, whose picture hangs in the current dean's office, had served as an officer in both world wars and looked and acted the part, carrying himself ramrod straight (as he still does in retirement in Duxbury, Mass.). As his successor, Byron Trippet said about him: "When Kendall was Dean, all he had to do to stop a riot was show up." Here was a wonderful and tough-minded human being. For example, one of the new members of the English Department in the 50's (Owen Duston, I believe) gave George Kendall a copy of Arthur Miller's play *Death of a Salesman*. When Duston later asked him if he didn't think it great drama, Kendall replied, "Great drama, bah! Why if I met that Willy Loman, I'd kick him right in the (censored)."

That reminds me of the reaction of another tough-minded man to the plight of Oedipus. This was a blast furnace superintendent from Inland Steel who, in one of the sessions of our program for businessmen, said: "What is this guy Oedipus screaming about? So he killed his father and married his mother! That's the way the cookie crumbles."

In 1949, the dean of the college and dean of students was Byron Trippet. He also represented all that was finest and best in this College. I cannot do justice to him in this limited space and will leave this task to others.

The business manager of the College (and professor of economics) was Fergus Ormes. Ormes had helped nurse the College through the depths of the depression, and he was having difficulty adjusting to the free-spending habits of President Sparks. Fergus looked on a College dollar spent by anyone for any purpose as a personal defeat. I had an office at that time in what is now Center Hall 206, and Kendall's office was just one thin connecting door away. About once a week Fergus

Ormes would come crashing into Kendall's office, shouting: "Do you know what that madman Sparks has done today?" Ormes was also official guitarist for the Division III faculty picnics. At one such session, Professor Wendall Calkins, who had just arrived on campus, asked him if he could play "Ora Lee." Fergus, whose repertoire ran more to the "Erie Canal" and "The Bastard King of England," looked blankly at Calkins, then at his guitar, and said: "If you mean, can I make this damned thing play by blowing on it, the answer is no."

The faculty of the College then was composed largely of real veterans in service to Wabash. Most of them had joined the faculty during or just after World War I. They were pleasant to us young upstarts, but I always had a feeling that they were also leading us into conversation just to find out how much we were getting paid. The rumor had gotten around that some of us were getting a salary on which a family of four could live for a year, which meant automatically that we were getting more than most of the senior members. Fortunately, perhaps, for the peace of the faculty, this rumor wasn't true.

Those first months, I lived in mortal fear of those crusty ancients and particularly of their acknowledged leader, Insley Osborne. Osborne had gone on from his undergraduate days at Wabash to Oxford as a Rhodes Scholar and returned after World War I as a professor of English. He was worshipped by many of his students and hated and feared by others, in part because of his acid tongue. There was a faculty meeting in which President Sparks brought in a proposal from a prominent graduate of Wabash who was also a member of the board of trustees. The proposal was not to the faculty's liking, and when Sparks asked for comments, there was a dead silence. Insley Osborne then raised up his long, lean frame and said: "I have sometimes regretted that Mr. X [the board member involved] was not a graduate of Ball State." He sat down and the proposal was a dead duck.

At that time, faculty meetings were held in the big South Room on the second floor of Yandes. The chairs were arranged in rows, and it was understood that new faculty members would sit in the back rows and speak only when spoken to. This I think is much to be preferred to our current arrangements. We now meet in the Goodrich Room in the Library and, in sitting at the oval table, the new faculty member gets the feeling that he is just as good as the rest of us. He may even be led to question the nature of the current Wabash curriculum as the revealed Word of God! Put them in their place, I say!

Yandes, like the Library, with its stacks disappearing into the dusty shadows at the top of the center well, had a certain sinister charm to it. It looked like the kind of place in which Edgar Allan Poe might have written "The Pit and the Pendulum" or the "Fall of the House of Usher."

Now that we're on buildings, let me briefly recall Old South Hall. Had I been Professor Strawn's insurance agent when Strawn was assigned an office on the second floor of that building, I would have cancelled his policy. The Scarlet Inn was in a room on the first floor, and the odor of stale hamburger grease mixed nicely with the aroma from a six-inch layer of bat guano in the attic.

The College dining hall was operated in Kane House, under the direction of Professor Bedrick, of the Classics Department. The boys told me that they had hamburger about five days a week, but each time under a different Latin name.

Kingery Hall housed most of the football players in those days, as part of a full-room-and-board arrangement. Sparks was pursuing an aggressive policy on football on the not-unreasonable assumption that a winning football team would help him raise money for salaries of English teachers. In the fall of 1951, Wabash and DePauw came up to the final game, both undefeated. As it turned out, the game was not even close—final score: Wabash 41—DePauw 12. Naturally, salaries of English teachers went up 10 percent the next day. The stars of that game were two young men named Huntsman. In spite of the fact that he has had the best record as a track coach in small colleges in America in the last nineteen years, Owen Huntsman is still not certain whether it was his productivity as a track coach or as a father that led Sparks to hire him in 1949.

Unlike the situation now, the faculty in those years included a few eccentrics. One was the longtime teacher of mathematics George Carscallen. A chapel speech by Carsy might include a selection on the violin, a brief, acted-out lecture on the manly art of self-defense (he was a boxing buff) and a few kind words for the Soviet Union.

Another was an instructor who was to receive the "outstandingness" award for the year from Dick Banta, Minister without Portfolio to the College and Assistant to the President. This young man soon left

Wabash to join a ballet troupe in New York City. Banta's award was based on the arrest of this professor by the local police for an interesting method of garbage disposal. He lived on the second floor of one of the business buildings on North Green Street. Each evening he would collect his day's accumulation of garbage and, with a graceful pirouette, toss it out the window onto the sidewalk next to the Elston Bank.

Another was John Forbes, teacher of history and owner of an ancient yellow Rolls-Royce, who gave his Saturday morning lectures on Pan Hel weekend in formal dress—full tails, opera hat, the works. He once wrote a letter of recommendation for a Wabash student to the University of Chicago Law School that is still remembered at that institution. He wrote: "This young man is not very bright and his work for me has been mediocre at best. At the same time, he's smarter than all but two members of the Montgomery County Bar Association and I recommend you take him."

Another teacher of history stands out in my own mind. He was a pure scholar with a very sensitive ego. He came into my office in my first week in the dean's office and demanded that I expel from the College one of his C.C. students. The charge was insolence. It turned out that he had sent his C.C. students to look at an exhibit of wood carvings then on campus. Then they returned to the classroom and wrote an essay on what they had seen. The professor, livid with rage, asked me to read the offending lines in the young man's essay. They went something like this: "Personally, I think all this a bunch of bunk. The carvings didn't do a thing for me. Now I know that it's hard to do such carvings, but it's also hard to stack beebees in a corner and no one calls that art." Some on campus, especially those on the faculty who knew this professor well, wanted to give the young man a medal, but at least he wasn't expelled.

Well, enough is enough, if not perhaps too much. I have treated Old Wabash lightly here, but I want to assure you that this has not been for lack of basic respect. Those men—the Frank Sparks, the George Kendalls, the Byron Trippets, the Fergus Ormes, the Ted Gronerts, the Insley Osbornes, the George Carscallens, the Frederic Domroeses, the Doc Bechtels, the Doc Howells, the Norwood Brigances, the Neil Hutsinpillars, and others—in spite of an inadequate physical plant, and with a love of Wabash that transcended questions of salary and teaching loads—maintained the traditions of this College as a fine place of learning and as a rewarding place for young men to spend four years of their lives. Without the base they helped to maintain and to expand, neither students nor faculty would be here today, because we would not think this a worthy place to be.

It is still not certain that those of us now on this campus—students, teachers and administrators alike—will do as well for this college of ours.

An Entry in the Business Citizenship Competition

The ideas of economists and political philosophers, both when they are right and when they are wrong, are more powerful than is commonly understood. Indeed the world is ruled by little else. Practical men, who believe themselves to be quite exempt from any intellectual influences, are usually the slaves of some defunct economist. Madmen in authority, who hear voices in the air, are distilling their frenzy from some academic scribbler of a few years back. I am sure that the power of vested interests is vastly exaggerated compared with the gradual encroachment of ideas. Not, indeed, immediately, but after a certain interval; for in the field of economic and political philosophy there are not many who are influenced by new theories after they are twenty-five or thirty years of age, so that the ideas which civil servants and politicians and even agitators apply to current events are not likely to be the newest. But, soon or late, it is ideas, not vested interests, which are dangerous for good or evil. —John Maynard Keynes, *The General Theory of Employment, Interest and Money*

I. The Nature of the Problem

The proposal to be outlined below will be based on the assumption that Keynes was essentially right—that, in the long pull, it is ideas that count. Witness the influence of Keynes's own ideas on the current

Source unknown, no date. Reprinted by permission of the Rogge estate.

economic policy of this country. Witness the influence of the ideas of that thoroughly defunct economist Karl Marx on the lives of all of us in the world of the 1960s. In the presentation to follow, the confrontation between the Communist and the relatively free societies will be seen as primarily a struggle for the minds of men.

None of this should be taken as minimizing the importance of the associated and current problems of military defense. To be free, one must first of all be alive. The ultimate persuasion of freedom would be severely muted in a Communist-controlled world. In this area, the American business firm can make its contribution in the traditional way—by continuing to be the most efficient agency for production in the history of the world.

Some leaders of business may wish to go beyond this and partici-pate personally in the discussion of optimum strategy for the politico-military conflict. This is quite appropriate in a free society, but the issues are complex, and the sheer amount of technical knowledge required for efficient decision-making is staggering. Here the expert in the armed forces or in the civilian branches of government or in the universities and related agencies is likely to continue to be the dominant figure. But again it is not only appropriate but necessary that every citizen— whether businessman or no—continue to be involved in the choice of fundamental strategic policy for the not-so-cold war. Disagreement there will be—even among committed anti-Communists—over the choices to be made here—for example, over the usefulness and wis-dom of military intervention in a Vietnam. But this dialogue must go on, and the individual businessman as citizen can make his own con-tribution, whether limited or substantial. The business firm, however, as a complex collection of individuals and lines of authority and re-sponsibility, does not seem to be an appropriate unit for extended par-ticipation in the discussion of politico-military strategy.

Moreover, if Keynes is right, it is not in the rice paddies of a Vietnam or in any other field of hot war that the decision will ultimately be made. Even the most sanguine would not argue that a clear-cut military vic-tory in Vietnam or in similar struggles in the years ahead would assure us a world based on freedom under the law. It might even be plausi-bly argued that if the Communist leaders of every leading Commu-nist nation in the world today were to be deposed by politico-military maneuvering, the threat of communism as ideology would still be with us. In fact, if history is any guide, in the very process of this maneuvering, the relatively free societies might themselves be led to adopt many of the ideas and techniques of authoritarianism. (For example, I would argue that American economic and military aid to other countries, extended in part as an element in cold war strategy, has led directly to an expansion of the role of government in the economic life in every one of the recipient countries, encouraging a socialism that is ideologically of the exact same family as communism.)

The ultimate bastion of freedom is in the mind of the individual human being who is committed to a society of individual freedom, limited government, and private property. Take away this commitment, and the military struggles can decide only *who* shall rule, who shall administer what particular form of authoritarianism. To repeat, the great battlefield is on the terrain of ideas.

II. The Strategic Elements in the Struggle for Men's Minds

Some would deny the primary role that is here assigned to ideas, but almost none would deny that the battle for men's minds is of substantial importance. But many who admit its importance despair of winning this battle, because they see it as a question of numbers and they are aware of the indifference, the lack of knowledge, and the low levels of perceptivity of most human beings on questions of principle and ideology—not only in the so-called backward parts of the world but in our own developed societies as well. Indeed their pessimism would be justified if it really were a problem of numbers. To convert the masses to anything but an unstable, emotional hatred of what is called communism is an almost hopeless task, and to convert the masses to a sophisticated, knowledgeable understanding of and commitment to freedom *is* a hopeless task.[1]

---

1. I am not using the word *masses* in a pejorative sense; as a matter of fact each one of us belongs to the masses on all but a few issues within the range of our special competence.

Fortunately, the problem is not one of numbers.[2] As a matter of fact, the masses can never be converted to a sophisticated, knowledgeable understanding of and commitment to communism either. They tend to be followers of those who, by whatever means, have established themselves in leadership roles. The problem then is a problem that relates to the leadership and not to the masses—and at once the problem becomes, by no means easy, but by no means inpossible.

Here again the problem can be easily misinterpreted. "Leader" can be read as political leader only—as congressman or member of parliament or president or premier or what have you. Now, in fact, these men may be leaders in the sense in which the word is used here, but even these apparent leaders are more likely to be followers of the true leaders, to be reflections on the surface rather than the surface itself. By the very definition of the problem used here, the true leader is the man with the ideas, the man whose thinking is reflected ultimately in the religious, political, social, and economic arrangements in the society.

This man, then, is our target. But how can he be recognized? Where does he work? What titles and degrees does he hold? What is his distinctive coloration? The answer is that he might be found anywhere, in almost any employment, with or without revealing titles or degrees. Only the perceptive observer of each local scene can identify him, but, often, the apparent leader is not the true leader at all.

Fortunately, though, there are some rough guides to identifying this man, or at least the man who has the potential to play the role of true leader. He is most likely to be found in the school or college classroom, or among the authors and playwrights, or working for a newspaper or a magazine or a radio or television station, or among those who are involved full-time in serving one of the religions of the society. Not only do such positions promise important exposure, but they tend to attract the men of ideas, the ones who are capable of analyzing complex phenomena and perceiving and creating abstract systems. They might well be called "intellectuals," if that word is taken to be descriptive only

2. My own thinking here has been largely influenced by the work and writings of Leonard Read, president of the Foundation for Economic Education, Irvington-on-Hudson, N.Y. See his *Elements of Libertarian Leadership*.

of those who are at home in the world of ideas and not as implying a specific degree-holding fraternity of men.

However difficult the problem of identification, these are the key men in the battle for the minds of men. If a sufficient number of sufficiently effective such men around the world were to become committed to the philosophy and practice of freedom, the world would eventually be a collection of free societies. It would be utopian indeed to expect such a state of affairs to actually be realized in the forseeable future. It is not utopian to see the possibility of a world in which the balance is sufficiently on the side of freedom that those societies which are relatively free can exist in relative security.

III. How Can a Business Firm Participate in This Struggle for the Minds of Men?

The target has been identified. The question now is how an American business firm can affect the thinking of the true leaders around the world. Obviously it need not work alone at this task, but the question is whether there is any role for the business firm in this vitally important contest.

Various American firms have long recognized the critical role of these men (whom we will now refer to as the "intellectuals") and have worked alone or in concert to convince them of the merits of the free society, or at least of the American business system. Unfortunately, most of these attempts have been propagandistic (selling) in technique, and the fine (and usually sensible) words have fallen on deaf ears. Putting signs lauding free enterprise in store windows will have little or no effect in Maintown, America, and none at all in Calcutta. Even the hired spokesman (intellectual) for the business point of view makes few converts among the men in whom we are interested here. The response is, in effect, "I can not hear what you are saying because what you are is pounding in my ears."

This reveals at once one of the central problems in the battle for men's minds and at the same time the greatest opportunity for the individual business firm to participate in the battle. The plain fact is that for most intellectuals around the world today, on both sides of the Iron and Bamboo curtains, even among those who believe themselves on the side of freedom, the free market economy is not looked upon as an essential ingredient in a free society, and the business firm itself is regarded as at best a necessary evil and at worst a symbol of the greed and exploitation in the American way of life.

I believe that the exact opposite can be demonstrated. I believe it can be established that the free economy is an absolutely essential ingredient in a free society and that the business firm is the very best concrete illustration of the way in which free men use their creativity and energy in serving not only their own interests but the interests of others as well.

It is in the struggle for men's minds that the business firm can play a meaningful role. This derives from the fact that the business firm, as a type, is close to the center of the problem. The intellectuals around the world, whose allegiance we need in the long-run confrontation with communism, are generally suspicious of, if not actually hostile to, the American business firm. The businessman, as the personification of the business firm, shares in this general hostility. (For example, I have seen no book or play or film from foreign hands in recent decades where such American businessmen as appear are permitted to be other than knaves or fools. As a matter of fact, much the same could be said of the work of Americans in recent years.)

This hostility to the business firm and the businessman is then transferred to the free market economy generally. Most intellectuals around the world seem to have an instinctive preference for public operation of economic activities and for closely regulated private firms. Thus even the anti-Communist intellectuals around the world tend to reject the free private enterprise approach to economic organization and, through their influence, move their own countries further and further toward the Socialist-Communist model of economic life. If my assumption is correct—that a free economy is a necessary ingredient of a free society over the long pull—this trend is likely to move the world progressively further toward authoritarianism and thus in most cases to a more sympathetic and congenial relationship with the outright Communist countries.

The nub of the matter, then, seems to lie in the distorted image of the American business firm and the American businessman in the minds of the intellectuals in the non-Communist world. I am suggesting that it is to the changing of this image that an individual American business firm can meaningfully dedicate some of its resources. The appropriate technique here is not elaborate propaganda systems but the truth—the truth as it can be perceived by one who has been permitted to see the actual workings of an American business firm at first hand and to know the American businessman as human being rather than caricature. Thus the proposal.

It would be foolish to expect immediate and universal miracles from the plan presented here—or from any other approach. Changes of mind-set come slowly, and a road-to-Damascus-type conversion is rare indeed. If this program were set in motion, not all who participated would come to see the American business firm in what we believe to be its true light, nor would such changes as might take place in the minds of others be immediately apparent.

But if the business firm really believes in the significance, the basic morality, the essential rightness of what it is doing; if it believes as well that man through his reason is capable of recognizing that which is right; if it is willing to expose itself with complete candor to "men of reason" from around the world; it might be able to work that most astonishing of miracles—a change in the minds of men, of men who count. It might be able to make a really meaningful contribution in the struggle of the relatively free societies with today's most virulent form of authoritarianism—Communism. It would thus have contributed to the making of a better world for itself, its owners, its leaders, its workers—and for all who prefer freedom to slavery.

Economic Education

Interview with Dr. Benjamin Rogge

GREG MCDONALD: This is Greg McDonald, and in this week's segment of *Economics 101*, we have with us as a guest Dr. Benjamin Rogge. Dr. Rogge is a Distinguished Professor of Political Economy at Wabash College in Crawfordsville, Indiana. Dr. Rogge, your business is educating students and the public in the area of economics. What do you see as one of the greatest problems in developing this kind of education?

DR. ROGGE: I think it is the general lack of understanding of the way in which the market process works, of the way in which alternatives to the market have proved themselves to be just something not workable and not able to produce the results, the consequences, that society hopes to achieve. As a consequence, I've spent a good part of my life attempting to improve the level of economic literacy of those with whom I come into contact. It seems to me of particular importance that this be done on the college campuses, not simply with the students but with our colleagues from those campuses as well, because most of the economics that is taught in this world is not taught by professional economists—it's taught by ministers and by teachers of Spanish or philosophy or political science. It is necessary, then, for all those who are in a position to influence

Transcript of an interview from *Economics 101*, an American Broadcasting Network radio show hosted by Greg McDonald. Recorded November 15, 1979, aired December 1979. Reprinted by permission of ABC News Radio.

public opinion to be reached if possible—or at least as many as possible—with what seems to me to be a more complete and objective understanding of how the market works.

GREG MCDONALD: Is a simple technical education enough? Is there some kind of moral basis that needs to be developed to have a complete understanding of the free enterprise system?

DR. ROGGE: I think ultimately the acceptance or rejection of the free enterprise system is going to depend on whether the masses see it as an essentially moral, ethical, and just way of organizing economic life. The economic education in many ways is simply a first stage, a first step, in coming to understanding how the free enterprise system works. But the complete understanding requires the moral understanding, the moral basis, of freedom itself and not just simply the question of whether or not the marketplace can handle an energy problem—which by the way it can.

GREG MCDONALD: Do you find that most of the colleges and universities around the nation are prepared to teach the principles of the free enterprise system?

DR. ROGGE: I think there are many campuses where there is a full understanding of the enterprise system that I hold to be the correct one. It is not necessarily presented to the students. At the same time, I think it is very clear that among professional economists, the marketplace is winning. That is, I think there is a growing skepticism about whether or not the state, the government, can function in the multitudinous roles that we have assigned it and a greater awareness then of the necessity of using the marketplace. So I am really fairly optimistic about economic education on the campuses, in the departments of economics, in the long run. But still there is a need for more teachers, better material, and better ways of presenting that material in the years ahead.

GREG MCDONALD: How receptive do you find economics students or students that come into your economics classes to the principles which you advocate?

DR. ROGGE: Well, again, on my own campus, I encounter perhaps a more accepting environment than I would on other campuses by the very nature of the selection process. It's a small, liberal arts college for men only. Young people come out of midwestern middle income and upper income families, and most of them lean instinctively in this direction. But at the same time, I think on campuses around the country, there is today an openness to these ideas if we can but take advantage of that openness and find the right way to present them and get them in front of the students so that they can better understand them.

GREG MCDONALD: Do any of these students come prepared with any kind of understanding of the free enterprise system from the high school level?

DR. ROGGE: A few, a few do. Not just simply from the high school but from their own homes. I think the home is an enormously important educating influence on the life of a young person.

GREG MCDONALD: Do you see in the next decade a shift away from what we would call the "Keynesian" theory of economics which is taught on most college campuses to the "Friedman" or "Monetarist" school, or "Austrian" school?

DR. ROGGE: As I said before, I think the general Friedman point of view is winning. At the same time, the forces that have been set in motion by the economic policies of the last fifty years continue to move us away from the marketplace and the real world where decisions are made. These changes that are taking place on campuses are typically not going to be felt for another ten or fifteen years, so while I think the developments on campuses are encouraging, we still face a tremendous problem in the society at large of slowing down the forces moving us to the left.

GREG MCDONALD: Thank you very much, Dr. Rogge, for being with us today.

Economics in Schools: Discussion

If I had the courage and if I were not so fascinated by the sound of my own voice, I could now establish a meaningful precedent in economic discussions. I could say: "I have read the papers prepared by Professors Lewis and Bloom and I agree with what they have to say." Then I could sit down.

That I do not do this is symptomatic of one of our faults that makes us less than universally popular. We talk too much, too often, and too long. We are too interested in our places in the shifting hierarchy of the profession and too little interested in the relevance or significance of what we are saying. We play at a scholar's version of Stephen Potter's "one-upsmanship," with our major ploys reserved for the footnotes. We are less desirous of communication than we are afraid of "ex-communication."

It is little wonder that our students find us dull, that our campus colleagues find us amusing, and that the general public is delighted when our predictions prove to have been wrong.

I have found us playing this same game of thrust and parry—of "status, status, who's got the status"—in the Workshops in Economic Education designed to inform the uninformed and excite the unexcited. I have watched the expression on the face of a forty-year-old teacher of American history as she sat, still panting from a postdinner game

Excerpt from a panel discussion reprinted from *American Economic Review* 47 (May 1957): 687–88, by permission of the American Economic Association.

of badminton, listening to a bright young economist as he tried hard to communicate but even harder to protect himself from the scholarly error of oversimplification which his colleagues could chide him about over the uniced highballs that evening. She seemed to be feeling as E. B. White once described himself as feeling: like a reluctant conspirator in a plot he did not understand.

Now let me protect myself. I do not believe that accuracy of statement is unimportant or that communication comes before knowledge of the material to be communicated. I do not think that economists are incapable of communicating or that all or even a majority of economists need be brilliant expositors to lay and professional audiences alike. But I am convinced that the profession is guilty of excessive preoccupation with minutiae, with trivial refinement of trivial propositions, of massive expenditures of time, effort, and money on the gathering of data to answer trivial questions. I am convinced that these characteristics are produced by a selection principle within the profession (and particularly on college campuses) which overemphasizes so-called scholarly achievement and underemphasizes communication skills. The young scholar who wishes to make progress is almost forced to jump into the scholarly publications race, even if he has nothing really significant to say at the moment. Nor do I see any real hope for economic education of the kind we are talking about here so long as this selection principle is applied. Certainly it is discouraging to find younger economists apologizing for their participation in activities such as the Workshops in Economic Education. As one of them once said to me: "This is a pretty low-level operation, but I couldn't turn it down, because I needed the money."

The formation of a standing Committee on Economic Education in the American Economic Association is an encouraging note, and particularly so in light of the high caliber of the men appointed to that Committee. But it is revealing that the sessions on economic education at the annual meetings are always scheduled on the afternoon of the last day of the meetings. Thus those who have to leave early will not miss anything of importance.

I would like to propose the creation of an American Association of the Teachers of Economics, with membership drawn from the high schools as well as the colleges and with strong emphasis on the participation of those who are teaching economics in the teacher-training institutions. Such an association could do something to reduce the insularity of each of the various groups now engaged in teaching economics and could serve to give greater recognition to the role of the teacher and to the man whose primary contribution is in the teaching role. It could also give economists a continuing opportunity to make the case that Lewis and Bloom have made so well today: that much of what passes for economic education in the high schools and teacher-training institutions today is certainly not economics and may not even be education.

I make this proposal in spite of my instinctive suspicion of and lack of confidence in do-gooder, crusading organizations. However, the need for some kind of action is clear, and this might be a forward step.

Part 4   *Microeconomics, Labor Issues, and Political Foibles*

The Myth of Monopoly

I'm honored to again be invited to speak in your von Mises series and am delighted to have again found my way to Hillsdale, Michigan—a city which seems to be equally inaccessible from all major airports in the Midwest. It's good to see my good friend and longtime colleague George Roche again. George is the only man I know who would rather play catch with his daughter in the backyard than be a United States senator. I'm embarrassed to be giving this presentation, though, with George in the audience; not only has George heard this speech many times, he's given it several times. When he and I were on the lecture tour for the Foundation for Economic Education and one or the other couldn't make it, we gave each other's lectures.

I stand before you tonight as a licensed, certified, practicing professional economist, and I am about to practice my trade. But at the same time I stand before you as an open, admitting, professing apologist for that system of economic organization known as capitalism. Moreover, that which I preach is not the gospel of the capitalism of the capitalist-based but mixed economic system. What I preach is the gospel of pure *laissez-faire*. It would be reasonable to assume that my attachment to *laissez-faire* capitalism derives from my work as an economist—reasonable but wrong. My position on any question of public policy is fully determined by moral judgment and needs

Reprinted from *Champions of Freedom*, Vol. 6 (Hillsdale, Mich.: Hillsdale College Press, 1979), 53–77, by permission of Hillsdale College Press.

no support from the work of Ben Rogge or any other economist. My moral judgment (in questions of social organization) proceeds from my assumption that each of us comes into this world with the right to do anything that's peaceful, and to do it singly or in pairs or in groups as large as the Mormon Church or General Motors. Given that basis for moral judgment, capitalism as a system of *voluntary* exchanges is marked as a moral system right from the beginning, and socialism as a system of *involuntary* exchanges is marked as immoral by that very fact. That really is all I need to know for my own decisions.

To give you a more precise example—government intrusion in wage and price setting of the kind that we now see practiced in this country and that I think you will see in less-voluntary manifestations within six months; that kind of intrusion into wage and price setting stands condemned as an immoral act by its very nature. It's an intrusion by government in what would otherwise be a series of voluntary exchanges among willing partners, and that's all I need to know to know that it stands condemned. I do not need to ask that it be twice condemned on the grounds of inefficiency—although it is grossly inefficient.

Well so much for Ben Rogge the Economist. Who needs him? Not even Ben Rogge seems to need him. Fortunately there are those who do. Fortunately there are those who need Ben Rogge the Economist because that is indeed the way I make my living. And who are they? Well these people who need Ben Rogge the Economist are of that great multitude of doubters and worriers who fear that the freedom I preach would not work in practice, who fear that instead this freedom would unleash any number of unspeakable horrors on society. What unspeakable horrors? Great depressions! Violent inflations! Massive unemployment! Starvation for many! Consumers deceived and destroyed! Workers exploited and in danger! And everywhere the tyranny of the private monopolist. These are the kinds of images that are brought forward. These are said to be the consequences of "turning things loose," of really attempting to put freedom into practice.

And of course it is a frightening thing. If Ben Rogge would really push the button and eliminate all that he would like to see eliminated in the present relationship between our government and its people, a good share of the familiar economic landscape of this country would disappear. Not only would the minimum wage laws disappear, not only would the social security system disappear, not only would the Food and Drug Administration disappear—but even, God help us all, even Michigan State would disappear! To tell you how hopeless it is, even that part of the local public library supported by public funds would disappear. And of course (as I am going to argue tonight) so would the anti-trust laws. You can say I can't really mean it. But I do. People would really be free to do that which is peaceful; this is what is implied. But would it *work*?

The first way to answer the attack on freedom in terms of whether or not it would be workable is simply to say that if it is right in principle— if the freedom principle is indeed correct—then it is going to work. Unless the world is a tale told by an idiot, whatever is right in principle is going to work, and whatever is wrong in principle isn't going to work. Thus if this principle of the freedom of the individual to do that which is peaceful is indeed correct, obviously it is going to work if you put it into practice.

That would be the first answer, but it would be convincing only to somebody who shared the principle. The second way of answering attacks on the workability of freedom is much more time-consuming and cumbersome. It consists of taking each of the charges in turn and proving it wrong. Would freedom mean inflation and depression? Quite the contrary. It has been government mismanagement of the money supply that has visited upon us every one of the great depressions and the great inflations in the history of man. It is not freedom that we have to fear but interventionism. Each one of these could be taken down the line. Is it the free market that brings unemployment? No. Why are 80 percent of the young people in the south Bronx out of work? Because that is inherent in capitalism? Not at all. It's because they have been priced out of the labor market. They have been protected out of the labor market. What I am saying is that I think it is possible to take each of the charges against the free market and prove it to be wrong. But obviously I do not have the strength, and you certainly do not have the patience to sit here as I go all the way down this list, so I am going to pick one.

Tonight I have chosen the particular assignment of responding to the charge that under *laissez-faire* capitalism many of the markets would not be competitive but would instead be under private monopoly control. It is typically argued (and not just by the enemies of capitalism, but by the better part of its friends as well) that the tendency to monopoly inheres in capitalism itself and that only strong action by government can prevent this from happening, or can correct the situation which has already developed, or can substitute government regulation or ownership for the discipline of the market. On the way to the airport today I heard an interview with the current head of the Federal Trade Commission, and he said that he had been looked upon by many as an enemy of the business system and of capitalism, but in fact in his planning to become ever more vigorous in acting in his role as director of the Federal Trade Commission, he saw himself as the ultimate defender of capitalism. He said that he was the one who was going to keep the markets of the economy truly competitive, and that was what capitalism was all about. I am certain that he is absolutely sincere. I don't doubt his sincerity in the slightest. He sees himself in his rulings defending capitalism, purifying capitalism. Now, I think, as a matter of fact, he is wrong. I think that almost without exception what he does reduces competition rather than enhances it. I think that almost everything that he does works in the long run to the disadvantage of the consumer without enhancing the possibility of a better life for the consumer. But I do not doubt his sincerity. Nor do I doubt the sincerity of most who make this charge against capitalism. The mere fact that it was also made by Marx does not alone condemn it. This is an ancient charge against capitalism and deserves to be taken seriously.

What I am going to argue is that I believe that competition inheres in the very nature of human beings, the very nature of the marketplace, and that as a matter of fact only strong action by government can prevent markets from being competitive. Or to put it another way—all that government has to do to see that markets are competitive is to get out of the way, to not create monopolies. Well here is the issue, and I want you to note that this is not an issue in value judgments. These are not normative questions of good or bad, but simply questions in positive economics. What is the nature of things? Does competition inhere in the nature of the marketplace or does it not? Does it have to be created? Is it an artifact or is it inherent in the human system? These are questions of analysis and of fact, not questions of value judgment. Is IBM a monopolist, as it is now charged with being? Surely the economist can give you an answer. Is the Topps Chewing Gum company guilty, as it has been charged, of monopolizing the baseball picture card industry? These are questions of fact. At the same time, these questions can be very easily answered by reference to the principle that I have enunciated. If individuals do indeed have the right to do as they please so long as it is peaceful, even in groups as large as General Motors, then obviously there can be no real monopoly in a true free market. How can we condemn any organization simply because it has become very successful at certain kinds of voluntary exchanges? At serving other people as those other people are willing to pay to be served? How can we possibly condemn an organization for being so successful at serving others that it stands out far ahead of its rivals? If we insist on breaking up General Motors, should we not then be consistent and demand, for example, that Heifetz be required to play a violin with two strings missing? Or perhaps Wilt Chamberlain be forced to undergo vertical dismemberment? Or that Jack Nicklaus be permitted to play in only two tournaments a year? Why should success in pleasing others stand condemned as a matter of social policy? "Ah, yes," you say, "but when Jack Nicklaus gets that good it is hard for a Ma and Pa kind of golfer like Ben Rogge to compete with him." True, so true. But I don't remember coming into the world with a slip entitling me to win 50 percent of my matches against Jack Nicklaus. The only right that is relevant is my right to be free to try, to be free of coercive restraint in my attempts to succeed at golf or car making or grocery retailing or what have you. This would be the answer on principle. On principle if they got there by peaceful action they cannot stand condemned by society. But this principle is convincing, of course, only to those who share that principle. And so let's go on. Let's go to work as economists.

How can we tell whether or not IBM is a monopolist? How can we look at a company and say, "Aha, that is a monopolist! That is a competitor." How do we know? Well let me give you one piece of advice. If you are going to get a totally unambigious, clear-cut answer, do not go to the decisions of the United States Supreme Court dealing with issues of this kind. A second piece of advice, do not go to the economists either! We economists are not yet in agreement. We economists have not yet even agreed upon the first-stage question, what is a monopolist? Or the reverse, what is a competitor? How do you tell one from the other? What I want to do tonight is to give you three of the more widely recognized answers to this question of how do you tell a competitor from a monopolist. The first one I'm going to call the generally accepted, orthodox "textbook" definition of competition and monopoly, and I'll explain the kind of public policy that tends to go with it. This is the one you would find in most textbooks in most colleges in the country. That doesn't mean that you will find it at Hillsdale, because as you know this is a rather different kind of place. But in most textbooks around the country, you would find this particular kind of definition of competition and monopoly, the "textbook" definition.

The second is an approach to this kind of question on the part of that self-admitted genius of social policy John Kenneth Galbraith. And the third is the truth. I will identify it as the Schumpeter-Rogge Model of competition and monopoly. Some of you know about Schumpeter; some of you do not. I'll describe him in a few minutes, but if he were here he would not call it the Schumpeter-Rogge Model; he would call it the Schumpeter Model. But he is dead and I am here.

In the typical textbook in economics, the author begins his discussion of this topic by describing what he calls "pure competition." This is the pure thing. There's nothing better. This is it. This is the ideal. The first requirement for pure competition is that each firm be so small that by its own actions it can have absolutely no effect on the market. It is infinitely small relative to the market. One wheat farmer in Kansas, yes—General Motors, obviously no. This is the first requirement. What it does is to direct the attention of the students to the issue of smallness. If the "pure" is small, then obviously bigness is suspect, isn't it? You look at General Motors and you say that is a big—and hence bad—company. The second requirement for pure competition is that a unit of output from one firm be exactly identical to a unit of output by any other firm in the market. This may be true of two bushels of number 2 winter wheat of a certain moisture content, but of course they can never be exactly at the same place and hence are always differentiated in part by geography, if nothing else. What this does is establish a suspicion of all attempts to differentiate. If one aspirin maker says, "I want to call my aspirin 'Bayer,' and I think there are things I do to it that make it different in one way or another," he immediately comes under suspicion. Somehow it isn't right. The student gets the idea that those who differentiate their products, who try to make them distinctive, are somehow non-competitors, that this is withdrawing from the competitive market and is contrary to the well-being of the consumer.

The third requirement for pure competition is ease of entry. What does this mean? What does this imply? The fact that there are already firms in a given industry that are successful at serving other people does indeed make it more difficult for new firms to enter. As a matter of fact, there are Supreme Court decisions in which, in effect, the Court has said that the reason this company is at fault under the law is that it is so successful at serving the consumer that it makes it difficult for any one else to get in there to do it. Its sin is that it is very good at serving the consumer.

The next requirement for pure competition is independence of action—no getting together, no collusion of any kind. The final requirement—and the real kicker—for pure competition is full knowledge. If a market is to be truly competitive, then every person participating in that market must have full knowledge of all of the relevant data, both as of the present and on into the future. Where do you find those all-knowing people in the modern world? The only man who has that much self-confessed wisdom is John Kenneth Galbraith. Most of the rest of us do not know. As a matter of fact, by the very nature of the human condition, we will always see as through a glass darkly. Every decision we make in our lives is based on something less than full information, every single one. Not just the choice of toothpaste, but the choice of college, of wife or husband, of religion, of which tie to wear on Monday morning. Every decision we make in life is based on something other than full information. As a matter of fact a good part of life is involved in the search process. How do we find out? And "finding out" costs money. How do you find out which college to go to? How many campuses do you have to visit? Ten, twenty, thirty? Each visit costs money. In other words acquiring information is one of the most important things we spend our lives doing. As a matter of fact much economic practice in a capitalist world that is often looked upon as wasteful (the use of brand names, for example) is simply a way of getting information less expensively. What does Holiday Inn advertise? "No surprises." When you are out driving along the road, what is the function of Holiday Inn as a brand name? By golly, you go in there and you know it is at least going to be reasonably decent. And in all probability you are not going to be assaulted in your room. Well you can't be sure of that. But almost. Why do we parents send our young people to college? For one reason, to reduce the search costs of finding an appropriate mate. A good share of our life we spend in trying to "find out." We *never* know in full, because that isn't given to the human being.

Here is the description of pure competition: the infinitesimally small firm, producing an absolutely homogenous product with reference to every other firm, with absolute freedom of entry at a moment's notice, absolute independence of action, and perfect knowledge. You, the student, take that as your description of competition and go out in the real world. How many such markets do you find? Not a one. So you come back and report to your teacher; you say, "I've got a problem; I went out into the real world and I didn't find any of these." "Aha," replies the teacher, "that is true. I will now describe *other* kinds of markets for you. Way over here is monopoly. The real monopolist you can tell because there will be only one of him. There will be only one firm; no one will be able to get into the market, and there will be no substitute for what the firm produces." So you go out into the real world, look for a pure monopolist, and find very few, because there are very few things in this world for which there are no substitutes. Young people sometimes say, "Aha, how about the telephone?" My reply: There are people in this world who have gone through their entire lives without a telephone. There *are* other ways of communicating. You can even write letters. (To the Rogge children, the only way to communicate is by telephone—*and collect*.) So the student finds very few cases of pure monopoly.

But the "textbook" teacher is not at a loss. He next describes a market type that he calls *oligopoly*. This is the rule of the few, a few firms and difficult entry. So you look around and see that you see oligopoly everywhere. How many banks in your hometown? How many automobile makers? How many big steel companies? How many cereal producers? (By the way, you are being exploited by monopolists in the cereal business, according to the United States government. You didn't realize that in Battle Creek and elsewhere here in Michigan you are harboring enemies of society in the form of breakfast-cereal makers.) So you look around and find oligopoly almost everywhere.

There is one other category, and this the textbook identifies as "monopolistic competition," which is not very complimentary. Monopolistic competition is a market situation in which there are many small firms and it is easy to get in and out, but each firm differentiates its product a little from that of each other firm. As in what? Fast food chains. Burger Chef, Burger King, A&W, all of them. They all buy their hamburger at the same plastics factory as far as I can tell, but they are slightly differentiated. This is called monopolistic competiton.

The textbook economist then goes ahead to show that as a market moves further away from pure competition over toward monopoly, it produces less-desirable outcomes. That is, it is charged that as the markets move in that direction, there is less efficiency, less equity in the functioning of the economy. Therefore, the focus of public policy should be to try to push markets back in the direction of pure competition, knowing that you can't get there but using it as the benchmark. If the firms are getting too big, what do you do? You pass a law saying they cannot acquire, they cannot merge, they can't grow any bigger. You say to a firm, you know, if you have 90 percent of the market, that automatically is too big, and we may have to break you up. The pressure then is back toward smallness—and toward sameness. In the pharmaceutical industry and elsewhere, we are going to see this attempt to allow us to buy everything the way we used to buy crackers, just in a barrel, unmarked—you just reach in and pull out your penicillin or whatever it is you are buying—without brand names.

It also means that there's a constant concern that each of us in the marketplace does not have enough knowledge to make our own decisions, and hence we must have somebody forcing knowledge upon us or standing *in loco parentis* over us telling us what to buy, what not to buy.

This is the public policy of the United States today. A significant part of our anti-trust legislation is based upon this kind of thinking. Not all. There are many things in the current laws that even the textbook economists would join me in condemning. But this is essentially the kind of thinking that has led to the public policy of America today.

What does John Kenneth Galbraith say about all this? I think he starts off correctly by saying, "It's amusing, is it not, that if you go into the front offices of a major U.S. corporation you might find there two groups from government. One would be a group of young bright lawyers developing an anti-trust case against the firm; the others, the

purchasing agents from all the major departments of government."
Why are they there? Because that's where the action is; that's where
the efficiency is. Now what is Galbraith saying? He is saying something that I think is perfectly sensible. It just does not make sense in the
modern world to insist that we ought to have 125,000 makers of automobiles in America, or steel companies. In other words, it is foolish to
talk about breaking them up to get back to some unattainable ideal of
atomistic competition.

But does that mean you let these big companies alone? Oh, no, no,
no, says Galbraith, that doesn't mean you let them alone at all. How
does he go about his analysis? He asks, who runs each firm? Who runs
General Motors? If you look inside, you will find what he calls the technostructure. This is made up of the people at General Motors who know
how to design a car, how to plan for the making of a car, how to hire
the workers, get the capital, how to market it. These are the people who
know how to get things done. This is what many of you are preparing
yourselves to be—parts of the technostructure.

Now, the question is, who controls the technostructure? Do the consumers control it? Do we have what is called consumer sovereignty?
To this Galbraith says no. These large firms cannot wait upon the consumer to validate the decisions that they had to make five years, eight
years, ten years earlier. They have no choice but to control the consumer, and this they do, with their allies on Madison Avenue. In other
words, says Galbraith, rather than the businessman being the pawn of
the consumer, as the old myth would have it, the consumer is in fact the
pawn of the businessman and his allies on Madison Avenue.

Is the technostructure under the control of the stockholders? Nonsense! They don't have any idea what's going on in General Motors anyway. Is it under the control of regulating agencies? No, says
Galbraith—and here, by the way, I would agree with him. In most cases,
he says, after a while the regulating agency, if one exists, becomes the
pawn of the regulated, serving *their* interests rather than the interests
of consumers.

As in what? The Civil Aeronautics Board. We're having some pretty
dramatic evidence of that right now. As with the Interstate Commerce
Commission, where the estimates are that as much as four to eight to
ten billion dollars is wasted each year in transport costs. In other words,

says Galbraith, the regulating agencies do not necessarily regulate. Well, then, who does control the technostructure? The answer—no one.

The technostructure at General Motors is a self-perpetuating dynasty controlled by no one. Well, what's wrong with that? Are they competent people? Of course they are. Are they generally well-meaning people? Of course they are. What is wrong with them? They do not know what is best for society. What they do they do efficiently, but they're doing the wrong thing. What is the solution to that problem? The solution is to put them under the control of those who do know what is best for society. Who are they? John Kenneth Galbraith and people like him— exactly—and particularly those of us in the academy, in the intellectual world. He identifies this explicitly. Why? Because we spend our days and nights contemplating the public good. We are the ones most likely to know what is best for society, and, therefore, we should be put in charge. How do you do it? Well, he's not very explicit on details. He admits now that it might take some outright socialization, but he's far more attracted, from what I can see in his writings now, by the kind of thing Ralph Nader and others are pressing for as well, and that is that on the boards of directors of the major corporations there be placed representatives of the public interest with the power of mandate and veto. Thus when the board of directors of General Motors is meeting to decide what kind of car to make for two years hence, some associate professor of English from Wayne State University attends as the representative of the public interest. The directors say, "We are not going to make any more of these small cars; the people want the big dudes back again." But the professor of English says, "That isn't what we're going to do at all. I have decided that it is not in the public interest to do it that way. We're going to do it my way." That's exactly what Galbraith has in mind. The major decisions of the major economic units in society must be placed in one way or another under the control of those who know. The rule of the philosopher kings.

The moment I am told that intellectuals are going to make the decisions, I know it won't work. If there's anything a group of intellectuals, a group of faculty members, are incapable of doing, it's making a decision. I don't know whether the students here are permitted to go to faculty meetings, but in a typical faculty meeting everything gets sent back to committee. In Galbraith's world, everything would get sent back to committee. But this is what he has in mind—and it's enormously popular. Why? Because the "word people" are going to run the world and who are the word people? They are the ones who acclaim social policy proposals or criticize them and, hence, shape public opinion. And here is a man saying to the word people of the world, I want to turn it all over to you.

That's John Kenneth Galbraith, and I think many of the things that are happening in America are taking us in that direction. Now comes the truth. Joseph Schumpeter is the man whose work under the heading "Can Capitalism Survive?" in *Capitalism, Socialism and Democracy* I talked about when I was here a number of years ago. I talked about Schumpeter's prediction that capitalism was not going to survive because its very success would undermine the social institutions which protect and that eventually there would be a transition into socialism without necessarily anybody saying, "Let us go there."

In this same book Schumpeter takes up this question of what is the true nature of competition under capitalism. Why does he feel compelled to discuss it? Because he has asked the question, has capitalism in fact worked? He examines the history of capitalism, and he sees that it has indeed worked, in the sense of putting more bread on the table of the masses than any other economic system in the history of man. Then he asks the question, has this system that has been so successful at any time been characterized by the pure competition of the textbook? His answer of course is no. In other words, here is a system that, according to the textbook prediction, could not possibly have worked. But when you look at the facts, you see that it has worked magnificently. As Schumpeter puts it, "If your facts and your theory are not in agreement, it is better to throw away your theory." In other words, if you really want to understand competition in the real world, what you must do is throw away your textbook—just literally. Not only is it not relevant, it is actually misleading. It will lead you to look at the wrong phenomena. It will lead you to ask such questions as: How many firms are there in the industry? How big are they? What is the concentration ratio? (That's a number where you find out how much of the total output is produced by the top few firms.) What are the profits of the firms in the industry? These are the things that the textbook approach would lead you to ask Schumpeter, and I say that none of that is in the slightest way relevant.

None of that is relevant in any way to the question of competition. But how can that be?

Well, it's the question again of what do you mean by competition. Schumpeter says if you want to understand competition, you have to start by understanding what capitalism is all about, what freedom is all about. What is freedom? It is an opportunity for each individual human being to act in response to his own preferences, his own needs as he sees them. In response to these felt needs, individuals in freedom go out and try to find the way to best serve those needs and at the same time to respond to this inner creativeness that is in all of us. In other words, what capitalism is all about is innovation. It is the constant search of individual human beings acting individually or in small groups or in large groups to come up with better ways of doing it, whatever it is. This is what capitalism is all about.

But how does this translate into a definition of competition? To Schumpeter, competition is the inevitable consequence of this perennial search for the better way, with neither the "finder" nor the "way" predictable—to be Henry Ford. If somebody had said "We've got to come up with a great new invention in the automobile industry. Let's pick these people who are ten years old who look like they will be the ones to get it done," would they have picked Henry Ford? Would they have picked Thomas Alva Edison, whose only education was three months in the public schools of Port Huron, Michigan? See, we don't know; we haven't the faintest idea of who's going to do it.

But somebody like Henry Ford comes up with an idea, and he gets way out ahead because people like it. And when he gets way out ahead, he makes a lot of money. At one time in the early twenties, it is rumored that for something like thirty-eight straight days he made a million dollars a day for himself, clear, after taxes. And the textbook writer might say, "It's just incredible. Nobody can be worth that much." Schumpeter would say, "nonsense." The fact that he was making that money, that is what sent tens of thousands of individuals into their garages trying to build cars. And throughout southern Michigan, northeastern Indiana, northwestern Ohio, in fact, all over the country, people were looking at that million dollars a day and saying, "I want some of that," and pretty soon somebody else comes along and they leapfrog. They go over the top. Moreover, to the man who had the first success, the very way he made that success may later prove to be his handicap. Henry Ford got to the point where people said to him, "Henry, somebody might like a car that isn't black." He said, "But that's how I made all that money." And so other people start leapfrogging. And then somebody else comes along and leapfrogs, and this is the way it really works. At any given moment if you do what the textbook would have you do, if you take a time slice right down the market, you would find to your horror that somebody was out ahead—the way you would if you went to the race track and kept shooting with the old Brownie camera, then went home and developed it; you'd take it out and say, "Oh my God, those two horses are way out ahead." But, if you have a movie camera and you keep following it, it's a race that never stops; the horses just keep running around the track with new leaders, and some of the old leaders die. Why? Because they don't anticipate innovation. The American Woolen Mill people were once among the top ten companies in America. But they didn't think the synthetic fibers were going to make it. So they dropped dead somewhere on the backstretch. Baldwin Locomotive—where is it? It didn't think that the diesel was going to make it. So, it's over there by the seven-eights pole. This is the way it is. It's a never-ending game of leapfrog, and that is what competition is all about.

Does it make any difference how many firms are in the market at a given moment? No. How much money they're making? No. This is the way the game is played. Even if there's only one firm in the market, that one firm has to keep running; it keeps hearing footsteps behind it, even though nobody's there. Because if it doesn't, there soon will be.

Schumpeter says this kind of competition disciplines before it even attacks. There is always somebody out there in a garage trying to do you in. And here you're in the vacuum-tube business, and you're one of the only two vacuum-tube firms in all of America in 1946, and you say, "We've got it made"—and then what happens? Some character in a garage comes up with a transistor, and you're out of business. Or you're the Keuttel and Esser Company. Do you know what they make? The slide rule. And what do engineers and school kids now carry? Pocket calculators. Well, this is what competition is all about, says Schumpeter.

There is supporting evidence, by the way, in a source you would never expect. This is Alvin Toffler's book *Future Shock*. If you want to read what this is all about, read this book. Toffler's thesis is that changes of this kind come along so rapidly that our defense mechanisms can't cope with them. And he talks about the fact that fully 55 percent of all of the items now sold in the typical supermarket did not even exist ten years ago. The year 1968 saw ninety-five hundred new items in the consumer-package-goods field alone, with only one in five meeting its sales target.

Well now, what happened to the Galbraithean idea that the businessman can just simply manipulate the consumer as he sees fit? All Galbraith would really have to do is look out the window. If he'd just look out the window, he'd see what really happens out there. Do they try to manipulate us? Of course they do. But does it work?

I've got a response to anybody who talks about pawns on Madison Avenue. I ask, "Are you yourself a pawn of Madison Avenue?" And I've never yet met a human being who himself or herself was a pawn of Madison Avenue. My college friends say, "No, Rogge, but you know you and I have Ph.D.s. I was thinking of common laborers and filling station operators." So, I am talking to my filling station operator one day, Bill Sabens (and Bill Sabens did not go to college; he resigned from Crawfordsville High School with the full cooperation of the administration), and Bill says to me, "Rogge, you college professors shouldn't be let out without a keeper." I say, "What do you mean?" He says, "Well, a lot of your friends, they listen to this stuff about additives. They'd have additives in the air of their tires if I didn't stop them." See, it's always other people who are the fools. Don't misunderstand me. I don't mean we don't make mistakes. I don't mean we aren't influenced by other people. As a matter of fact, the very evidence that we are a free society and a free market is the advertising—the attempt to persuade us. You don't have to persuade in a controlled society. They don't have to advertise in Russia—take it or leave it. You see, the fact that people are trying to persuade is the evidence that we are living in a free world.

Well, in any case, this is the way the process goes along—unless what? Unless somebody's position in the market is buttressed by government. If you're out ahead and you can somehow do something to stop the process, the next would-be leapfrogger is cut out. Schumpeter says that unless buttressed by government this process goes right on and on and on forever.

But doesn't it cost the consumer a lot? What about that million dollars a day? Nonsense. You know what this really costs you? Nothing. You subtract all those failures, the Edsels, all of the mistakes, all of those four-out-of-five that didn't meet their sales target, subtract those losses from the gains, and the net might well be zero or even less than zero.

So what is the cost of this attempt to come up with something that will better serve us? Nothing. But the critics ask, "What about collusion? Aren't people going to get together to 'fix' the market?" Of course they are going to try. But it doesn't work. Suppose Professor Gerhart Niemeyer and I get together and we go up to Roche and say, "From here on out any lectures we give at Hillsdale College will be $5,000 a lecture." All we are doing is asking for what we are worth. But there might be a consequence of that, to wit, a shrinkage in quantity demand to zero. I know what Niemeyer would then do. He would go around to Roche and say, "If you hire me I'll make a contribution of $2,000 to Hillsdale College." And I would have to make it $3,000. We would keep on bidding like that until we got down to the market price of $25. Farfetched? Not at all. I do not know of a single cartel that has been successful *without the aid of government,* not even the cartel that we attempt to run in higher education, known as the National Collegiate Athletic Association. It's designed to do what? Hold down the cost of athletes. Thank God it doesn't work, because if it did it would hurt the poor families the most because they turn out more athletes. The reason it doesn't work is that every college in America cheats. At least Wabash and Hillsdale don't cheat very effectively.

There are many types of cartels in America that are successful because they have the support of government, including, very importantly, trade unionism. That's the kind of cartel that has the government on its side. The authorities even let the union use violence in many communities. But there are also business organizations that get the government behind them—doctors, lawyers, bankers, farmers. The farm program is the greatest cartel in the history of man, run by government at the expense of the consumer. One of the strongest pieces of evidence that a cartel can't last without government is the almost frenzied attempts that those who run a cartel will make to get government to back them up, because otherwise it doesn't work.

"Do you mean, Rogge, there's no need for anti-trust?" That is right. No need for anti-trust at all. For example, anti-trust keeps trying to break up IBM. But here are some IBM ads: "IBM System 370 grows again to meet tomorrow's needs"; "IBM offers processor to buck competition"; "IBM offers faster computer processor and cuts prices of its older model." Is that the way a monopolist behaves? If you want to know how a monopolist behaves, look at the post office. Their idea of a new service is to close down on Saturday.

In my opinion anti-trust is contrary in both philosophy and practice to the idea of the free market. It says to the businessman, "If you do exactly what you were hired to do, come up with a better product, expand your share of the market, or make more money, we are going to send you to jail." What is the businessman supposed to do? Somehow apparently society is saying to him, "If you get too good at doing what we want you to do—we are going to send you to jail or fine you or whatever." This just makes no sense.

You heard me mention Topps Chewing Gum as a monopolist, and you probably thought I had made that up. Here is a report: "Find baseball picture cards monopolized; tied with bubble gum and marbles. In the estimate of the Federal Trade Commissioner Examiner Herman Tocker, Topps Chewing Gum of New York City, the world's largest manufacturer of bubble gum, is monopolizing the baseball picture-card industry. Tocker said that Topps has been hustling around, collecting the rights to use the player's pictures, pretty well cornering the major league players. Players get $5 for a five-year contract." Now who could compete with a company that's willing to throw money around like that?

What are your questions?

Putty in the Hands
of the Image-Makers

Are you and I the victims of advertising? Are we but helpless pawns in the hands of the medicine men from Madison Avenue? So the critics of capitalism would have us believe. My own first answer to these critics is to ask if they themselves are pawns of Madison Avenue. So far, I have yet to encounter a single human being who is willing to admit that he personally is but putty in the hands of the image-makers. An intellectual colleague sometimes responds, "No, Rogge, but then you and I have Ph.D.s. I was thinking of common laborers or filling station workers, or those who just aren't prepared by intelligence and training to make correct decisions in today's complex, technological world of goods and services." Several years ago I talked to a filling station operator. He did not have a Ph.D.; my memory tells me he resigned from the local high school many years earlier with the full cooperation of the school administration. His statement to me that morning: "Rogge, some of these buddies of yours out at the college shouldn't be let out without a keeper. They listen to all this stuff about additives and they'd have additives in the air in their tires if I didn't stop them."

Somehow it is always the other person who needs the protection, who needs to be shielded by the government from the temptations of the marketplace. Am I arguing that you and I never make mistakes in our choices in the marketplace? Not at all. Of course we make mistakes—because we are human. To be human is to make every decision in life on the basis of less-than-perfect information. To be human is to find it

Reprinted from the *Indianapolis Star*, October 19, 1980, by permission of the Rogge estate.

necessary to use trial and error as the method of searching for the right product, the right service for our particular needs at a given moment in time.

Advertising is one of the ways in which those search costs are reduced, as is the use of brand names, chain stores and worldwide hotel-motel operations. "No surprises" is the slogan of one such well-known chain, and that is precisely what such arrangements tend to produce. They reduce the search costs of all of us and make the marketplace more efficient.

"But," say the critics, "doesn't advertising also create wants? And if a want has to be artificially created, it can't be a real honest-to-goodness want that deserves to be satisfied!" In other words, doesn't the capitalist marketplace serve spurious rather than real wants? As a matter of fact, in the way in which the critics use the word here, all specific wants are spurious because they have to be created. No one comes into this world asking for a bowl of Post Raisin Bran or for a membership card in the Baptist Church or for a copy of the latest edition of the *New Industrial State* by John Kenneth Galbraith. All specific wants arise out of the influences, including explicit advertising, to which each of us is subject.

In the free market, all such influences must be persuasive in nature. In a controlled economy, with free choice removed, there is no role for advertising. Advertising then is a symbol of freedom in the marketplace and an important element in the efficient functioning of that marketplace.

Debating the Gold Standard

Will the American dollar soon again have a tie to gold? Some of the statements in the Republican Party platform quite clearly point in that direction. Of course, a party platform is more a rhetorical device than a statement of firm intent, but political parties do sniff the political winds, and the Republicans seem to have detected some unease among voters with the current monetary arrangements.

Who determines what serves as money in a given society? The Republican platform statement implies that the government so determines. But we must always be on our guard against the easy assumption that it is the rooster's crow that brings up the sun. In the realm of money systems, governments do indeed propose, but do they also dispose? That is, does the fact that government proposes that such and such serve as money dispose of the matter?

Not necessarily, and for reasons that are clearly seen in the very definition of money. Money is anything that is generally accepted in exchange for goods and services. A metal coin or a piece of paper or whatever may have stamped on it, in large letters, "This is money"; the legal tender laws may require that it be accepted in payment for all debts and obligations; the government may threaten to place in jail or even to put to death those who do not accept it as money. But if in fact it is not generally accepted in exchange, it isn't money. If the dog

Reprinted from the *Indianapolis Star,* September 14, 1980, by permission of the Rogge estate.

won't eat it, it isn't dog food. If the people won't take it, it isn't money, period.

How does this relate to the gold standard, an arrangement under which the money in circulation has some tie to gold? Over the centuries, governments have gone on and off silver standards, gold and silver standards, tobacco standards, etc. But the peoples of the world seem never to have really "gone off" gold. Throughout history, the would-be buyer with gold to offer has had little difficulty in arranging exchanges for what he wished.

Tolstoy caught this universal aspect of gold when he wrote that gold is "coined freedom." Let the politically persecuted or discontented have nothing to trade within or without his own country but the paper currency of that country, and his freedom to escape it is severely limited. But give him gold, and he can literally go anywhere in the world and find willing partners in exchange—and hence, survival. This is one of the reasons that the governments of the world from ancient times to the present have resented the discipline of the gold standard. The citizen who has gold is a potential troublemaker or at least a potential exile and can be embarrassing to the government in either role. Another reason that a government frets under the restrictions of the gold standard is that if it is profligate in its spending, producing inflationary consequences within the economy, the country will become a worse place to buy and a better place to sell for all, and gold will start flowing out of the country.

This is what the late, great Austrian-born Harvard economist Joseph Schumpeter meant when he said, "Gold is that naughty little boy who insists on telling the truth." Let the government be indiscreet in its fiscal policies, and gold, that inveterate tattletale who can never be silenced, by flowing out of the country, will sooner or later trumpet out the government's indiscretions.

It should now be obvious why those in government typically resist the gold standard, or any other monetary arrangement that reduces their discretionary control of the money supply.

The gold standard or any similar arrangement is a restraint on the power of those in government to do as they please. It should also be obvious why the members of society have an almost instinctive attachment to gold. They simply do not trust their governments. Or rather, they have come to know through ancient memory that they *can* trust their governments—to inflate the money supply and to use the control of money to control human beings.

Will the American dollar soon again have a formal tie to gold? I doubt it. Have the governments of the world "gone off" the gold standard? Yes. Have the peoples of the world "gone off" gold? Neither now nor ever.

Job Creation . . . Whose Job Is It?

I have been somewhat bemused by the topic of this particular session. I do not intend to argue finally that the question is absurd. Yet phrased in a slightly different way, it *is* patently absurd.

Suppose we were to put the question this way: Whose task is it to see that there is work to be done in this world? No one's of course. Because this task was accomplished in the act of creation, however long and involved that act of creation may have been. A creature of limited talent and energy was placed in an environment of limited physical resources, and then, as if he were to be deliberately tested, this same creature was given (1) a virtually unlimited capacity to want the things of his world and (2) a passion that gave him the power to increase his own kind almost without limit.

Create work for this creature? But how absurd. His own appetites give him no choice but to work. In the sweat of his brow is he to eat his bread. And, paradoxically, as his supply of bread is to increase, so is his desire for it—not perhaps in the same forms, but in ever new and expanded shapes and designs. Give him bread in plenty and he still knows no rest. He must then catch the 7:15 train to the city and the 5:23 home, carrying a briefcase of homework, all so that his children can have color television or a college education or the latest album of the Beatles.

Address before the Joint Meeting of the Clergy-Industry Relations Committee and Clerical Advisory Council, National Association of Manufacturers, in Rye, N.Y.; reprinted from *NAM Reports in Depth*, Washington, D.C., January 18, 1965.

Ah, but you say he doesn't need this kind of bread, nor do his children. You may be right or you may be wrong, but the point is quite irrelevant. This is the way man is, period. Give or take a few saints, this is the way he has always been, and this is the way he will always be.

How many of you in this room now have all you want for yourselves and your families? Can't even you heed the advice of Ruskin when he said, "The true progress of a nation consists in extinguishing a want," or of Gandhi when he said, with prophetic vision, "Today man wants to visit England; tomorrow he will want to visit the moon."

What I have just described to you is what the economist calls the economic problem. It is simply the existence of a gap between what people want and what they are able to get. Does this gap still exist? Have we not, in America at least, already achieved the affluent society?

Admittedly most of us now have more than enough to stay alive and far more than most of our ancestors. But this does not mean that the gap has been eliminated—probably not even that it has been narrowed. Such is the elasticity of human wants that an American family living in affluent suburbia may feel no less of a passion for things it cannot afford (a trip to Europe or membership in the country club or season tickets to the opera) than did the less affluent grandparents on the farm (a telephone, inside plumbing or a trip to the World's Fair in St. Louis).

Even Professor John Kenneth Galbraith, author of the book *The Affluent Society*, cannot and does not really say that the gap between what we want and what we are able to get has been eliminated. What he is really saying in his book is that Americans have more of the things they want than he thinks they need (such as tail fins on cars) and produce too little of the things he thinks they should want (such as education and hospitals).

Whether he is right or wrong is not at issue. What is at issue is whether people are now able to have all of the things they do want or even all of the things they should want. The answer to this question is no, and (I would insist) will always be no.

Whose task is it to create jobs then? No one's; the jobs to be done are implicit in the wants of the consumers. The only problem is to find the appropriate mechanism for bringing workers and jobs together. The title of this session should really be "What are best ways to bring workers and jobs together?"

Let us begin our answer to this by reviewing the answer traditionally given this question in America. The answer was the marketplace, and it is useful to review the model of how the marketplace is supposed to solve this problem.

Consumers, in asking for goods and services, are calling for work to be done. Sometimes these calls are answered directly, as by a cleaning woman or a hairdresser or piano teacher. But typically the calls are answered indirectly through the unit known as the firm. The entrepreneur organizes the work to be done, sending out calls of his own for laborers, from those who sweep out the plant to executive vice-presidents. Laborers, impelled by their own desires for goods and services, answer the calls, and jobs and workers are brought together automatically and without coercion.

In this model, whose task is it to see that a given worker has a job? Why his own, of course. If what he has to sell is tomatoes or books on theology (that is, the product of his labor), it is his task to find the buyers. If what he has to sell is his own labor services, it is his task to find the buyers.

But what if there are no buyers? We have already said that there must be buyers of work to be done in the general sense because there are human wants. Now there may not be buyers who want to buy the particular kind of labor a given man wants to perform or at the place where he would like to perform it or at the price he would like to receive for it. But in this model no man is assured that he can do what he would like to do, where he would like to do it and at the price he would like to receive. He is told only that there is work to be done of some kind, some place, at the price that consumers are willing to pay for having it done. He is told that it is his responsibility to make whatever adjustments in kind of work or location or price that will bring him and a job together.

Of course, each man is free to take less of one element to gain more of another—for example, he may choose to work in one given place at some sacrifice of income or of choice of type of work. The choice is his, but so is the responsibility for bringing himself and a job of some kind together.

Oh, but you say this is a very cruel business indeed. Perhaps so, but perhaps no more apparently cruel or arbitrary than most of the other choices he confronts in life—such, for example, as the choice of a wife.

Let us look for a moment at the most obvious alternative. Suppose we say that a job is to be created for each man of the kind he wants, where he wants it and at the price he would like to receive. Of course, consumers will not voluntarily pay for this, and it can be put into effect only by the use of force. Businessmen can be ordered to provide such jobs, under threat of being sent to jail. Or they can be bribed to provide them by subsidies from the government. But the subsidies must be raised by taxation, and taxation, whatever else it is, is a forced taking of money.

I am not arguing that all taxing is evil; I am simply arguing that the alternative to letting the marketplace bring jobs and workers together is that of using sheer force. This might be pleasing to the worker as a worker, but it could hardly be pleasing to him as consumer or taxpayer.

But, of course, this is only a model, isn't it? Perhaps it doesn't apply to the world we're talking about here. Certainly no marketplace in the real world works perfectly, because it is given life by human beings, and human beings are imperfect. Certainly not all workers or employers have full knowledge of what's available. Certainly it takes time for changes in skill to be made, and some men and women may never be able to make great changes in work skills. At the same time, it isn't necessary that all workers have complete knowledge or mobility. Most adjustments require only that there be some workers who have decent knowledge of the alternatives and some willingness to move in space or vocation.

I would argue that in the absence of interference American labor markets today would operate in a manner substantially like the one I presented earlier.

What then can account for the fact that we seem to be enough worried about a shortage of jobs to hold this session? I would argue that the shortage of jobs existing now and predicted for the future is closely related to various interferences in the workings of American labor markets and that most of those interferences have been introduced, or at least encouraged, by the government.

The first and most obvious kind of interference is the setting of a minimum wage by law. Given a minimum wage, some workers of low productivity or high personnel costs to a firm are going to find that they are prohibited by law from arriving at an agreement on the price of their services that would secure them employment. What kinds of workers would we expect these to be? Well, the young people just entering the work force, with no experience and with high personnel costs for handling; women, who are more expensive than men because of high turnover, high absenteeism, and so forth; members of minority races, with few developed skills and high handling costs because of the tragic prejudices of other workers; old people, with uncertain futures and high handling costs.

Is this just a model, or have I identified precisely those groups in which we now find a high level of unemployment?

The second kind of interference is the setting of minimum wages for all kinds of work, not by law, but by trade unions, which in turn have acquired their economic power under special privileges and immunities granted by government. This kind of wage-setting acts as a brake to many of the adjustments that the labor-market process would otherwise handle. For example, it makes it more difficult for displaced workers from one industry or area to find employment in other industries or areas. The increased supply of labor to an industry or area can often be absorbed only if there is some softening of the wage structure or, at least, if wages do not continue to be forced up by union action.

Moreover, we would expect aggressive trade union action to produce as a long-run effect an adverse response on employment in the industry or area involved. The real world is complex, and many causes are at work at one time, but I find it difficult to believe that there is no connection between the long history of aggressive trade union action and the current problems of unemployment in such areas as the New England textile towns and the mining regions of Appalachia.

I could go on, but time would not permit a thorough documenting of my position in any case. What I am saying is that a significant part of the apparent "shortage of jobs" in America today is a direct result of government-enacted or -encouraged interferences in the workings of the labor market.

These interferences in many cases have made it difficult for the individual to act on his own inherent responsibility for bringing himself together with a job.

The apparent helplessness of these individuals has in turn induced demands for further government action to (1) employ these unemployed workers directly, (2) train them for jobs they won't be able to get if wage rates are not permitted to reflect their availability, (3) bribe private businessmen to employ them in specific areas and (4) to take action to increase total dollar spending in the economy by government budget deficits to produce enough inflation to offset the unwarrantedly high money wage rates—which in turn will be successful only if those money-wage rates are not increased as rapidly as prices and which will bring a whole host of undesirable side effects.

In summary, I have argued that jobs do not need to be created—they inhere in the very nature of man. The only problem is to bring jobs and workers together, and this is best done through the marketplace, with each individual free to make his own decisions and responsible for finding his own particular job. I have argued that various interferences in the labor market have reduced the ability of many individual workers to find their own jobs. The proper approach, then, should be one of reducing the interferences in the labor market, rather than adding new governmental interferences to old.

The labor-market process may seem harsh, but I am convinced that it is, on balance, far less harsh and cruel than the processes that are likely to be resorted to over time if we continue to move away from the market.

Workers are not yet ordered to work in one specific place at one specific task, but this is a not unlikely climax to a policy of increasing interference with the workings of the marketplace. When all is said and done, only through the market process can consumers, employers and employees alike retain that individual freedom of choice which has long distinguished this free society of ours. The "vulgar" marketplace is still the most humane means man has yet discovered for solving the problems of who's going to do what, and where and at what price.

People, Problems, and Progress

The most important economic problem of this country right now and for the years ahead is the problem of wage rates. The reason that wage rates are a problem is that in important segments of the economy they are being determined outside the marketplace; that is, the wage rates set do not reflect the underlying reality of the supply-demand relationship.

The forces that have brought this problem into being are complex, but at least three can be clearly identified. The first is the direct intervention of the government in the setting of wages through minimum wage laws and through the Walsh-Healey and Davis-Bacon Acts. The second is the influence of labor unions operating under special legislated privileges and immunities. The third is the fact that many businessmen have deliberately chosen to set wages on some basis other than the market criterion of what they must pay to get the quality and quantity of workers desired. I shall return to each of these in turn in a moment.

First let me identify the problems that I believe to be directly related to the non-market-oriented elements in the wage structure. The first problem is that of unemployment. If tomatoes are overpriced, some tomatoes are going to be unemployed; that is, not purchased. If labor is overpriced, some workers are going to be out of work. At the risk of oversimplification, I would say that the problem of unemployment in

Remarks before the 68th Annual Congress of American Industry's Panel Session on Industrial Relations, sponsored by the National Association of Manufacturers, New York, December 6, 1963. Reprinted from NAM press release, "News from NAM."

this country today is a direct result of the continous overpricing of labor in specific areas and industries and for specific kinds and qualities of labor. In effect, you show me a depressed area, and I will show you an area with a long history of aggressive and successful trade union activity.

The second problem is that of misallocation of our available capital resources. I am prepared to argue that we have had uneconomic use of capital in many industries in the sense that the capital-labor coefficients have been brought to higher levels than would have been true had labor been priced on the basis of supply and demand. For example, had the wage rate in coal mining in the last thirty years been permitted to reflect the true supply of labor to that industry, some part of the accomplished mechanization of coal mining would not have been undertaken because it would not have been economic to do so.

We Americans are so impressed by mechanization and automation that we tend to applaud it even when it represents a gross misreading of the capital-labor ratios in the industries involved. I might add that this problem has reached absurd proportions in a number of underdeveloped countries in the world, where scarce supplies of capital are being squandered daily in mechanizing industries that would be much more truly efficient if they utilized capital-saving, labor-intensive techniques. In effect it is not necessarily wise to install an electric toothbrush in a house that has as yet no inside plumbing.

The third problem to which I have time only for a passing reference is the impact of above-market wages on the competitive position of United States firms in the world market.

The fourth problem associated with overpriced labor is a derivative of the first two. Above-market wage rates produce unemployment and an apparent continuing shortage of capital, both of which in turn produce almost irresistible pressures to inflate the money supply. To a certain extent and under appropriate, though special, circumstances, both problems can indeed be eased by inflation. If the printing presses can keep ahead of the wage demands, unemployment can be relieved and some additional money may find its way in the short run into the loanable-funds market. This approach reminds me of my father's advice when I was young and had hurt myself, which was to sit on the red-hot cookstove and then I would soon forget the cut on my finger.

The current demand for inflation through a budget deficit is an entirely predictable consequence of the overpricing of labor in recent decades. I say with some real confidence that such demands will be a regular part of the economic life of this country in the years immediately ahead of us.

Given the overpricing of labor, our choice is between chronic unemployment and chronic inflation. This might lead a few cautious people to ask if we must take the overpricing of labor as a constant factor. This question in turn brings us back to the forces that have produced the non-market determination of wage-rates. Must these forces be taken as given, or is there an alternative in each case?

The first of the forces identified earlier was that of direct government intervention in the labor market to set wage-rates. The most obvious case of this is of course in the setting of the minimum wage. However, given the importance of the government as a buyer and the wage rules governing firms selling to the government, the most significant wage-setting may come through this channel. In any case, the federal government is explicitly responsible for the overpricing of labor in many of the labor markets of the country. The alternative here is clear and obvious. Let the government get out of this kind of price-setting. Let the market, not the Congress or a bureaucratic expert, set wage-rates. This kind of government fixing of wage rates is usually presented as protection to the low-paid worker. This is patent nonsense. It causes the low-productivity, low-paid worker to lose his job or to be pushed into less-productive, lower-paid employment in the uncovered industries, particularly into subsistence agriculture. Government wage-setting is really protection for the high-wage sectors of the economy against the lower-wage sectors and is of exactly the same order as a protective tariff. If you don't believe this, just study the geography of the loudest demands for higher minimum wages in the last or in the next session of Congress.

The second of the forces is that of government-supported collusion in the labor market; that is, of trade unionism. The union has been given special privileges and immunities granted to no other group in our economy and has been permitted to use techniques of enforcing its demands that make a mockery of the laws against assault. Whatever else you might say about this, it is a clear denial of the fundamental legal principle of a free society, of equality before the law. In America today, trade union members (and to some extent farmers) are encouraged, assisted and at times forced to do precisely that for which businessmen are sent to jail; that is, to work collusively for the manipulation of market price. The blindfolded Goddess of Justice has been permitted—nay, encouraged—to peek, and she now says with the jurists of the ancient regimes, "First tell me who you are, and then I'll tell you what your rights are."

The answer here is also clear and obvious, and it does not call for laws prohibiting trade unions nor even for right-to-work laws, which after all represent another government intervention in the employment relationship. It calls only for us to eliminate the legislation of the last forty years that has given trade unions special privileges and immunities. You may think this unrealistic, but it is no more unrealistic than assuming that we can live forever with the choice only of chronic unemployment or chronic inflation.

The third force is the well-meaning businessman who consciously chooses to pay wages above the market. Admittedly there may be good reason for this at times, perhaps with the thought of attracting a better quality of workers (which of course would mean that the wages would *not* be above the market) or to attempt to forestall union organization of employees. However, there are many businessmen who are simply embarrassed or who feel guilty about paying wage-rates that are no higher than what is needed to attract the workers they want. These men are usually operating under the influence of the modern doctrine of the "social responsibility" of the businessman.

The true social responsibility of a businessman is to make money for his stockholders, period. If a businessman were sole owner of a firm and had no need or real desire for money, and wished only to serve his fellow man, he could still choose no better guide to action than that of maximizing his profits. The profit signal is the signal sent out by his fellow human beings, acting as consumers, and, in fact, if he doesn't listen to the signal, he is certain to be acting at odds with their wishes. Production for profit is production for use, and for the use of others as those others wish it to be. If you can't accept this, you simply can't accept the free market system.

The answer here is also clear and obvious. Let the businessman heed the market in the setting of wage-rates as he does in all his activities.

In summary: I have argued that the central economic problem in America today is the overpricing of the services of labor in key industries and areas. I have said that this overpricing has presented us with a choice between two evils: chronic unemployment and chronic inflation. I have argued that we can escape from this dilemma only by returning the setting of wages to the marketplace. This would involve, among other things, eliminating direct wage-fixing by government, eliminating the special privileges and immunities of trade unions and denying them the right to break the law against assault with impunity, and counteracting the influence of the doctrine of the social responsibility of the businessman.

This is as negative-sounding as any prescription you might hear these days, and I make no apologies for it. I am absolutely convinced that only by saying no to the government can the individuals in our society receive a yes to their request for freedom and plenty. Or in the words of my favorite economist of the last century, Henry David Thoreau, the famed author of *Walden Pond*, "Government never of itself furthered any enterprise, but by the alacrity with which it got out of its way."

Union Wage Hike: An Economic Yes and No

Our question for the day: Do trade unions raise wages?

Our answer for this or almost any question in economics: Yes and no.

Does this mean that we economists are equivocating fools? Not necessarily. True, there is much about economic life that we do not fully understand, but our yes-and-no answers often derive not out of ignorance but out of the nature of things.

For example, trade unions can indeed cause the wages of some workers to be higher than they would otherwise be. But in that very same process they cause the wages of other workers to be lower than they would otherwise be. The two opposite effects are not equally visible to the general public.

To make clear why this is so, let me lay out the argument that underlies the yes-and-no answer I have given to the question for today. The workers in a trade, such as the automotive industry, by use of their combined power in a union can cause their wage rates to go to a higher level than the free market would have produced.

But as with tomatoes or teacups, the higher the price, the fewer the units purchased, other things being equal. Moreover, the longer the time period, the greater will be the decline of the sales as American buyers turn to foreign-made cars or make do longer with old cars. As the inventories in the hands of the dealers and in the plants of the

Reprinted from the *Indianapolis Star*, October 26, 1980, by permission of the Rogge estate.

producers start climbing, the producers reduce output and, hence, employment.

If this condition persists, thousands of workers find themselves out of work. As they eventually turn to employment in other industries, the labor supplies in these other industries increase and the wages go down, or at least fail to rise as rapidly as they would otherwise have done.

Who have been the gainers and who the losers in this process? Those automotive workers who continue to be employed gain substantially and point to the union as their great benefactor. Those who have had to find new jobs and those who receive lower wages because of the shift of former automotive workers to their industries are the losers.

The gain to each of the gainers is substantial. However, because the workers who shift to other employments spread themselves across the entire economic landscape, the loss to any single loser is small. The distinguished economist Milton Friedman has estimated that because of trade unions something like 10 to 20 percent of the working population has had its wages raised by something like 10 to 15 percent, with the other 85 to 90 percent suffering rate reductions of something like 4 percent.

Thus the benefits of union action are there for all to see; the losses are visible only to the perceptive few. Of course, some employers in the automotive industry suffer at least short-term losses from the higher labor costs and never cease to petition the general public for relief from the competition of their lower-wage rivals in other countries. At the same time, the employers in the industries who have benefitted from the shift of workers enjoy at least temporary gains.

The consumer at large loses because workers have shifted from higher to lower productivity employments, but this too will be recognized by only the perceptive few. The consequence of all this is that unions will have gained public acclaim for having raised the wages of the deserving working man. In fact, the most probable net effect of trade unions on the real wages of American labor is to have made them lower than they would otherwise have been.

It is high time we took a look at the special privileges we have granted to trade unions. Those privileges have been well described by the late Edward Chamberlin of Harvard University:

If A is bargaining with B over the sale of his house, and if A were given the privileges of a modern labor union, he would be able (1) to conspire with all other owners of houses not to make any alternative offer to B, using violence or the threat of violence if necessary to prevent them, (2) to deprive B himself of access to any alternative offers, (3) to surround the house of B and cut off all deliveries, including food, (4) to stop all movement from B's house . . . and (5) to institute a boycott of B's business. All of these privileges, if he were capable of carrying them out, would no doubt strengthen A's position. But they would not be regarded by anyone as part of "bargaining"—unless A were a labor union.

Barriers on the Road to Employment

The *Wall Street Journal* has just released the report of a staff group that was assigned the task of explaining the high rate of unemployment among black teenagers. The essence of the report was that there seemed to exist no causes that could explain this personally tragic and socially disruptive situation.

Is there a plausible explanation for the differentially high rate of unemployment of black and other minority teenagers? I believe there is and that it can be constructed from the following case study.

Several years ago the *New York Times* carried a report on the sentencing of a man who had quite obviously violated various state and federal laws. The judge, in announcing his punishment, expressed his regret that he could do no more than levy a fine against the archfiend, when he would really prefer to have him publicly horsewhipped.

What heinous crimes against society had this man committed? In an attempt to make money in the garment trade, he had hired black and Puerto Rican children after school to make small embellishments for women's dresses. The place of employment was a loft in an old building, and the children were paid largely on the basis of output. Within two weeks or so of starting this enterprise, the owner was arrested, the loft padlocked and the children rescued from this gross exploitation. And except for the owner, everyone lived happily ever after.

Reprinted from the *Indianapolis Star*, September 28, 1980, by permission of the Rogge estate.

Or did they? I would argue that a different interpretation could be placed on the facts in this case. How had this work affected the lives of the young people involved, both immediately and over the long pull? First, for many of them it was probably the first chance they had ever acquired that sense of personal worth that comes with earning a dollar—not being given it, stealing it or winning it in a numbers game—but actually earning it as reward for their own personal effort.

Next, the employment opportunity provided the young workers with a sense of the discipline of work life, a sense so absolutely necessary to continuing progress in employment. The judge seemed to be particularly incensed by the petty rules of behavior and performance imposed on the young workers. Yet one of the continuing benefits of the work experience may have come directly from the acquired habit of obeying the rules of the work game.

Government training centers for older teenagers report that trainees who have had no early work experience, who have developed no sense of work discipline, are much more difficult to train and much less likely to hold on to such jobs as may come out of the training.

Finally, the pay for the work done, though not great by absolute standards, must have made a real contribution to the incomes of the families involved, many of which were relying on the earnings or benefit payments of a single parent, female head of the family.

Here again, the evidence is clear that the low-income families in this country have made progress by what economists call "multi-family-member participation in the labor force"—or as my immigrant father put it, "By God, in this family, everybody works."

The high level of unemployment among black teenagers is the direct result of legislation enacted by well-intentioned people. The most important legislative enactments have been those that impose minimum wages, restrict child labor and add heavy fringe costs to the employment of all workers.

The evidence on the adverse employment effects of minimum wage laws on employment opportunities for marginal workers of whatever skin color is so unambiguous as to be totally convincing to all but those who approach such questions with emotion-blinded bias.

As the Nobel Prize–winning liberal economist Paul Samuelson has put it, "What good does it do a Negro youth to know that an employer must pay him $1.60 per hour [the legislated wage at the time], if the fact that he must be paid that amount is what keeps him from getting a job?"

The obvious fact is that the great curse of today's young people is not exploitative employment but the terrible, soul-destroying idleness that has come as an unintended by-product of the well-intended actions of political society.

I offer as final evidence a question that returns to the case study from New York City. Once the great-hearted judge has saved these children from what he saw as vicious exploitation, what did those children then do after school? Did they skip home, pick up a copy of Shakespeare and listen to Beethoven? Or did they take to the streets, learn the art of the switchblade knife, the niceties of gang warfare, drug pushing and arson for fun and profit?

The road to unemployment in this country has indeed been paved with good intentions, and good intentions alone are never enough.

Racial Discrimination
and the Market Place

The relationship that I wish to examine is that between various kinds of economic arrangements and the extent and character of racial discrimination. The thesis I intend to present is that the freer and the more competitive the market, the less severe will be the discrimination, both in quantity and quality. Or to put it another way, I intend to argue that various interventions in the market place, both public and private in origin, have added significantly to the severity of the problems confronting minority races in this country.

I shall begin the argument with a statement of those things I take as given to the American society. First, I take it for granted that all responsible elements in the society sincerely desire to see an improvement in the lives of the members of the minority racial groups, which means of course, most importantly, the American Negro group. Next, I take as an initial given the existence in many elements in the society of racial prejudice, and particularly of prejudice against the Negro. Some of those who hold such prejudices believe in and practice active discrimination; for example, they prefer segregated schools, segregated employments, segregated transport facilities, segregated housing, etc. When carried to the extreme, this point of view can create a virtual police state to enforce segregation and to suppress all those who argue against it.

Reprinted from *Money, the Market, and the State: Economic Essays in Honor of James Muir Waller,* ed. Nicholas Beadles and Aubrey Drewry (Athens: University of Georgia Press, 1968), 146–56. © 1968 University of Georgia Press. Used by permission of the publisher.

Others who hold such prejudices do not believe in and practice active discrimination, except perhaps in choice of close friends and dating partners for their children. They do not oppose integration and, in fact, may support it in particular cases. Many seem honestly to wish to see the worst forms of discrimination eliminated. Yet some element of prejudice does exist and does influence the decision-making of these people.

I would estimate that at least three-fourths of all white Americans are prejudiced against Negroes in one of these two ways. I consider this prejudice, of either variety, to be both unwarranted and tragic in its consequences. But my purpose here is not to deliver myself of a polemic against racial prejudice. My purpose is to accept this prejudice as current datum and ask, as a social scientist, which social, political, and economic arrangements are most likely to reduce the extent of prejudice over the years and/or to reduce the severity of its impact on the minority groups which are the objects of the prejudice.

This is clearly to be an exercise in normative social science, yet I wish to minimize the need for my own personal values to be determining and maximize the range within which positive social science can be employed. For example, I do not wish to debate the rightness or wrongness of the various civil rights laws. For your information, and so that my biases can be known and not just guessed at, I approve of some sections of these laws and disapprove of others. Quite briefly, I believe it to be quite appropriate for the federal government to demand absolute equality before the law in its own jurisdiction *and* in all lesser jurisdictions and to strike down all discriminatory practices in the use of public property. At the same time, I believe it to be quite inappropriate for any level of government to force *either* segregation or integration in the use of *private* property. Moreover, I would define private property as including all privately owned and operated establishments except those that have been granted exclusive franchise arrangements. As you can see, this would strike against a number of particular sections of the current law.

The questions I wish to discuss, in a sense, reach beyond the impact, whatever it may be, of the current law. I know of no one, however sanguine he may be about the outcome of civil rights legislation, who argues that such legislation can quickly change the total environment in which minority groups must live or that it can alone ensure full social and economic opportunity to all. It is appropriate then to ask what else we as social scientists can contribute to an understanding of these phenomena and what practical lines of further action might be suggested by that analysis.

My own suggestion is that we examine carefully the impact of various distortions of the market process on the economic opportunities of minority groups and on the extent of racial prejudice itself. I have taken my cue here from the work of a number of men, and let me begin the analysis with a quotation from one of them. The man is W. H. Hutt, formerly Dean of the Faculty of Commerce of the University of Cape Town, South Africa, and the quotation is from his book *The Economics of the Colour Bar.* I might add as further preface that Hutt is a man absolutely without racial prejudice and a man whose freedom was often in jeopardy in South Africa because of his well-known views on the racial policies of the South African government.

In the closing chapter of his book he writes as follows:

> Throughout the description and analysis of South African developments the reader will have perceived the interaction of two sets of opposed forces, the first tending powerfully to liberate the non-white peoples of the world from inertias and coercions which would otherwise perpetuate historical inferiorities of occupation, training and status, the second tending to maintain or strengthen the coercions which hold the non-whites in economic subjection.
>
> The liberating force is released by what is variously called "the free market system," "the competitive system," "the capitalist system" or "the profit system." When we buy a product in the free market, we do not ask: What was the colour of the person who made it? Nor do we ask about the sex, race, nationality, religion or political opinions of the producer. All we are interested in is whether it is good value for money. Hence it is in the interest of business men (who must try to produce at least cost in anticipation of demand) not only to seek out and employ the least privileged classes (excluded by custom or legislation from more remunerative employments) but actually to educate them for these opportunities by investing in them. I have tried to show that in South Africa it has been to the advantage of investors as a whole that all colour bars should be broken down; and that the managements of commercial and industrial firms (when they have not been intimidated by politicians wielding the planning powers of the state)

have striven to find methods of providing more productive and better re-
munerated opportunities for the non-whites.

The subjugating force is universally exerted through what we usually
call, when writing dispassionately, the interventionist, collectivist, authoritarian or "dirigiste" system or, when writing tendentiously, by euphe-
misms like "the planned economy." Unchecked state power (or the private
use of coercive power tolerated by the state) tends deliberately or unin-
tendedly, patently or deviously, to repress minorities or politically weak
groups. Thus the effective colour bars which have denied economic opportunities and condemned non-whites to be "hewers of wood and drawers
of water" have all been created in response to demands for state intervention by most political parties (although in some of the most blatant cases,
to pressures from those who have claimed to be "syndicalists," or "Marx-
ists"). Of course, the extension of state control need not necessarily involve
discrimination on the grounds of race, color, caste or creed; yet in practice it
does seem always to discriminate against the politically weak; and by reason of history, the non-whites have (so far) usually fallen into this class.

Competition is essentially an equalitarian force. In a country of racially
homogeneous population, it tends, unless obstructed by sectionalist law
and administration or the use of private coercive power (as by labour
unions or business monopolies), to bring about the classless society. In a
multiracial society, it tends, because of the consumers' colour-blindness, to
dissolve customs and prejudices which have been restricting the ability of
the under-privileged to contribute to, and hence to share in, the common
pool of output and income.[1]

I am currently at work on a book in which I will explore this thesis
as it applies (or does not apply) to this country. Much of the research
remains to be done, and I am presenting here only a very tentative first
statement. At the same time, I have as yet found very little that would
contradict and much that would confirm the validity of Hutt's thesis
for this country's experience.

Let me deal with a few specific examples, beginning with minimum
wage laws. We would expect the employment effect of such laws to fall
most heavily on those groups who come to the labor market with low
net productivity, either because of low personal productivity or because

---

1. W. H. Hutt, *The Economics of the Colour Bar* (London: Andre Deutsch Limited, 1964),
173–75.

of high handling costs. For the moment, the question is not who is to blame for the handicap, but does it exist? It does of course exist for the young workers, who bring no developed skills and high handling costs to the labor market; for women workers, whose handicap is principally high handling costs; and for members of most racial minority groups, and particularly Negroes. Not only do they bring low productivity because of inadequate education and training (for which they may not be responsible), but they often bring high handling costs as well because of the prejudices of fellow workers (for which they again are not responsible). But responsible or not, they come to the labor market with a handicap, and they will stand under the employment effect of arbitrary wage standards as will any other marginal worker.

Here are statements from two men who have worked in this general area for some time, and this is what they report.

First, from Arnold Rose, a sociologist at Washington University in St. Louis, in his book *The Negro in America,* which is a condensed version of the report by the committee chaired by Gunnar Myrdal, the report itself entitled, of course, *An American Dilemma:*

> During the thirties the danger of being a marginal worker became increased by social legislation intended to improve labor conditions. This legislation included, among other laws, the Wages and Hours Law, the National Labor Relations Act, and the Social Security laws. The dilemma, as viewed from the Negro angle, is this: on the one hand, Negroes, much more than whites, work under imperfect safety rules, in unclean and unhealthy shops, for long hours, and for sweatshop wages; on the other hand, it has largely been the availability of such jobs that has given Negroes any employment at all.
>
> As low wages and substandard labor conditions are most prevalent in the South, this danger is mainly restricted to Negro labor in that region. When jobs are made better, employers become less eager to hire Negroes, and white workers become more eager to take the jobs from the Negroes. There is, in addition, the possibility that the policy of setting minimum standards might cause some jobs to disappear altogether or to become greatly decreased. When labor is no longer cheap, mechanization will come in and wipe out many types of jobs.[2]

2. Arnold Rose, *The Negro in America* (New York: Harper, 1948), 130–31.

As we might expect, this does not lead Rose to condemn the minimum wage laws; quite the contrary. But he never questions the fact that such laws can and usually do have an adverse effect on employment for Negroes.

A case study in the tobacco industry is reported in Northrup, *Organized Labor and the Negro*. Here is what he writes:

> The principal reason for the decline in the proportion of Negro tobacco workers since 1930 has been the introduction of machinery into the stemming department where the bulk of the Negro women are employed. Prior to 1933, the low wages of these employees discouraged mechanization. As a result of the NRA, however, the average hourly earnings of hand stemmers employed by tobacco manufacturing companies increased from 19.4 cents in March 1933 to 32.5 cents two years later. Many of the larger companies thereupon installed stemming machines, which displaced a considerable number of Negro workers. For example, at the R. J. Reynolds plant in Winston-Salem, 1,000 were reported to have lost their jobs; and local union officials claim that the former labor force of 3,500 at the Liggett & Myers stemmery in Durham has been more than halved since 1933.
>
> Unlike the employees of manufacturers' stemmeries, those employed by the independent were not covered by NRA codes. Thus, whereas the wages of the former increased by 40 per cent, those of the latter remained very low. In May 1934, the median hourly earnings of workers in independent stemmeries were 12.3 cents; of workers in cigarette companies' stemmeries, 25 cents. In September 1935, stemmery employees were still among the lowest paid in American industry, with average earnings of 16 cents per hour and $6.92 per week.
>
> Following the passage of the Fair Labor Standards Act, many of the independents mechanized their stemming operations. For example, in 1935 ten such stemmeries surveyed by the Bureau of Labor Statistics employed no machine stemmers; in 1940–41, the identical ten plants reported that 54 per cent of their employees were working on machine stemmers. Hence it was the adjustments to the NRA and the Wage and Hour law which caused a decline in the proportion of Negroes in the tobacco industry during the 1930's.[3]

3. Herbert Northrup, *Organized Labor and the Negro* (New York: Harper and Brothers, 1944), 108–9.

I don't wish to press this any further until I am in a position to present more adequate data. However, I find it difficult to believe that there is *no* relationship between minimum wage standards and the high level of unemployment among Negroes, Puerto Ricans, and Mexicans in this country. This is precisely what elementary economic analysis would lead us to expect, and I have at least found no evidence that would dispute this alleged relationship.

It might now be argued that this is no argument against minimum wage laws but rather a reason to take action to eliminate the handicaps with which the member of a minority group comes to the labor market. This may be true, but it is difficult to conceive of *any* action, however vigorous, that would quickly eliminate lifetimes of educational deficiencies and lifetimes of accumulated prejudice against racial minorities. We might well wish reality to be different than it now is (and we may well work to change it), but it is hardly sensible to proceed now as if the wished-for state of affairs were already in existence—particularly, if the principal sufferers in the short run are to be precisely those we are most anxious to help. It is cold consolation to the Negro unable to find work because of minimum wage standards to be told that in a better and different world he would be able to compete successfully with the white workers in the market place.

And unfortunately, the employment search of the better-educated, better-trained Negro is also dependent for success on an appropriate structure of wage rates and on free access to the market place. At this point, the Negro encounters a second set of institutional barriers to employment, this set associated with the trade union. The trade union acts to restrict employment opportunities for Negroes in two ways: (1) by erecting explicit or implicit racial barriers to membership in unions and hence to employment, and (2) by demanding equal pay for apparently equal work, thus preventing employers from recognizing skill differentials and the higher handling costs associated with the fact of prejudice in the white worker group.

The first effect is summarized by Alfred Marrow in his book *Changing Patterns of Prejudice* as follows:

> Unions North and South exclude Negroes, or deny them apprenticeships and Jim Crow them the lowest paid and least secure jobs. The AFL-CIO

has not appointed one Negro head of a department. The big building trades unions are still essentially lily-white, others have segregated locals. In January, 1962, New York City had *three* Negro apprentice electricians and *one* Negro apprentice plumber. Of all apprentices in the country, only 1 per cent is Negro."[4]

It is difficult to determine the amount of implicit exclusion now practiced, but let me quote from the one comprehensive survey of explicit exclusion. This report is from Northrup again, in his book *Organized Labor and the Negro.*

At least fourteen American unions specifically exclude Negroes from membership by provisions to that effect in either their constitutions or their rituals. In addition, eight unions permit Negroes to join and give them the privilege of paying dues, but limit their participation to "Jim Crow" auxiliary bodies which in one way or another prohibit them from having a voice in the affairs of the union, from negotiating their own agreements, or from having an opportunity to advance in the occupational hierarchy.

In most instances the exclusionist and discriminatory practices of these unions have been in effect for many years, and there is no doubt but that they have the support of the majority of the membership of the unions. For despite the efforts of a number of members in several of these organizations to have the anti-Negro provisions erased, only two unions, the Commercial Telegraphers and the Hotel and Restaurant Workers, both AFL, which once adopted racial restrictions, later completely removed them from their laws. Nor does it seem necessary to discuss at great length the underlying motives which bring them into being. Undoubtedly racial prejudice plays a part and particularly so on the railroads, because railroad unions came into being as fraternal and beneficial societies. To admit Negroes to their ranks on an equal footing would be, in the minds of many white members, tantamount to admitting that the colored man is a social equal, and this the majority of white railroad workers has always refused to countenance.

But it is much more important to note that nearly all the unions practicing discrimination—and railway labor organizations are no exception—are organizations of skilled craft unionists. It seems likely that economic interest, or, as Spero and Harris so well put it, "the desire to restrict

4. Alfred J. Marrow, *Changing Patterns of Prejudice* (Philadelphia: Chilton Company, 1962), 89.

competition so as to safeguard job monoply," is the major contributing factor. To exclude Negroes, these craft unionists have found, is a convenient and effective method of limiting the number of sellers of a particular type of labor or skill, and that, in turn, enables the white craftsmen to obtain a larger share of the available work for themselves and/or higher wages.[5]

It is quite true that most, if not all, unions have now eliminated exclusionist clauses and direct exclusionist practices. However, the tight trade union control of entry in many skilled trades, under which preference in entry is given to family members or friends of current members, has had the effect of barring Negroes from those trades—witness the figures on apprenticeships cited above.

It is also quite true that trade union leadership (particularly at the national level) has been outspoken and aggressive in supporting the idea of equal opportunities for Negroes. Yet even when the motive is sincere, the practice may be different, and the very nature of trade union wage policy may well work against employment opportunities for Negroes.

Let me refer again to Hutt's book and to experience in South Africa. Here is what he says:

> The "rate for the job" was the vital principle in the most powerful yet most subtle colour bar that has ever operated. Equal pay for equal work (i.e., for identical outputs of a given quality) is a result of the neutrality of the free non-discriminatory market. It is no method of achieving such a market. When the standard wage-rate is forced above the free market level (whether through legal enactment or the strike threat), thereby reducing the output which can be produced profitably, it must have the effect of preventing the entry of subordinate races or classes into the protected field or of actually excluding them from it. This has been by far the most effective method of preserving white privileges, largely because it can be represented as non-discriminatory. Whereas some of the policies of the Labour-Nationalist Pact amounted to blatant discrimination (such as the deliberate dismissal of non-Whites in order to employ Whites in government service), the effects of the "civilised labour" restraints have been far more important. They have rendered much more formidable those restraints imposed by custom and prejudice that have debarred non-Whites from avenues of economic advancement. They have, indeed, had

5. Northrup, *Organized Labor and the Negro*, 2–6.

a more unjust impact than "influx control" and "job reservation" under *apartheid*.[6]

Again the evidence is incomplete, but again I find some support for the following description of one of the dilemmas of the Negro. The typical immigrant group in America has followed a progression from common laborer to skilled laborer to higher incomes to greater social acceptance to whatever levels of economic position individual talents might permit. The Negro in a sense was in the "immigrant" position in the decades immediately following the Civil War. In that period, the Negro was a "hewer of wood and drawer of water," as were the Irish, the Germans, the Scandinavians, and later the Eastern Europeans and the Italians. However, from the 1890's on, these other groups were able to make the transition to the skilled trades, while, in general, the Negro was not. To some extent, this was caused by pure prejudice on the part of the employer or fellow employees. But also in part this was associated with the rise of craft unionism in this period in almost all of the skilled trades. The craft unions tended to be lily-white, out of a combination of prejudice and the desire to protect employment from competition. (It is interesting to note that the large industrial unions, with little chance for job control, have been much more enlightened in their approach to Negroes than the craft unions.) There is some evidence that in some skilled trades (such as barbering) Negroes actually lost ground in the period from 1900 to 1960. Even though most of the formal barriers have been removed in recent years, various trade union practices, including the dictum of equal pay for equal work, continue to operate to deny the Negro full access to the skilled trades. This in turn denies the Negro the kind of path to full social and economic participation that has been followed by most of the white minority groups in this country. In sum, whatever the words that are uttered by trade union leaders, trade unionism in practice would seem to have been an important barrier to economic progress for the Negro in America.

I could take up other types of interventionist action, but space does not permit. I shall content myself in closing by presenting a summary thesis: in general, the freer and the more competitive the markets of the

6. Hutt, *Economics of the Colour Bar,* 72–73.

country, the more economic opportunity there tends to be for members of minority races.

Milton Friedman has phrased this as follows:

> No one who buys bread knows whether the wheat from which it is made was grown by a Communist or a Republican, by a constitutionalist or a Fascist, or, for that matter, by a Negro or a white. This illustrates how an impersonal market separates economic activities from political views and protects men from being discriminated against in their economic activities for reasons that are irrelevant to their productivity—whether these reasons are associated with their views or their color.

> As this example suggests, the groups in our society that have the most at stake in the preservation and strengthening of competitive capitalism are those minority groups which can most easily become the object of the distrust and enmity of the majority—the Negroes, the Jews, the foreign-born, to mention only the most obvious.[7]

One interesting illustration again comes from Hutt and South Africa. Under South African law, whites and non-whites have quite unequal standings, and all orientals were for many years considered to be non-whites. However in the post–World War II years, South African trade with Japan has grown tremendously, involving numerous visits to South Africa by Japanese businessmen. Under the pressure of preserving a flourishing trade, the South African government has recently declared that henceforth all Japanese are whites.

I don't wish to push this thesis to absurd limits. Obviously, free markets alone are not going to bring the end of prejudice. Obviously, the Negro would have found his economic viability less than perfect even without minimum wage laws and trade unions. Obviously we are dealing with a complex problem that will admit of no single solution.

But I am prepared to say that as social scientists concerned with this problem, we should not let presupposition pass for research and analysis in evaluating the effects of social legislation on all groups in the society. If a handicap to minority groups *is* one of the predictable consequences of passing minimum wage laws and Walsh-Healey Acts and of officially encouraging trade unions (and I am not saying that I have

---

7. Milton Friedman, *Capitalism and Freedom* (Chicago: University of Chicago Press, 1962), 21.

proved this beyond any doubt), then surely this should be put into the equation of normative social science developed to evaluate such public policies.

Perhaps the world should be different than it is, but even here it might be well to remember that it was Plato who first said, "Trade is the great persuader."

The Welfare State against the Negro

The question that I wish to discuss this afternoon is precisely this: Does or does not American capitalism deserve the support of the American Negro? Or to put it another way: Has the move in recent decades away from a rather uninhibited, free-wheeling kind of capitalism toward an interventionist, welfare-state system assisted or inhibited the American Negro in his striving for economic and social progress? Has capitalism been a help or hindrance? This is the fundamental question I want to examine. I assume that I need not talk in this group of the tremendous significance of this question, but I want to point out that these are questions of analysis and fact. They are not questions of value judgment. They are questions for analysis and fact, and hence, they are appropriate questions for the social scientist and particularly the economist. And they have received increasing attention from social scientists, including economists, in recent years; as a matter of fact, these questions have been an important part of my own research for approximately eight years. This afternoon I want to give you a sampling of what I think to be the relevant evidence as it relates to this question, followed by my interpretation of that evidence.

Given the all-too-apparent fallibility of economists, I need hardly issue the caveat that of course I could be wrong. My interpretation could be wrong, but it would not be a question of intent or motive; I would

Reprinted from *The C. A. Moorman Memorial Lectures at Culver-Stockton College,* September 23, 1971, by permission of Culver-Stockton College.

simply be wrong as a professional. But, of course, the social scientist must always deal with probabilities and never with certainties.

The first problem that we confront in dealing with this question is one of choice. The government has been involved in the economy of this country now in an increasing way for a number of decades, and so we have to choose among these multitudinous interventions, deciding which ones we are going to examine to see what has been the impact of these interventions on the economic viability of the minority groups in America and particularly of the American Negro and the Negro family.

Your analysis tends to lead you in the direction of those kinds of evidence that you think would be relevant. My own work here and the work of others has led me to believe that the most important problems of the Negro family in America relate to the acquiring of income rather than to the spending of it. Now, that is not to deny that such questions, for example, as the prices paid by low-income and, particularly, ghetto families are of no importance, but the evidence available indicates that whatever problems the low-income family faces in the spending of income are minor relative to its problems in acquiring income. By the way, if you're particularly interested in this question of whether ghetto families are being exploited as buyers and as spenders, I refer you to the work of Professor Yale Brozen, of the graduate school of business at the University of Chicago, and particularly to a recent rather substantial monograph of his on ghetto economics and its implications. I think it is not yet published but is available by writing directly to him. His findings and the findings of a staff that has been working with him in the Chicago area would indicate that as a matter of fact most in-ghetto and out-ghetto prices are approximately the same, and that where in-ghetto prices or rentals are higher than out-ghetto prices or rentals, they do no more than reflect the higher cost of retail and housing operations within the ghetto. And he asks the logical question: If there are indeed great profits to be made by exploiting the residents of the ghetto through retail trade and service or through rental property, why is it that retail merchants and landlords are leaving such areas rather than flocking to them? Again this is not my topic, but if you are particularly interested, there is a substantial amount of research work going on. And I emphasize to you again, particularly to all of you young people, the importance of not simply taking intuitive impressions but of actually taking a look at the facts and what they mean.

But now we turn to the question of Negro family income. I have chosen for you seated here this afternoon, as an illustration of the kind of thing I have been doing and others have been doing, four kinds of government action that seem from the evidence to have had some real impact on the income flow to Negro families in this country. They are (1) minimum wage legislation, (2) child labor legislation, (3) attitudes and actions related to trade unions, and (4) the direct transfer of income under social security and related welfare programs. These are the four that I want to discuss with you—rather, to give you a sampling of my studies here in terms of the impact of these kinds of government action on the income possibilities of the Negro family in America.

We start first with minimum wage legislation. If we look only to the opinions of most Negro leaders and of others active in championing the cause of the Negroes in America, I think we would be led to conclude that laws setting legal wage minimum must serve the interest of the Negro family; that is, most of these people are actively involved in urging not only that we maintain such legislation but that we progressively increase the dollar figure. And in many a picket line, there will be people parroting them in demonstrations—racial demonstrations—carrying signs demanding, for example, a $2.00 an hour minimum wage. If my findings (which are not unique to me and are really a summary of the findings of many others) are correct, those who hold these views about the impact of minimum wage laws on Negro family income are not only wrong but tragically wrong.

As Professor Milton Friedman of the University of Chicago has put it, "Of all the laws on the statute books I believe the minimum wage law does the Negroes the most harm." This position is not taken only by economists of conservative persuasion. As many of you know, Professor Milton Friedman is probably the best-known economist of conservative persuasion in America today.

But let me read to you two other statements on the minimum wage law. (In a moment I want to talk to you about some of the evidence here; statements are never conclusive, because they are simply the opinions of particular people.) I've read to you the opinion of Milton Friedman, the recognized leader of conservative economic thought in

America today; let me read you a statement from a man of somewhat different basic persuasion, who says that the Wages and Hours Law— that is, the minimum wage law (this is really the Fair Labor Standards Act passed in 1938) "tends to spur mechanization by raising wages. It goes without saying that *the Negroes are, and will continue to be, the main sufferers in such a development.*" This man in his book goes on to document this by pointing out the great number of job losses that could be traced directly in the late 1930's (and from an earlier experience with minimum-wage-setting under the NRA in the mid 30's) to minimum-wage-setting. The job losses in the South were concentrated particularly among non-whites. Now who is this man? This is from Gunnar Myrdal's book *An American Dilemma,* a book that many believe to be the truly seminal work in defining and outlining the tragic race problem of this country of ours. And Gunnar Myrdal is by no means a compulsive conservative. He is, on the contrary, a lifelong socialist and economist-sociologist from Sweden, and his conclusion is precisely the same as that of Milton Friedman.

Let me read you another one. "Minimum wage rates: these often hurt those they are designed to help. What good does it do a Negro youth to know that an employer must pay him $1.60 per hour if the fact that he must be paid that amount is what keeps him from getting a job." By the way, we need not just say Negro youth there; what good does it do any young person to know that an employer must pay him $1.60 if that is the fact that keeps him from getting the job at all? Where is this statement from? From the seventh edition of *Economics* by Paul Samuelson. Paul Samuelson is the high priest of modern liberal economics and was just recognized as the first Nobel Prize winner in economics. His conclusion is again precisely the same as Milton Friedman's.

Here then we have three economists coming at it from quite different basic persuasions, all arriving at the same conclusion: that the minimum wage law, by restricting employment opportunities and causing employment opportunities to dry up altogether, hurts those it is designed to help, and that its impact on the minority race group member in this country may be particularly severe. This is the thesis that I have attempted to explore by examining not only some of my own research work but all the existing research work on this particular question that I could find in the literature, and with one exception

I do not find any significant piece of research that does not support this conclusion.

Now let me again make clear why we would expect this conclusion. In general, a minimum wage is going to restrict the employment opportunities of all those who bring into the market what is thought by employers to be lower productivity than that dollar figure. Now who are these people likely to be? The young, for example. I'll point in a moment to some of the studies that have indicated that after every single increase in the minimum wage since WW II, within six months, there has been a dramatic rise in teenage unemployment among both blacks and whites, but again with the incidence particularly severe among black teenagers. But why? Because again the minimum wage would discriminate against those who enter the labor market with any handicap, including the tragic handicap of race, but also of age—of being old or young—and of gender—being female; when you bring any kind of handicap into the labor market a minimum wage is going to reduce your employment opportunities, and the evidence establishes very clearly that this has been true in the period since WW II.

Now what kinds of evidence do we find? Well, again there have been a great many attempts at formal investigations of this, as I have said, and they all indicate precisely this. Again Yale Brozen, at the University of Chicago, has been one of the important investigators here, and Brozen, in examining this, finds that very clearly there has been a positive and demonstrable relationship between the high rates of unemployment among the unskilled, both black and white, and the minimum wages set under the Fair Labor Standards Act. For example, he undertook a very interesting kind of study. He said he expected that the minimum wage law, by reducing employment opportunities for Negro women in Southern industry, would lead to there being greater availability of such women for domestic work in Southern cities and smaller towns. So he planned to investigate what happened to the availability of domestic household workers in Southern cities within six months to a year following each increase in the minimum wage. And so he took the Department of Labor material, and what did he find? Precisely what he would have expected. That by reducing employment opportunities and manufacturing, the minimum wage squeezed more of these people back on the domestic household work market, and at lower wages by the way, significantly lower wages, than they were making before the increase in the minimum wage in manufacturing.

Another kind of study is the direct interviewing of businesspeople, of, for example, the American Federation of Business, an organization made up largely of small retail establishments, laundries, nursing homes, restaurants, etc., that were not for many years covered under the minimum wage law. The minimum wage law coverage came into these occupations, and the wage was raised (in particular in February of 1967). By mid-1967 a poll indicated that there may have been as many as 700,000 jobs lost just within these smaller business firms in America because of the imposing of the minimum wage. And what I have here is a whole list of the responses by these businessmen running small firms, one after another saying, because of the minimum wage, I have had to cut down on my employment.

At Wabash College, for example, where my colleagues are suspicious of these findings because they contradict their liberal propensities, they have direct and dramatic evidence of the impact of the minimum wage, because in February 1967 the minimum wage for the first time was applied to colleges—and within a week we had an announcement from the administration that from that time on they were abandoning all student help in the cleaning of buildings, and henceforth, buildings would be cleaned only every other week rather than every week. A notice then went to all students who had been employed by the college telling them that their jobs no longer existed. Again, in the attempt to help, what has happened is that we have denied individuals employment opportunities altogether. In a sense we seem to be saying to people in America, "Rather than see you employed at a dollar an hour, we would see you unemployed at $1.60."

Again, here's a long article in the *New York Times* in mid-winter 1967 (following the covering of farm labor under the minimum wage law). The headline in the *New York Times* says, "In the Mississippi Delta More Pay Means Less Work." They go on in the next part of the column to say that as a direct result of the minimum wage law 100,000 people in the Delta region of Mississippi may lose all income because the farmers will have no choice but to use mechanical devices for cotton-picking and weeding, and as a consequence, employment opportunities are going to virtually disappear. As a matter of fact, within six months, it was precisely in this group where there came to be evidence of virtual starvation as a result of these families losing all income and having no alternative available to them.

Here, for example, is a study of minimum wage laws in Puerto Rico. America imposed minimum wage laws on Puerto Rico. Why? Because the Puerto Rican workers were demanding it? No. Who demanded minimum wage laws for Puerto Rico? American trade unions competing with products coming from Puerto Rico and American businessmen competing with products coming from Puerto Rico. They said we must protect the Puerto Rican worker from exploitation. What they meant was we must protect ourselves from competition. Studies by Lloyd Reynolds—longtime chairman of the Department of Economics at Yale, expert in labor economics, one of the great figures in modern liberal economics in America, and a strong figure in the Kennedy administration behind the scenes—indicate that absent the minimum wage law in Puerto Rico, manufacturing employment at the end of the 1950's could well have been some 50 percent higher than it actually was— which would have meant then that many of these people could have found employment opportunities in manufacturing and industry. They could have seen their levels of living improving while staying in their homeland of Puerto Rico rather than moving to the strange social and economic environments of Gary, Indiana, New York City, Cleveland, Ohio, and so forth. Again good intentions are never enough; we must always look at what are going to be the consequences of those actions.

I indicated to you that there was one set of studies that would tend to contradict this conclusion. Those studies have been made by one agency, the Department of Labor of the United States government, which is the agency charged with administering this law.

Let me read what one professor says of these studies. "In the detailed studies and controversies, which have raged over minimum wage effect studies, a very important fact has been overlooked. The actual statistics of labor department industry studies show declines in employment following minimum wage increases though the stated conclusions of those studies are to the opposite." He concludes, "As so often happens what is hailed by the Department of Labor as a triumph of facts over theory proves on closer scrutiny to be the triumph of bold assertion over the truth." In other words, he said that the Department of Labor was simply wrong. Its own statistics did not bear out its conclusions. Now this is from Professor Tom Sowell, a distinguished teacher of economics now at the University of California at Los Angeles, the author of a new textbook that I am using. Interestingly enough, in terms of my particular topic, he is black. He is black, deeply committed to the capitalist economic process by the way, and a very interesting and very brilliant man. I urge you to get to know his work better. In other words, the only significant piece of evidence that seems to contradict these conclusions, upon investigation by people outside the agency itself, would tend to indicate that the findings are essentially contrary to the data from which they drew the findings.

My conclusion then: I think there is a very, very high probability that minimum wage setting in this country has seriously reduced the employment opportunities of low-productivity workers and of workers who enter the labor market with a handicap. For the non-whites in the American labor force, government-imposed minimum wages seem to have been an almost unmixed tragedy.

Now I want to relate this conclusion to my next topic: child labor legislation. I realize we're touching on grounds where many of you have strong emotional reactions. Why is it particularly a handicap for the young person (whether black or white) not to be able to find employment? It is not simply that he or she loses the income; it is that he or she loses the opportunity for acquiring work skills, for acquiring a sense of work discipline, for getting ready for full entry into the labor force. This is why it is not simply the loss of income (although for many a student in this room, your summer employment opportunities would have been significantly improved had there not been a minimum wage law). What particularly hurts for those on down the line, for the teenagers who are denied employment opportunities by the price set upon their services above their productivity, is that it denies them this chance to get into the labor force. And precisely the same thing is brought on, I think the evidence indicates, by the excessive zeal with which we have passed and enforced child labor legislation in America.

I realize that many of you are immediately shocked. Am I saying that child labor legislation hurts the poor? I think precisely so, at least the way in which it has been interpreted in America. As a matter of fact, I am also convinced that most people in America really believe in child labor. Most of the parents of the young people in this room believe in child labor, don't they? Didn't they when you were around home? In Crawfordsville some of my college faculty colleagues (because I have been there many years) come to me and ask for help in finding employment for their children during the summer. Now these are the same people who are very much in favor of strong anti–child labor legislation, but who then come to me and say, "Rogge, can you help me get my boy a job this summer?" I say, "Well, how old is he?" They say, "Well, he's almost 14 now." I say, "I thought you didn't believe in child labor." He says, "Oh, it will do him good." And of course it will. I say, "Well look, it will have to be in an area not covered by the minimum wage." He says, "I don't care what he gets paid. I know he isn't worth much." And if he can't get that young person a job that way, what does he do? He gets him up at 5:15 in the morning, puts him on a bicycle with 70 pounds of newspapers, and sends him out on icy roads to deliver newspapers for a net income of around 38 cents an hour and considers the family fortunate because the young person is acquiring an understanding of the worth of money.

I have here a statement by a man on this topic, again one you would not expect to be on this side of the fence. This man is saying that he delivered milk at the ages of 12 and 13, pumped gasoline in a garage at 14, and worked with a road construction crew at the age of 16, and that today all of these operations would be against the child labor laws, and that the nation has far too many such laws coddling children and denying them employment opportunities. And who is the author of this statement? Abraham Ribicoff, former Secretary of Health, Education, and Welfare in Democratic administrations, and one of the leading liberals in America. Interestingly enough, a number of states have begun to modify their legislation; Kentucky last year modified legislation dealing with child labor. At whose urging? At the urging of the social welfare workers in Kentucky who said it is handicapping our families, the ones with whom we are working, in getting an income supplement from their children's earnings. And they said we ask you, we beg you, to make it easier for these young people to work.

There is a story that tells much of this from an article I saw in the *New York Times* a year or two ago. The article was reporting a trial in which the judge was saying to the criminal, "I regret that I can only fine you. I would like to have you publicly horse whipped."

Now what was this man's crime? He was a member of a minority race who had never been very successful, but he saw a chance, if he could get some very low cost labor, to make a little item for women's dresses. And so he hired Puerto Rican children to work after school in an old loft where they made this little gimmick, whatever it was. And he paid them 35, 50, 70 cents an hour, depending on how much they produced. But, of course, within two weeks about fifteen agencies of government came down on him, and he was up in front of the court. Now, my question is this, what do you suppose these Puerto Rican children are doing now that they have been saved from this vicious exploitation? Do they now go home after school and sit down and read Shakespeare while listening to Beethoven? They go back on the streets of New York, and they learn the art of the switchblade knife and the art of the Molotov cocktail.

So, many times in our desire to be helpful, we have prevented people from doing precisely those things that have been the traditional way in which people have risen up out of poverty. For many people, and particularly for non-whites, if they do get on these first rungs of the ladder, they have difficulty going further. Why can't they move? Why are our Negroes so grossly underrepresented in the skilled trades of America, particularly, for example, in the construction trades? There used to be—there is still—a thesis going around, that that's in part because the Negroes can't do that kind of work, or they don't want to do that kind of work, or what have you. Nuts! One way to test this would be to find out if Negroes at any time in the past played an important role in the skilled trades in America. What I did was go back to the post–Civil War period. And I found a number of studies that had been made on this, in this period. And the facts are these. Who do you suppose did the skilled labor on the plantation? The white masters? Don't be ridiculous. There are reports that Negroes were doing all the skilled labor. For example, here's a report: "Among the slaves are found: tailors, shoe makers, carpenters, smiths, turners, wheelwrights, weavers, tanners, and on, and on, down the line." And these were people brought directly over from the jungle, many of them.

Now who do you suppose was doing the skilled labor, particularly in the South, in the 1860's, 1870's, and 1880's? The Negro. Negroes were well established in every single skilled trade in the South in that period of time, including the railroads. Almost every fireman on a Southern railroad in the 1870's was Negro. What happened; what happened? Well, a young sociology professor at a university in Atlanta went out and made some studies, and here's the kind of thing he reported. For example, what happened on the levees where the Negroes had been doing the skilled work? "The effective organization of white laborers was closely followed by the driving of Negroes from the levees at the muzzles of loaded rifles." Now what reactionary professor made that kind of finding? His name: W. E. B. DuBois.

In the late 1880's and the 1890's, when with favorable government treatment, all up and down the line in most cases, trade unionism really took over the skilled trades of America, particularly the construction trades and the railroads, the Negro was driven out of skilled employments where he had gotten himself firmly established. And as Herbert Hill, the labor secretary of the NAACP, says, "Labor unions frequently were the instrument that forced Negro workers out of the jobs that they had held for many years by replacing them with white workers after union organization." And he goes on to say, "The harsh discriminatory racial practices of the A. F. of L. affiliated unions and the railroad brotherhoods were decisive factors in developing the pattern of Negro job limitation that was to continue for many generations."

I'm not trying to say this is the total explanation, but there is good evidence that employers were perfectly willing to use them; they were well-established everywhere, but with the coming of trade unionism and the special privileges that we granted it, the Negro was effectively denied participation in the skilled trades in America. And think what a difference it could have made in their lives, and in your life and mine now, had the Negro been permitted to play the role in the skilled trades that he was playing in the 1870's and 1880's. Because once you get on that level, you have the platform from which you can go on. In most of your families, the one who first came over from the old country probably didn't go to work as the president of a bank. The Irish came over here and were beasts of burden in building the Union Pacific Railroad, or what have you. But then they went on to the skilled trades, and from that they got a foundation on which they could build a secure family and move up out of poverty. The Negroes have been effectively denied that, and one of the important barriers throughout this whole period of time has been, and still is, the trade union. And by the way, this has had a tragic double or triple set of consequences.

Why is it so difficult to get decent low-income housing in the typical American city? In part because of the fantastic construction cost and the fantastic delays—all kinds of featherbedding, all kinds of rules passed by local councils on zoning and on housing requirements that make this housing far more expensive than it need be. And so these people who are denied access to these unions then have to turn around and pay the price for it in less-adequate housing than they would otherwise have.

Many of these unions are under strong pressure now to change, but it's very difficult to bring the change about even though the top leadership of American unions is, in the main, I think, very responsive to this situation and anxious to do something about it. But often they say, "Well, they can't pass our tests." I want to read you a little of a test that was constructed by a plumbers' union. You may have seen it in *Fortune Magazine* a year ago. Here is a test, an apprenticeship test being used by a plumbers' union: "Aztec is to Mexico as Maya is to Peru, Guatemala, Haiti, or Uruguay. Blank is to phlegmatic as vivacious is to blank. Fill in from husky, rheumatic, pneumatic, sluggish, elusive, pouting, exuberant, and gripping. Blank is to composer as Longfellow is to blank. Fill in from Dali, Van Gogh, Riley, Haydn, musician, poet, entertainer." You know, George Meany, the president of the AFL-CIO, holds a plumber's license, and if he had to pass this test right now, he'd be out of the labor movement. But the unions say, "Well these people can't pass our tests." Or they say, "Well look, anybody can get into this union, all you have to do is have a relative who is in the union." That's kind of difficult for Negroes.

The situation in 1971 is not significantly better than it was in 1890. And the answer to this is not to pass more laws, but to reduce the special privileges that we have given trade unions, including essentially the privilege of engaging in violence. As the president of the University of Illinois said recently, "How can we deny our students the right to use violence in what they believe to be good causes when by our example in the nation at large we have permitted trade union members to use violence in serving their cause?" And he referred specifically to the cutting of telephone cables in the recent Bell strike in Illinois. Well, that's another two or three chapters on the trade union, and I'll tell you, it's a pretty frightening story. Here are some recent clippings which tend to show that it's still going on: "The United Steel Workers Discriminating," "The United Automobile Workers Resurgent Racism," "N.A.A.C.P. Official Sees Building Job Threats," and so on. Well, that's what you get all down the line.

A quick comment on another kind of government program or government action that has hurt the poor: urban renewal. Here is a statement on urban renewal from the *Chicago Defender,* which is a Negro paper in Chicago: "Nothing has been more difficult to contend with than the newest strategy of racial discrimination—the device called urban renewal." Who gets kicked out when they go into your city or mine and decide to engage in urban renewal? Do you? Do the Rogges? No. In the city it's the poor, and in the last ten years or so, two-thirds of those removed by urban renewal projects have been non-whites.

And where do they go? If you listen to the government you get the impression that they all go to at-least-as-good housing. Well, a man by the name of Martin Anderson, formerly a professor of finance at Columbia University, has written a book called *The Federal Bulldozer,* and if you haven't read it, read it. He points out that if you go back and study the statistics, you find that that just ain't true. In most cases, these people end up in worse housing and under more-crowded conditions than they started out in. There are some good studies of what happened in Cleveland on exactly this. For example, of the 4,487 families who lived in these apartments and duplexes that were torn down, only 114 found their way into public housing. The goverment keeps saying, "Well, they go out of here, but then they get into public housing." But how many go back into the urban renewal area? Last year the average rental of new apartments opened in urban renewal areas was something like $235 a month. How many of the Negroes who were forced out, how many of the little people who had little shops in there were able to reestablish? Good intentions are not enough. You and I may like urban renewal because they tear down old, unsightly areas, and it doesn't offend our sensibilities anymore to have to drive through those areas. But what about the people who get moved, these poor in whom we are so interested?

Let me close here by reading to you what seems to me to more or less summarize the Rogge thesis, that so often the government ends up doing more harm than good. I don't mean that this is because government people are inefficient, corrupt, ruthless, or anything else. I'm just saying that by the very nature of their action, most of the time, they end up doing more harm than good. Here's a statement from a book by a remarkable woman who is not a conservative by any means. She's a bohemian from Greenwich Village by the name of Jane Jacobs. She's written a book called *The Death and Life of Great American Cities*. And she starts like this,

> There is a wistful myth that if only we had enough money to spend—the figure is usually put at a hundred billion dollars [it's now a trillion]—we could wipe out all of our slums in ten years, reverse decay in the great, dull gray belts that were yesterday's and the day-before-yesterday's suburbs, anchor the wandering middle class and its wandering tax money, and perhaps even solve the traffic problem.
>
> But look what we have built with the first several billions: Low-income projects that become worse centers of delinquency, vandalism and general social hopelessness than the slums they were supposed to replace.

Right or wrong? Right,

> worse . . . than the slums they were supposed to replace. Middle-income housing projects which are truly marvels of dullness and regimentation . . . Luxury housing projects that mitigate their inanity . . . with a vapid vulgarity. Cultural centers that are unable to support a good bookstore

and on and on and on. And she says, "This is not the rebuilding of cities. This is the sacking of cities."

She goes on to talk about a visit she made to a section of Boston called the North End, which apparently was one of the early slum areas in Boston. But without any government aid whatsoever, as the people got more money, they de-slumed it. She tells about a trip she took through the North End in 1959, the first time she had been there in thirty years or more. She was amazed by the wonderful vitality and buoyancy of life in this old city district, where nothing had been done by government standards. It was just amazing what had been done and that the people had been doing this themselves. So she went into a bar and called a Boston city-planner that she knew. And he said, "Why in the world are you down in the North End?" And she asked him, "Well, have you spent any money down here?" And he said,

"Money? Why, no money or work has gone into the North End. Nothing's going on down there. Eventually yes, but not yet. That's a slum!" She said, "It doesn't look like a slum to me." He said, "Why, that's the worst slum in the city. It has two hundred and seventy-five dwelling units to the net acre! I hate to admit we have anything like that in Boston, but it's a fact." She said, "Do you have any other figures on it?" He said, "Yes, funny thing. It has among the lowest delinquency, disease, and infant mortality rates in the city. It also has the lowest ratio of rent to income in the city. Boy, are those people getting bargains. . . . The death rate is low, 8.8 per thousand, against the average city rate of 11.2. The TB rate is very low, less than 1 per ten thousand, can't understand it, it's lower even than Brookline's [the fancy suburb]. Of course, they must be strong people. Well it's a terrible slum." She said, "You should have more slums like this. Don't tell me there are plans to wipe this out, you ought to be down here learning as much as you can from it." "I know how you feel," he said. "I often go down there myself just to walk around the streets and feel that wonderful, cheerful street life. . . . But of course we have to rebuild eventually. We've got to get those people off the streets."

This is the kind of thing we are facing in America today. All of us, in our well-intentioned way, are going to save all the others from their own situations. And Rogge's thesis is that most of the time we end up making their lives not nobler, not more dignified, but more hopeless and less bearable, and that this is part of the sickness of the modern American society: Not that government has done too little, but that it has done far too much.   .

Motivation and the Cost Squeeze

Ladies and Gentlemen—I know why you are here; I do not know why I am here. This topic and I are not a good match. I am not engaged in motivation research; I am not even motivated to engage in motivation research. I do not know what is now being done in your stores, factories and mills. I'm not even certain that I know what is being done at Wabash College. I am innocent of any special knowledge, training or experience.

If you seek that magnificent objectivity which comes only from ignorance, that I can bring you. If you seek the arrogance, the oversimplification, the easy solution of the unread and the uninformed, that I can bring you. If you wish to be assured again that the ivory-tower professor is a babe in the woods of the real world, you've come to the right meeting.

You might be tempted to ask now, "Why then did you accept the assignment?" To begin with, I accepted because I am fascinated by the sound of my own voice in a large meeting room. But I accepted as well because I thought that in spite of my ignorance of detail I might have something to say that you would find useful. That something does not relate to the details of technique and of program; it relates rather to a suggested frame of reference to use in discussing motivation and motivation problems. To anticipate, the central thesis of my comments is to be that the motivation techniques employed by American business

Speech given in Minneapolis, Minn., April 17, 1958. Reprinted by permission of the Rogge estate.

firms should be consistent with the continued vitality of the American private enterprise system.

I would like to begin by examining the significance of the fact that we are here at all to discuss this particular topic. First let's take the words "the cost squeeze." To put it bluntly, would it not seem that to a well-managed firm, there is always a cost squeeze? Isn't the well-managed firm constantly seeking ways of cutting costs? Why should one set of external circumstances or one period of time be different from any other? Can it be that the firms you represent are just now suddenly aware of costs and of the need to reduce them?

Well, of course, it could be. Even that best-managed of all colleges, Wabash College, has just launched a cut-the-costs campaign. When the management consultant firm that is working with us on this project reaches the dean's office, I'll be available for speeches of this kind whenever you want me. As that famous Scottish psychologist Adam Smith said, "It is the interest of every man to live as much at his ease as he can." But that same man, as an economist, also said that this ease would not be possible in a regime of competitive economic freedom.

From the fact that we seem to have been taking our ease it would seem to follow that we are not living in a regime of competitive economic freedom. In other words, the very fact that we are here would seem to be an open admission that the firms we represent are not under continuous competitive pressure. For if they were, the cost squeeze would be an everyday fact of life rather than a topic for a special conference.

I want to return to this topic in a minute, but first I'd like to suggest another possible reason for the relative lack of cost-consciousness in American industry in the post-war period. In general this has been a period of inflation, and certain traditional accounting practices tend to give all business firms a sense of well-being in an inflationary environment. I am referring particularly to the practice of computing each year's depreciation charges on the basis of historical rather than current costs. The resulting overstatement of profits (and of the net national product of the country as well) gives to business management a general feeling of well-being and sets the stage for an almost panicky reaction, not just to a downturn in prices but even to a failure of prices to continue to rise. We have at last had the good sense to use LIFO for inventory valuation, but most depreciation accounting is still based on the delusion that a dollar is a dollar is a dollar.

I don't want to get sidetracked on this topic, but I do want to present this as one explanation of the relative lack of cost-consciousness in American firms in the post-war period. Realistic accounting would have shaken many a management out of its life of ease.

But now let's return to the subject of market structure, this time in relation to the word "motivation" in the conference topic. In the really free labor markets of the textbooks in economics, such as the one by Van Sickle and Rogge, motivation isn't much of a problem. Each worker knows that he is dispensable and that his continuing in the job and his chances for higher wages depend upon his individual productivity. At the same time, the freedom of workers to move from one job to another forces each employer to pay those wages and create those elements in the work situation that will permit him to keep his workforce. From top management on down, motivation is built into the free labor market process itself. Fear of loss of the job (or position) and hope for advancement keep everyone humping each hour of the work day. Competition for labor and competitive pressures from the product side force each employer to keep the work environment in a productivity-inducing posture. In sum, the principal instrument for moving men to action is the economic pressure of the marketplace.

I realize that the reaction of the modern industrial psychologist to the description I have just presented is that he doesn't know whether to laugh or cry—laugh at it for the absurd fairy tale that it is (in his opinion), or cry at the brutality of the process, at its treatment of the labor of a human being as a commodity. Nor am I unaware of the motivation research that has tended to cast doubt on the efficacy of market pressures in inducing the motivation required for performance in modern industry. Even though I am an economist by training, even I have heard that man is a complex organism, that a group of men is also a complete organism and that motivation is itself a complex phenomenon. I hope that I have some awareness of the dangers of oversimplification, of relying on simple answers to many-faceted questions.

Yet I cannot escape the conclusion that the motivation problem *is* less serious in a truly free labor market situation. I am convinced that direct economic pressure, while it may not alone produce the desired level of motivation, is a very potent force, and indeed that any motivation system constructed without it is almost certain to fail. I am also convinced that the fact that we are discussing this topic testifies to the extent to which both labor and management in this country have rejected the free labor market. To make my point by exaggeration, we are moving away from the society of contract in the employment relationship and toward a society of status, of a form of industrial feudalism in which both employers and employees are substantially sheltered from the cold blasts of the open labor market. The relationship between the two is not unlike that of marriage partners, tied to each other by bonds that are not easily or peacefully broken. In a society of status, as in marriage, problems of human relations are terribly important, and motivation is a great and obsessing challenge.

I find support for my thesis that problems of human relations and of motivation increase as the force of labor market pressures diminishes in explicit or implicit form in almost every book on industrial psychology that I examine. For example, Mason Haire, of California, in his book *Psychology in Management,* writes as follows:

> The internal organization of our industrial plants has changed, too, and these changes put increased pressure on our human-relations techniques. When a given man is hired, now, it is much less likely than formerly that he will be let go for having failed to work out well on the job. Formal labor-management relations and contractual obligations make it harder and harder to eliminate individuals from the work force for any reason other than a general reduction in personnel. This is not to suggest that these changes are not beneficial in a general social sense. In many cases they have forced the revision of personnel policies that were arbitrary and whimsical. However, they have added problems to our relationships.
>
> At the simplest level, it means that people are going to be around longer on any given job, and with a continuing relationship, the nature of the relation and its fruitfulness become more important. Two other very important things come from this development of more certain tenure, however, which will have to be developed in more detail later. In the first place, it means that management must count more on utilizing the skills and abilities that are present in or can be developed in the present work force. It is less and less possible to rely on replacement to improve the quality of the work group. This means an additional emphasis on training and leadership in the development of people on the job, and this in turn puts more weight

on the problems of the relationships among people. Still more pressure is put on the problem of the relationships by the fact that as a worker begins to feel secure in his job and sure of his continued pay, other things—his feelings about his superiors, about his fellow workers, and about himself and his job—become more important to him. All these things combine to force us to pay more attention to our human-relations techniques, and to ask ourselves searchingly whether we are developing the requisite skills fast enough to keep pace with the developing problems.

You will note that Haire, like most industrial psychologists, is quite willing—nay anxious—to live with this turn of events. In the writings of some of his colleagues, I find such statements as these: "Except in very general ways the law of supply and demand no longer applies to labor" (Norman Maier, *Psychology in Industry* [1955], 6). "In general, management as well as labor is becoming less and less dependent on the so-called 'law' of supply and demand as a basic factor in determining wage rates" (Joseph Tiffin, *Industrial Psychology* [1952], 362).

And so it goes. As Kenneth Boulding, the Michigan economist, has said, everywhere he turns he finds labor economists and industrial relations specialists jumping up and down on the corpse of supply and demand and proclaiming, "The labor market is dead; long live human relations!"

Among my conservative friends it is popular to say that the labor market (in fact the free market generally) has been killed by the wicked trade unions and their allies, the fuzzy-headed denizens of the intellectual world. I have even heard this point of view expressed by the president of a company in my hometown, which at that very moment had a non-vested pension plan for its employees and was participating in a quiet and occasionally effective non-pirating agreement among the firms in the town. The fact is that American business firms, while insisting that their workers should confront the labor market in all its fury, have themselves liked the cozy security of a workforce isolated from that same labor market. The employer who speaks of "my men," who wages vigorous and continuing loyalty campaigns, who does everything he can to tie his workers to the company, should not be surprised if his workers insist that in return for becoming the property of the company they at least be given the job security of the medieval serf. I do not mean by this to say that rejection of the labor market is an exclusive invention of employers or that trade unions have done nothing to restrain the workings of that market. On the contrary, while they insist that employers should compete vigorously for labor, they have usually demanded a series of protections for the individual worker against that same labor market. Rigid seniority systems, closed shops, guaranteed annual wages, restrictive work rules—all these and many more devices attest to the pressure of unions for greater job security, for property rights in the job. Given these demands, the unions should not be too surprised if the employers ask as a quid pro quo that they acquire property rights in the workers.

Nor would I excuse the intellectuals of all responsibility. There has been a tendency for many of them to look with horror on the competitive struggle of the marketplace and on the conflict of employer and employee over division of the product, to imagine that the "right" system of industrial relations can be developed which will generate in each firm such a feeling of togetherness that hand in hand employer and employee will march joyously into the New Jerusalem.

Now I am not really completely out of sympathy with the goals which each of these groups seeks to attain. Personal experience alone convinces me that it is not unnatural to wish oneself to be protected from the marketplace while all others are fully exposed to it. Nor can anyone completely reject the dream of a world free from conflict.

But I am nonetheless convinced that neither employer nor employee nor intellectual will like what he will get if we continue to move away from the labor market. If the employer does succeed in insulating his own workers from the temptations of the marketplace, he will find that he must then take care of them through thick or thin, that the guaranteed *annual* wage will have to give way to the guaranteed *lifetime* wage. He will also find that his motivation problems have assumed staggering proportions. Good human relations or lousy human relations, the worker you can neither fire nor promote on the basis of performance is going to be a hard worker to stir into action.

But the worker too will find his security a very mixed blessing. To discover too late that he has a made an unwise first decision and yet to be condemned by the weight of seniority and other considerations to that job is likely to be a frustrating experience. The old freedom to pick up and move will be gone, because of course to move would be to threaten another man's job and hence his property. Even the union that administers this job security system will find it a mixed blessing. The workers will now turn their ambitions to control the controller, and the fights for power within the unions will be bitter and bloody. Moreover, the amount of power exercised by the leadership over the economic process will be so tempting that cases of corruption and racketeering will be commonplace. These circumstances may in turn engender such a great amount of public ill will that the unions will find themselves more and more under the control and guidance of government.

Even the intellectual will be disappointed to find that competition and conflict can go on outside the marketplace. In fact the non-market conflict is likely to be more personal and hence more degrading than the old market-channeled conflict.

In sum, neither the employer nor the employee nor the intellectual is likely to approve of what he will get if he gets what he now seems to want.

You are probably restive by now at this recital of things to come and ready to insist that things certainly aren't that bad yet. And of course you're right. Things are far from being that bad at this moment. The labor market is not dead, and universal security has not been established. But it is also true that we are meeting here today to discuss motivation, and we would probably not be giving it the amount and kind of attention we will be giving it if there had not been a progressive weakening of labor market power in recent decades.

But equally disturbing is the trend I note both in the writings of the experts and in the practices of companies and unions toward solving the motivation problem by techniques that move us even further from the truly free labor market. Specifically, a very popular approach is to say that if we first give each other security and firm status, we can then work together and find ways of expanding output, cutting costs, and the like. In other words, the answer is being sought in moving even further from the free labor market rather than toward it. Moreover, the kind of security that is being granted can be granted only by firms that are themselves sheltered from drastic changes in the product markets. Thus, movement away from the free labor market seems to induce and demand movement away from the free product market. If this be true, the implications for the survival chances of a vigorous, competitive enterprise system are obvious.

What does all this signify for the discussions in which we will be involved in the next few days. Well, perhaps I've been wrong from start to finish and it signifies nothing. A man with a wife and a teenage daughter is certainly aware of the fact that he is not infallible. But if I have been even partly right, it would seem to signify that as we discuss motivation techniques and programs, we would do well to ask as one of our questions whether the technique or program under study will move us away from or toward the free labor market, whether it is of such a nature as to be consistent with the long-run survival of the free enterprise system.

Of course we do not now have that perfect system of the economics textbooks. Our competitive enterprise system is not fully competitive and probably never can be. Our labor markets are not completely and ideally free and probably never can be. Even if market pressures were alone sufficient to provide adequate motivation for one and all (which is quite unlikely), those pressures can never be mounted fully and universally. There will always be need for supplementary pressures for efficiency and high productivity. In other words, there will always be room for the human relations expert, the industrial relations officer and, yes, the trade union in our industrial society. But as we recognize this, let us also recognize that if we rely too heavily and too exclusively on these agencies, and if in our search for an answer to the motivation problem we move even further away from the free market, we can do our system of economic organization irreparable harm.

In closing, I would like to answer one question that many of you must be asking. To wit, if he's so smart why doesn't he propose a system of supplementary motivation that will work and that will be consistent with the free market system? If I were really smart, I would avoid answering that question at any cost. But I'll stick my neck out halfway by suggesting a scheme developed by someone else. I have been much intrigued by the ideas on this subject of Norman Martin, a professor at the School of Business at the University of Chicago, and Bennett Kline, Director of Management Training and Development for Inland Steel Company. These two have collaborated on a paper that will appear in the May-June issue of the *Harvard Business Review*. I have read the paper, and I have heard them discuss their ideas on several occasions. Each man has had long personal experience with the motivation and other problems of modern industry. I am certain that their judgment of what will work, while not infallible, is much better than my own and that you too will be in a better position to judge than I.

But what intrigues me about their approach is that not only is it consistent with the free market but, in fact, if it were accepted, it would enhance the general public acceptance of the free market system.

They begin with this idea: "It appears to many millions of Americans that, while they live in a free society, earning and using their incomes in a free economic system, they spend most of their working hours in authoritarian institutions playing the role of the managed. The employing institutions do not match the market system in their use of freedom."

In other words, the worker is told that he is fortunate because he is a free man in a free society, yet every day when he reports to work he is told what to do and where and when and how to do it. This they believe has contributed substantially to a less-than-thoroughly enthusiastic public endorsement of the so-called free private enterprise system.

But more than that; the primary effect of the authoritarian structure of the typical business firm is to institutionalize ignorance. As Kline and Martin put it,

> The chief characteristic of the command hierarchy, or any group in our society, is not knowledge but ignorance. Consider that any one person can know only a fraction of what is going on around him. Much of what that person knows or believes will be false rather than true. And many of the directions he gives to those beneath him will be misunderstood. At any given time, vastly more is not known than is known, both by one person in a chain of command, and by all of those in the organization.
>
> It seems possible then, that in organizing ourselves into a hierarchy of authority for the purpose of increasing efficiency, we may really be institutionalizing ignorance. While making better use of what the few know, we are making sure that the great majority are prevented from exploring the dark areas beyond our knowledge. While we progress, our increasing knowledge is more than matched by the emergence of new areas of ignorance, and the trappings of status are substituted for the dignity which naturally crowns achievement. At least, that is how it seems to millions down the line.

It follows then that we may have a double dilemma. Our system stresses freedom; our employing institutions stress authority, direction and control. Our progress depends on expanding knowledge and increasing the "accidents" of discovery and invention; our institutions foster the maximum use of existing knowledge, deliberately organizing to inhibit creativity and innovation.

They proceed from this to a recommendation that business managements think and act in terms of the principle of granting freedom rather than of delegating authority. My first reaction to this was that I had heard it all before, that we had had participative management and decentralization and invented pyramids and industrial democracy and so on and so on. But as I read further, and as I talked to these two men, I became convinced that what they are proposing is a much more thoroughgoing revamping of the philosophy of management than any of the others.

Moreover, I became convinced by the sheer strength of their own belief that it could be made to work. On these questions, I will not presume to speak for them; if you are interested, I suggest that you read the article when it appears. I have given you this tantalizingly brief review of this idea, not to try to convince you that it is clearly and undeniably the answer. Rather, I have presented this idea to show that there are men who are professionally trained and well-versed in the actual workings of modern industry who do believe that motivation techniques can be found that reinforce rather than reject the labor market and the free market system.

If such techniques can be created and if we are interested in preserving that system, then I believe that we have a duty both at this conference and elsewhere to attach some importance to the question of whether any given proposal is or is not consistent with the operation of a free market system. If we fail to ask this question, then I personally would join with Archy the Cockroach in saying that there seems to be more reason to be optimistic about the past than about the future.

Of Turnips and Energy Scarcity

Is the energy shortage real? The answer to this question is yes and no. Yes, it is very real to the householder who has difficulty getting attached to the local supply of natural gas for heating his home. Yes, it is very real to the electric utility that is required to convert from gas or oil to coal. And yes, it is real to all of us who are now paying higher real costs for the energy we use today than we did a few years ago.

But from a more fundamental point of view, these "shortages" are quite unreal, in the sense they are not the inevitable consequence of nature's niggardliness in supplying us with resources. Nor are they a reflection of an inherent weakness in the capitalist way of going about such things as energy provision.

On the contrary. The energy-supply problems we now confront are the predictable consequence of unwise public policy, of policy decisions made in courts, in legislative halls and in administrative agencies over the course of the last fifty years.

The essence of these mistaken policies has now been given concrete substance in the Department of Energy. The way in which agencies of this kind work is such that were we to create a Department of Turnips today, we would soon be facing a shortage of turnips, requiring that we stand in line to buy or that we acquire a certificate of necessity or social importance from the Department of Turnips to qualify for our share of this scarce resource.

Reprinted from the *Indianapolis Star*, September 21, 1980, by permission of the Rogge estate.

What should the government have done in the past to assure us of ample supplies of energy at decreasing real costs? What should it be doing now? The answer is to be found in the words of that famous citizen of Concord, Mass., Henry David Thoreau, writing well over a hundred years ago, "Government never of itself furthered any enterprise, but by the alacrity with which it got out of its way."

In other words, the best way for the government of our country to assure all of us of ample supplies of low-cost energy would be, for today as in the past, to get out of the way of those who stand ready to apply their creativity and their capital to the task in the hope of profit.

Would such a policy mean that the government should stop being concerned with such problems as air and stream pollution from energy-provision sources? Not at all. The government should keep me from throwing my garbage in your backyard, whether that garbage comes from my kitchen table, my coal-fired furnace or my nuclear reactor.

A "hands-off" policy for government in energy provision means only that in administering the law of trespass it should be neutral among energy sources. In other words, it would not relax or stiffen its treatment of one energy source as opposed to another to further some bureaucrat's idea of the proper energy source.

For example, the Price-Anderson Act, under which the government subsidizes some part of the insurance cost of firms using nuclear methods of energy provision, is a non-neutral position. Let the would-be users of any energy source pay the full costs of provision; only in such a way can the market process yield efficient results.

But how can we be certain that the market process will work alone and unaided by government? Will our new energy supplies come to us as manna from heaven? I haven't the faintest idea, nor does anyone else in the world, not even the well-meaning people who staff the Department of Energy.

The very necessity for letting the market process work arises out of the essential human ignorance of the outcome of the trial-and-error process through which the efficient solutions to all such problems emerge. We do not know, nor can we ever know enough to determine collectively what will prove to be the best energy sources nor who will bring them into being.

Can a Thomas Edison be identified in advance? Hardly. A Department of Energy in his day would not have been likely to place its bets (with the taxpayers' money) on a man whose entire formal education consisted of three months in the elementary schools of Port Huron, Mich.

But men such as Edison, permitted to give free rein to their creative powers, bearing the costs of their failures and allowed to keep the fruits of their successes, solved one problem after another in ways that no one man or group of men could possibly have foreseen. Were we to create these same conditions today, the so-called energy problem would soon be a thing of the past, and our friends in the oil-producing nations would be up to their burnooses in oil.

Yes, America, There Is an Energy Problem, But . . .

The energy crisis is real, according to Dr. Benjamin A. Rogge, Distinguished Professor of Political Economy at Wabash College. The nature of that crisis and its remedy, however, are not as they have been outlined in the President's national energy plan, Prof. Rogge said in an interview with the *Wabash Street Journal*.

Prof. Rogge's assessment of the energy problem and his discussion of the proper remedies are reprinted in full in the following paragraphs.

QUESTION: *Isn't the world (including the U.S.) rapidly running out of resources, particularly those used in energy production?*

ANSWER: Nonsense! Both analysis and history suggest exactly the opposite. If resources and energy markets were permitted to be even partially free in the years ahead, there is every reason to believe that the *real* cost of energy would continue to decline over the next 100 years, as it has over the last 100.

Q: *How can you say that, when we are told that we can anticipate a serious shortage of natural gas this coming winter? Won't this shortage be real?*

A: Of course it will be real!—but totally unnecessary. As Professor Milton Friedman has said recently, "Economists may not know much, but there is one thing they do know how to do and that is how to produce a shortage or a surplus. Set a price *below* the market price and a shortage is created; set a price *above* the market price and a surplus is created."

Reprinted from the *Freeman* (November 1977): 656–58, by permission of the publisher, Foundation for Economic Education, Irvington-on-Hudson, N.Y. All rights reserved.

The existing "shortage" of natural gas is the predictable (and predicted) consequence of the ceiling price on natural gas at the wellhead that was imposed in 1954 and that continues to this day. Estimates have been made that at a free-market price (that would still leave gas the lowest-cost source of energy for most uses), our natural gas reserves should be adequate for another 1000–2500 years of full and expanding use.

Q: *But, whatever its cause, don't you agree that we now face an energy problem and that we need to conserve our currently available energy supplies?*

A: Of course we need to take conservation measures—which is precisely why I am urging an immediate deregulation of the prices of basic energy materials. The market has its own magnificent incentive to conservation—an increase in price!!

Moreover, the market way of conserving permits each individual householder, businessman, farmer, car owner, or the like to conserve in the way that is best suited to *his* special circumstances. To conserve on heat use, one householder may wish to add insulation, another may wish to close off unused spaces, another may wish to turn down the thermostat, buy sweaters for everyone and order his daughter and her boyfriend to take up the old courting practice of bundling.

In addition, the market method of inducing conservation, in contrast to the government-ordered method, also encourages suppliers and would-be suppliers to redouble their efforts to add to the supply of energy.

Q: *But how do you* know *that that will happen? Exactly where is all this new energy supply going to come from? Nuclear? Solar? Geothermal? Gasification of coal?*

A: I do not know; James Schlesinger, our energy czar, doesn't know. *No one* knows, because the very essence of the free market operation is the unpredictability of the specific outcomes. The market process is a never-ceasing *search* process, carried on by literally millions of participants, each trying to serve his own purposes by finding new and better ways of producing and making efficient use of energy.

The number of variables in the energy equations is literally in the billions, and it is for this reason that any attempt to "solve" the problems involved by government direction is predestined to failure. The miracle of the market consists precisely in its capacity to make use of these billions of bits of special information in getting the world's work done efficiently—and in the interests of the consumers.

Q: *But isn't the cost of this so-called miracle a significant factor? What about the windfall profits the big oil and mining companies would enjoy in the meantime?*

A: *All* profits and losses are "windfall" in nature, in the sense that they arise out of a concurrence of events that no one could have foreseen in perfect detail. At the same time, these windfall profits will be the carrot hanging in front of every possible producer of energy and hence will be precisely the agent of a continuing solution to the energy problem—in the process of which the profits will tend to return to normal.

How can we encourage people to try to produce energy for us, with a warning that, if they fail, they must bear the losses, if we don't also assure them that, if they succeed, they will get to keep their winnings?

Q: *But how can people like Ralph Nader and others be so wrong in what they propose as solutions to the energy problem?*

A: For one thing, Nader has had a lot of experience at being wrong— witness the Corvair episode. But most important, in their approach to the energy problem, they seem to me to be largely giving vent to their dislike of industrialization, economic growth, suburbia, economic success, cars—especially big, comfortable cars—and (for some) the whole capital process itself. The energy problem is simply the reason-of-the-moment for an attack on the establishment and its system.

Q: *You sound pretty biased yourself. But, however that may be, wouldn't turning the market loose lead to an explosion of prices and real damage to the low-income families of America?*

A: The groups in America that have the most to gain from the free market approach are precisely those with little money and even less influence with the powers that be. The world of government controls and rationing is a world made to order for those who have money or influence. For the man on the street, it is a world of disaster and frustration.

Q: *But surely you wouldn't deregulate everything right away!*

A: Oh, but I would! Don't cut off the dog's tail an inch at a time.

Part 5

Macroeconomics:
Policies and Forecasts

Keynesian Policy

Keynesian economics is, of course, much more than a set of policy prescriptions for specified ailments. It is at once a value system, a language, a set of assumptions, and a general policy orientation. Nor is it possible to speak of *the* Keynesian policy. Yet it might still be argued that had Keynesian economics not included a policy framework capable of commanding the loyalty in the whole (if not in each of the parts) of a large number of people, it would never have assumed an important and controversial place in economic thought. The specific advice to governments was the élan vital of Keynesian economics, the magnet that attracted economists and laymen alike. Even today, when Keynesian economics is at once something more than and something less than *The General Theory*, it is still the kind of advice which Keynes included in his famous letter to President Roosevelt, which, explicitly or implicitly, keeps the professional journals filled with neo-, non-, and anti-Keynesian articles, replies, and rejoinders. However much he may value his "scientific objectivity," the average economist is still more easily moved to action by questions of policy than by questions of abstract analysis.

It is with a certain amount of relish, then, that we turn to a discussion of Keynesian policy. To add to the pleasure of the game and to try to identify the real issues in public policy, we shall review the continuing

Unpublished paper written while Rogge was a visiting professor of economics at Escola de Sociologia e Politica de São Paulo, São Paulo, Brazil. No date. Reprinted by permission of the Rogge estate.

controversy between those of "orthodox" orientation and those of Keynesian orientation. This is an exciting but dangerous project. It is dangerous, first because it is difficult to avoid some heroic oversimplification of the issues. Various shadings of opinion must be lumped together and contrasted with other lumps composed of equally diverse materials. It is also dangerous because no person undertaking this work is likely to be completely neutral in the controversy he is describing. I must warn you that I am not a neutral in this controversy. My particular bias should soon become obvious, and you must be on guard against the distortions my prejudgment may prevent me from recognizing. Finally, it is dangerous because it emphasizes the disagreements among economists, rather than the substantial consensus on many important issues that may prevail; this can lead the uninformed to reject all economic analysis because of the apparent inability of economists to agree on certain issues. However, if we keep these dangers in mind, we may still find this a useful undertaking.

The Nature of the Ailment

The first task is that of identifying the economic disease for which the therapy is intended. This is not as easy as it might seem, and it might be well to identify various "diseases" for which the Keynesian remedies might be suggested as cures.

The economic ailment that is most commonly associated with the Keynesian remedies is the one in which a given country is confronted with an actual or threatened volume of unemployment substantially larger than that which would be expected to exist because of various frictions in the adjustment processes of the economy. No competent Keynesian has ever proposed his remedies as a cure for so-called frictional unemployment—that is, the unemployment associated with seasonal variations in the demand for workers in various employments, with the delays that mark transfers from one job to another, and so forth. "Full employment" is usually defined in such a way as to recognize the existence of the frictionally unemployed. As the noted Keynesian Abba Lerner once said to the author, "To improve the adjustment mechanisms is not to bring full employment, but only to raise the level of full employment."

The significant feature of this use for the Keynesian remedies is that it is of a curative rather than a preventive character. In other words, it is a suggested answer to the question, What should a country that is faced with unemployment do? and not to the question, What should a country do to prevent this problem from arising?

This immediately suggests a second use for the Keynesian remedies: as preventive medicine to keep the patient healthy rather than as treatment once he has become ill. We shall see that the Keynesian medicine chest is said to contain this type of medicine as well. It might be noted that there is much less agreement on the value of the Keynesian remedies for preventive purposes than for curative purposes.

A third use for which Keynesian remedies have been suggested is to treat an economy that is chronically ill, specifically, an economy that faces the problem of chronic underemployment of resources. This problem is usually related to the famous "stagnation thesis." Most non- or anti-Keynesians (and even many Keynesians) deny that this problem even exists (or need exist) in modern economies, but it must be included in any listing of the problems for which Keynesian remedies have been proposed.

The problems listed above have one thing in common: a concern for unemployment or deflationary tendencies. Does the Keynesian medicine chest contain remedies for inflation as well? Because the Keynesian remedies were first developed to meet deflationary problems, Keynesian economics has often been designated "depression economics." However, most present-day Keynesians resent this label and insist that the Keynesian remedies can be used to treat inflationary problems as well.[1]

In recent years, another problem has been added to the list of those that can be treated, in part, at least, with Keynesian remedies. This is the problem of the underdeveloped economy.

It should be obvious that the Keynesian medicine chest has different remedies for different problems and not one magic elixir that will

---

1. "Far from being 'depression economics,' modern income analysis has many of its most important applications in connection with the process of inflation and what can be done about it." Paul A. Samuelson, *Economics,* 2nd ed. (New York: McGraw-Hill, 1951), 288.

cure any and all ailments. This makes it necessary that we examine the specific policies proposed to meet the specific problems listed above. Fortunately the discussion centered around the first problem will have substantial relevance to the later topics, and this will permit briefer treatment of the later topics.

What to Do When Unemployment Threatens

The first problem to be discussed is the one that existed at the time Keynesian economics was brought into being: the problem of a country faced with large-scale unemployment (or threatened with this possibility). For easier, more precise handling, the public policy question might be phrased as follows: what (if anything) should be done in a situation in which the level of effective demand has fallen below the level needed to provide full employment at existing prices and wages? Let us see first what answer might be given by more-or-less orthodox economists and then review the Keynesian reasons for rejecting these answers.

Reductions in Prices and Wages

The first answer that might be ascribed to the orthodox economist would be to take no action: the pressure of unsold goods and idle men (by forcing reductions in both prices and wages) will permit the market to be cleared of both goods and men by even the lower total of effective demand. While few modern economists of generally orthodox persuasion would be content with this one recommendation, most of them would insist that *some* downward flexibility of prices and wages is essential to proper full-employment policy. Let us leave the answer in its extreme, unqualified form, though, and review the Keynesian reasons for rejecting this proposal.

The first and most telling answer is that even were it desirable for money prices and money wages to be reduced it is not a practical or workable solution to the problem. In modern industrial economies, strong trade unions and equally strong industrial combinations (for example, cartels and semi- or fully monopolized markets) resist wage and price reductions so effectively that they will not be made even in the face of serious unemployment and idle facilities. Nor can these

pressure groups be "atomized," or neutralized, over the short-run period for which policy must be formulated. Note that this does not eliminate the possibility of reducing the power of the organized pressure
groups over a longer period of time; thus, we shall have to return to
this topic when discussing preventive medicine for the unemployment
ailment.

But Keynesian economics goes further than this. It argues that it
would not be possible for workers to bargain for lower real-wage rates,
even if they were willing to do so—and it is real-wage rates that must
be lowered if unemployment is to be reduced. In its least sophisticated
form, the argument is as follows: wages are costs to employers, but they
are also incomes to workers; to reduce worker incomes is to reduce effective demand. Now, in this form, the argument is patently false. The
dollars not spent on wages must still be held by someone, and a dollar
spent by a profit taker is no less and no more than a dollar spent by a
wage earner.

This means that the argument must be presented at a more sophisticated level. One possibility is to argue that a redistribution of money
resources from wage earners to non–wage earners will reduce aggregate demand, because of the lower marginal propensity to consume of
the second group.

Another possibility is to argue that wage (and price) reductions will
set in motion psychological reactions on expectations that will lead to a
continuing deflationary spiral. Only under very special circumstances
will wage-price reductions restore full employment. We shall return to
this later.

Keynes himself emphasized the fact that if wages and prices fall in
the same proportion, real wages will not be reduced and unemployment will still exist. But the orthodox model has usually been one in
which wages are to fall more than in proportion to the fall in prices,
thus reducing real wages, restoring profit margins to firms and bringing the economy to full employment. The argument here could be taken
to greater level of sophistication, particularly by introducing the controversy over the "Ricardo effect," but let us stop here. Few economists
would recommend wage-price reductions as the only remedy for existing unemployment while taking no action to counter the fall in aggregate demand. Given a substantial volume of existing unemployment

and a general deflationary environment, most modern economists would agree on the necessity of taking expansionist action of some kind. The dispute centers around the form of the action to be taken.

Monetary Policy versus Fiscal Policy

This dispute is often said to be one between those who would rely on monetary policy (the more orthodox position) and those who would rely on fiscal policy (the Keynesian position). In fact, though, this is a false dichotomy. If monetary policy is interpreted in its broadest sense—that is, as any policy proposing to change either the quantity of money or the velocity of circulation of money or both—then Keynesian fiscal policy is nothing but one technique (among many) for implementing monetary policy.

Even if monetary policy is restricted to manipulation of the quantity of money, the usual variety of Keynesian fiscal policy is still subsumed under monetary policy. By "the usual variety," I mean a policy of government deficit spending, the deficits to be financed by borrowings from banks with excess reserves. Only the balanced-budget model would be excluded, if it is designed to work primarily on the velocity of circulation of money by redistributing money resources.

The Keynesians have created much confusion by trying to deny these aspects of their policy; the denial has taken the form of assigning to the quantity of money only a role in determining the interest rate and then ascribing to the interest rate a very modest role in influencing aggregate demand. In fact, given the rigidity assumptions of the Keynesians, the quantity of money can be shown to exercise an important influence on aggregate demand and, hence, on output and employment. (See Modigliani on this in *Readings in Monetary Theory*.) In fact, the usual variety of Keynesian fiscal policy is an implicit acceptance of the importance of changes in the quantity of money in Keynesian policies.

The only way the distinction between monetary and fiscal policies has any real meaning is as a distinction between competing techniques for changing the quantity of money (or the product MV, if the broader interpretation is used). In this sense, monetary policy should be thought of as action taken by, or though, the central bank—perhaps with the cooperation of other agencies with some power over the individual banks—to influence the quantity of money in circulation. Fiscal policy is similar action initiating in the spending and taxing decisions of the legislative agencies in the country. But even this is more confusing than enlightening, because fiscal policy can indeed change the quantity of money in circulation only if it has the cooperation of monetary policy or is not countered by monetary policy, and vice versa.

The real issue, in the setting of our current discussion, is whether the needed expansion in total spending can be secured by some combination of, for example, open-market operations, reserve requirement, or rediscount rate changes—that is, by some combination of the weapons traditionally at the disposal of the central bank. Economists have long recognized that it is easier for a central bank to curb an unwanted expansion in the quantity of deposit currency than it is to induce a desired increase in that quantity. The central bank can increase the ability of the banking system to expand loans and deposits, but it cannot do much to increase the opportunities to do so. If potential borrowers do not appear, the added potential to loan is of no consequence.

In effect, fiscal policy is nothing more than a provision of the opportunity for banks to increase loans and, hence, deposit currency in circulation; the government does the borrowing and spending that private firms are not willing to undertake. This is the rationale of government deficit spending in a period of deflationary tendencies. But this makes it clear once and for all that fiscal policy is not a substitute for but, rather, is a supplement to monetary policy (in the narrow sense).

Now most economists today accept the desirability of deficit spending under the circumstances outlined here: a large volume of existing unemployment and strong deflationary pressures. They would admit that central-bank policy alone is inadequate to deal with such a situation. In this sense, almost all economists in the world today are Keynesians.

Preventive Medicine

But this does not imply acceptance of the Keynesian remedies for long-run, preventive uses. For these uses, the defenders of monetary policy or wage-price flexibility take a stronger anti-Keynesian position.

In the first place, the argument that wages and prices cannot be made flexible need not be accepted if the time period is long enough to permit a reorientation of public policy. The defenders of the wage-price flexibility position would argue that much can be done to eliminate the barriers to a more flexible economy. They point to the fact that the governments in most industrial economies have done much to "rigidify" the wage-price structure, both directly and indirectly (for example, price supports for agricultural and industrial products, wage supports through specifications for government contacts). What the government has done, it can stop doing and perhaps undo. What is needed is a firm and well-known position against wage-price rigidities and the devices that bring them about.

But few non-Keynesians would argue that this is all that need be done to assure full employment in the future. Most would admit that the economy can never be made so flexible that it can adjust to changes of any magnitude in the product MV (or aggregate demand, if the Keynesian language is preferred). What is needed as well is a monetary framework which will keep fluctuation in MV within modest hands.

To some this means a return to the gold standard (or some commodity standard), with its alleged automatic brake to movements of MV in either direction. To others this means the adoption of a 100 percent reserve banking system. These men argue that the wide swings of M that have characterized fluctuations in the past have been due to the perverse elasticity of the supply of deposit currency under fractional-reserve banking. The proper solution is to eliminate fractional-reserve banking. This is the position of the Chicago school—Mints, Simons, Friedman, Brozen, and others. To others it means only a stronger central bank, supplied with weapons that will permit it to check inflationary and deflationary changes in the quantity of deposit currency. There are many varieties of monetary policy in this total grouping; the unifying element is the belief that a wiser monetary mechanism (coupled with greater wage-price flexibility) will largely eliminate the need for manipulation of the government budget to attain a more stable economy.

A second unifying element is the belief that a wiser monetary mechanism can prevent the inflationary excesses that generate the deflationary reactions; if this be true, the alleged inability of monetary policy alone to cope with strong deflationary pressures is of no great consequence.

Two factors lead the Keynesians to reject this type of solution. The first is their belief that a flexible wage-price structure, coupled with elastic expectations, would produce a violently unstable economy, rocketing from wild inflation to equally wild deflation. The second is their belief that monetary policy can at best influence the quantity of money and that changes in the velocity of circulation of money must be offset by a stronger medicine if the economy is to be stabilized at full employment.

The most extreme statement of the Keynesian position is found in the writings of Abba Lerner. Lerner's "functional finance" is the clearest presentation of Keynesian policy as a long-run remedy for economic instability. The old budgetary principles are to be scrapped; the government is to tax only to take money out of the hands of the public and to spend to put money into the hands of the public. The government budget is the "steering wheel" of the economy, keeping it from falling into either the inflationary or the deflationary ditch. (See Lerner's *Economics of Control.*)

Now it cannot be denied that, in theory, the government budget could be so manipulated as to stabilize the level of effective demand at any desired level. The problems that surround this proposal relate to the practical problems of achieving this result without serious side effects in a modern democracy.

The first problem is that of the political temperament. The politician is almost always willing to spend borrowed money—in fact, he prefers it to spending money that is taxed away from a sensitive electorate. This suggests the first criticism of the functional finance proposal: if politicians are freed from the restraining influence of a philosophy of balanced budgets, they are likely to expand government activity far beyond the level that would be deemed desirable on grounds of economic necessity and efficiency. Experience in both the United States and Brazil suggests that this is a very real danger and not just a figment of the conservative imagination. The balanced budget may be just a fetish, but it may be a very important fetish in a world of imperfect men and imperfect politicians.

This suggests a related criticism of the functional finance proposal: politicians will be willing to spend borrowed money when deflation threatens, but will they be willing to tax away money and not spend it when inflation threatens? Isn't the most likely outcome of such a program creeping (or galloping) inflation? Again experience does not permit us to answer this with a categorical no.

But even if the political temperament were completely attuned to the needs of the program, success would not be assumed. There would still exist at least the two problems of budgetary flexibility and forecasting. The spending and taxing programs of a government cannot be changed as easily or as quickly as the steering wheel analogy suggests, particularly in a democracy where these programs are the result of legislative processes. An economist-dictator might be able to enlarge this and reduce that, stop this project, increase those taxes, and so forth, without much delay. But the legislative bodies in the United States and Brazil are more likely to take weeks or months or years to agree upon the steps to be taken, and then the legislative decisions have to be implemented by bureaucracies that are not noted for fast action in either country.

This criticism reinforces G. D. H. Cole's argument that Keynesian policy is best adapted to a socialist economy, in which a central planning agency is capable of acting quickly and completely to implement any agreed-upon policy. This conclusion might not disturb an Abba Lerner, but I am certain that it would be distressing to the great body of nonsocialist Keynesian economists.

They hope to solve this problem, at least in part, by the use of "built-in" stabilizers, such as are found in the operation of a social security program and a progressive income tax–rate structure. If deflation threatens and money incomes fall, social security payments to persons automatically increase while social security withdrawals from persons and income-tax yields automatically decrease. It is argued that these built-in stabilizers can be expanded in scope and effectiveness to reduce the need for deliberate action to modify the government budget. Few Keynesians, however, would argue that such automatic stabilizers could alone handle the stabilization problem. Most would admit that some discretionary action by legislative groups will usually be necessary.

This action is admittedly slow, but it can be effective if it can be based on fairly accurate forecasts of the shape of things to come. By "the shape of things to come" is meant not only whether the level of aggregate demand is likely to be above or below the full-employment level but also by approximately how much it will be above or below this level. Excessive countering action can often be more serious than the original problem itself, as experience in the United States in 1946–47 indicates. Economists had forecast a substantial volume of unemployment for the immediate postwar period, and this, in part, led the government to adopt an expansionist program for the postwar period.

The result was actually a period of fast-moving inflation. Now, perhaps the forecasters were right in predicting that the level of effective demand would be below the full-employment level during this period, but they certainly erred in estimating the extent to which this would be true. The result was to give an inflationary bias to the economy, rather than stability.

This is exactly the kind of problem that functional finance must deal with, and there is as yet little evidence that governments (or economists) are ready to solve it. Any program that depends on even approximate forecasts of future shifts in the economy is resting on a rather uncertain base. As Milton Friedman has demonstrated so clearly, unless there is a high ratio of "right" to "wrong" actions, the program will do more harm than good. (See "The Effects of a Full-Employment Policy on Economic Stability: A Formal Analysis," in *Essays in Positive Economics*.)

To this could be added the problems arising out of the actions of pressure groups under a guarantee of full employment. Trade unions, particularly, are likely to take advantage of such a situation to drain off the increases in aggregate demand into their own incomes, with the result being inflation with unemployment.

Now the fact should be clear that many of the problems of functional finance identified above would confront any stabilization program. A monetary program under a central bank would also need fairly accurate forecasts of the shape of things to come and would also have to confront lags in the responses to actions taken. Nor are trade unions likely to distinguish between a rising aggregate demand produced by open-market operations and one produced by fiscal policy.

In other words, there seems to be little possibility that any program for stabilizing MV (or aggregate demand), whether Keynesian or non-Keynesian, can hope to bring even approximate stability at the full-employment level. The most that a realist can hope for is that extreme swings in aggregate demand can be eliminated, that the amplitude of the fluctuations can be reduced. It is this which leads Friedman to say, "The brute fact is that a rational economic program for a free-enterprise system (and perhaps even for a collectivist system) must have flexibility of prices (including wages) as one of its cornerstones" (Friedman, "Effects of Full-Employment Policy," 144).

But if this be true, how to deal with the problem of elastic expectations? A partial answer might be that the mere announcement of a program of stabilization would tend to reduce the elasticity of expectations. If prices were to start rising or falling, people would expect the government to step in to reverse the trend, and this means less elastic expectations. If the government (or pure luck) is successful in actually reversing the trend a few times, the elasticity of expectations might be sharply reduced. While I cannot prove it, I am convinced that something like this has taken place in the United States in the last ten years.

One more issue in the dispute between the orthodox and Keynesian positions might now be identified. In general, orthodox economists insist that policies be designed to work by pure rule of law and not by rule of men. That is, in their general distrust of arbitrary action by governments, they would refuse to grant discretionary powers to any agency of the government. The action to be taken must be built into the legislation, and the decision must not be delegated to administrative agencies.

Now of course this would rule out even a central bank possessed of discretionary powers. It would seem to compel an endorsement of a return to a pure gold standard with 100 percent gold reserve banking. However, it might be consistent with a program in which the administrative agencies are forced to act in specified ways whenever certain signals are flashed (such as a fall in a price index below a certain level). It is also roughly consistent with the built-in stabilizers of Keynesian policy, and it is interesting to note that those orthodox economists who are not wedded to the balanced-budget principle generally accept the desirability of budget surpluses or deficits that arise out of the working of these automatic stabilizers.

In summary, I would conclude that no stabilization program can do more than reduce the amplitude of the fluctuations in aggregate demand. It follows that full employment can be maintained indefinitely only if prices and wages are somewhat flexible and if the elasticity of expectations can be reduced to around one. This may mean, in fact, that continuous full employment without inflation is a goal that cannot be attained in free-enterprise democratic society (or even in a collectivist but democratic society). This, however, does not mean that nothing can be done to reduce the amplitude of the movements away from a stable-price-level, full-employment position. On the contrary, much can be done, and the choice is not between monetary and fiscal policy but rather between different combinations of monetary and fiscal policy. The two are supplementary rather than competing. As a general rule, the more experienced and dependable the administrators of public policy, the greater the use that can be made of policies that grant discretionary powers to those administrators; the more restrained the politicians, the greater can be the departure from the principle of a balanced budget. From what I have seen of Brazil, I would say that Brazilian economists would do well to emphasize central-bank policy (rather than the manipulated budget) and nondiscretionary programs (rather than discretionary programs) for attaining stability. I think economists everywhere would do well to stress that even approximate continuous stability at full-employment is an almost unattainable goal, or a goal that can be attained only at great sacrifice.

In other words, I do not believe that there is any program (perhaps not even a completely authoritarian program) that can assure even approximate stabilization of effective demand at the stable-price, full-employment level. Like Friedman, I believe that even the Keynesians would do well to give some attention to creating a more flexible economy.

Chronic Underemployment of Resources

Even the ailment here is controversial; many economists (including many Keynesians) deny that the problem exists or even threatens. Others admit that the problem may arise but identify the cause as excessive government intervention in the economy, a cause that can be eliminated without use of the Keynesian remedies. Others, like Schumpeter, believe that modern industrial economies may stagnate but that the causes are sociological and not economic. Only a limited number of men ever argued that because of the disappearance of the external frontier, the decline in the rate of population growth, and the slower rate and altered nature of technological change in the future, these economies were likely to confront a persistent problem of inadequate effective demand and chronic underemployment of resources. (Keynes himself placed considerable emphasis on the operation of diminishing returns in gradually reducing the marginal efficiency of capital.)

The general picture is one of a mature and wealthy economy in which the propensity to save is high and the propensity to invest is low. The ex post equality between savings and investment is attained by a drop in income (and, hence, effective demand) below the level needed for full employment.

The first reply of the classicist would be that even if the original thesis be true the lower level of money demand need not produce unemployment if prices and wages adjust to this lower level. (In the article referred to before, Modigliani shows that the stagnation thesis, like all of Keynesian economics, really rests on the wage-rigidity assumption.)

A second reply would be that the situation described would simply induce a lowering of the interest rate until ex ante savings and investment were brought into equality. Given an inverse relationship between savings and the interest rate, this would mean that the mature economy would become a high-consumption economy.

To this the Keynesians reply with the concept of the liquidity trap. At an interest rate low enough to induce the needed investment, holders of resources might prefer to hold cash rather than noncash assets. Thus, large-scale hoarding might be the outcome.

But the classicists usually rest their case on the argument that the stagnation thesis (the low marginal efficiency of capital) is itself unsupported by either logic or experience. The arguments here are too well known to require repeating. I would say that post–World War II experience in the two countries that were singled out as most likely to stagnate (the United States and Great Britain) is so overwhelmingly contradictory of the stagnation thesis that we are not likely to see a real revival of this thesis for some time.

However, let us ask what some Keynesians have proposed to do about chronic unemployment if such were the problem. The one path is the investment path, with government continually supplementing the low level of private investment with public investment financed by borrowings. This specter of a continuously rising public debt has frightened the balanced-budget element in the world and has been one of the important factors in the emotional rejection of Keynesian economics by the more conservative groups in the United States and elsewhere. Actually, if we ignore the possibility of political abuse of the unbalanced budget, the Keynesians have the weight of logic on their side in this dispute. The size of the national product is more important than the size of the national debt, and a rising public debt is not an evil per se.

A second part of the investment approach would be a low-interest-rate policy on the part of the monetary authorities, the goal being that of stimulating private investment.

The outstanding "stagnationist" Alvin Hansen, however, has largely rejected the investment path to full employment. For various reasons, he supports the consumption path to full employment. That is, the proper offset to a diminishing marginal efficiency of capital is a diminishing marginal propensity to save. This can be accomplished (it is said) by redistributing income from the high-income, low-propensity-to-consume segments of the economy to the low-income, high-propensity-to-consume segments.

Now of course this is equally frightening to the conservative elements. However, this thesis has become almost dogma with many elements in the United States. The trade unionists and the farmers alike cry that they must be given a larger share of the national income to maintain the purchasing power needed for prosperity and full employment. (As a matter of fact, recent studies have demonstrated that the effectiveness of income redistribution in increasing the propensity to consume is very limited, that only a heroic and far-reaching redistribution can have a significant influence.)

What I would like to draw attention to is the fact that both of the elements in Keynesian policy that have accounted for much of the conservative layman's fear of Keynesian economics are related to the uses of that policy to combat chronic unemployment. Those two elements are, of course, a continuously rising public debt and a radical redistribution of income. This has brought under the cloud of conservative disapproval even the moderate Keynesian who proposes no radical redistribution of income (and more and more Keynesians are coming to this position) and a cyclically balanced budget rather than a continuously rising public debt. Those who have urged the use of Keynesian policy for countercyclical purposes only have been seriously handicapped by the stigma attached to the stagnation-thesis uses of Keynesian policy. If I were a Keynesian today, I would be regretting that the stagnation thesis ever came to be associated with Keynesian economics.

Keynesian Anti-Depression Policies

A convenient way to summarize the antidepression policy possibilities suggested by Keynesian analysis is to group them according to the component of total spending to which they apply. These components are of course, consumer spending, private investment spending, net government spending (expenditures minus receipts), and net foreign spending.

I. Consumer spending may be increased by
    A. Raising the economywide average propensity to consume by
        1. Redistributing income;
        2. Placing a tax on idle money;
        3. Better consumer-credit facilities.
    B. Raising the disposable income of consumers by
        1. Reducing direct or indirect taxes or both;
        2. Increasing social security payments.
II. Private investment spending may be increased by
    A. Raising the marginal efficiency of capital by
        1. Creating a favorable "climate" of opinion among potential investors;
        2. Creating a tax structure favorable to investment;
        3. Reducing the risk factor in investment.
    B. Lowering the interest rate through
        1. Central-bank monetary policy;
        2. Direct lending by agencies of government at low interest rates;
        3. Larger supplies of debt instruments that are almost as liquid as money itself;
        4. Reducing the risk factor in lending.
III. Net government spending may be increased by
    A. Increasing expenditures more than receipts; or
    B. Reducing receipts more than expenditures.

Note that the increased expenditure versus reduced taxes controversy is one of the important intra-Keynesian controversies. Those
more-or-less orthodox economists who accept the usefulness of fiscal
policy usually prefer the reduced-tax approach. Their argument is that
increased government expenditures often involve an unwise extension
of government activity and may serve to drive up the costs of certain
types of materials and labor (in the construction industry, for example)
and thus discourage private investment spending.

IV. Net foreign spending may be increased by
   A.   Raising exports; or
   B.   Reducing imports

Most Keynesians (including Keynes himself) retain the free-trade
prejudices of classical and neoclassical economics and are reluctant
to recommend protectionist devices as a remedy for unemployment.
However, this must be modified in a number of ways.

First, this reluctance to recommend protectionist policy is more
pronounced among Keynesian economists in the more industrialized
countries of the world, particularly in the United States and the United
Kingdom. In the so-called underdeveloped countries, the effective demand arguments for protection are usually supplemented by other
pressures for protection. Keynesian and non-Keynesian economists
alike in these countries tend to be rather more protectionist than their
colleagues in the more industrialized countries.

In the second place, the practical effect of Keynesian policy in the
real-world setting is often that of forcing Keynesians to accept protective measures as the least of a number of evils. One of the first principles of Keynesian economics is a rejection of the method of fluctuating
price levels as the equilibrating mechanism in international trade. At
the same time, the income path to equilibrium must be rejected, at
least to the extent that it calls for a reduction in money incomes, in the
country (or countries) suffering from a balance-of-payments problem.
This leaves a freely fluctuating exchange rate as the only alternative
in the free market tradition. And whether desirable or not, this alternative seems to be impractical and unlikely in the political economies
of most countries. Thus, two non–free market alternatives seem to

remain. The one most usually adopted is that of meeting balance-of-payments difficulties by direct and indirect controls over imports and exports: multiple exchange rates, import licenses, quotas, subsidies, and the like. The one most usually recommended (for example, in the United Nations' National and International Measures for Full Employment) is an international scheme under which surplus nations would be committed to making their currencies available to deficit nations, a more-or-less forced equilibrating of international balances. The odds against this second solution ever being accepted are large. As a practical matter, then, Keynesian economic policy, with its concentration on a stabilized (or expanding) effective demand in every country, is not consistent with even approximate freedom in international trade. This is a dilemma that every Keynesian has tried to escape from but so far with little success (except on paper, as in the proposals of the United Nations group). It is not surprising then that many a Keynesian has "solved" this problem by simply ignoring it.

Actually, of course, even the non-Keynesians who would use, say, monetary policy alone to stabilize MV confront the same dilemma. Most of these men have escaped by frankly urging freely fluctuating exchange rates (Friedman and Williams, for example). This may permit them to be logically consistent, but it does not solve the problem of the conflict between stabilization programs and healthy international trade in a real world that does not permit exchange rates to follow the market. Nor does it solve the serious problems in the international capital market that would be created if exchange rates were free to follow the market. This does not mean that all other considerations must be sacrificed in the interests of international trade and capital movements. But it does mean that economists should stop fooling themselves and the public by pretending that it is possible to have the advantages of every arrangement and the disadvantages of none.

Economics—Some Relationships
of Theory and Practice

In *The Failure of the New Economics*, Henry Hazlitt, whose economic analyses and interpretations have become well known over the years, has set himself the ambitious task of exposing the fallacies in one of the major contributions to modern economic orthodoxy—John Maynard Keynes's *The General Theory of Employment, Interest and Money*. Those to whom Keynes's views are sacrosanct are not likely to be impressed by the results. Even those economists who have generally rejected the Keynesian analysis may wish to quibble over some of the handling of technical details of the argument. However, Hazlitt has had the courage to say bluntly what some of these men must often have wished to say, to wit, "The emperor has no clothes."

He charges Keynes with having moved from fallacious premises to false conclusions and outright dangerous proposals for action by government. This would seem to be sufficient, but he also charges Keynes with poor writing, sloppy and inconsistent handling of definitions, and a chaotic development of his theme. Strangely enough, he is able to quote most of the prominent followers of Keynes in support of his complaints about style and use of language.

Reviews of *The Failure of the "New Economics": An Analysis of the Keynesian Fallacies*, by Henry Hazlitt (1959); *The Classical Liberalism, Marxism, and the Twentieth Century*, by Overton H. Taylor (1960); and *The Economic Point of View*, by Israel M. Kirzner (1960). Reprinted from *The National Book Foundation*, February 15, 1962: 1–4, by permission of the publisher.

In brief, the Keynesian argument runs as follows: (1) the level of employment is determined by the level of total dollar spending in the economy; (2) changes in the level of total dollar spending in the economy are largely produced by inconsistencies in the saving and investing decisions in the economy (e.g., if savers decide to save more than investors decide to invest, the result will be a drop in national income and a drop in employment); (3) the automatic adjustment mechanisms (in which the orthodox, pre-Keynesian economists placed their faith) do not work to remove such inconsistencies; (4) the government should stand ready to use its own spending and taxing to correct the inconsistencies wherever they threaten to appear, and thus keep the economy on an even keel at a level of full employment. In addition, Keynes predicted a *chronic* tendency for the economy to fall below the full employment level of total spending (the famous "stagnation thesis"), thus requiring of governments never-ending supplements to the spending stream through continuing budget deficits.

Hazlitt meets Keynes head-on at each point in the argument. He charges Keynes with ignoring the fact that full employment can be achieved with *any* level of total spending, provided only that the wage-price level is appropriate, both for the whole economy and in each of its sectors. He demonstrates that the Keynesian thesis of the possible inconsistency of savings and investment decisions was arrived at by definitional sleight-of-hand.

He reminds the reader that pre-Keynesian economists had always recognized that their conclusions on saving and investment would not follow if the adjustment mechanisms (particularly the interest rate) were not functioning—and he argues that these mechanisms could work if they were not prevented from working by various government interventions, including inflating of the money supply. Finally, he argues that the Keynesian policy proposals would not only not remove the true sources of instability in the economy (which are said to lie in unwise monetary policy), but would actually prevent the necessary and desirable adjustments in wages, prices, and interest rates from taking place. In addition, the Keynesian policies, if long continued, would produce continuous inflation and an ever-more-socialized economy.

Hazlitt is a skilled expositor, and rarely is the layman given this kind of opportunity to peer over the shoulders of the professional economists as they debate the policies from which he (the layman) will benefit or suffer.

A second opportunity for the non-professional to come to a better understanding of today's issues is provided in Professor Taylor's book *The Classical Liberalism, Marxism, and the Twentieth Century*. The book consists of four lectures delivered in 1958 at the Thomas Jefferson Center for Studies in Political Economy at the University of Virginia.

In the first lecture is a genealogy of the central themes in the American tradition—individualism, free market economics, and liberal democracy. He traces these themes back through Adam Smith and Locke, to St. Thomas Aquinas, and to their Greco-Roman and Judaic-Christian beginnings.

The second lecture is a similar treatment of socialism, with particular emphasis on the contributions of Karl Marx to the socialist tradition, and provides a particularly clear and readable primer of Marxian analysis.

In the third lecture, he describes the challenge that modern socialism presents to American liberalism today, including an analysis of the differences between mid-twentieth-century communism and classical Marxian communism. In the final lecture, he discusses the need for a revised and revitalized liberal philosophy to meet the communist challenge. In particular, he asks for renewed concern with an "all-inclusive vision of the whole and the grasp of fundamental, general principles without which we lose our way and become victims of growing and multiplying, intellectual and moral confusions."

The third book, Israel Kirzner's *The Economic Point of View*, can be recommended both to the specialist and to those intrepid amateurs who are willing to struggle with its style and its numerous references to the literature in the field. It is probably the best single reference book available on the history of the discussion of what constitutes "the economic point of view." Kirzner traces the discussion from approximately the time of Adam Smith, when economics was thought to be a wealth-centered study, through the period when it was thought to be centered on man in his wealth-getting activities, to the more modern definitions of economics as a science of human action (the *praxeological* view of economics, associated particularly with the name of Professor Mises).

Those who are tempted to ask, "What difference does it make how economics is defined?" would do well to read this book and find out. For example, the early definitions of economics in terms of wealth-getting were partly responsible for the low repute of the science. Its concern seemed to be only with the "vulgar" activities of man, or when he was operating at his worst. The praxeological view, in which economics is viewed as the study of man in the process of making rational choices among alternatives, relieves economics of much of the stigma that was once attached to it for definitional reasons alone. This is a reference book that every economist, professional or amateur, should have on his shelf—after reading.

The Outlook for the
American Economy

The dedication of a new facility is an appropriate time for stocktaking by those whose efforts have brought the building into existence and by those who will use the services provided there. It is equally appropriate, then, that the speaker on this occasion engage in stocktaking, and that is what I propose to do. Where does the American economy stand today, and what are its prospects for the years ahead?

Obviously neither your speaker nor any other mortal man really knows what lies ahead. At the same time, both curiosity and necessity lead us to attempt (hopefully) informed guesses as to the future course of events. Given the role of government in the American economy, the making of such guesses involves speculation on (1) the purposes that the government will attempt to serve in economic life, (2) the devices available to government in the service of those purposes and (3) the likely consequences of the actions so predicted.

(1) With reference to goals, I assume that not only the current administration in Washington, D.C., but any administration likely to be in power in the next two decades will assign first priority to avoiding a major, economy-wide depression. It will do this because we, the majority, have made it abundantly clear that we will vote out of office any administration that permits even a sharp recession to persist for any length of time. At the same time, we will ask that inflation be avoided

Address given in Winchester, Ind., at the dedication banquet of the new banking facility of Peoples Loan & Trust Company, December 4, 1970. Reprinted by permission of the Rogge estate.

or kept at a moderate pace, but I am assuming that we, as citizens, in assigning lower priority to this goal than to avoiding depression, will cause any administration of any political party to do the same. This does not mean that an administration will be able to ignore the problems of inflation; it means only that it will feel required to fight inflation by means that seem unlikely to bring on recession or depression. The consequences of this are of central importance, as will be noted later.

Other goals of lesser priority will be involved as well, including those of avoiding serious balance-of-payments problems, encouraging economic growth, expanding domestic welfare programs, etc., but in the time available to me here, I wish to concentrate on the problems posed by the case of the economy being required to steer between the ditch of inflation on one side of the road and the ditch of depression on the other, with orders from the passengers to avoid both ditches, but in particular to avoid the depression ditch.

(2) We turn now to the question of the steering mechanisms: What are they? How well can they be expected to work? What are the likely consequences of government attempts to employ one or more of these mechanisms to serve the purposes identified earlier?

Economists do not speak with one voice on the question of which dials, which levers really steer the car in one direction or another. Traditional orthodox economics of the kind associated with Adam Smith, David Ricardo, the Austrian School of late 1900's, Irving Fisher of Yale, etc., placed primary emphasis on changes in the money supply as the primary cause of movements in the general level of prices, production and employment. They also tended to distrust government control of this steering wheel and favored a self-adjusting steering wheel such as was alleged to be the case under a true gold standard. These people explained the historical occurence of business cycles or other fluctuations as arising out of government intervention in the money system.

This point of view was sharply challenged in the 1930's, with the leadership of the challenge coming from the late English economist John Maynard Keynes. Keynes argued that the money supply was of much less significance than the spending, saving and investing decisions of households and firms. He also argued that destabilizing changes in these decision patterns were to be expected under capitalism and that, in particular, it was not only possible but probable that depressions similar to the one of the 1930's could become a chronic problem for the capitalist economies. He recommended a variety of measures to combat this tendency, including redistribution of income to increase consumer spending, governmental direction of investment, etc., but urged that primary reliance be placed on the use of the government's power to tax and spend to offset anticipated, destabilizing changes in private spending decisions. If needed, the central government might well run a permanent deficit so as to bring total spending up to the level necessary for full employment.

This is the famous fiscal policy that has tended to dominate public policy in this country in the 1960's, but with earlier influence on the actions of the Roosevelt, Truman and Eisenhower administrations.

Throughout history (from the Code of Hammurabi to the Edicts of Diocletian to the death-penalty-for-price-increases of the French Revolution) many, both within and without the ranks of professional economists (but more without than within), have insisted that the obvious way for a government to stop inflation is to pass a law forbidding price increases, just as the obvious way to stop deflation is to pass a law forbidding price decreases. This is the dial of direct controls. If you wish to attach the name of an economist to this dial, you can associate it with John Kenneth Galbraith.

Here then are the three dials: the money dial, the fiscal dial and the direct-controls dial. Which one really controls the general level of economic activity? This is still under debate. My own conviction is that it is the money dial. As a matter of fact, under the leadership of Professor Milton Friedman of the University of Chicago, a growing number of economists are becoming "monetarists," i.e., convinced that it is the quantity of money that really counts. Those of us in this grouping believe that turning the fiscal dial has an impact on the overall level of economic activity only if it induces the government to turn the money dial. For example, a government deficit is not inflationary if it is financed by the sale of securities to those who have real savings; it is inflationary only if the securities are purchased with newly created money, made possible by government actions in the money supply area. We also reject wage-price controls as being no more effective in controlling inflation than breaking the thermometer can be in curing a fever. In addition, we believe that imposing such controls, which silences the signal system of capitalism, is the single most anti-capitalist action that a government can take.

We turn now to a different question. Whatever the control device or devices to be used by government, how effective can we expect it to be in steering the car of the economy between the ditches of inflation and depression? Some four or five years ago, such administration economists as Walter Heller were proclaiming that particularly by use of the fiscal dial, we were now in a position to "fine tune" the economy. Translated to our analogy, this would imply a driver of great wisdom and skill and perfect foresight driving a perfect piece of equipment right down the middle of the road—forever.

To understate my true feelings, I believe this to be a slight exaggeration of what can in fact be expected. A better analogy would be that of a well-meaning drunk, driving a significantly unreliable piece of equipment down an unfamiliar road in the dead of night, with strong and unpredictable winds buffeting the automobile. In particular (a) the driver cannot really anticipate either the road or the winds ahead; (b) there is a time lag between the time the driver turns the wheel and the time the car responds, and the length of this time lag varies from one time to another and (c) the lag is different for one part of the vehicle than for another.

It follows that the driver of the car is likely to be zigging when he should be zagging and vice versa. Admittedly, he does have enough control that when he gets way over into either ditch, he can yank himself out, but he can't avoid getting into the ditches now and then—nor can he get out of one ditch without the probability that he will skid clear across the road to the other ditch.

Given this analogy, how would we expect the driver to behave? Given his instructions from the passengers to never get too deeply into the depression ditch, we would expect him to hug the inflation side of the road and correct only when an apparent political necessity.

(3) We are now in a position to predict the course of events in the ten to twenty years ahead. (a) There will be no prolonged, economy-wide depression; the government is under orders to avoid it and has just enough control of the economy to do so (probably). (b) There will be never-ending, year-in and year-out inflation, probably at an annual rate of 5 to 10 percent, with interest rates to match. (c) There will be occasional

short (but perhaps sharp) recessions as the government makes tentative moves in the monetary and fiscal areas to stop inflation. (d) The rate of inflation will probably increase over time, but probably won't really become runaway inflation in the next two decades; the driver does have enough control to keep this from happening and may just have enough will to exercise that control (by slowing down the rate of increase in the money supply). (e) Afraid to try to stop the continuing inflation by the only means that can really work (holding down the quantity of money), because to do so is politically painful, the driver will inevitably be pushed in the direction of direct controls. Within five years' time, it is probable that a fairly comprehensive system of wage and price controls (with the associated rationing) will be in existence.

The consequence of this will be an explosive increase in the control exercised by government over the economic decisions of all of us, including such decisions as those to build or not to build a new bank building.

A second consequence will be a progressively less efficient economy, a very low (or even negative) rate of economic growth, a multiplying of the frustrations and discontents of the average citizen, a growing clamor from the intellectuals for the government to take over even more functions from the obviously inefficient private sector; to wit—an accelerated movement away from economic freedom and economic prosperity to economic dictatorship and economic stagnation.

Is this course of events inevitable? Of course not; nothing in human affairs is inevitable. We are headed for trouble because of decisions made by human beings; we can save ourselves by decisions made by human beings. All that is really required is for a significant number of those who help to shape the destiny of this country to escape from the ancient myth that we can solve a problem, whether it be low profits or stagnation or high interest rates, or what have you, by the simple device of increasing the quantity of money. Failing this, with Archy the Cockroach, I am more optimistic about the past than about the future.

Misconceptions of the Cause and Cure of Inflation

The most probable course of events in the American economy in the next 10 to 15 years is the following:

- Continuing, in fact accelerating, inflation;
- No major depression, but occasional periods of reduced real output—and hence employment;
- Off-and-on price and wage controls;
- A rising pattern of interest rates;
- An increasing direction of private economic activity by public agencies; and
- An increasingly hampered economy, with an associated decline in its efficiency and its capacity to produce economic growth.

The most probable final outcome of all this is that the American economy will come to look very much like the English economy of today, an economy that one English observer has described as "sinking slowly under the sea, giggling as she goes down."

The reasons for this probable course of events are many and complex. They will be examined in two groupings:

- Those that relate to what I believe to be serious misconceptions about what inflation can and cannot produce; and

Editor's title. Address before the Wisconsin Bankers Association, July 18, 1974. Reprinted from *American Banker* (June 19, 1974): 1–13, by permission of American Banker, Source-Media Publications.

- Those that relate to the nature and attitudes of the businessman and of the intellectual in a mature capitalist economy.

Misconceptions about inflation—

The primordial sin in treating of inflation is that of assuming that interest rates can be kept at some desired level—usually "low"—by increasing the money supply; i.e., by an easy money policy. It is typically argued that high interest rates reduce investment, curtail output, reduce home building, penalize the debtor-poor to the advantage of the creditor-rich, etc., and that low interest rates are clearly to be preferred to high. This argument is filled with dubious connections, but the real trouble flows from the attempt to implement its thesis by means of continuous inflation.

The fact of the matter is that the level of interest rates is a market phenomenon, and not only is it undesirable for government to seek to control it, but it is largely impossible for it to do so as well. It is true that by adding to or subtracting from the rate of change in the money stock, temporary changes, particularly in short-term rates, can be achieved—and this illusion of effectiveness is the precise source of the problem. Suppose, for example that the monetary authority—i.e., the Federal Reserve System—were to bring about a significant injection of new money into the economic stream over a short period of time. The point of impact of the injection would normally be the short-term money market, and the rather immediate consequence would be a fall in the short-term rate of interest. However, over the course of the next few months, as this new money churned through the economy, there would be a tendency for spending of all kinds to increase, with consequent upward pressure on prices. This in turn would lead both businesses and individuals to wish to spend more now, to build up inventories or undertake expansion of plant or buy durables and homes now before prices go even higher. This increased propensity to spend would be translated into a sharply increased demand for loanable funds. This in turn would mean that the original increase in the quantity of money would be offset by the increased demand for loanable funds, and interest rates would start to climb. Moreover, as potential lenders would see prices rising, they would insist on an inflation premium in the interest rate; in other words, the supply curve of loanable funds would shift up and to the left, indicating that it would now take a higher rate to bring forth a given volume of loanable funds than was true before.

But why can't this countering effect be matched or more than matched by continuing injections of new money? Because this would mean continuing inflation, and this in turn would mean a continuing demand by lenders for an inflation premium on interest rates.

To try to "cure" the problem of high interest rates by increasing the quantity of money, i.e., by inflation, is like trying to cure a hangover by some "hair of the dog" the next morning. The temporary feeling of well-being is closely followed by a renewed attack of the problem; the alleged remedy is in fact not a cure to the problem but its precise cause. It is inflation that causes high interest rates, not the reverse, the Honorable Wright Patman to the contrary. There is one way and only one way to bring the market rate of interest back to the levels we tend to think of as normal, and that is to take the inflation premium out of interest rates by taking the inflation out of the economy—and there is only one way to do that, and that is by keeping the quantity of money from going up faster than the output of goods and services.

A related misconception is that it is possible to trade off any given degree of inflation for corresponding levels of unemployment, i.e., that we can purchase whatever level of unemployment we think bearable or desirable by paying the cost in the form of some predictable level of inflation. This is the famous Phillips Curve hypothesis of recent fame.

It can be demonstrated that this is true only if the specified level of inflation is unanticipated by the economic units in the society. Thus an unanticipated rate of inflation of 5% may be consistent in a given economy with a 3% level of unemployment. But of course a continued rate of inflation of 5% soon comes to be anticipated by wage earners, lenders and others in the economy; this in turn will lead them to demand an inflation premium in their wage rates, interest rates, etc., and the changing cost structure, given no change in the rate of increase in the money supply available for spending, would produce reduced outputs and rising unemployment. When this happens, the 5% rate of inflation comes to be associated with a much higher rate of unemployment, say 6%. To bring the rate of unemployment back to 3% would now require an additional and unanticipated inflation factor of, say, another 5%, for a total rate of inflation of 10%. In other words, as for the drug addict, ever-increasing dosages come to be necessary to achieve any given level of "high" or feeling of well-being. Any attempt to maintain unemployment at some given desired level by the means of a continuously easy money policy must mean not just continuous but accelerating inflation.

Another related misconception can be handled very quickly. It is the belief that the liquidity problems of individuals, businesses, governments and whole nations can be cured by increasing the supply of money within nations and worldwide. An economic unit can be said to face a liquidity problem wherever it can make necessary borrowings only at interest rates that are inconsistent with other parameters in its system, e.g., the family's income available for payments on interest and principal or the prices the business firm can charge for its product or the level of taxation a political unit feels it can impose on its citizens or the interest payment outflow that a nation's balance-of-payments position would seem to tolerate. The fact is of course that it is inflation itself which tends to produce this seemingly universal illiquidity. Borrowers are tempted to borrow for the very good reason of buying now before prices go even higher; lenders are tempted to lend by the ready insistence of borrowers and the rising charges they can impose on loans. One special feature of this process deserves mention here. In those periods of time when an easy money policy has brought about a temporary lowering of the short-term rate relative to the long-term, those institutions which tend to borrow short and lend intermediate and long—guess who—tend to expand both their borrowings and their lendings. When the inevitable rise in the short-term rate comes, they then find themselves with a most embarrassing problem of liquidity. At this point they never cease to cry aloud for a new injection of money to save them from a liquidity crunch or crisis. Again the proposed remedy for the ailment turns out to be that which brought the ailment in the beginning and also that which is certain to produce a recurrence of the ailment at a later date.

A liquidity problem, whether it be for Joe Doaks and family, the Widget Mfg. Co., the First National Bank of Everywhere, the U.S. Government or the countries of India, England, Italy and Japan, can never be solved by inflation, by creating more dollars or more pounds or more yen or more SDRs. The temporary relief so gained is purchased at the price of a certain recurrence of the disease, and almost certainly in a more virulent form.

Another misconception is that inflation is caused by something other than the money relationship and that it can be stopped by doing things other than that of bringing about a proper relationship between the stock of money and the output of goods and services.

One form that this misconception takes is the Keynesian one, the belief that changes in total spending in the economy are not as closely related to changes in the stock of money as to other variables, such as business and consumer propensities and the fiscal actions of governments. For example, in the mid-60s, the Keynesians who were advising the Johnson administration assumed that in urging a more restrictive fiscal posture on the government, they had taken the important step in fighting the developing inflation and that they could then feel free to recommend a somewhat easy money policy. Although their advice was not followed in all details, the course of action was roughly what they called for—but the consequences were what Friedman and the monetarists were predicting, i.e., rising inflationary pressures under the influence of excessive monetary ease.

Another and more disquieting form that this misconception takes is what might be called the Galbraithian one. It is the belief that inflation is really produced through the domino-effect of price and wage increases triggered by powerful business, labor and farm groups in the economy. This point of view is supported neither by common sense nor theory nor the facts. Professor Paul McCracken once said of this idea that "it is still common among uneducated people. Galbraith's view is unusual only in being held by the president of the American Economic Association and in being described by him as new" (Washington Post, July 28, 1971).

It is indicative of the nature of the problem we are facing that this self-same McCracken was to publicly defend a system of wage-price controls instituted by his president just three weeks after he, McCracken, wrote the above statement.

Strong groups within the economy may be able to divert spending in various anti-social ways, but they cannot bring about an increase in total spending, which is what inflation is all about. Trying to stop inflation by wage and price controls is like trying to cure a fever by breaking the thermometer. The observed wage and price increases are but symptoms of the disease. The real problem is the heat in the body economic, and this can be reduced only by reducing the rate of increase in the quantity of money.

A final misconception about inflation is that it should be, and is, possible to stop an inflationary process without cost to anyone in society, except perhaps the very rich, who deserve their comeuppance in any case.

The fact is that once inflation lasts for any length of time it will come to be anticipated in the decisions of a greater part of the society. If inflation is stopped, those anticipations prove to have been in error, and the decisions based on those anticipations now have painful consequences: unemployment for the workers who had demanded the higher wages, losses for the firms who had contracted to pay the higher costs, financial loss to all who had purchased assets, directly or indirectly, in anticipation of rising prices, financial distress to all who had borrowed long-term money at high interest rates, etc.

The fact is that we can find not one single case of a society that has been able to stop an inflationary addiction without serious withdrawal pangs, in the form of higher rates of unemployment, lower real output, declining profits, etc. Moreover, the experience indicates that the longer and more rapid the inflationary surge, the more painful the withdrawal process.

The prophecy: We turn now, to my not-so-Delphic forecast of things to come. We have before us most of the ingredients on which I base my specific predictions.

We will have continuing, in fact accelerating, inflation in the years ahead.

Reasons: It would be too painful to stop it. Not only would it be painful to many of the citizenry, but because it would be painful to the citizenry, it would be political suicide for any administration that really attempted to do it. I am saying that I doubt if any administration could stay in power long enough—or continue to have power enough—to carry through to conclusion a really successful struggle to end inflation.

For the same reason, the administrations in power, of whatever political party, will find it necessary to jump up the rate of inflation from time to time to avoid the letdown that continuing a fully anticipated rate of inflation inevitably brings.

We will not have a major depression in the next two decades.

No administration could tolerate it and the alternative—a step up in the rate of inflation—is much less dangerous, politically, than a major depression. However, because of the imperfect nature of all attempts at control, and because of the necessity from time to time of taking half-hearted steps to slow down inflation, there will be occasional periods of recession—of the kind we have been experiencing. These will be marked by reduced rates of real growth, perhaps even negative real growth, higher unemployment, etc., but not by lowered levels of prices and wages. The descriptive word is "stagflation"—stagnation with inflation.

We will have off-and-on wage and price controls.

Too many people believe the Galbraith myth, and the pressure on administrations to do something—or to seem to be doing something—about inflation will bring recurring trials with direct controls. Each new return of controls will be greeted with huzzahs and cheers—even from the business community—only to fall victim to the inevitable frustrations and conflicts of the economic anarchy produced by those controls. Each repeal, though, will leave a larger part of the economy under some form and degree of direct controls.

The combination of continuing—accelerating—inflation and on-again, off-again controls will make it increasingly difficult for economic calculation to take place with any degree of efficiency.

The subsequent inefficiencies, shortages, frustrations and inequities will lead to increasing demands for even more detailed control of the private sector. In banking, this may well take the form of governmentally assigned quotas of lending to identified groups and for identified purposes at levels of interest rates well below market. This in turn will mean that the government will itself become an ever more important guarantor of loans and fund source of last resort.

The increasing control of economic life by government can have but one effect on the vitality and strength of the economic process—and that is to sap the vitality and diminish the strength of the most productive economic system in the history of man.

With the size of the pie either growing more slowly or diminishing, the conflicts over its division will increase in intensity. As the English experience so clearly demonstrates, these conflicts—particularly in the form of labor disputes—can make the efficient functioning of an integrated economy virtually impossible.

All of this in turn will reduce the capacity of this country to compete in world markets. Our fate, as England's, will then be chronic balance-of-payments problems, continuing loss of faith in the currency in the world money markets and periodic crises of increasing dimension. If this analysis be at all accurate, then we can say, with Archy the Cockroach, that there is indeed more reason to be optimistic about the past than about the future.

The forecast revisited: But must things turn out this way? Will there be none who will see the danger and fight it vigorously and successfully? What of the businessman? Won't the traditional American system find a defender in him?

In answer, I turn to the second part of my analysis of the processes I see at work in the American society, to the changing attitudes toward what may be called capitalism on the part of the two key groups, the businessmen and the intellectuals. Here I draw on the work of one of the most perceptive men of this century, Joseph A. Schumpeter. In his *Capitalism, Socialism and Democracy,* written in the early 1940s, he asks himself whether capitalism can survive in the long run and answers that question in the negative. Briefly summarized, here is his argument:

- Contrary to the Marxian and related analyses, capitalism has been a magnificently effective system for increasing the welfare of the masses of the people, not because of government intervention in the capitalist economics but in spite of such intervention.
- However, "criticism does not arise out of grievance and cannot be turned by justification." Capitalism must be defended in the arena of values and emotions, and here it is almost certain to lose.
- The businessman, if moved to defend capitalism, will be ineffective because of the very nature of what he is. Here are his words: "A genius in the business office may be, and often is, utterly unable outside of it to say boo to a goose, both in the drawing room and on the platform. . . . There is surely no trace of any mystic glamor about him, which is what counts in the ruling of men. The stock exchange is a poor substitute for the Holy Grail."

In other words, even if strongly moved to do, the businessman would be largely ineffective in the doing so. But, says Shumpeter, as capitalism matures, the businessman tends also to lose his will to defend the system of which he is a part. Why? Because the team man replaces the individual leader, group research, the one-man discovery and collective, anonymous ownership, the one-man or one-family firm. With these changes, the businessman loses that gut sense of ownership so typical of the entrepreneurial class of the past and comes to care little whether the technical ownership of the firm lies in the thousands or millions of invisible stockholders or in the thousands or millions of invisible citizen-owners.

These forces alone would not mean the end of capitalism. A defenseless fortress may still survive if there is no enemy. But this, too, a mature capitalism provides in the form of the class of intellectuals. What is an intellectual? In Schumpeter's words, "Intellectuals are people who wield the power of the spoken and written word and who have no responsibility for practical affairs." This definition would include, among others, teachers, preachers, poets, novelists and people of the media.

But why would such people necessarily be critical of capitalism? Why indeed. First, they are critical because "the intellectual's main chance of asserting himself lies in his actual or potential nuisance value." He is by nature a critic of the established system, whether he be in the United States or in Russia. The difference is that in Russia he is not tolerated whereas he is more than tolerated under mature capitalism. According to Schumpeter, the businessman is by nature tolerant and pacific. He wishes to trade with people rather than send them to Siberia.

Moreover, some part of the enormous affluence of a mature capitalist country will almost certainly be lavished on education, with the result that the number of intellectuals will be increasing rapidly. In fact, their numbers will be so increased that there will no longer be employment opportunities for all of them in positions with income and prestige appropriate to their self-evaluations. For this, the intellectuals will hold the capitalist system responsible, which will but add fuel to their already burning critical fires. Their favorite target will be the businessman, their favorite allies the bureaucrats of government with whom they share a common education and a common adversary relationship to the business community. In fact, the intellectuals will have a vested interest in expanding the governmental bureaucracy because of the job opportunities for themselves in such an expansion. In addition they will woo the trade unionists and the more militant minority groups within the society.

But what of those great beneficiaries of the capitalist process, the masses of the people? Won't they rise to defend the system responsible for their affluence from the attacks of those whose ways are forever at odds with their own? Not at all, says Schumpeter. The masses do not connect their affluence with the capitalist system; they are in fact incapable of understanding any economic system, whether capitalism or socialism. They are more aware of their daily frustrations under the system than of the long-run benefits. Finally, they are taught not to love the system by the intellectuals.

But won't the businessman finally recognize the danger and rise to the defense of the capitalist system? Quite the contrary, says Schumpeter. Here are his words:

> Perhaps the most striking feature of the picture is the extent to which the bourgeois besides educating its own enemies allows itself in turn to be educated by them. It absorbs the slogans of current radicalism and seems quite willing to undergo a process of conversion to a creed hostile to its very existence.

I call your attention to the many business leaders who have enthusiastically endorsed the idea of the social responsibility of the businessman. The traditional—and correct—view was that the businessman best served society when he made a profit out of correctly anticipating what consumers were going to want and be willing to buy. The new view, that the businessman should make primary—or at least of equal importance to profit-maximizing—some amorphous idea of the good society, is both an unworkable guide to business decision-making and destructive of the very basis of the capitalist economy.

In the same way, the business demands for direct controls in the months before August 1971 give evidence of a basic loss of confidence in the workings of the marketplace. In fact, the general response of the businessman to threatened or realized encroachments by government into his domain has been similar to that predicted by Schumpeter and similar to the response of the native girl to the advances of Lord Jim in

Conrad's novel. Conrad describes her response as follows: "He would have ravished her, but for her timely compliance." Need I say more?

Whatever else may be said of it, is it not true that what I have been saying here constitutes a rank form of defeatism? Schumpeter faced the same charge and answered as follows:

> I deny entirely that this term is applicable to a piece of analysis. Defeatism denotes a certain psychic state that has meaning only in reference to action. Facts in themselves and inferences from them can never be defeatist, or the opposite whatever they might be. The report that a given ship is sinking is not defeatist; only the spirit in which this report is received can be defeatist. The crew can sit down and drink. But it can also rush to the pumps.

As you would guess, I am suggesting that now is the time for as many as are inclined to rush to the pumps.

Political Incentives
and Continued Inflation

Let me begin with some opening comments on the introduction. My first comment is on that title of mine, Distinguished Professor of Political Economy. What does that signify? That's the kind of thing they hand out at small colleges like Wabash instead of cash. Actually, every good bank has titles of that kind tucked away for similar use.

I want to apologize to those of you who have been in my classes up at Madison if I didn't recognize you. Were you to let your beards grow, take off those coats and ties, slouch down in your seats, and go to sleep, I could pick you out in a minute. Some of you who have not been to Madison think all these men do is drink and carouse at night. I want to tell you that many of them are serious scholars up there. In fact, some of them have endangered their eyesight reading their lessons at night. Of course, the light's pretty damn bad in the Dangle Club.

I know that some of you have heard me give talks before on the economic outlook, and for me to come back into a group where there are those who have heard me before runs directly contrary to the fundamental principle of my profession as a forecaster, and that fundamental rule is the same for economic forecasters, for patent medicine salesmen—in fact, for confidence men of all kinds. It is that you go into town, you make your pitch, you get your money, you get out of town, and you never go back. Never go back? Well, here I am. I am also uneasy because this talk is being taped. If you will send that tape to me,

Editor's title. Speech to the General Meeting of Robert Morris Associates, Chicago Chapter, January 18, 1977. Reprinted by permission of the Rogge estate.

I will have my secretary, Rose Mary Woods, run a transcript. I am also a little nervous about being with a commercial lending group, sort of like attending a stockholders meeting at Penn Central right now.

Well, my assignment is to tell you whether or not capitalism is going to survive. In other words, to take a look into the future. I want to begin with the same disclaimer that some of you have heard me make before, and that is that I do not know what is going to happen to the American economy. And secondly, if I really did know, it would cost you one hell of a lot more than you're paying here tonight to find out. You'd come down to Crawfordsville one at a time as a matter of fact and line up.

Will capitalism survive? Some of you have asked me, survive what? Is it going to survive Jimmy Carter, for example. And you've asked me what do I think of his victory. As a matter of fact, I was delighted with his victory. Because for a number of years now I've been predicting that the economy was going to continue going to hell, and I feel absolutely safe for the next four years. As a matter of fact, I feel that he is a man of eminently good intent and a man of real intelligence. What bothers me is what bothers many others, I think, who have observed him, both before and now. He reminds me of Tell Binkley's nephew. Now Tell Binkley's nephew was created by a Hoosier humorist by the name of Kin Hubbard. He had a creation of his named Abe Martin, and Abe Martin came out with magnificent one-liners in the twenties and thirties. In one of his one-liners, he had Abe Martin saying that Tell Binkley's nephew was being interviewed by the Plum Creek School Board last week for the position of schoolmaster, and when they asked him whether the Mississippi River flowed north or south, he replied that he could teach it either way. But, I think, as a matter of fact, that Jimmy Carter does not have strong principle positions on economic questions. I think he can indeed teach it either way, and what bothers me is that I think most of those he has gathered around him are convinced that the Mississippi River flows north, or that it could be made to flow north by enough government spending.

At the same time, he is a most fortunate president. I think, as many others have noted, he is taking over a ship in very good shape. And this is going to be demonstrated in what happens in the next year or two, regardless of what Jimmy Carter does. I don't see how he could lose in the next year or two, as a matter of fact, in terms of the basic shape of the economy. I think 1977 is going to be an increasingly good year; I think 1978 is going to be a strong boom year. I think a year from now you people are going to be back in business. They are going to be at your window again. Now, why? Well, in large part, because he inherited the work of Jerry Ford and that administration.

By luck or courage, or maybe foolishness, Gerald Ford kept right on fighting inflation right to the end. He thought that a modern American president could fight inflation and still be reelected, and I don't think that's true. I don't think it can be done. I think the primary reason he lost was because of the state of the economy. Had it been really a booming, hot economy he would have been reelected. I think, as a matter of fact, had he had a stronger candidate against him, he would have lost by an even wider margin than he really did. But now, Jimmy Carter is inheriting this economy, in which the Ford vetoes and other Ford policies and the policies, in the main, of Arthur Burns, that much maligned man, have given us a dramatic drop in the inflation rate. The cost has been a slowdown in economic growth, but right now the economy is moving back in the other direction; 1977 and 1978 I think ought to be damn good years. Contrast that with what Nixon inherited.

I think Nixon took over exactly the opposite kind of economy in 1968. He took over an economy under very strong inflationary pressure brought on by what I think to have been the mistaken policies of his predecessors. Enormous inflationary pressures had been built up by the monetary and fiscal policies of the mid-sixties, and he took over the ship at that moment. As some of you have heard me say, his position was somewhat like the captain of the *Titanic*. Suppose that right after the ship hit the iceberg, the captain of the *Titanic* had turned to his second in command and said, "Now you've always wanted a ship of your own." And of course, Nixon had always wanted a ship of his own, and what he took over was a ship under very strong inflationary pressure. So Carter is going to have two good years, and then what's going to happen? What does it look like for the years ahead, including the survival of capitalism?

I think that in the years ahead we're going to see the following. Government spending and deficits are going to increase. We are not going to have a major depression at any time within the next four to eight years. The rate of inflation is going to head back toward double digits, reaching that, I forecast, sometime perhaps in late 1978. We will have wage-price guidelines reintroduced, in spite of what Carter has said, sometime in 1978. Included, I think, as part of that and as part of the general trend of events, the years immediately ahead will see an ever-increasing role by government in your economic decision-making and mine, as private individuals and as as businesspeople. The government is going to become involved in the details of to whom we may loan money, to whom we must lend money. This is going to be true for all sectors of the American economy. And as a result of this and other things, the American economy is going to become less efficient, less capable of producing economic growth. In the long run, the American economy is going to come to look very much indeed as the British economy does today. As one British commentator has described it, England is sinking slowly under the sea, giggling as she goes down. That is essentially my forecast.

Now once again, somewhat more slowly. Why are we going to have a return to inflation? Because, I think, it hurts too much to try to stop it. Because there are still too many pressures for government to spend and for it to reduce taxes, too many pressures for the deficit to increase, too many pressures that are going to be applied to the monetary authorities to keep the money supply loose, for the Fed to be accommodating. If Arthur Burns does not accommodate, I think there will be enormous pressure put upon him to get the hell out before his term as chairman runs out. Some of you have heard me say this before. Paul McCracken tells me he doesn't think Arthur will leave. He thinks Arthur has grown too fond of the office; he's grown too fond of having someone in a big, black car pick him up every morning and take him to work, and they don't do that on college campuses. But there will be enormous pressures put on him and on the Fed, and I think the Fed will accommodate. And that means by late 1977 on into 1978, we are going to have cumulative pressure of too much money again chasing too few goods, and the inflationary spiral will be well under way.

In fact, we are into the very early stages of this right now, and in the early stages it feels very good. Sales pick up, employment picks up, inventory accumulation starts again, business borrowing picks up, profitability goes up; the economy feels good. And that, of course, is the terrible, seductive attraction of inflation. Because when you first start it up again, it feels so darn good; it's only later that the price has to be paid. But there's a temporary price to slowing the monetary growth and eliminating the inflationary pressures, and I don't think we're willing to pay that price. The lesson of Ford's failure to be reelected is going to be clear to those who run in the future. How do the American people reward you for having fought inflation? They kick you the hell out of office. So that means we will undoubtedly again move to those devices for trying to stop inflation that will never work—wage and price guidelines, then full-scale controls. And when these devices come, as in the past, the greater part of the business community will be out there applauding in the vain hope that they will save them from the pressures on the wage rate, on labor costs, and so on, but, of course, that won't work. This is the kind of pattern that we will see repeated in the years ahead. Somewhere along the line, by the turn of the decade, somebody will again make a very strong attempt to control inflation by the more feasible means of again curtailing spending, curtailing the rate of growth of the money supply; and again we will have a sharp slowdown in the level of economic activity. As soon as that comes, there will once again be strong demands to get the economy moving, and away we go again, and each time we go up to a higher level. So by the end of the decade, we will have long-term double A rates of 12, 13 percent, maybe higher. Say, oh my God, that cannot happen here. Of course it can. Anyone who would have said that we're going to have long-term rates of 7 or 8 percent a few years ago would have been laughed out of court. You know, I think we're almost certain to have them. Then what you have sitting there in your portfolio isn't going to look very good again. Every time that happens, you can thank God that the bank examiners do not make you list your long-term bond holdings at market value, because a lot of you would be bankrupt, as would a great many of the pension funds of America. What else do you put it into; I don't know. I am only a diagnostician; I don't know what you do about any of these problems. I am just your friendly, neighborhood diagnostician; therapy comes from someone else. Again, if I really knew how a bank or person could hedge against these possibilities, I couldn't afford to be here tonight; I'd be too busy, but I don't know.

What about capitalism itself? Is this economic system going to survive all of this? Well, I want to talk about that in closing here, and I want to talk about it by reviewing what I hope some of you will have heard before: an analysis of the future of capitalism developed by a man a number of you have heard me talk about in the classes up at Madison or perhaps elsewhere, a most remarkable Viennese-born economist by the name of Joseph Schumpeter, who died in the 1950's, having taught at Harvard for many years after a distinguished career in Austria. He was the only man in higher education in America whose ego matched that of his colleague at Harvard University, John Kenneth Galbraith. I've had a request to repeat my description of John Kenneth Galbraith, and I'll do so. If you're not reading Galbraith, by the way, you really must because he continues to be the single most influential social scientist now at work. I have described him as an intelligent, literate, articulate, persuasive, arrogant, wrong-headed son of a bitch, and he continues to be precisely all of those things. He himself, of course, would argue only with the "wrong-headed" part of it. But his colleague Schumpeter was equally vain and arrogant, but I don't mind that when it's on my side. A friend of mine said to me, "Rogge, people like Galbraith who think they know everything are a very real trial to those of us who really do." He's quite a man. Schumpeter was as well.

In 1942 Schumpeter published a book called *Capitalism, Socialism and Democracy* in which he asked the question, can capitalism survive? and his answer was, No, I don't think it can. Why not? Because it was going to fail as an economic system? No, no, no. Strangely enough its success was going to be its undoing. How could that come about? Well his analysis runs like this. The first question is, Has capitalism, in fact, succeeded? Well, how do you measure how an economic system has succeeded? You can measure it by whether or not it puts bread on the tables of the masses. There are other criteria that we can use, and people do use, in evaluating economic systems. But he says fundamentally the question societies ask of an economic system is, By God does it get bread on the tables of the masses? His answer to the question, Has capitalism succeeded in doing that? is an absolutely, unambiguous, emphatic yes. In fact, he says that it is the only economic system that has ever succeeded in so doing, and he says it does it not by coincidence but by virtue of its very mechanism. He said look wherever they try it around the world—it works. You know, you can say, Rogge where is your hard data; where is Schumpeter's hard data? It's not too easy to come by, but

I think as a matter of fact there is some enormously persuasive evidence around the world and has been for some long time. How do we know whether you get more bread on the tables of the masses in East Germany than in West Germany? You take a look at which way those guns point. Why do the guns point to the East if the exploited workers from capitalist West Germany are trying to sneak into East Germany? They never do; it's always the other way. And as you might know, they've just announced a new device by which they can scan automobiles to make certain that no one is hanging someone on the bottom of the car trying to get into West Germany. You see how people vote with their feet. Or take it another way: which way are they swimming around Hong Kong at night? How many of them are headed for mainland China? Never one; it's always the other way. What has Hong Kong got going for it? Not a thing. Not a thing but freedom—no resources, no anything, really. All it has got going for it is the freest economy in the world today. Some of you may know far more about it in detail than I do. It really is an amazing place. It has absorbed a great flood of refugees from all over the Far East, and still the standard of living goes up more rapidly than anywhere else in the East, with the possible exception of the other areas that are trying capitalism in one form or another, Taiwan, South Korea, and Singapore. But Hong Kong is really the showplace of the world in terms of capitalist achievement. They have absolutely nothing going for them but freedom and capitalism, yet you see people risk their lives every night trying to swim from the workers' paradise of mainland China to get to Hong Kong. This is the evidence that I see all around me that capitalism has indeed worked.

Now Schumpeter says people say this was pure luck. You Americans, for example, were very lucky you found all those resources lying there. But as Schumpeter points out, resources are only objective opportunities, possibilities; they mean nothing until they are put to use. A couple of million, at the most, American Indians live lives of desperate poverty right on top of those same resources from which about 220 million of us now derive what Galbraith calls the affluent society. The resources didn't mean a thing. I used to fly over Saudi Arabia during the war, and you look down and there are these nomads living in poverty on top of black gold. Some of those people now have the highest per capita income of any in the world, but it took capitalist techniques, capitalist money to give it any meaning. It isn't by coincidence that people say, well, it's because the government brought it about. No, says Schumpeter, this rate of improvement in the well-being of the masses was going on just as rapidly, if not more rapidly, before the government got significantly involved in the economy. In fact, he said, the government involvement, if anything, held improvement back, as I think can be demonstrated.

If you've got a going economic system and one that he says can go right on producing liberty and economic growth in the years ahead, how can it possibly lose? How can people possibly reject such an economic system? Let us ask the question, Who is going to defend it? Will the masses who are the real beneficiaries of the system defend it. His answer is no. Why not? For one thing, they don't understand where the goodies come from. They don't tie their affluence to the capitalist system. They are far more conscious of their daily frustrations and insecurities under the system than they are of their long-run gains from it. More than that, they are taught not to like it. By whom? More of that in a moment. Why does that make any difference? Why can't the businessman defend the system? Why does the businessman need any help at all? Why can't he alone defend capitalism? Ah, says Schumpeter, even if the businessman is of the mind to do it, he's not very good at it. Why not? Well, says Schumpeter, many a genius in the business office is utterly unable outside of it to say boo to a goose—either in the drawing room or on the platform—that is, businessmen are simply not very persuasive. He says there is surely no trace of any mystic glamor about him, which is what counts in the ruling of men. The stock exchange is a poor substitute for the Holy Grail. In other words, what the businessman lacks is charisma. By the very nature of what you people do, you are logical, rational, pragmatic; these are not the stuff of what charisma is made. These are the stuff of good business decision-making but not what excites the masses of the people. Now, the businessman, in other words, even if he is of a mind to, is not a very good defender of capitalism.

Secondly, says Schumpeter, as capitalism matures, the businessman loses the will to fight. How does that happen? Well, the old, rough, tough entrepreneur who started the business is replaced by the next generations in his own family or by outside managers, by the organization people, and these people do not have this same gut sense of private property and the firm. The old man who started the bank or the mill or whatever it might be had kind of a Woody Hayes attitude—get the hell off my football field, get out of my plant, get out of my bank— whenever he was threatened by an intrusion. The modern manager is far more inclined to compromise, to find a way to accommodate, to go along rather than fight. And so as time goes on, the very nature of the businessman tends to change, and he finally doesn't really care whether he is reporting to these anonymous stockholders of the bank or the mill or the anonymous citizens in a socialized concern, so he tends to lose the will to fight.

So now you have no one defending capitalism. Does that make any difference if there is no enemy? No, but is there an enemy? Ah, says Schumpeter, capitalism produces its own enemy. In what form? In the form of intellectuals. Who is an intellectual according to Schumpeter? Intellectuals are people who wield the power of the written and spoken word and who have no direct responsibility for the conduct of practical affairs. That's what I am. That's right. That's what Schumpeter was; that's what Galbraith is; that's your priest, your minister, your rabbi, the people who teach your kids in school, the people who write the six o'clock news, the ones who write the dramas for television. Take a look at what they think of you. Take a look at what they think of the businessperson these days. The people who write novels, poetry, the lyrics for the songs the young people sing—we're all intellectuals, we live by words, and we have no direct responsibility for the conduct of practical affairs. Now why should we dislike capitalism? Well, in part, because we are by nature critics. Put us down in Eden, and two days later we've got a demand for reform. Put us down in Russia, and we're critics (but the Russians have a special way of dealing with critics). Put us down in capitalist America, by God, and we're critics. This is a most useful function in a way. We are made ever more critical under capitalism by what? In 1942 Shumpeter predicted that inevitably, as capitalism became ever more affluent, a significant part of that money would be directed into higher education, and there would be produced a great surplus of intellectuals. Absolutely accurate. Two years ago, we had one opening in the Department of English at Wabash College at low pay, and we had 325 applicants. Now as the 324 disappointed applicants tend bar, operate car washes, become minor bureaucrats, or what have you, and they see John Perkins drive up to the Continental Bank in his big car, they say, by God, there's got to be something wrong with this system. That man probably hasn't read a book all week. Now John may have read a book, as a matter of fact. But the intellectual then has to find some way to account for the success of the businessman, and how does he account for it? By hard work, intelligence, ambition, willingness to take a risk? Oh no, no, no. How do you get ahead in business? Take a look at how they portray you. How do people get ahead in business on television? By violence, by deceiving the customer, exploiting the worker, despoiling the environment, by outright dishonesty. Some of you have heard me give part of my lecture on dishonesty, where I argue that I think that actually a thoroughly dishonest man or woman can last far longer in college teaching or the ministry than in the used car business. I think that's true. There's no tenure in the used car business to the best of my knowledge. You see, this is the intellectuals' explanation. But when the intellectual critics claim businessmen are dishonest exploiters, the businessman not only doesn't fight these critics, not only subsidizes them, not only tolerates them, he ends up being educated by them and repeating their slogans.

Would time permit, which it obviously doesn't, I could pull out of the folder here an enormous collection I have made in just the last few years of statements by the leading businessmen of America that seem to me to be giving away the case. For example, talking about the social responsibility of the businessman, "Well by God, if you don't believe you serve society in trying to make a profit you don't really believe in the system." "I trust you characters only when you're out to make money, because then you're going to try to do it my way." "When you're out to do me good, then you're going to want to do it your way, and I don't want it done your way, I want it done my way." Thank God, most businessmen don't act on their platitudes. Thank God, most of them still try to make money, because the system would be in a hell of a shape if they didn't. But Schumpeter argues that ultimately the businessman capitulates. And again, I think there is evidence for precisely that point all around us. I don't mean that all businessmen capitulate, but again, this is the drift. The response of many businessmen to the encroachment of government tends to be very similar to the response of the native girl to the advances of Lord Jim in that book of Conrad's. Conrad describes her response to Lord Jim's advances in this way: he said he would have ravished her but for her timely compliance.

So there will be no one to defend capitalism, and over time the intellectuals will win. With whom will they make alliances? With the bureaucrats. Not with the workers; the workers and the intellectuals are simply different breeds of cat. When John Kenneth Galbraith goes skiing in Switzerland, does he go with George Meany? Or with Cesar Chavez or Leonard Woodcock or Jesse Jackson? No, no, no. Do you know with whom he goes? Bill Buckley. Two of the greatest egos in the modern world up there on that mountaintop at Gstaad, Switzerland. Because, you see, they're the same breed of cat. The intellectuals make their alliances with whom? The bureaucrats. Why? Because they all went to college together, and the bureaucrats have power, and it is being used in general to regulate business and that's good. As a matter of fact, where are intellectuals in the modern world going to find employment? In the bureaucracy. We have a vested interest in the growth of the bureaucracy. That's where we find pay, power, and prestige appropriate to our self-evaluations, as Schumpeter put it. So intellectuals have a vested interest in the growth of bureaucracy, and over time, the bureaucracy progressively stifles the functioning of the economy. When it can no longer be efficient at putting bread on the tables of the masses, we all say, well the system has failed. We have to try something different, and there we are.

Finally, Schumpeter takes up the question, is this a defeatist message? People always say, Rogge, in closing, for God's sake, say something cheerful, and I'm tempted to respond with one of my favorite Charlie Brown cartoons, where he's lost one of his baseball games and Lucy is trying to cheer him up, supposedly. Lucy says, "Charlie Brown, I know that these are your days of defeat, frustration and despair, but Charlie Brown just hold your head up high and keep on fighting and some day you'll win." He says, "Gee, Lucy, do you really think so?" and she says, "Well, frankly, no."

But even if Schumpeter didn't believe capitalism could survive, he was not a defeatist. In his preface to the final edition of his book, he denied that a piece of analysis could be considered defeatist. The report that a given ship is sinking is not defeatist. It's either right or wrong; it's not defeatist or its opposite, whatever that may be. What can be defeatist? The response of the crew. He said the crew can sit down and drink—that's defeatism. Or, he said, it can rush to the pumps. What I'm saying to you tonight is that if you want to give capitalism a better chance to survive, now may be the time for such of you as are inclined to rush to the pumps. Thank you.

The Political Economy of Inflation

At some time in what I hope will be the distant future, when my final
Personnel Performance Record is sent to the Great Evaluation Committee up there in the sky, pride of place will surely belong to the following entry: "Whatever his all-too obvious flaws and shortcomings, let it
hereby be recorded that on April 27th, 1978, in the city of Fort Wayne,
Indiana, said subject, B. A. Rogge, was involved in an activity in which
his name was associated with that of Herman B. Wells." Given the fact
that Herman B. Wells even now has many friends of great distinction,
both up and down in the Great Beyond, this should be helpful to me,
whatever the decision in my particular case.

My standing in the world academic community is to the standing
of Herman Wells as the association with which I am involved, Ladoga
Federal Savings and Loan, is to the Federal Home Loan Bank. Our only
claim to fame is that none other than Richard O. Ristine was once our
attorney and fellow board member. In fact his photograph once hung
on one of our walls—until the day after the gubernatorial election of
1964. Service on that board has been an educational process for me, with
the two principal lessons learned being these: (1) The lowest-earning
asset in an association portfolio is its stock in the Federal Home Loan
Bank; and (2) you have to be touched with a certain fine madness to

Herman B. Wells Memorial Lecture, delivered at the Annual Stockholders Meeting of the
Sixth District Federal Home Loan Bank, Fort Wayne, Ind., April 27, 1978. Reprinted by
permission of the Rogge estate.

really believe that, in an inflationary world, you can make money by borrowing short and lending long.

But enough of the preliminaries. I know that you are anxious to hear my incisive analysis of the course of inflation in this country in the decades immediately ahead. My assignment is just that: to tell you what lies ahead for the American economy. I have two statements to make about that assignment: (1) I do not know what lies ahead for the American economy; and (2) if I really did know, it would cost you significantly more than I'm being paid here today to find out. I do not know what lies ahead, nor does anyone else. Not Charles Schultze, Chairman of the Council of Economic Advisors to President Carter; not Arthur Burns, the just-retired Chairman of the Board of Governors of the Federal Reserve System—and if Burns did know, he wouldn't tell Jimmy Carter. I'll tell you how desperate things are: not even Milton Friedman knows for sure what's going to happen. The reason for this universal ignorance is perfectly clear: God did not see fit to endow any of us mortals with the power of perfect foresight. But plan we must and so guess we must as to the course of events in time yet to come.

My own guesses are presented here under the catch-all label "The Political Economy of Inflation." I have chosen this title in part because it recapitulates a part of my own title at Wabash College—Distinguished Professor of Political Economy. Let me hasten to caution you not to over-interpret that title; that is the kind of thing that small colleges hand out to senior faculty members in lieu of cash. The phrase "Political Economy" identifies to me a field of study that examines the intricate relationships between politics and economics in the real world off-campus. This in turn implies that political economy is a less rigorous discipline, less amenable to mathematical statement and verification, than is theoretical economics. Or to put it another way, by identifying himself as a practitioner of political economy, a man relieves himself of the necessity of proving the validity of any statement he might happen to make.

To give emphasis to the political content of my probes into the future, I am structuring my discussion in the form of an imagined meeting in that Holy of Holies of politics, the Oval Office of the White House. The purpose of the meeting is to assist the president of the United States in drafting a set of policy proposals for the nation's economy. I have chosen Jimmy Carter as the man in the president's chair, because to do otherwise would be confusing at this moment. But, as I shall reiterate, the course of the discussion and the proposals finally accepted are not really to be seen as a function of either the man or the party that fills that chair. More on this later.

As the scene opens, we find the president, seated (naturally) in the president's chair, practicing his smile. As he listens to the suggestions of some of his advisors, he's going to need that smile to keep from laughing right out loud. As is his preference on these occasions, the president has surrounded himself with various members of his personal and political family. Brother Billy is seated right, on an oil drum, sipping on a Ribbon—or is it a Billy Beer? Amy is there, and as a show-and-tell project, has brought her school class with her. Bert Lance is there, along with two of his Arab friends, one of whom has in his pocket a takeover bid for the Federal Home Loan Bank. And so on.

The president begins by identifying the topic for the meeting (economic policy) and by asking Charles Schultze, of the Council of Economic Advisors, to briefly summarize how things now stand in the American economy.

SCHULTZE: Mr. President, in spite of your brilliant performance in your first year in office, I must report to you that we still confront a high rate of inflation, a high rate of unemployment, a serious energy problem—and that the dollar has just fallen through the subbasement.

PRESIDENT CARTER: Picky, Picky, Picky. However, I suppose we do have to do something. What should receive top priority?

SCHULTZE: Mr. President, so that he can speak first and be hustled out of the room, I'd like to call first on a young staffer from the Federal Reserve Bank of St. Louis, which, as you know, Mr. President, is the inside-the-government statistical arm of Milton Friedman.

ST. LOUIS STAFFER: Mr. President, the number one problem now facing this country is clearly that of continuing inflation. Until, and if, it is solved, very little can be done to reduce our other problems. Mr. President, the analysis of what causes inflation and of how to stop it is simplicity itself. Inflation is caused by a too-rapid rate of growth in the money supply; the solution is for you to tell William Miller at the Fed to bring the rate of growth of money down to a lower level and hold it there through thick or thin.

PRESIDENT CARTER: If this were to be done young man, exactly what would happen and when?

ST. LOUIS STAFFER: If this were done immediately, the first noticeable consequence would be a rise in the short-term interest-rate structure; in six months to a year's time, the economy would turn sluggish, demand would fall off, profits would fall, unemployment would go up, and the economy would enter into a full-scale recession in 1979 and 1980.

PRESIDENT CARTER: To come in here with a suggestion like this indicates that you need help, young man, help and a mother's care. But a certain grisly fascination with your proposal leads me to ask this: When, if ever, would the economy start getting back on its feet?

ST. LOUIS STAFFER: With a little luck, Mr. President, by 1981 the inflation rate should be back down in the 1–3 percent range, and the economy should be starting on its way to recovery.

PRESIDENT CARTER: Yes and I would already be on my way to the Georgia poorhouse. Do you not know, young man, that there's an election in this country in 1980? Do you know how the voters of this country showed their gratitude to the last president under whom the inflation rate was cut in half? His name was Gerald Ford and they fired him. Mr. Schultze, bring on your next speaker.

SCHULTZE: Mr. President, I am pleased to present a student of your friend Walter Heller, a young man thoroughly versed in the ideas of Keynesian economics.

KEYNESIAN: Mr. President, I question your assigning top priority to stopping inflation. I believe that you should give at least equal attention to the problem of unemployment.

PRESIDENT CARTER: Humor me, then. If I am determined to fight inflation, how should I go about it?

KEYNESIAN: The cause of inflation and the cure are both immediately obvious. The cause of inflation is excess effective demand in the economy. The cure is for the federal government to cut its own spending and/or raise taxes so as to cut spending in the private sector.

JORDAN: [Hamilton Jordan now speaks. He had been sitting next to Patricia Harris of HUD, into whose blouse he has been absent-mindedly stuffing his ice cubes.] Did I hear you right, young man?

Did you honestly propose to the president that he go before the American people and tell them, not only that is he going to cut out some of their favorite programs but that he's going to raise taxes as well?

KEYNESIAN: That's right. He has no choice if he really wants to fight inflation.

JORDAN: Mr. President, can't we get rid of this whole gaggle of egg-heads and get down to business with people who really know the political score?

SCHULTZE: Mr. President, I have just one more speaker to present, and she may be more to Mr. Jordan's liking. She is a disciple of that self-acknowledged genius of social policy John Kenneth Galbraith.

GALBRAITHIAN: The two speakers who have preceded me, Mr. President, are splendid specimens of the dodo bird, one old and one new. The reasoning of each is impeccable but suffers from one distressing flaw—it is totally irrelevant to the political economy of the world around us. It is Euclidean geometry in a non-Euclidean world. Prices, wage rates, and interest rates in the real world are not set by the invisible hand of Adam Smith—or even by the union leaders of Keynes's dreamworld, who were aware of wage changes but oblivious to price-level changes. In the part of the economy that really counts, these so-called market phenomena are in fact not a product of the competitive market at all—which exists only in certain classrooms at a distinguished university on the south side of Chicago—but of the very invisible hand of the technostructures that now control the destinies, not only of General Motors and Exxon but, through that, the very nature of your lives and mine.

Mr. President, the choice is yours. America can go on being ruled—or rather mis-ruled—by this private power elite, or it can be ruled for the public good by its government, under the tutelage and guidance of those of us who have a clear perception of the social necessities and possibilities of the modern world. Your first step must be to impose a system of mandatory price and wage controls on at least the non-market-controlled sectors of the American economy.

PRESIDENT CARTER: Don't rush me. You are very persuasive, but let me ask you this: Are you telling me that it is not the government—not the president's office, not the Congress, not the Federal Reserve

System—that produces inflation? but rather the self-serving activities of private power groups, acting in flagrant disregard of the public interest?

GALBRAITHIAN: I am indeed, Mr. President.

PRESIDENT CARTER: Young lady, I like the way you think, but if I were you, I'd move over closer to Amy's school group and further away from Hamilton Jordan. But to return to the topic: Are you saying that the person who really causes inflation is the assistant manager of the A&P store who goes around erasing forty-three cents on a can of beans and writes in forty-seven cents? or the loan officer who announces an increase in the prime rate? or the leader of a Republican-voting construction union who demands a higher wage for his men? or how about the leaders of the OPEC nations, those crazy Arabs that no one likes anyway (sorry there, Bert)? Are these the real culprits who have visited the curse of inflation on this great country?

GALBRAITHIAN: They are indeed.

PRESIDENT CARTER: I like it, I like it. But wait a minute: Did you call for me to institute mandatory wage and price controls? Young lady, don't you know that I have taken a foursquare stand *against* doing that?

GALBRAITHIAN: Well, so had President Nixon—right up to August of 1971, with election time just a year away. As my mentor, John Kenneth Galbraith, said at that time: "Nixon has opposed wage and price controls all of his political life, but thank God in Nixon we have a president without principle and without scruple who will do whatever is expedient at the moment."

As a practical strategy, Mr. President, I would suggest that you begin, not with mandatory controls, but with a policy of ongoing voluntary restraint on the part of all those in the private sector who are the price- and wage-makers in the economy. This will clearly establish in the public mind that these private-sector institutional leaders do indeed have it within their power to stop inflation and that all that is needed is the will to do so in the public interest.

Then, if they flagrantly disregard your appeals to them to exercise restraint (as is quite likely), you will be in a position to go before the American people and say that in your great dislike of government intervention in our great free enterprise system you have insisted on following a policy of voluntarism, of giving each group in the American society an uncoerced opportunity to assist its country to Whip Inflation Now—but to no avail. A callous disregard of the public interest is everywhere to be seen, and you can no longer stand by and see this country's economy ruined and its dollar debased by the cancer of inflation. And then, just as Nixon did, announce that, as of that moment, all prices and wages are frozen for an interim period, pending the development of a program of full-scale direct controls.

PRESIDENT CARTER: But I really *am* opposed to direct controls— although of course, I have always said that I was opposed to such controls except in a case of dire emergency, such as war. And haven't I already identified our energy crisis as confronting us with "the moral equivalent of war"? I must confess, it's sounding better and better to me.

ST. LOUIS FED STAFFER (who has broken through the guards at the back of the room): Are you all mad in here? Don't you know that price controls have been tried for five thousand years—and have never worked? How can you cure a fever by breaking the thermometer? The wage and price increases are only the symptoms of the disease; the problem is too much money! Remember as well, what our great mentor, Professor Friedman, has said to us: "Nothing can more surely destroy a free enterprise system than long-continued wage and price controls."

PRESIDENT CARTER: Will the security officers please see that that man is removed from this room and not permitted to reenter. Now, where were we? Oh yes, we were discussing a strategy of combating inflation by a system of voluntary restraint. I like it. I can see a good set of lines even now:

> . . . it is a myth that the government itself can stop inflation.

> Success or failure in this overall effort will be largely determined by the actions of the private sector of our economy.

> I expect industry and labor to keep price, wage, and salary increases significantly below the average rate for the last two years. Those who set medical fees, legal and other professional fees, college tuition rates, insurance premiums, and other service charges must also join in.

Well, that takes care of inflation. What's next?

Patricia Harris, various congressmen and senators, spokesmen from other programs, and others all start shouting at once. In effect, what they are saying is that now that we've got inflation taken care of it's time to go ahead with the federally financed programs so necessary to solving the ills of this great country: urban redevelopment, water-diversion systems, rebuilding of the railroads, from Amy's group a demand for more federal money for school playgrounds—and on and on and on.

Included in the voices is that of George Meany, who is on a direct hotline with Secretary of Labor Roy Marshall, who indicates that his people will not submit to any wage-control system that denies them their just due. If the president is determined to go ahead with direct controls, he should at least order Bill Miller to open the money spigot and drive down that ungodly interest rate.

At this point the spokesmen for the Keynesian and Galbraithian points of view try to make their voices heard, saying, "Wait a minute, wait a minute. There are still levels of government spending and money creation that go too far." But it is too late. Finally the president restores order to the group and announces, in a stern voice, that in the interest of fighting inflation he stands ready to veto any new spending proposals or specific tax reductions that he didn't like in any case—such as the tax credit for tuition paid to private schools.

PRESIDENT CARTER SPEAKS AGAIN: We still have several other problems that demand our serious attention. For example, what are we going to propose to bring down the unemployment rate?

KEYNESIAN: Here's where I think I can be of real help. The high rate of unemployment in our country today is in significant part a reflection of inadequate effective demand. The answer is simple: you should propose that the federal government increase its spending and/or cut taxes.

JORDAN: Now you're talking sense, man. But is that alone going to do it? How can we convince the voters that this administration is going to see to it that there is a job for every American who wants to work?

At this point, various senators and congressmen from both parties, labor leaders, progressive, forward-looking businessmen, leading churchmen, and others press forward and lay on the president's desk a copy of one of the thirty-three existing versions of the Humphrey-Hawkins bill, saying in effect, "Voila!"

PRESIDENT CARTER: I was a great admirer of the late Senator Humphrey, of course, but I was disturbed by the section in the earliest version of this bill, which would have given an unemployed worker a right to sue the government for not providing him with the promised employment.

On receiving assurances that the later versions omit that section, he agrees to give it a try.

At this point, the St. Louis Fed man sticks his head in an open window and shouts, "Don't listen to them, Mr. President! If you really want to reduce unemployment, get rid of the minimum wage law, the laws against child labor, OSHA, and all laws that give special privileges to trade unions.

"Also, stop paying people more to *not* work than to work."

His further remarks are drowned in cries of disbelief and horror. Senator Javits proposes that those unsolicited comments be stricken from the record or, as an alternative, that the tape on which they were recorded be turned over to Rose Mary Woods for transcribing.

Order is again restored and the president speaks: "We have just one problem left: the falling value of the dollar in the world exchanges. How do we handle that?"

SECRETARY OF THE TREASURY BLUMENTHAL: My suggestion is that we go out and buy dollars, thus bolstering the demand for the dollar and raising its price as against other currencies.

At this point, those near a grating over a cold-air duct can hear the muffled voice of the St. Louis Fed man saying that that's like a tomato farmer trying to get rich by buying his own tomatoes.

BLUMENTHAL CONTINUES: Our problem, Mr. President, is that the governments of West Germany, Japan, and Switzerland are reactionary and almost totally out of step with the times.

PRESIDENT CARTER: What do you mean by that?

BLUMENTHAL: They won't inflate! And if they don't inflate as fast as we do, people around the world would rather have their currencies than ours.

PRESIDENT CARTER: Oh what a dastardly trick! I shall discuss this with their governments this very weekend, on my goodwill visits to Europe, Asia, New Zealand, and Antarctica. Well, I guess that just about wraps it up. The only item left on the agenda is energy and I've already created a department to take care of that.

My thanks to all of you, with the possible exception of the man from the St. Louis Federal Reserve Bank.

Well, enough is enough—or perhaps too much. Enough of the White House scenario. How much difference would it have made if I (or rather, the American voters) had put Gerald Ford in that chair instead of Jimmy Carter? My own answer: Very little. You could have put Ronald Reagan or Ted Kennedy or Governor Stassen in that chair, and it wouldn't have made much difference—assuming that he (and/or his party) were running for office in two years' time. The fact of the matter is that an addiction to inflation, like any addiction, once fully acquired, is extremely difficult and painful to shake. From an attempt even to slow the rate of inflation, the pain comes now—and the good feeling sometime later. When an economy is sluggish, a new, unanticipated burst of inflation, like the first drink of the day, restores health and vigor to the constitution in short order—and the pain comes the next morning.

With these thoughts on the political economy of inflation in mind, I hereby offer you my own guesses about the course of events in the next ten to fifteen years.

(1) We will have no major depression in this economy in that period of time. No political leadership group could afford to be identified with one and by heroic feats of public spending and money creation can keep it from happening.

(2) We will have never-ending inflation during that period of time. The rate-of-inflation pattern over time will be a now-familiar one: an upward-tilted sine curve. Each new high will be higher than the one before; each new low, higher than the one before.

We have now learned the painful lesson that the supposed trade-off between inflation and unemployment is a snare and delusion. Once the economy adjusts to and comes to expect a given dosage, it no longer produces that wonderful feeling of euphoria in which profits are rising, unemployment is falling, and all's right with the world. Only a new and larger and unanticipated dose can get the job done—and then its effects wear off as well.

I do not see the American people as willing to go all the way through the tunnel of self-denial and unequally distributed pain for a long-enough adjustment period to drive the inflationary forces and expectations out of the economy. Long before the other end of the tunnel would be reached, they would be shouting, "Get us out of here!" I fully expect us to see inflation rates of 15 to 20 percent within the next five to eight years.

(3) This belief of mine is strengthened by my conviction that the federal budget of this country will not be balanced within the lifetime of anyone in this room—with the possible exception of Herman Wells, who just may have found the secret of eternal life. We have been running budget deficits of $40 billion to $60 billion during a strong recovery; what will they become in the next downturn?

An unbalanced budget is not per se inflationary, but it creates an almost irresistible pressure on the administration to favor an easy money policy (and hence temporarily lower interest rates)—and that *is* inflationary.

(4) It is also strengthened by my conviction that the unemployment rate is going to continue indefinitely to be higher than is politically palatable. For whatever reasons, we seem determined to price most of our young people—and particularly our minority-race young people—out of the labor market. Moreover, as Senator Abraham Ribocoff—in an unguarded moment—once put it, after recalling many of the things he did to earn money as a boy, "We have too damn many laws coddling children." The great curse of America's young people today is not overwork but idleness.

Their idleness, together with that of those whom we will pay more to not work than to work, is a constant challenge to the society to do something—and that something is almost inevitably inflationary.

(5) Yes, the forces now at work in this economy—and, in fact, in the world economy as well—produce a strong bias toward inflation. God knows that inflation creates problems for various sections of the economy; God knows that it makes economic calculation difficult. But perhaps paradoxically, I share Milton Friedman's concern that we may have more to fear from the things that are done in an attempt to stop inflation than from the disease itself. He has in mind, as I do, the powerful political enticement of direct controls of wages and prices. I attempted to spell out the nature of that enticement in the Oval Office melodrama. By imposing direct controls, the political leaders of the country absolve themselves from responsibility for inflation and point the finger of guilt at the private sector. In other words, the perpetrators of the crime fasten the blame on its victims—a neat switch indeed. My own guess is that we will have a system of direct controls of prices and wages imposed on the American economy sometime in the summer or fall of 1979.

What does all this signify for the mortgage-lending business of this country?

(1) Interest rates will escalate. If mortgage money can be had at 3–4 percent in a price-stable situation, in a situation in which the price level is expected to rise by 5–6 percent a year, the rate will rise to 8–10 percent (as it has in recent years). In a situation in which the price level is expected to rise by 10–12 percent a year, the rate will move to 13–16 percent.

(2) Uncertainty about the future course of prices, interest rates, and public policies will be increased.

(3) Both of these factors will lead to increased use of hedging devices in the mortgage-lending field—indexed interest charges, short-term (say 3, 5, 8, or 10 years) with, for example, negotiable renewal of balloons. When I was in Argentina recently, where they were celebrating the fact that inflation was *only* 120 percent a year, rather than the 700 percent of the year earlier, I asked some financial people I met if there was a long-term money market in existence. Their reply: "Of course. You can get 30-day money here—at ten percent a month."

(4) Wild swings in short-term money-market rates will arise out of the stop-go policies of the monetary authorities. Regulation Q will have to go, as will the one-half percent advantage we now have over other financial institutions.

(5) "Direct controls," as applied to mortgage-lending institutions will probably involve some control of lending rates but will also include much more specific regulation of to whom we loan how much for what purpose. In my opinion, we are even now being required to invest the other people's money under our guardianship in ways that are a direct denial of the requirements of the prudent construct at law. This will get worse.

(6) To summarize, in the immortal words of Archy the Cockroach, when asked for his views on the human prospect, "I believe that there is more reason to be optimistic about the past than about the future."

But be of good cheer; the system may still survive. I close with the encouragement given us by my mentor, Adam Smith, writing in 1776,

> The uniform, constant, and uninterrupted effort of every man to better his condition, the principle from which public and national, as well as private opulence is originally derived, is frequently powerful enough to maintain the natural progress of things toward improvement, in spite both of the extravagance of government, and of the greatest errors of administration. Like the unknown principle of animal life, it frequently restores health and vigour to the constitution, in spite, not only of the disease, but of the absurd prescriptions of the doctor.

Part 6 *Foreign Policy and Economic Development*

Should the United States Be in Vietnam?

Let me begin by saying that I prefer *this* method of examining the issues to that of carrying placards through the city streets. For me to join in a street demonstration of any kind, for any purpose, would be for me to publicly proclaim that I have largely abandoned hope of the possibility of a civilized society—and this I have not done. In further explanation: Although I oppose our intervention in Vietnam and although I oppose the military draft, I do not intend to urge you young men to tear up your draft cards. On the contrary, when the discussions have ended and the decisions have been made, I believe that each of us has more to gain by abiding by the decisions of our country than by openly flouting them—at least until that point is reached where our country, on balance, represents the anti-civilization—and that point has by no means been reached as yet. To do otherwise is to court not freedom but chaos. I trust that I do not need to add that my position does not reflect any liking for the social and economic philosophies of the Vietcong and North Vietnamese. I am spending a good part of my life attempting to defeat those ideas.

My conviction that we should withdraw our troops from Vietnam does not rest on any expert knowledge of Southeast Asia. Rather, it derives from the same set of presuppositions that lead me to my non-interventionist position on economic and social issues in this country. For me, as for a somewhat more distinguished social philosopher—Plato—civili-

Panel presentation given in 1969. Reprinted by permission of the Rogge estate.

zation is the victory of persuasion over force. I start then with a tremendous presumption against the use of force. You may say, "Yes, so do I," but let me itemize the price we pay for the use of force in Vietnam.

First, there are the specific Americans who will die in exercising it. As someone once said, "After all, it is not so much to die—but young men think so, and these men were young." Next, there are the specific South Vietnamese who must die, including the women and children in the village which happens to be in the path of the poorly aimed shell. I even confess some concern at the fact that specific Vietcong and North Vietnamese must die, even though I might say, "Well, they asked for it." There is at least a grain of truth in the old Arabian adage "He who strikes the second blow, starts the fight." I doubt if we can take much satisfaction in the killing of these basically primitive people, most of whom probably know little more than that they are again fighting some kind of foreign devil.

But the price of fighting in Vietnam cannot be measured solely in the destruction and despoiling of human life. We are paying (and will pay even more severely in the months ahead) in the narrowing of freedom in our own country. Societies at war are rarely attentive to the cause of liberty. Witness the concentration camp treatment of the Japanese in California during World War II—an operation, by the way, that was encouraged and supervised by the man who was until recently the Chief Justice of the Supreme Court of the United States. I point this out, not to single out Earl Warren for attack, but to illustrate how even the apparently most judicious of us can be ruled by the anti-freedom frenzy of wartime. If this war continues for another year or two, as it seems likely to do, we are almost certain to see a suppression of some of our civil liberties—including the right to publicly oppose the continuation of the war.

To this will probably be added other features of the garrison state, including new controls over the economy and the associated loss of economic freedom. National defense has been used before and will be used again as a reason for expanding the public sector of the economy—an expansion which if past experience serves as a guide, will never be completely undone in the post-war period.

In other words, in the proclaimed interest of defending freedom, we are always in danger of abandoning that freedom and becoming more and more like the enemy we oppose in the field.

This then is the *why* of my tremendous presumption against the use of force in the form of war. My instincts are those of the pacifist—but my logic does not lead me to pacificism as a final position. I believe that the presumption against the use of force can be overridden under two specific situations: (1) to defend ourselves from an actually existing (clear and present danger) use of force against us by others; and (2) to go to the aid of another people who face a clear-cut choice between freedom and oppression, who have expressed a clear-cut preference for freedom, and who have made it clear that they would prefer the death and destruction that our intervention would entail to falling to the enemy that threatens them.

I would argue that reason 1 cannot be advanced in the case of the intervention in Vietnam. The North Vietnamese are not preparing to invade U.S. territory nor are even their allies, the Chinese Communists. Even were the Chinese Communists to control all of Southeast Asia, which by the way I think unlikely and which, if achieved, would be more a source of trouble for them than of strength, they would not be at war with the U.S. If we are in Vietnam only because of a chain of hypothetical consequences that might at some time in the future threaten our own survival, then the killing in Vietnam is not only wasted but immoral. What right have we to be involved in the killing of thousands of primitive peoples on the off chance that it might conceivably serve our own interests at some time in the future?

No, if there is a justification for our intervention, it must rest on reason 2. But let us examine each of the clauses of the sentence in which I defined reason 2.

Do the South Vietnamese face a clear-cut choice between freedom and oppression? Were they a free people before the current struggle began? Would they be likely to be a free people after the struggle, if we were to win? No one of the pre–armed-intervention regimes seems to have been precisely freedom-loving. It was not an England faced by a Hitler that we intervened to save, but a right-wing dictatorship faced by a left-wing dictatorship. If we were to win, it seems certain that we could preserve freedom for the individuals in the Vietnamese society only by a more-or-less permanent military occupation, with the native leaders being permitted to be no more than American puppets. Given the characters who have paraded through the leadership roles in South

Vietnam in recent months (including the one who prefers to take Hitler as his model), it seems unlikely that we could take any great pride in these puppet rulers of the future or in our role in keeping them in power.

But now to the second clause: If given a choice would the people of South Vietnam clearly choose the leaders we have been fighting to save to the leadership of the rulers of North Vietnam? No one knows, of course, but we were apparently unwilling to take a chance on an election, perhaps because we believed it couldn't really be a free election or perhaps because we were aware of how shaky was the South Vietnamese opposition to the Communist rulers of the North. Without us, a victorious South Vietnam would almost certainly be ruled by a right-wing dictator; with us, it would be ruled by an American puppet. Given the nationalism of the people, it is doubtful if these people, in a free election, would select an American puppet and American-enforced freedom over one of their own, even if he were a dictator of the Communist left.

If these propositions be true, can we have any certainty that the people of South Vietnam really prefer the death and destruction that our intervention entails to the consequences of a takeover by the North Vietnamese? Lacking that certainty, we have assumed a terrible burden in urging on and joining these innocent, largely primitive people in the killing of their own, in the largely vain hope that freedom can somehow be brought to Vietnam. If to be an internationalist is to use our economic and military might to "set the world straight," then I am an isolationist; if to favor all peaceful interventions, then I am an internationlist.

I have argued that the presumption is always on the side of non-intervention in the affairs of other people, that the costs of armed intervention (i.e., of war) are terrible indeed, both to them and to us, and that we must never undertake armed intervention unless the case for intervention is overwhelming. I have insisted that the case in this situation, far from being overwhelming, is shaky indeed, whether viewed from the viewpoint of our own national security or from the viewpoint of preserving freedom for the Vietnamese. My conclusion is that our troops do not belong in Vietnam and should be withdrawn.

East-West Trade

I begin with one of the simplest propositions in economics—yet one that seems to be commonly ignored. It is this: In any *voluntary exchange*, both parties must expect to benefit. This is so obvious that I am always embarrassed when I feel compelled to explain it. The failure to recognize this simple fact was at the heart of the ancient mercantilist sin that Adam Smith went to such great lengths to expose; it is at the heart of many of the economic errors of the modern liberals; I regret to report that it also seems to be involved in the attitude of many conservatives on East-West trade. In every article condemning this trade, I read only of the goods that we have sent to Russia—never of the goods that we have received in return. What of the manganese, the chromium, the ore, the furs, the fish and fish oils, and yes, the gold, that we receive in return? Are these of no value to us?

Ah, but you say, "We are sending them machinery and equipment that is directly related to their military potential, while we get caviar in return."

In the first place, not all that we receive is caviar. What of the manganese that is critical to some of our own war production, of the chromium—used in rifle linings—that Union Carbide recently announced it is now buying from Russia, and of the oil we buy that permits us to conserve our own underground reserves?

This paper was originally presented at a meeting of the Intercollegiate Studies Institute in Indianapolis, Ind., in December 1967, and subsequently published by the Cato Institute (Cato Essay No. 4, 1980). Reprinted by permission of the Cato Institute.

But all of this is of no real significance anyway. To worry about the exact composition of the trade makes about as much sense as instructing a beggar that you will give him a dollar if he promises not to spend it on liquor. He may indeed spend your dollar on food—and with the dollar now released from that necessity, he heads for the nearest grogshop.

If we were to sell the Russians nothing but wheat and they were to sell us nothing but caviar, resources would still be released in each country that could then be turned to military purposes.

I repeat: If the Russians benefit from trade with us, by the same token we benefit from the trade with them.

Here you may want to argue that this isn't strictly true, that some part of our trade with Russia is on credit, and credit of a dubious quality. In the first place, our exports to Russia and Eastern Europe in 1966 of $198 million were almost balanced by our imports from these countries of $178 million, so the amount of credit was small. In the second place, the credit that is being granted comes largely from our Export-Import Bank—a bank that I feel shouldn't exist in the first place and that certainly should not be making loans to such doubtful credit risks in the second place. If the problem is the dubious policy of a public lending agency, the answer is not to stop all trade, but to get rid of or correct the agency.

Let me make it clear: I am against *any* government-supported long-term credit to another country, on either side of the Iron Curtain. But I don't think that this is the crux of the issue, because I think that American business, as it has proved throughout its history, will find a way to trade, anywhere in the world, government-guaranteed credit or not.

One final objection: What of the sale to Russia of machinery embodying essentially new processes, i.e., of machinery and equipment that it really couldn't get elsewhere because of the advanced technology involved? Let's take the case where the machinery is not directly related to weapons systems. If a private American firm feels that it is getting a fair price for its advanced technology, why should the government stop the sale? After all, the technology does not belong to the United States government or the American society; it belongs to the firm that produced it. Admittedly, the Russians have a long record of pirating patents, but if a private firm sells the Russians a prototype machine with full knowledge that it may have difficulty protecting the patented devices or processes, why should we then listen to its cries of dismay if and when the Russians *do* pirate the patents?

But what of the case where new technology is involved that has military applications? Should we permit the sale to Russia of our latest missile or missile-defense hardware? Here I would say no, for the very good reason that the technology involved has been produced directly or indirectly by the government, and it has a perfect right to refuse to sell its secrets to anyone—including a potential hot-war foe. Admittedly the exact dividing line is often difficult to draw, but it can be and has been drawn.

But with this one exception, it seems obvious to me that we have as much to gain by trading with the Russians as do the Russians. If this is not true in this case, it is not true in *any case* of international trade, and we should go back to the mercantilist world or even the world of the medieval scholastics, to whom trade was a low and vulgar business in which one man always benefited at the expense of another. Fortunately, the whole of modern history proves the mercantilists and scholastics to have been wrong. Voluntary exchange does indeed benefit *both* parties to the exchange, even if one be an American and the other a Russian.

But now it might be argued that, in trading with Russia we are not involved in real, market-type trading, and for two reasons: (1) the obvious lack of sense in the Russian costing and pricing systems; and (2) the fact that all Russian trade is under state control, and hence, all international transactions will be political moves in the Cold War.

This lack of sense in Russian economic practices is true but irrelevant. All that counts in a voluntary exchange is whether the buyer and seller can agree on a price. Nothing else—including "true costs"—really counts.

In the same way, it makes no difference whether a storekeeper is modifying his terms for me because he's courting my daughter or whether the Russians have dark political motives in mind in selling to America. The charge of "dumping," for example, is irrelevant. The Russians are not likely to win the world by selling their meager output of goods and services at below cost. This kind of charge usually comes from someone in this country who wants to be protected from *all* competition from abroad, whether Russian or not. An example is the tobacco grower in Shreveport, Louisiana, who argued that "if we continued to import

Yugoslavian tobacco for American cigarette blends, all the Christians will be persecuted and the women raped and little children sent to slave camps" (*Department of State Bulletin,* June 12, 1967).

I repeat, we have as much to gain in a direct way from trading with the Russians as they do. But even if this were not clearly true, even if there were some possible damage to our so-called national interest from this trading, it would still be dangerous for those who believe in maximizing freedom to propose that we stop trade by governmental coercion. This precise argument—damage to the social or national interest—is precisely what the modern liberals are using to demand that we *not* trade with Rhodesia or South Africa. It is precisely this argument that is used to justify telling an employer whom he must hire (under Fair Employment Practices Acts), a businessman to whom he must sell, a homeowner to whom he must rent or sell (under open housing laws). I am losing patience with conservatives who oppose (and rightly so) the interference with freedom of Fair Employment Practices Acts and open-housing laws, but who then accuse businessmen of being unpatriotic for trading with the Russians—and want to prohibit their doing so by force of law. Either you believe in the right of people to engage in voluntary exchange or you do not. If you are for it when it fits in with your own prejudices (e.g., buying South African lobster tails) and against it when it means buying Polish hams, you do not really believe in freedom. Freedom to enter into voluntary exchanges is the essence of economic freedom, and it is presumptively immoral for the state or any other agency to interfere with such exchanges.

Advocates of embargoes on American trade with South Africa and Rhodesia also use a Cold War argument. The modern liberal does not advocate cessation of trade merely because he doesn't like the way the South Africans and Rhodesians govern their country or because he swallows the Communists' and Black Africans' argument that white government in South Africa is a threat to the peace and that therefore the United States should try to undermine it. Nor does the modern liberal argue solely on the grounds that the United States has a commitment to adhere to the decisions of the United Nations. He argues that to trade with South Africa will tend to disrupt American relations with non-Communist, black governments throughout the world, and that if we are to maintain our stature in the Third World and our alliances with these non-Communist governments, then we must join in their "holy war" against the white government in South Africa. I will not discuss the factual basis of any of these modern liberal arguments, because I will not admit that they are relevant to the question of trade restrictions. But if nonlibertarians accept that the lines of argument are relevant to the question of trade restrictions, if they insist that the Cold War arguments apply in the case of Russia, then they are going to have to debate the same Cold War arguments on their merit in the case of trade restrictions against Rhodesia and South Africa, and I need not remind you that questions of this kind are not always decided on an entirely rational basis. But if you expect the issues to be decided by a Cold War argument in the one case, then you have to expect that they will be decided by a Cold War argument in the other case.

I turn now to the second part of my argument, to the reciprocal relationships of trade and peace as between people and nations. Plato said it all when he said, "Trade is the great persuader."

If you prefer Marx to Plato, here is the way he put it:

The bourgeoisie, by the rapid improvement of all instruments of production, by the immensely facilitated means of communication draws all nations, even the most barbarian, into civilization. The cheap prices of its commodities are the heavy artillery with which it batters down all Chinese walls, with which it forces the barbarians' intensely obstinate hatred of foreigners to capitulate. It compels all nations, on pain of extinction, to adopt the bourgeois mode of production; it compels them to introduce what it calls civilization into their midst, i.e., to become bourgeois themselves. In a word, it creates a world after its own image.

If you prefer Ludwig von Mises to either Marx or Plato, here are his comments:

The idea of durable peace was one of the main points in the body of nineteenth century liberalism as consistently elaborated in the much abused principles of the Manchester School. . . . In their eyes free trade, both in domestic affairs and international relations, was the necessary prerequisite of the preservation of peace. . . . In the philosophy of the Manchester School, free trade and peace were seen as mutually conditioning one another.

I would put it this way. The process of voluntary exchange tends to be "civilizing" in its social impact on the parties involved, including a greater awareness of each other's basic humanity and a reduction in sheer uninformed prejudice. This civilizing influence, combined with economic interdependence created by trade, tends to reduce conflict between the parties involved and to make for more peaceful relationships, both within a country and between countries.

An instructive example is to be found in the century preceding World War I—a century marked by freer trading among nations than ever before or since—and also a century marked by fewer armed conflicts among nations than any other in the history of man.

But during that period there was a continual ebbing of free trade, especially in the United States, which had never divested itself of the high tariffs instituted during the American Civil War. The period ended in World War I. I do not want to make this case of Marxist determinism, to say that if there had been free trade, there would never have been a war. Life is not so simple. However, the developing autarky was a contributing factor to World War I, which in turn paved the way for World War II. (Parenthetically, the rise of protectionism accompanied the rise of the welfare state in many countries, largely because the welfare state does not function well under free international trade. The welfare state helped to push these countries in the direction of autarky.)

It would be a mistake to make too much of this period, but it seems to me that everything we know about human beings argues in favor of the plausibility of my thesis on the civilizing influence of free trade.

Here is the way Winston Churchill put it in the early 1950s:

> I do not feel that there is any incongruity between building up the strength of E.D.C. and N.A.T.O. and associating with it under the conditions which have been set forth a powerful German contribution on the one hand, and faithfully striving for a workaday understanding with the Russian people and Government on the other.
>
> There is one agency, at any rate, which everyone can see, through which helpful contacts and associations can be developed. The more trade there is through the Iron Curtain and between Great Britain and Soviet Russia and the satellites, the better will be the chances of our living together in increasing comfort. . . .
>
> Friendly infiltration can do nothing but good. We have no reason to fear it and if Communist Russia does not fear it, that in itself is a good sign.

All of this may sound reasonable, but is it really applicable in the situation in which we now find ourselves? Are we not, in the case of the Russians and the Red Chinese, dealing with the fanatics of a secular religion, prepared to wage a holy war on all those who do not accept the true faith?

I would like to cite a recent experience of my own. In September of 1967, at a conference in Rapallo, there was a meeting between economists from behind the Iron Curtain and from this country. At the end of the conference, Milton Friedman, who had participated in it, came over to the Mont Pelerin Society meeting and gave us a report. He said the Rapallo meeting was one of the most exciting things he had ever seen. He found more good words being said about the market economy by the economists from behind the Iron Curtain than he had ever heard in America.

I am prepared to argue that there are forces behind the Iron Curtain that make this moment propitious for us to use the weapon of free trade to build up those in the Communist bloc who are interested in economic efficiency and economic decentralization, interested in a higher standard of living, and interested in a new technology. I read a statement recently by Senator Warren Magnuson (D-Wash.), who is a strong advocate of free trade, who said in essence: If you are a Communist state in Eastern Europe, and have an unquenchable thirst for the products and know-how of the West, some interesting things will happen. For one thing, in selecting managers, you become less concerned with party loyalty and become more concerned with ability and ambition, that is you become more concerned with profits, a word which begins to gain respectability. Then, you will turn to marketing incentives. Labor and management will be rewarded not solely for producing the quota, but for producing quality. The export executives must learn English. They must travel in the West. In sum, Magnuson concluded, we will have a stake in a new breed of Communist traders, because they will have a stake in us.

I agree with this. I do think there is a "new class" developing behind the Iron Curtain. And I think that our new technology and East-West trade is helping to develop that class. For example, our new technology, if by itself transfused to one of those countries, will have little or no meaning, because most of what is new in American technology is just about useless without the capital markets and the other market structures of capitalism to go along with it, and the people behind the Iron Curtain are going to find this out. They are going to discover that advanced technology requires economic decentralization, and then they are going to find out what the modern liberal still has not found out, that there is a significant relationship between economic decentralization and political decentralization. If you lose economic freedom, whether in this country or anywhere else, you lose political freedom as well. But the converse is also true, and when they import our technology, they are going to find that they have also imported some of our capitalism, or a closer approach to capitalism than they now have.

I think we have to recognize that the present generation of Soviet leadership is not going to last forever. Someone is going to take its place. That "someone" is going to rise from the middle echelon of the Soviet bureaucracy, just as Kosygin and Brezhnev rose from the ranks. Increasingly, successive generations of leadership are going to be bred in the economic system (Kosygin himself was a textile economist), and if we can get through to the economic structure by way of infusing our new technology, I think we are going to impose some "liberalizing" influence on the future Soviet leadership. It may be the only possible way that there can come a breaking down of the monolithic structure.

Whether any one man regards the Russians and Chinese as secular fanatics is probably less a function of his knowledge of the true state of the minds of the Russian and Chinese peoples (about which no one can speak with perfect assurance), than it is a function of his basic view of man and of the human drama. It has always seemed to me that conservatives (as well as modern liberals) tend to take a somewhat romantic view of the human drama, seeing it as essentially a contest between the forces of unlimited good and unlimited evil, acted out by men who can be classified as either heroes or devils.

I offer as evidence of this a statement by my colleague Richard V. Allen: "In the past, our [United States] exercise of national power has been for the interests of mankind, and not for selfish and 'imperialistic' interests dominated by any one group." This is a curious reading of American history and one that some Mexicans, Filipinos, Hawaiians, Nicaraguans, and Cubans might be prepared to challenge.

In the same way, the conservative approach often leads to an almost cult-like worship of men like MacArthur, Herbert Hoover, and Chiang Kai-shek. As a libertarian, I do not question the good qualities of such men, but I am also aware of some of their tragic mistakes. Essentially, the libertarian's view of man and the human drama is an unromantic one. He tends to see the drama as a series of conflicts among imperfect men, with very few pure devils to be found. He is more inclined to see the root cause of conflict in ignorance—in ignorance of each other as human beings, in ignorance of the relative effectiveness of various means for serving goals that are usually common to all men.

He sees the long-run solution, then, as residing in increased mutual understanding and the short-run expedient as demanding increased toleration of those who are different or in opposition. The libertarian would need to be hard-pressed indeed to launch a holy war against the nonbeliever (whether the nonbeliever be Christian or Moslem or Roman Catholic or Protestant or what-have-you). He is genuinely skeptical of the value that can come from one imperfect man subduing another only-slightly-more imperfect man, at the cost of thousands or even millions who have no idea what the leaders are even fighting about.

As I read him, the modern conservative is saying that the Communist is a devil with whom a righteous people can never coexist, a devil that must be exorcised if the world is to be saved. I might note that this is precisely the same view that modern liberals have of the governments of Rhodesia and South Africa. They have forced American businessmen to stop dealing with the Rhodesians, but would encourage them to trade with the Russians. I personally would have us trade with both.

I could never be interested in a holy crusade to free South Africa from its Afrikaner leadership. In the same way, I am not interested in a holy crusade to save the South Vietnamese from the N.L.F., or the Cubans from Castro. We have fought too many holy wars in the history of this world, and each has itself produced the new fanatics against whom the next crusade must be launched. Lenin, Stalin, Hitler, and Mussolini were uniquely the products of World War I. Russian control of Eastern Europe is uniquely the product of the holy-war advisers around Franklin Roosevelt, who demanded unconditional surrender and the pastoralization of Germany—thus inducing the Germans to a last-ditch effort that gave the Russians the excuse and the time to over-run Eastern Europe.

I am not so foolish as to be a pacificist, but I am not a holy-war crusader either. Let me bring it out into the open so that all may know how total is my sin: *I am a builder of bridges.* I wish with all my heart to see bridges built between East and West. I believe that the people of the East earnestly desire to see such bridges built and moreover that there is a possibility—though not by any means a certainty—that their leaders can be brought to accept and work for these bridges as well.

Even though this is just a possibility, it seems to me to be clearly preferable to the almost-certainty of war that comes with *not* building bridges. I am a bridge builder, and I am for expanded free trade between the Americans and Russians not just because it is dangerous to ask the government to interfere with voluntary exchanges, which would be a sufficient reason by itself, but because trade is now and always has been one of the greatest of bridge builders. I repeat: In spite of the fact that I am as convinced of the error of the Socialist-Communist way of life as anyone could be, I favor building bridges between our world and theirs.

I think the greatest threat to the world today is not the Russian people, or even the Russian government, but rather the concept of collectivism. I think that the best way to combat it is to work for the disintegration of monolithic governments everywhere, not to introduce yet new forms of collectivism or political restrictions into our own system.

If we are really convinced that our capitalistic, free-society medicine is more potent than their socialistic, authoritarian medicine, we should welcome the opportunities that trade would afford to open the eyes of the Russian people to the error of their ways. To ban this trade (and to take similar actions in other areas) is to resign ourselves to the ultimate desirability and necessity of a holy war between the two societies. This I refuse to do.

A Letter from São Paulo: They've Got an Awful Lot of Rogges in Brazil

Editor, *The Bulletin*

Sir:

A reporter for *Time* can usually size up a country by talking to the cab-driver on the way from the airport to that "quaint little hotel" (probably a bawdy-house)[1] where *Time* reporters always stay. I have been in Brazil exactly 12 days, 8 hours and 15 minutes (Jungle Saving Time), and I now have an intimate knowledge of Brazil and the Brazilians. However, I did not acquire it from talking to the local cabdrivers: the typical Brazilian cabdriver is a deaf-mute who couldn't find the Great Pyramid from over a block away. The only thing I've learned from the cabdrivers is that he who tips less than five cruzeiros[2] gets a car door slammed on his leg.

Nor are we living at a "quaint little hotel." Rather we are living at one of the new hotels, ultra-modern in design, so typical of this fast-growing city. Also typical is the nattily dressed manager who can add extra charges to a hotel bill in seven different languages. I am learning about international economics the hard way. (Personal note to any of my creditors who may read this: I have something good in the sixth race at the São Paulo Jockey Club this afternoon. If it comes in, you're still in good shape.)

Reprinted from the *Wabash Bulletin* 51 (May 1955): 1–3, by permission of Wabash College.

1. Dr. Rogge obviously means *boarding*-house. His typing is not very accurate.

2. One assumes that a "cruzeiro" is a local coin: those familiar with the author's tip-ping habits estimate its value at something like ¼ of a cent, U.S.

But I am getting ahead of my story. I know that all of you "homebod-ies" back "stateside" are just dying to hear about our thrilling airplane trip to São Paulo. At New York's Idlewild Airport, after a last hand-shake from Mayor Bob Wagner, we boarded a Pan American Airways Clipper for the flight South. They don't use the very latest equipment on tourist-fare[3] flights, but those good old tri-motored bi-planes are still pretty serviceable.

As soon as the two stewardesses saw our four lovely children, they insisted on taking complete care of them on the trip. Mother and I just went to the other end of the cabin and relaxed over a bottle of J. W. Dant I happened to have in my briefcase. Two hours later, for no apparent reason, one of the stewardesses leaped (or was pushed) out of the emergency exit hatch.[4] Except for this amusing little incident, the flight was quite uneventful.

When we landed at São Paulo we were met by a large crowd of peo-ple, television cameras (so help me, we were!) and newspaper men. Some of the people made the natural mistake of thinking I was a Hol-lywood movie actor,[5] while others insisted that I was either John Foster Dulles or Eleanor Roosevelt. Quite a number wanted my signature on their copies of Van Sickle and Rogge, *Introduction to Economics*. It wasn't until after our younger boy bit a cameraman on the leg[6] that we even had room to breathe.

We had no trouble with customs, but I did have to get firm with one man who wanted to test us all for hoof-and-mouth disease. Then we were rushed to our hotel, where the manager met us with a big smile and a bill for the dinner we would have eaten there had the plane been on time. (Personal note to my creditors: Your hope of repayment just threw his jockey at the three-quarter pole. Remember, money isn't everything.)

---

3. Taking a "tourist-fare" flight is one of those amusing little peccadillos for which Dr. Rogge is famous.

4. One wonders if the body of the *other stewardess* was ever found.

5. All theatre-goers will recall *The Dead End Kids*.

6. "Younger" boy is redundant. It is well known about the Wabash campus that the older Rogge boy is at a time of life when, having lost his milk teeth, his bite would not affect a cameraman.

Now about my work: My primary assignment is as a visiting lecturer at the Escola de Sociologia e Politica de São Paulo, associated with the Universidade de São Paulo. I gave my first lecture this morning to an enthusiastic group of six students,[7] one of whom later turned out to be a janitor who was trapped in the room when I locked the door. I deliver my lectures in English, while the students understand only Portuguese. However, economics is often more interesting and intelligible when presented in a language one does not understand, so it's nothing to worry about.

The language problem is more difficult when we try to arrange the ordinary details of life. My wife ordered peanut-butter sandwiches for the children the other day, and they brought each child a big bowl of peanut butter and a spoon. Our second morning here we ordered breakfast brought up to the room. The order included two coffees and a large pitcher of hot milk for the children. They brought us a large container with coffee for five, a small pitcher of hot milk and two cups and saucers. In fluent Portuguese, I carefully explained to the waiter that we needed five[8] cups altogether and a large pitcher of hot milk. He nodded his head enthusiastically, left and soon returned with the following: Another large container of coffee, one cup and saucer and another small pitcher of hot milk. With the old Rogge bulldog determination, I tried again. This time he brought us a small container of coffee, another small pitcher of hot milk and five cups and saucers. Even the floor now being covered with containers of one kind or another, I reluctantly conceded defeat. (To those who argue that this is a steal from an old Ring Lardner story called "Large Coffee," I can only say that it really happened.)

My language difficulties have also reduced my effectiveness as an "ambassador of good will" for the State Department and the American people. I go around from dawn to dark with a jolly expression on my face and an outstretched hand, but somehow I don't feel satisfied. I have drunk coffee until the very smell of it causes my toes to curl. I follow all the local customs, whatever the sacrifice—even that of sleeping for two hours after lunch every day. To all you taxpayers who

7. The word "hundred" was probably omitted between "six" and "students." Dr. Rogge has always been handicapped by his overweening modesty.

8. The youngest Rogge uses a bottle.

are supporting me down here, I can only say that I will do my best (or even better!) to justify the confidence that you have placed in me.

I know that you are all waiting for my incisive analysis of the Brazilian economy. To an economist brought up on the old-fashioned idea that two plus two equals four, the Brazilian economy would be incomprehensible. Fortunately I was brought up on the economics of Henry A. (for Agrarian Reformer) Wallace and Madame Francis Perkins, and it's all as clear as crystal to me. Let me give you an example: To save the poor coffee-grower, the government buys the entire coffee crop, destroys most of it and sells the rest for a price substantially higher than that paid the growers. (Note: They supposedly destroy coffee by pouring kerosene on it and burning it; actually, they pour kerosene on it and then give it to our hotel for use in the hotel restaurant.)

This has worked wonderfully; in fact it has made a millionaire out of every coffee grower in Colombia and El Salvador. The profit made by the government is used to buy kerosene from the U.S. for burning the excess coffee and to subsidize the import of other petroleum products. In fact, gasoline is so subsidized in Brazil by this process that American gasoline costs much less here than in the U.S. This is interesting because they have prohibited the further import of cars, and they have no parts to fix the cars that are already here. If they had the cars and parts, they still would have no roads negotiable by any car other than a Jeep or a Model T. This leads to a great demand for bus and streetcar service, so of course the government has prohibited the importation of buses and streetcars. To compensate for this, the government has placed a ceiling price on bus and streetcar fares of around two cents a ticket. Thus no company or city operating transport services wants to buy a bus or streetcar anyway. The result is that the average Brazilian spends two to three hours a day waiting for a bus or streetcar, which gives him a lot of time to reflect on the glorious accomplishments of his beneficent government and to contemplate his navel. Are there any questions?[9]

One last word about the school: The school now has no organized athletic program, but I have remedied this in part by organizing a faculty Ping-Pong team, in the spirit of the one and only Warren W. Shearer. I hope to teach them something about intercollegiate sports,

9. No.

and they may soon be offering some 7'2" Neanderthal from the jungle a scholarship covering room, board, tuition and spending money. After all, it's the American way. Also I am now having painted on the wall of the main building the new school motto, "Escola de Sociologia e Política de São Paulo sempre luta."

Write when you get work.

—Ben

P.S. Note to my creditors: All is not lost. I have just heard that a horse named Heliotrope is a cinch in the fifth tomorrow. Wire me another five hundred and we're all in the clear.

Haste Makes Waste
in Economic Development

Let's get started with the great economic problems of our era. Without hesitation, I would name as the number one economic problem of our world the exaggerated importance attached to economic well-being itself and the associated unrealistic expectations of rapid, continuous and universal economic progress. This may sound as if I am a traitor to my own profession, but I assure you that I am completely sincere in making the statement that I am not doing it just to impress you and my colleagues with my objectivity. If there has been one central theme running through the material presented here in the last eight months, it has been the theme of the great complexity of the human problem. In the literature, the poetry, the philosophy, the history, the psychology, the political science, the religion that you have explored, the theme has been apparent again and again: man does not know why he is here, or what god or gods he should serve, or what happiness is or how to attain it, or what he is capable of becoming. You have read of good coming out of evil, and of evil coming out of good; of men who are willing to die for freedom, but who do not know how to live under it and who are just as likely to toss it away to the first strongman who comes along. You have seen that to the individual human being, the great social problems of the day are as nought compared with the problems of his relationships to the handful of people with whom he is living his days and nights.

Editor's title. Speech to the Inland Steel Academy at the Professional Development Program, May 27, 1958. Reprinted by permission of the Rogge estate.

No fact should be more readily apparent to even a casual observer than this complexity of the human problem. Yet our current world seems to be acting on the assumption that paradise can be regained by the simple expedient of increasing the output of goods and services, that the key to the New Jerusalem is a higher per capita income. The Communists sell this line and sell it very effectively, as befits the followers of that great economic determinist Karl Marx. But we who are supposedly non-Marxists sell the same line of merchandise. We sell it by precept but also by example. Do you remember that set of readings on what foreigners think of us—a set of readings that made you and me both uncomfortable and at least a little irritated?

To many of these men, Americans seemed to behave as if they thought life could be beautiful if only they could get that raise, that promotion, that new home, that pastel-colored toilet stool, that beauty cream, that new bicycle for the children. We expect far too much from economic well-being alone, and so great is our appetite for it that even as we achieve a higher level, we are already dissatisfied with it and pressing on hurriedly to reach an even higher level.

But we are far from alone in this. Throughout the world there is a desperate, obsessive concern with economic progress. The relatively high income countries are pushing hard for even higher income levels, and the relatively underdeveloped countries have made a religion of it. There is a feeling abroad in the world, a feeling that both Russians and Americans have each fostered with claims that its economic system can best achieve the goal of allowing both the nomad in the desert wastes and the naked savage in the steaming jungle to rapidly attain that level of economic well-being now attained by the citizens of Indiana.

The concrete problems that flow from this world state-of-mind are both numerous and serious. Let us begin with the international problems that are involved and with their impact on the free world. I would like to choose as my example here the country of Brazil, where I spent some nine months in 1955. This country is in many ways far advanced over other areas in South America, particularly over areas in Asia, Africa and the Pacific islands that are aspiring to economic development. Yet even in Brazil the problems can be clearly seen. The obsession with economic development is apparent the minute one enters the country.

The papers are full of it, the politicians talk of nothing else, the conversations of the intellectuals are filled with it. My first two lectures in the school where I taught had titles that identified them as discourses on the nature and method of economics, and I lectured to a polite gathering of five or six students each time. In response to some strong hints from the chairman of the economics department, I selected as the title for my third lecture "The Conditions of Economic Progress"—and my lecture had to be moved to the school auditorium to accommodate the crowd. Some of the people in the audience understood not one word of English, yet apparently such was their interest in this topic that they were content to be in a room where it was being discussed even in a strange tongue.

I closed my lecture by commenting on the time dimensions of economic progress, making the point that at best it is a slow process and can proceed no faster than the institutions of the society can adjust and adapt to meet the demands of progress. This was not smart; it set off a violent argument, mostly in Portuguese (of which I understood not a word), and the department chairman told me later that most of them had agreed that there was no point in listening further to a man who talked in terms of the next generation rather than the present one.

In this climate, it is not surprising that the politicians tried to outdo each other in their promises of economic development. As a matter of fact, each new regime for years has put in its own plan for economic development (usually without bothering to dismantle the one of the preceding regime), and the result was that in 1955, Brazil had five master plans for economic development (one laid on top of the other). Since then a new president (Juscelino Kubitschek) has taken over, and I understand that he has added a sixth layer to this already confused accumulation.

Because of their impatience, the Brazilians have little use for schemes that emphasize the cumulative effect of small, day-by-day, year-by-year improvements in products and processes—the clear way of economic progress. Rather they emphasize the spectacular—such as the Steel Mill at Volta Redonda, which in spite of fantastic subsidies and tariffs is still producing steel that costs more than steel imported from East Chicago or Belgium.

Because of this impatience, they are forever unhappy with the United States and its unwillingness to concentrate all of its economic aid in South America or, more particularly, in Brazil.

Because of this impatience, the calm, wise heads that do find their way to positions in government do not last long. When I arrived in Brazil, a really brilliant man was the finance minister. But because he tried to fight the inflation that is continuous and rapid in Brazil, he was quickly forced out of power. He was replaced by a charlatan who readily assured the Brazilians that they could have their cake and eat it too.

In fact, perpetual inflation is the natural outcome of this impatience. The true savings of the country are never adequate to support the grandiose schemes of government, and so the government finances these schemes by the simple expedient of printing more money.

Because of this inflation, the Brazilian unit of money (the cruzeiro) is constantly deteriorating on the world market. Thus, the best way for a Brazilian who has some money to protect is for him to send it abroad. The goal of every successful Brazilian is a dollar account in a New York City bank. Thus even such domestic savings as are developed tend to flow out of the country rather than being put to work at home.

At the same time, in the industrialized areas such as São Paulo, the impatience of the workers to catch up with their U.S. brothers, combined with the softness of the politicians, leads to legislation that makes of those workers who have found work in industry a very privileged group indeed—with real incomes five to ten times as high as those in the rural areas a few miles away. This vision of what could be is to the great rural proletariat a constant source of frustration and stimulation. These shirtless ones are the rich feeding-ground for the would-be strongmen, the demagogues and the Communists.

The Communists (though technically outlawed) move through all segments of the society, capitalizing on every misfortune, urging on every anti-American feeling, using every trick in their well-written book to set the stage for the day when they can come out in the open and take control of the country.

This same story is being repeated in one underdeveloped country after another. And our response is so often of a nature that it encourages the most unrealistic dreams of these peoples.

The Role of Government in Latin American Economic Development

To an economist, Brazil is one of the most exciting countries in one of the most exciting periods in world history. In this country are to be seen all of the hopes, accomplishments, and frustrations that make up the central theme of this era—*economic development.* The low-income, underdeveloped countries of the world are striving for rapid transformation into high-income, industrialized countries; the high-income countries are striving for even higher levels of economic development. Never before has the economist lived in a world so acutely conscious of the materials of his calling; never before has he been pressed so hard and so continuously for answers to questions, for solutions to problems, for guides to action.

This is an intoxicating atmosphere for the usually neglected, often-reviled student of the "dismal science." It has encouraged a new boldness among economists, a new willingness to expose their complicated brainchildren to the hitherto critical or uninterested policy makers. In particular, it has induced economists to develop plans of great subtlety whereby the governments of the underdeveloped countries can squeeze from their countries the maximum of economic development. Needless to say, they have found a receptive audience in a public already convinced that it is the *government* which must bring economic progress, and in a governing group always ready to accept anybody's mandate that it assume more power.

Reprinted from *Inter-American Economic Affairs,* Winter 1955: 45–66.

It is not the purpose of this paper to criticize the peoples of the underdeveloped countries of the world for desiring a fuller life. Nor is it designed to dash their hopes of achieving this goal. Nor even is it designed as a defense of a complete *laissez-faire* policy on the part of the governments of the underdeveloped countries. Rather, the primary purpose of the paper is to suggest that the governments of these countries are not capable of performing all (or even most) of the ambitious tasks assigned to them in the typical plans for economic development; it is to argue that the typical plans for development are unrealistic because they are not based on an appraisal of the performance levels to be expected of the governments of the underdeveloped countries.

To illustrate: In a book with the title *The Industrialization of Backward Areas*, the well-known and very competent economist K. Mandelbaum has outlined an elaborate and complex "model" of industrial development, calling for equally elaborate and complex action by government. In the introductory chapter, he makes the following statement:

> The intensive development of backward parts of the world assumes the existence in these parts of reasonably stable governments capable of advance planning and strong enough to overcome the resistance of interested groups. It requires the building up of new institutions in many fields, including general education and technical training. All these social and political problems are outside the scope of this book.[1]

Now of course it is perfectly legitimate for an economist, as a preliminary exercise, to construct a "model" of economic development, even one calling for far-reaching government activity, without considering the question of whether the government involved is *capable* of undertaking the prescribed activities. But in such cases, it is dangerous to even permit the inference that the "model" so constructed is directly useful as a guide to public policy. Yet this is precisely what has happened in so many cases.

In developing a "plan" for economic development to serve as a direct guide to public policy, the economist cannot act as if "the social and political problems are outside the scope" of his study. On the contrary,

---

1. K. Mandelbaum, *The Industrialization of Backwood Areas* (Oxford: Basil Blackwell, 1945), 19.

these problems should occupy the central position in his analysis. Paradoxically enough, the choice among different techniques of economic organization must be made on the basis of "social and political" factors, rather than on the basis of economics elements *per se*. Economics is a study of the administration of scarce resources to achieve only dimly perceived and conflicting ends. The central question of economic organization *in a free society* is which form of economic organization will achieve the greatest success in perceiving and reconciling the goals of the people and in administering the scarce resources in accord with those goals.[2]

Or, more realistically, in deciding which activities the government should and which it should not undertake, the expected efficiency of the free market process must be weighed against the relative efficiency of government action. Economists have directed most of their attention to the expected efficiency of the market process, relative to some absolute standard, and little or no attention to expected levels of efficiency of government action. Because of this, they have tended to call for a much larger role for government than seems to the author of this paper to be consistent with the actual performance level of most governments of underdeveloped countries.[3] *The central thesis of this paper is that the peoples of the underdeveloped countries of the world who grant to their governments broad powers to promote economic development are likely to have their hopes frustrated and their basic freedoms endangered. The corollary thesis is that the best chance for economic development cum freedom will exist in a country whose government undertakes little more than the limited but very important task of creating an environment in which all the constructive*

2. In an authoritarian society, the problem of ends is not involved, because the ends are determined directly by the members of the ruling group (unless, of course, there is conflict among the rulers, as in the recent consumer goods–producer goods dispute in Russia which led to the downfall of Malenkov). However, even in an authoritarian economy, the problem of administration still exists.

3. It is often said the free market system "looks good in theory but won't work in practice." In the author's opinion, this is the reverse of the actual case. Anyone familiar with the theory of the market economy is aware of the many, many ways in which, *in theory*, the market economy will fail to serve the interests of the society. Also, it can be shown that, in theory, state intervention could improve the situation. It is *in practice* that the free market system works and the state-controlled system fails.

forces of private initiative and private enterprise can be released for the tasks of economic progress. A defense of these theses will be presented following a brief review of the role assigned to government in some of the more widely accepted plans for economic development.

Role of Government in Economic Development Plans

It might be well to start this review with one of the best-known reports in this field—*Measures for the Economic Development of Under-Developed Countries: Report by a Group of Experts Appointed by the Secretary-General of the United Nations.*[4]

The authors of this report are not doctrinaire "planners" or socialists, and they explicitly recognize the importance of private enterprise in promoting economic development. At the same time, they outline a minimum program of government activities of significant proportions. The following list of recommended government activities is representative rather than complete: market research; prospecting; establishment of new industries; creation of financial institutions "to mobilize savings and to channel them into desirable private enterprise"; operation of public utilities, of agencies for marketing agricultural produce, of factories for processing the output of small farmers; confiscation of "unearned increments" that arise in economic development; land reform; "creating credit institutions and insurance schemes which satisfy the farmers' legitimate needs for credit"; some compulsory standardization of products in particular industries; planning and organization of "industrial centers"; compulsory consolidation of land holdings; "influencing the movements of resources in directions which it considers to be more appropriate," including the location of industry; control new building by restrictive licensing; act as guarantor for particular investments; licensing of new investment; and perhaps controlling the consumption of the rich.

These and other duties of government are *in addition to* the traditional functions of government—maintaining internal law and order,

4. *Measures for the Economic Development of Under-Developed Countries,* United Nations, Department of Economic Affairs, New York, May, 1951.

maintaining a military establishment, postal services, roads and waterways, etc. In fairness to the authors of the report, it should be said that they do not recommend that each of the activities listed above be undertaken by the governments in all countries and under all circumstances. At the same time the list is incomplete, and some of the more extreme interventions suggested to meet particular problems were not even included. In a rough way, it is representative of the most widely accepted view on the role of government in economic development.[5]

These views have been expressed in one "plan" for economic development after another; they appear in the reports of innumerable development committees, councils, and boards that have flowered in the intoxicating atmosphere of the time. They are reflected in the host of new economic activities undertaken by the governments of the underdeveloped countries. In many of these countries, one "plan" has been succeeeded by another and yet another; governments have launched into ambitious projects, only to drop them and turn to other equally ambitious projects. The many obvious failures have proved no deterrent; the response to failure has usually been, "Our plan was faulty; now we must draw up new plans." The idea that the basic fault was in relying on government to do that which it cannot do seems never to have been considered. Thus, each nation has gone about piling one improvisation on top of another, making a new mistake to correct an old, adding one new function after another on the shoulders of an already overburdened government, in the firm conviction that economic development must be "planned" and that the only problem is to find the right plan. The few voices that have been raised in protest, that have suggested more freedom and less planning, have been brushed aside as the voices of reaction, of men trying to relive the 19th century. The triumph of government planning and government intervention in economic life has been almost complete; and any underdeveloped nation without at least three commissions and half-a-dozen plans for economic development is "backward" indeed.

---

5. For a review of development plans, see *An International Survey of Programs of Social Development*, United Nations, Department of Economic Affairs, May 11, 1955.

The Case for Freedom

Let it be said immediately that the case for freedom does not rest on any absolute assurance that economic freedom will automatically produce the desired degree and form of economic development for each and every country of the world. In the first place, the free market mechanism can do nothing about irrevocable deficiencies in the natural resources needed for economic development. It could not transfer the continent of Antarctica into an economic Eden. In other words, there are many parts of the world which are simply incapable of supporting a large population at a high-income level.[6]

In the second place, the market mechanism, even when working perfectly, may fail to take into account certain costs and benefits of considerable importance to the individuals in the society. Thus, a free market would not necessarily lead to the development of private military and police forces adequate to maintain internal and external order. The traditional functions of government are generally associated with this inadequacy of the market mechanism.

In the third place, the market mechanism is always something less than 100% efficient. It must operate through men and man-created institutions and will reflect the imperfections in man himself. At the same time the evidence is clear that given even a halfway appropriate institutional setting, the free market is capable of serving as a powerful vehicle for economic progress. Canada, starting as a raw-material-producing colonial enterprise, has become one of the highest-income nations in the world under a basically free market system and without any widespread government intervention in economic life.[7] Argentina achieved its most significant economic progress in the years when it was functioning with a free market economy.[8] The examples of the United States and England are too well known to require comment.

6. This point is forcefully made in the United Nations Report, *An International Survey of Programs for Social Development.* The authors of the survey suggest that underdeveloped countries too often set development standards and objectives which are unattainable.

7. See, H. M. H. A. van der Valk, *The Economic Future of Canada* (Toronto: McGraw-Hill, 1954), especially Ch. I.

8. See Miron Burgin, "Argentina," in S. E. Harris, *Economic Problems of Latin America* (New York: McGraw-Hill, 1944), 225–42.

Now of course these examples prove nothing other than that economic progress is *possible* under a free market system; they do not prove that it is inevitable or that it will work under any and all circumstances. At the same time, these examples do exist; whereas history has yet to reveal the case of even one nation that has secured both economic progress *and* personal freedom through the technique of government economic planning and control.

The case for economic freedom rests on the *relative* efficiency of the free market system as compared with a system of substantial government direction and control. Admittedly the typical underdeveloped country is deficient in many of the factors that make for a highly efficient, competitive market system.[9] It is this fact which has prompted so many economists to recommend substantial government intervention in economic life as the proper technique for bringing economic development. But what these economists overlook is that most of these same deficiencies—widespread illiteracy, inadequate mobility of labor, strong influence of custom, kinship relations, etc., primitive folkways— operate against the likelihood of the government performing in the necessary manner. *In other words, if the environment of a particular underdeveloped country is not congenial to a highly efficient market economy, it may be even less congenial to a highly efficient system of government control.*

The United Nations report referred to before touches lightly on this topic, but then the experts proceed to ignore their own warnings. "The first thing that is demanded of governments is that they should be efficient and honest. This is hard to achieve in any country, and is particularly hard in some underdeveloped countries where skilled technicians and administrators are scarce, and where traditions of honest administration are lacking."[10]

---

9. From his brief contact with the Brazilian economy, the author has gained the impression that Brazil is a more congenial climate for an *efficient* private enterprise economy than most other underdeveloped countries. A critical factor is the quantity and quality of entrepreneurship available in the economy, and here Brazil seems to be unusually blessed. The author has been enormously impressed by the skill, the vision, the daring, the competitive vigor of the leaders of business and industry whom he has met here. He has also been impressed with the extent to which their creative talents are dissipated or frustrated by the network of government interventions in their activities.

10. *Measures for the Economic Development of Under-Developed Countries,* 17.

Government in Latin America

This admission by the United Nations experts is certainly supported by the available evidence on government administration in the various countries of Latin America. Thus one observer describes the tradition of Latin American government as "control for special privilege without even the saving grace of a professed idealism."[11]
Another has written:

> government is the goal of every ambitious individual. Government employment is the refuge of everyone incapable of earning a living in any other fashion. It is far more profitable than agriculture or industry. Naturally, there are in South America, as in every other country, eminent and honest statesmen who attempt, Canutelike, to stem the tide of corruption, but generally with as little prospect of success as the Danish monarch faced by the English Channel. . . . Graft is a habit rendered sacred by custom and success. State employment ensures political adherence, so economy on any big scale is impossibe. . . . Municipal, state and federal payrolls are crowded with names representing sinecures."[12]

Mexico

Specific evidence on the performance of a Latin American government when it attempts a "rational" and complex program to promote economic development is to be found in Mosk, *Industrial Revolution in Mexico*.[13]
First, on a program of selective and rational protection for Mexican industries:

> It is true that almost everyone pays lip service to the point of view that protection should be applied with discrimination, that it should be extended only to industries which are "economically justified." No public agency,

11. Isaak Bowman, *Limits of Land Settlement* (New York, 1937), 300, quoted in Simon G. Hanson, *Economic Development in Latin America* (Washington: Inter-American Affairs Press, 1951), 461.
12. Rosita Forbes, *Eight Republics in Search of a Future* (London: Cassell and Company, 1933), 6. Quoted in Hanson, 462.
13. S. A. Mosk, *Industrial Revolution in Mexico* (Berkeley: University of California Press, 1950).

however, shows any inclination to determine which industries should or should not be given favorable treatment. It is difficult to imagine any public official in Mexico suggesting the withdrawal of tariff protection from anything but the shakiest of the small industries established during the war years. Protectionism is more thoroughly entrenched in Mexico now than at any time in the past. (73)

Next, on a program of channeling investment by declaring certain industries to be "saturated" and thus not open to new investment:

There is absolutely no evidence that the government made careful studies of the structure of any of these industries before acting to close them against new firms. To open the door again will not be easy because the established concerns will fight hard to maintain their privileged position. (98)

In reviewing the government program for the cotton textile industry, Mosk writes: "It must be concluded that the cotton industry has strong supporters in Mexican political circles." (130)

On a government-operated fertilizer-producing company:

The same writer also criticizes Guanos y Fertilizantes for failing to provide guano in larger amounts and at more reasonable prices than those charged thus far. He finds the performance of Guanos y Fertilizantes to be disappointing in every way. After more than two years of operation, Duran contends, Guanos y Fertilizantes has had no perceptible influence on Mexican agriculture, and he concludes that through Guanos y Fertilizantes "the government is spending large sums of money to little advantage."

We shall probably never know whether Duran's appraisal of the early work of Guanos y Fertilizantes is correct. The fact is that the project is dear to the heart of the Mexican government, and the government has a large financial stake in it as well as a prestige investment. Guanos y Fertilizantes will be strengthened, not abandoned. (153)

On a government-encouraged project for the production of Kraft paper:

The Atenquique project, like that at Altos Hornos, will continue to command the support of the Mexican government, and for similar reasons. The government's prestige investment, as well as its financial stake in Atenquique, is too great to allow an obvious failure, and the project will go on. It will be given whatever protection it seems to require from foreign competition. (165)

On a program of granting "temporary" tax-exemption to new industries:

The process of granting tax exemptions has tended to become cumulative. Pressures to extend the scope of the law by administrative decision are hard to resist.

Vested interests have been created, and thus there has been a tendency to establish tax exemptions on a more permanent basis than was originally intended. A generous attitude on renewals in the year 1946 shows a departure from the original policy of making temporary concession to help firms through the initial period of new investment. (197)

On the land-reform program:

Most, if not all, students of Mexican agricultural questions would also agree nowadays that a major shortcoming of agrarian reform has been the creating of holdings that are too small to support a family unit. (212)

On the effect of "welfare" legislation:

the Mexican Revolution has brought into operation many social and economic experiments since 1911. Prominent among these have been agrarian reform, strong labor laws, social legislation, and the expropriation of foreign oil companies. Not only in their effects have these measures been far-reaching but some of them have been applied in a kaleidoscopic manner. They have helped to sustain the atmosphere of uncertainty created by the civil warfare. However laudable these measures may have been in themselves, it must be recognized that they have greatly affected the economic psychology of the Mexican people, in particular, of those persons whose incomes allow for savings. The practice of hoarding has been fostered. (228–29)

On the effect of the government-sponsored and strong trade-union movement:

A much more important reason, undoubtedly, has been the fear of labor disputes and of the encroachment of labor on the functions of management. We cannot go afield to examine the difficult question of what merit there is in this position. What matters is that it is widely held among those persons in Mexico who have capital to invest. It has unquestionably retarded industrial investment. (229–30)

On the operation of the government lending agency, designed to promote economic development:

(1) The financieras have failed to initiate industrial undertakings. They have done very little promotional and organizational work.

(2) Lending has been a more important operation than investment.

(3) They have emphasized short-term rather than long-term lending.

(4) Their loans have financed commercial, often speculative transactions, instead of supplying circulating capital to firms engaged in the production of goods.

(5) They have done very little to create a market for industrial securities among Mexican investors.

(6) They have diverted central bank credit, intended to stimulate production, into commercial lending. (253–54)

On the effects of the government-induced inflation:

It is clear from the preceding discussion that the mass of the Mexican population has suffered an economic worsening during the inflation which has plagued Mexico since 1941, to say nothing of the earlier inflationary development. Only a handful of persons have derived benefit from the inflationary spiral. No one has stated this more clearly or admitted it more candidly than Minister of Finance Ramón Beteta. In his 1947 address to the Mexican bankers, already referred to, he reviewed the inflationary situation that had developed after 1941, and then concluded with the following remark:

"In summary, it can be concluded that the general picture of the war years in Mexico was one of a business boom, which was reflected in the expansion of numerous fortunes and in the well-being and comfort of a relatively limited social group."

The rising price of foodstuffs has naturally been a special source of distress to the Mexican consumer. Official statistics indicate that the wholesale price of goods rose 175 per cent from 1939 to 1948, while the wholesale price index for all commodities went up by a lesser amount (153 per cent). The index of food prices, however, fails to give an accurate picture of how much more the consumer has had to pay for food as inflation has advanced. There can be no question but that the index understates the true increase. During the war the Mexican government attempted to keep prices in hand by fixing maximum prices for certain basic items and by setting up a yardstick agency to retail food products at appropriate prices. Both measures were failures. The government stores were too few in number and too poorly stocked to be effective, while the other price regulations were violated openly. Black-market operations were dominant. Thus the actual prices paid by consumers were very much higher than the official prices. The price index, however, is based upon legal prices, and not upon the prices which really prevailed for most transactions. (286–87)

This is but a small part of the evidence on the nature of government economic action in Mexico. After himself presenting all of this evidence on the inefficiency of government action, Mosk then proposes to solve the problems by more government planning! "What is needed in Mexico at the present time is perhaps best described as economic planning"(307). In other words the fault is always with the plans or the planners and not with planning itself; all that is needed is a *new* plan, a *wiser* plan, one prepared by *experts*, and the future is assured.

Brazil

The author has spent but a brief time in Brazil, and he hesitates to make any use of his very inadequate understanding of this country. At the same time, just the reading of the daily newspapers has impressed him with the extent to which Brazilian experience argues against ambitious government intervention in economic life.

Some of the evidence relates to the apparent inefficiency of government-operated enterprise in Brazil, such as the government-owned railroads, Brazilian Lloyd, etc. Some of the evidence relates to the almost daily reports of dishonesty on the part of public servants. But more significant is the evidence that, in undertaking an ambitious program of subsidies, price supports, and other interventions, the government has not been able to do an efficient job of operating those services which are essential to any country which wishes to encourage economic growth and which are rightly and traditionally a function of government.

Thus, "Rio's police chief told a director of the Commercial Association last week that approximately 10,000 individuals sentenced to prison terms for thefts are in freedom owing to lack of space in prisons."[14] The salaries of policemen and police officials in most cities are apparently too low to attract the best candidates (although many good men are undoubtedly continuing to serve, even at a considerable financial

---

14. *Correio da Manha,* June 25, 1955, 7.

sacrifice). The low salaries also make it difficult for the average man to resist the temptations that always confront policemen.

Education is another area where government expenditures seem to be much too low if the goal of the country is a better-educated, more efficient, more productive citizenry. In 1950, some 57% of all Brazilians over the age of four could not read or write.[15] The long-run chances for economic development could certainly be improved by vigorous action to correct this deficiency. Illiteracy reduces mobility, slows down the spread of improved techniques of production, makes for inefficient factory operation, etc. And yet this problem cannot be given adequate attention if available revenues are committed to the operation of an expensive program of government subsidies and other interventions in economic life.

Another area for government action is the road and highway system. All reports on problems of economic development in Brazil have stressed the obstacle imposed by an inadequate system of roads for truck transport. Newspaper reports indicate that as much as 25% of the foods produced in Brazil spoil before reaching market because of the inadequate road and transport system. Here is another vital activity of government that cannot be given adequate funds and attention if available revenues are directed to other, less-central purposes.

In fact, revenues have been completely inadequate to cover the expenses of government, and the result has been recourse to the printing press. This in turn has contributed to inflation, and inflation itself has made it more difficult for the government to carry out the traditional functions of government so important to creating a proper environment for economic development.

Inflation also has had a serious effect on the public utilities, that is, precisely on those industries upon whose growth depends the rate of economic development. As Yale Brozen has said:

> The industries operating under the greatest handicap in inflationary periods are those providing electricity, gas, public transportation, telephone communication, and water. These are the regulated industries whose prices are governmentally controlled and whose return on investment is restricted to levels varying from six to twelve per cent in most countries.

---

15. *Annuario Estatistico do Brasil*, 1954, 390.

If inflation is proceeding at the rate of fifteen to twenty per cent, those engaged in trading ventures find they can earn fifteen to twenty per cent a year by just holding capital in the form of commodity stocks. Regulated industries which can offer no more than twelve per cent are unable to obtain capital since it can earn more in even the most unproductive alternative uses.

Not only do regulated industries suffer from a restricted rate of return. They also suffer from a regulatory lag. Their costs are forced up by inflation, but their prices cannot be increased until permission is obtained from the regulatory body. In the interval, their earnings drop far below even the poor level to which they are legally entitled.

For these reasons, it is a common complaint in economies undergoing inflation that the utilities are not doing an adequate job. The quality of service is poor and there is usually a great shortage of service. Because the utility companies are not able to obtain capital, they cannot keep up with growth in demand. Because they cannot even replace equipment with the depreciation funds available, since the price of equipment goes to levels far beyond the original cost returned by depreciation, they must maintain old, wornout equipment in use and buy cheap, inferior apparatus when it becomes absolutely necessary to replace or add facilities.

The poor service and shortage of facilities caused by restricted rates of return give rise to complaints that private enterprise fails to provide the community with the services it needs. This is treated as an excuse by governments to begin the operation of state enterprises or to nationalize the utilities. This, then creates more insecurity for private enterprises and investment and further slows the progress of the economy and the rate of capital formation.[16]

In light of this analysis, it is interesting to observe that the Board of Brazilian Traction, Light and Power Co., Ltd., has recently announced that it will distribute no dividends on its common stock at this time. While the high cost of dollars was an important factor in this decision, even this could be said to be associated with the inflation. Thus, at the same time that all observers agree on the importance of more electric power to Brazilian economic development, one of the most important

16. Yale Brozen, "Causes and Consequences of Inflation in Brazil," *Estudos de Economia Teorica e Aplicada* (Escola de Sociologia e Politica de São Paulo) no. 9, December 1954, São Paulo, 49–50.

companies producing and distributing power in Brazil is unable to pay a dividend on its common stock! It hardly seems likely that this will encourage the needed flow of capital into this critical industry.

The pattern is clear: Over-ambitious government action in the economic sphere reduces the efficiency with which it carries out the necessary and traditional functions of government, and leads almost inevitably to government deficits and the associated inflation; inflation in turn adds to the difficulties of the agencies entrusted with carrying out the traditional functions of government and brings with it a whole host of other difficulties which reduce the possibility of economic progress. Thus *the net effect of government planning and control for the purpose of promoting economic development is likely to be less rather than more economic development.*

Note: Throughout this section, the author has been referring to the governments of various countries in Latin America, particularly of Mexico and Brazil. It might be inferred from this that, in the author's opinion, the people who are a part of the governments of these countries are inherently less efficient, less intelligent, and less honest than their counterparts in other parts of the world, such as the United States. This inference would be wrong; on the contrary, the author is convinced that *efficiency and honesty in government are not a function of race or country but rather a function of the extent and nature of government action.* Certainly, his own country, the United States, is not to be held up as an example of honesty and efficiency in government. On the contrary, evidences of dishonesty and inefficiency have been found in every government since the founding of the Republic.[17] Even England, that model of democratic, honest, and supposedly efficient government, has known its scandals and cases of gross inefficiency.

There may be degrees of efficiency and honesty in public service but history shows that every government which has attempted important interventions in economic life has been plagued by inefficiency and dishonesty. These unwanted manifestations are not related to

17. See, for example, D. H. Stewart, "The Press and Political Corruptions During the Federalist Administrations," *Political Science Quarterly,* September 1952, 426–47.

peoples, but to the circumstances which bring them about. To say that the government of a particular country is dishonest and inefficient is not to say that the *people* of that country are inherently dishonest and inefficient. Rather it is to say that the government is undertaking functions which no government can serve in an efficient manner and which create many opportunities for personal gain to government officials.

Contrary to popular opinion in such cases, the solution does not lie in "throwing the rascals out" and replacing them with "honest" men. This is a temporary expedient at best, and the "reform" government, if forced to function in the same capacities, soon comes to be in need of reform itself. The solution lies in reducing the functions of government to a level that will permit them to be financed out of the available resources and that will permit the individual citizen to serve as a "watchdog" of his and his country's interests. This level may be slightly lower for an underdeveloped than for an advanced country, but the principle is the same in both cases.

Nor does the solution to inefficiency in the broad, economic sense lie in a reform of public administration organization and methods. It is important that a government be organized and staffed so as to permit efficient operation in the technical sense of carrying out the orders of the legislative and executive branches of government. But, as the British experience indicates, technical efficiency in this narrow sense does not assure efficiency in the broad economic sense, if the government undertakes far-reaching interventions in economic life.

The ill-fated African "ground-nuts" venture of the British government was probably administered with an efficiency that would satisfy the most demanding professor of public administration. The fault was in the conception and not the administration of the scheme—a deficiency that is more or less inherent in government economic action.

The Weaknesses of Government

The reasons for the inefficiency (and frequent dishonesty) of government interventionist action lie in the very nature of that action. These weaknesses can be summarized under the headings of *knowledge, motivation,* and *temptation.*

Knowledge

Most of the present-day plans for economic development assume, either explicitly or implicitly, that the government agencies will be possessed of an astonishing amount of information, both as to means and as to ends. In fact, the amounts and kinds of information needed for appropriate government action are not available even to the governments of those countries with excellent statistics-gathering services, let alone to the governments of most countries labelled as "underdeveloped." Nor can the problem be solved by improving the efficiency of the statistical services. As F. A. Hayek has said:

> the "data" from which the economic calculus starts are never for the whole society "given" to a single mind which could work out the implications, *and can never be so given.* The peculiar character of the problem of a rational economic order is determined precisely by the fact that the knowledge of the circumstances of which we must make use never exists in concentrated or integrated form, but solely as the dispersed bits of incomplete and frequently contradictory knowledge which all the separate individuals possess."[18]

The unique feature of the free market system is that it "plans" the use of resources without any one person or group needing to have knowledge of either the total process or of the goals that are to be served.

It is particularly difficult for government action to be based on adequate knowledge of the "goals" of the individuals who make up the society—to know how much of a sacrifice of present consumption goods the people are willing to make to permit an increased production of capital goods, for example. For this reason, much "planned" economic development has been authoritarian in form (even in democratic societies), with the "goals" imposed from above.

This may solve the problem of "goals," but the choice of means still confronts the planners, and the evidence of history (current and past) on the efficiency of government planners in selecting the proper means is certainly not favorable to the cause of government planning. Even the most honest, intelligent, and dedicated public servant cannot

---

18. F. A. Hayek, "The Use of Knowledge in Society," *American Economic Review,* September 1945, 519. The italics are my own.

make correct decisions when the decisions call for knowledge of all the complex ways in which phenomena are related in economic life.[19] The market mechanism has a rough-and-ready way of reflecting these inter-relationships without any one person needing to know more than a fraction of the total knowledge involved, and this is its unique virtue.

Motivation

The problem of knowledge is the central problem confronting "planned" economic development. But even if this problem could be solved, there would still exist the problem of motivating the planners to put this knowledge to its best uses. In this area the underdeveloped countries are under a greater handicap than a country like England, with its *tradition* of a dedicated civil service. I stress the word "tradition" because the political and sociological traits that produce a "dedicated" civil service cannot be developed in one night, or even in a few years. It is a long process, as the English experience indicates; experience in the United States would indicate that it is a process which may never take place! If the typical underdeveloped country devises economic plans on the assumption that it will soon be possessed of a dedicated civil service, it is destined to experience disillusionment and frustration.

Temptation

To inadequate knowledge and inadequate motivation must be added a third factor limiting the efficiency of government action in the economic sphere—the temptations that inevitably confront men who make decisions involving large amounts of money and who can expect little personal gain or loss from the consequences of their decisions. Consider the case of a civil servant making a few cents a month who is in a position to grant or deny an import license to a firm which stands to gain thousands of contos from an affirmative decision. If he yields to

19. The author does not share Celso Furtado's optimistic belief that the new "input-output" techniques developed by W. Leontief will solve this problem of planning. See Celso Furtado, "A Técnica do Planejamento Econômico," *Revista de Ciências Ecônomicas*, ano XI, no. 70, Marco 1954, 3–14.

the natural temptation to profit personally from his decision, is his dishonesty not a reflection on a system which creates greater temptations than the "average" person in any society will be able to resist for any length of time?

A program of government planning requires of men a level of morality and personal integrity not likely to be attained by any people in the foreseeable future. The free market process is based on the mildly cynical (but eminently realistic) assumption that men are neither devils nor angels, and that the best way to protect against the frailties of mankind is to associate the power to make decisions directly to the gains or losses arising out of these decisions.

To repeat, the failure of government action in the economic sphere is inherent in the very nature of that action, in the inadequate knowledge and motivation of the decision-makers, and in the powerful temptations to which they are exposed.

Guides to Public Policy

Now that this has been said, let it be said immediately that countries can no more dispense with government action than with fire or water or any of the other elements at once dangerous but essential. There exists in every country certain fundamental needs which are best fulfilled through government action. These needs relate primarily to the traditional functions of governments, but they may involve extensions into new spheres of action related to the problems of economic development.

In other words, the author of this paper does not adopt the categorical position of denying to government all activities that fall outside the traditional functions of government. His position is that *decisions about the role of government should be approached on the assumption that government action is a very blunt instrument,* and not the delicate scalpel wielded by an expert surgeon that it is assumed to be in the typical plans for economic development. This approach would undoubtedly lead to an adverse opinion on many of the activities now undertaken by the governments of the underdeveloped countries of the world, but not necessarily on all such activities.

Which activities should be continued and which should be discontinued? This question cannot be answered in a general way; it can be answered only in relation to the unique problems confronting a particular country. And for a given country (say, Brazil), the answer should best come from the people of that country and not from a visiting "expert" who knows little of the country, its people, and its economy.[20]

The only specific advice that would seem to follow from the arguments presented here is that the people of an underdeveloped country should first ask their government to concentrate on the traditional functions of government—to provide the police force, the legal system, the monetary system, the roads, the schools (to the extent that a public school system is desired), etc., so necessary to economic development. Only after these activities have been carried to a high level of efficiency, and only after the performance of private enterprise has been studied in this context, should the people then decide what additional activities might be undertaken by their government.

In the author's opinion, this would represent a significant improvement on the sequence of action in most Latin American countries. This sequence is described by Simon G. Hanson in his *Economic Development in Latin America:*

> In 1950 the governments were accounting for more than one-fourth of the economic activity of the Latin American countries, but this did not measure adequately the influence of the governments. Government expenditures commonly run 15 to 25 per cent of the national incomes of individual countries and were tending to advance more rapidly than national incomes. Long before they had fulfilled the ordinarily-accepted functions of government such as creation of elementary public health facilities, schools, flood control, water supply and the like, the governments were expanding steadily into the more controversial spheres of activity—steel mills, international aviation lines, petroleum exploration and exploitation, motion-picture production, chemical manufacturing.[21]

20. An example of the pitfalls into which the visiting "expert" can fall is to be found in the famous *Report Submitted to the Brazilian Government,* by Sir Otto E. Niemeyer in 1931. As Normano indicates, "Niemeyer neglected the fact that each country has its particular problems based upon its special political economic and financial needs, customs and conditions, and he neglected the interrelation between the social structure and finance." J. F. Normano, *Economic Brazil* (Chapel Hill: University of North Carolina Press, 1935), 209.

21. S. G. Hanson, *Economic Development in Latin America,* 456.

If this sequence is reversed, and if the peoples of Latin America come to look on government action as a very blunt instrument to be used only in the face of unqualified need, the hopes of these people for rapid economic development *cum* freedom may be realized in the remarkably near future. Most of the countries of Latin America have already made significant progress since World War II, in spite of the handicaps often imposed by unwise and unnecessary government action. With more freedom and less planning, there woud be every reason to expect an accelerated rate of progress, and no longer would it need be said, "Our country must grow at night, while the politicians are asleep."

INDEX

This book is set in 10 on 14 Palatino. Palatino is based on the humanist fonts of the Italian Renaissance and is considered easy to read because its lowercase is larger than usual for an old-style face. It was designed by Hermann Zapf and initially released in 1948 by the Linotype foundry.

Printed on paper that is acid-free and meets the requirements of the American National Standard for Permanence of Paper for Printed Library Materials, z39.48–1992. (∞)

Book design by Erin Kirk New, Watkinsville, Georgia
Typography by Apex CoVantage, Madison, Wisconsin
Printed and bound by Worzalla Publishing Company,
    Stevens Point, Wisconsin